The COLOR of GOD

America, the Church, and the Politics of Race

RICHARD D. DONKOR

Foreword by Dr. Mensa Otabil

Trilogy Christian Publishers
A Wholly Owned Subsidiary of Trinity Broadcasting Network
2442 Michelle Drive
Tustin, CA 92780

For information, address Trilogy Christian Publishing
Rights Department, 2442 Michelle Drive, Tustin, Ca 92780.
Trilogy Christian Publishing/ TBN and colophon are trademarks of Trinity Broadcasting Network.

For information about special discounts for bulk purchases, please contact Trilogy Christian Publishing.

Manufactured in the United States of America

10 9 8 7 6 5 4 3 2 1

Library of Congress Cataloging-in-Publication Data is available.

ISBN 978-1-64088-753-4 (Print Book)
ISBN 978-1-64088-754-1 (ebook)

ENDORSEMENTS

The Color of God: America, The Church and the Politics of Race calls Christians to look at their Christian faith rather than worldly principles to deal with our racialized society. We would be wise to take heed to this calling.

—George Yancey is professor of Sociology at the University of North Texas, specializing in race/ethnicity, biracial families and anti-Christian bias. He is the author, coauthor or coeditor of *Beyond Black & White*, *Beyond Racial Gridlock*, & *Dehumanizing Christians: Cultural Competition in a Multicultural World*.

The Color of God: America, the Church, and the Politics of Race by Rick Donkor is extremely rich with church history and context as to "how we got here." As an academic with a bachelor's degree in adult education, a master's in interracial/intercultural communication, and a doctorate in higher education: faculty leadership and college teaching, I strongly recommend this book as a tool to help lead adults into critical thinking and conversations about race, the church, scripture, and social justice.

It will make an excellent text for Christian Education class, Bible Study, book club, inclusion networks, and even textbook for many college level humanities, cultural studies, religious studies, and communication courses. People who fall anywhere in the spectrum from being well-informed to struggling to catch up and understand the current conversations around whiteness, white supremacy, racism, black power, black pride, social justice, and the long twisted road from the ideals of "liberty and justice for all" to our current state, MUST read this book.

Whether a pastor, employer, educator, community developer, citizen, or thinking person of any or no faith at all, this book will help you understand the cultural contexts and mantras that were selectively siphoned and perverted from Holy scripture to create the cauldron of our American Holocaust, our perpetual historic shame, and our current chronic struggle for racial inclusion, trust, and reconciliation across the color line. Thinkers who are not of the Christian faith will find this book very beneficial to gain understanding of how some of the teachings of the Holy Bible have been distorted, twisted, perverted, and politicized to support an inhumane and unholy agenda of subjugation of those kidnapped from Africa so long ago. The cultural beliefs of Western Christianity have often been derived from scripture, which is taken out of context. It is helpful for any change agent to thoroughly understand the true context of scriptures that have been used to support myths such as "The Curse of Ham" and "benevolent paternalism" of slavery, Jim Crow, and the vast networks of law and policy that have been developed (with purported support of Scripture) to protect these myths.

Reconciliation is the theme of the second half of "The Color of God." Mr. Donkor teaches how the multicultural church can "break the chains" by serving as a healing agent, "Having contributed actively to the creation of a fragmented culture, the Church cannot now remain passive or silent; it must engage the society in the effort to dismantle the vestiges of racism that still dots American institutions and cultural landscape" (Donkor).

This book is scriptural, historical, academic, comprehensive, and it is an easy read. It is one of the BEST compilations of factual information which synthesizes the facts of history, the distortions and true teachings of scripture (about race), and the lasting effects on our current social, political, economic, and spiritual condition. I have read this book through twice now, and it is still like drinking from a fire hydrant each time. I can't wait to get my hard copy and mark it up!

Thank you, Rick, for this brilliant work of critical analysis and spiritual insight. You are a gift!

—Dr. Angela Courage (EdD, MA, BA)

In recent years, America's race issues and our need for reconciliation have presented themselves like a disease, again and again. Of course, it is nearly invisible to some, except when another explosion occurs and our wounded soul lays there publicly in another bloody street or another burning community. For others, it is visibly, experientially present every day and is inescapable. In this generation, some believers are convicted that we cannot continue to ignore our condition, but instead, bring light to these matters and to set ourselves toward restorative justice. Love for God compels us and we cannot look away, at any price.

Oh, how greatly America, our world and the Church need to have a conversation about race! This uncomfortable subject has been centuries in the making, and we cannot grasp, resolve or move on with a speech, a conference or self-interest as our guide. But how do we proceed? Where do we start? Reason tells us we can start by listening, to get a better understanding.

In *The Color of God: America, The Church and the Politics of Race,* Pastor Rick Donkor brings an unusual background to the table and contributes to this conversation. This is an excellent tool to help those who love Jesus to intelligently begin to have such listening conversations in a meaningful way. I am privileged to be one of the few given the opportunity to read *The Color of God* in advance of its publication. Thank you!

—Pastor Frank Robinson, author of
Letters to a Mixed-Race Son

Rick Donkor's book is not only timely, but will also prove to be an essential manuscript in bringing racial reconciliation within the Body of Christ, consistent with the unity Jesus prayed for in John 17:21–23 and with one of three unalterable convictions of Every Home for Christ, the ministry organization I work for that: "Without unity, finishing the task of global evangelization is impossible."

As a Caucasian pastor and missiologist, I welcome Donkor's critique of the segregated church in America. I appreciate that he addresses the ills of church history with honesty and fairness. While he admits that the "white" population today is not directly responsible for the legacy of the racism of the past, he simultaneously educates the Caucasian church on our role and responsibility in fostering racial harmony and reconciliation.

As a white pastor, I accept my responsibility of not only advocating individually for healing and reconciliation, but also being a voice for social, economic equity, and justice for all races in America. This is the essential first step in seeing the unity of the Body of Christ take place, as we all work toward the evangelization of America.

I recommend this book to every pastor and church leader of every race. As leaders in the Kingdom of God, we all have a part to play, and Donkor's text is most assuredly the script that will bring about, not only racial reconciliation and harmony, but also usher in the much-needed unity that Jesus prayed for on our behalf.

—Rev. David Schaal is a pastor and a missiologist. He and his wife, Julie, have served as local church pastors for over twenty years. He currently serves in the US Ministries Department, at Every Home for Christ International, in Colorado Springs, CO.

Rick Donkor is in a perfect place to understand American racism from both *outsider* and *insider* perspectives. As a planter of cross-cultural and multiethnic churches, he understands what is necessary to bridge the divide separating various people-groups in America. He is more than a theorist; he is a practitioner. As such, he stands in a unique position to alter the course of a nation (and a church) whose opinions about our brothers and sisters throughout the world have been muddied by a systemic misconception, founded on outright lies, myths, and fear. Instead of pandering to these debased systems, Donkor calls us to something better, to a brotherhood of people knit together across ethnic lines.

Donkor's analysis of our current situation is a painful one to someone raised in white suburbia. He does not gloss over the history leading to our current situation, nor does he romanticize to make one side the hero over another. He paints clearly and accurately, the historical portrait leading to our current morass. Yes, he focuses on issues that many would prefer to forget or ignore, but the pain of rooting out these issues is a necessary pain, akin to that of a surgeon's scalpel cutting away years of accretion and atrophy accumulated within our collective soul. His intent is to cure, and the loving hand of a skilled minister is evident throughout his words.

Is there hope for America? Of course, there is! It is to be found in the instructions given us by the Great Physician. The prescription He proffers is one that requires the Church to be an agent of healing in the Name and power of Jesus Christ. Donkor calls us to engage ourselves in this destiny and manifest the transforming love we so desperately need. May it be, and may it be now!

—Rev. Brian D. Garner, Professor of Missiology at Biblical Life Institute, and author of Building the Carpenter's House, and Talking with the Father.

Pastor Rick Donkor's book, *The Color of God: America, The Church & the Politics of Race*, is an excellent work, scholarly, yet understandable to the reader that eagerly seeks the day when race, heritage, ethnic origin or the color of our skin will no longer determine the identity, the potential or the destiny of a person. With the resurgence of racial tensions in America, this book arrives at a time when a sober and wise perspective of the racial wars is very much needed, even as their pervasive innuendos of hate and discord have come front and center on the social and political scene. Rick presents foundational issues that have plagued America, but also affords viable solutions to eradicate the mind-set of hostility that has been perpetuated throughout the centuries. This book is timely in its release and, hopefully, will be used as a vehicle of healing and reconciliation. I applaud the quality and practical solutions presented by Rick.

—Pastor Lorraine Coconato, Leaves of Healing Tabernacle, Chatsworth, California

The Color of God: America, The Church and the Politics of Race is a captivating and provocative book, authored by the equally brilliant Pastor, Rick Donkor. The book highlights the confluence of race, religion and politics in American society and beyond. Pastor Donkor looks at the issues of the politics and dynamics of race in the US through missional lenses, as a scholar and cultural critic, bringing a wealth of research, experience and insight to bear on this toxic and often volatile subject—race. Labeling "race" a myth, Pastor Rick Donkor emphasizes that: "Racism is not just a Black or White thing; neither is it a 'Skin Thing,' but a 'Sin Thing.' At its core, it is a spiritual condition with overt physical, social, political and economic manifestations. Since the root of racism is spiritual, the Church, he emphasizes, is perhaps, the only entity with the divine capacity or wherewithal to, ultimately, bring healing to this global disease. What, however, if the moral vanguard of our society, the Church, itself, is complicit in the brutality visited upon the African or Black Man, and in the creation of a racially fragmented world, by extension, Pastor Rick asks?

The Church, through its manipulation of scripture and advocacy of theologically contrived doctrines, spoke to the genetic inferiority of all people of African descent, lending credence to the ideology of White Supremacy, Rick asserts. The inhumanity or sub-humanity of Blacks or Africans was, thus, touted from theology to biology and presented by many White racists as the results of scientific enquiry. Academically rigorous and intellectually stimulating, blending both secular and sacred insights into a wonderful mosaic of spiritual and social commentary and analysis, Pastor Rick Donkor calls for racial justice, healing, and reconciliation amid the tempestuous racial politics and polarization in America and beyond. Using the imagery of the black and white notes of the keyboard and the biblical narrative of "Joseph's Coat of Many Colors" as a paradigm, Rick buttresses his firm belief in the Creator's manifest love for all His creation, regardless of color or race.

Pastor Rick Donkor has been immersed in the politics and dynamics of race in the United States for over twenty-six years as a missionary evangelist and pastor.

For centuries, Africans, both on the African continent and in the diaspora, have been the victims of Western imperialist, colonialist and neo-colonialist intrigues often fueled by racist impulses. The "Scramble for Africa" and the subsequent domination of the African continent by European powers, ultimately, led to the Trans-Atlantic Slave Trade, Jim Crow in America, Apartheid in South Africa, and a plethora of unimaginable atrocities perpetrated by the "Whiteman" against Blacks, in general. Caught in the geopolitics and superpower rivalry of the Cold War era, several African leaders emerged with the avowed aim of liberating the African continent and ridding it of the vestiges of centuries of colonial domination and exploitation. Most notable among these revolutionary leaders were Dr. Kwame Nkrumah of Ghana, Patrice Lumumba of the Congo, Amilcar Cabral of Cape Verde, Steve Biko of South Africa, and the iconic statesman, Nelson Mandela. As the winds of change blew across the African continent, the fight for emancipation from slavery and Jim Crow (the American version of Apartheid), simultaneously, began in earnest in America, Europe, Latin America and the Caribbean. These freedom movements in the diaspora were equally led by descendants of African slaves, such as, Dr. Martin L. King, Marcus Garvey and W. E. B. Dubois.

I highly recommend *The Color of God* to every student of race, and to all on the frontlines in the fight against racial injustice, rancor and division, religious or otherwise. It is my hope that its contents will not only inspire and stimulate further enquiry, but also contribute to conversations on race in the halls of academia, serving as a resource in our libraries for public policy and advocacy groups, in discussion groups in our churches and places of worship, as well as in our homes, as we sit together around the dinner table.

—DR. PHILIP E. BONDZI-SIMPSON,
Professor and Founding Dean, Faculty of Law,
University of Cape Coast, Ghana. He currently
serves as Rector of GIMPA (Ghana Institute of
Management and Public Administration)

It is axiomatic in American discourse that to a very large extent, the constitutional right to life, liberty, and the pursuit of happiness, is shaped by two powerful elements—race and religion. This axiom is significantly palpable in politics, and political life. In *The Color of God: America, The Church and the Politics of Race*, Rick goes beyond the obvious by presenting a vivid picture of the antecedent conditions that have served as breeding grounds for much of the chaos in today's America, e.g., political divisiveness, racial discrimination, injustice, hate crimes, etc. As his contribution to literature on this subject matter, Rick boldly ventures into an otherwise "forbidden" area, by identifying and pin-pointing the Church as part of the problem. In a conscientious manner, he posits that the centrifugal forces that enabled the church to be a conduit of the existing problem can be contained and reversed by the same Church. The Church as a sinner, can thus, be "born again" and become a multicultural, multiracial, multiethnic and didactic conduit for the centripetal forces needed to achieve racial healing and reconciliation.

—Dr. Robert K. Manford Jr. Fulbright Scholar in Urban Planning and Adjunct Associate Professor of Environmental Planning, USC Price School of Public Policy

There are few issues that strike a raw nerve in America than race. From politics to the pulpit; from the posh streets of the affluent to the alleys of the poor, the festering sores of racial disharmony have been largely left untreated and unhealed. This burden is neither a Black or White burden. It is a Christian burden.

The "surgeon" who is qualified to treat and heal America's racial wounds—deep wounds inflicted by the weapons of hate, bigotry, prejudice, and emptiness of soul—is the Church of Jesus Christ. Yes, the Church united under the banner of reconciliation, mutual respect and love for one another.

In this book, *The Color of God: America, The Church and the Politics of Race*, Rick endeavors to bring the mission of God to the dysfunctional and unequal relationship between the races, cultures, and people groups in America. The Word of God implores the Church to be agents of racial healing and reconciliation. If America, Black, White, Latino, Native American, and all will recognize their common humanity, and love and respect their undeniable mutuality, then we shall be indeed a city set on the hill that cannot be hidden and manifest the words of Paul that "he has made of one blood all nations of men…"

—Dr. Frank Ofosu-Appiah, Pastor, All Nations Church, CEO, Advanced Life Inc

The next frontier the church of Jesus Christ must cross is that of providing well-researched and relevant answers to the pertinent and perplexing issues confronting the world today. With this book, Pastor Rick Donkor has taken the complex subject of race, which has been a thorny issue in America over the years, broken it down and provided a blueprint for the benefit of current and future generations. His liberal use of his life story has helped produce an easy-to-read, compelling book that everyone can read, enjoy and be challenged by. I recommend this book.

—Rev. Albert Ocran (Life Coach and Executive Pastor, ICGC Christ Temple)

The Color of God: America, the Church and the Politics of Race by Rick Donkor is a work of sheer genius. It's a bold, raw, transparent, thought-provoking, and powerful book that shoots from the hip and takes no prisoners.

It's an excellent read, expertly woven and presented. As I read through the pages I remember going through a conglomerate of emotions: amazement, anguish and intense anger, laughter and amusement, shock and awe, just to mention a few. I remember getting so angry when I read how a pastor declared Africans "beasts of the field" with no eternal souls, that I had to put the book down momentarily to recover. Intense emotions overcame me again when I read how "the church, the moral vanguard of society," the "light of the world" and "salt of the earth," chose to embrace eugenics in the name of modernity, thereby towing the larger society's quest for the creation of a "better" society. Incredible!

The book does a great job of making the reader aware that until the issue of race is confronted and addressed, true healing can never take place. Sweeping this deeply rooted American problem under the rug and pretending it doesn't exist will not solve the issue of racism. I concur with Pastor Rick that, America's "unfinished business" of racial healing and reconciliation in an increasingly multiracial and multicultural milieu makes the need for cross-cultural perspectives, particularly in the Church, an absolute necessity. Powerful!

—Benjamin Onyango is an actor, writer, and Musician. His film credits include *Heavenly Deposit, Beautifully Broken, God's Not Dead 1* and *2, Kwame*, in which he won the 2009 Best Actor Award, and *Tears of the Sun*, among others.

In his book, *The Color of God: America, The Church and the Politics of Race*, Pastor Rick, painstakingly, portrays the various races of the world represented in the American milieu as the colors God has created for his own pleasure. It is a divinely orchestrated gathering of diverse human populations, which should not be allowed to degenerate into unequal, discriminatory and hate-filled relationships. From this perspective, Rick is a march-on voice for the Church, for a new order in a world community seeking to foster peace and harmony among itself.

There is no mistaking the fact that racist behavior continues to trouble relations between persons, people groups and nations. It is foundational to most of the struggles of life today. The moral conscience of humanity, however, can by no means accept it. The Church as the body of Christ, is especially sensitive to this discriminatory attitude, but little seems to have been done to remedy it. The message of the Church, drawn from biblical revelation, strongly affirms the dignity of every person created in God's image, the unity of humankind in the Creator's plan, and the dynamics of the reconciliation worked by Christ, the Redeemer, who has broken down the dividing wall which kept worlds apart, to bring all persons together as one, in Himself.

This makes Rick Donkor's attempt to draw the attention of the Church to this pertinent issue, one to be taken seriously—by the Church. His choice of America, "the Salad Bowl," is the perfect case study for analyzing the challenges posed by race and the solutions needed to address them. America's multicultural stage, Rick conceives, is an opportunity presented by God to bring about racial healing and reconciliation, via the agency of the Church. I cannot agree with him more.

—Bishop N. A. Tackie-Yarboi, Victory Bible Church International, Presiding Bishop

A simplistic and reductionistic understanding of the politics of race in the United States has led, in most cases, to state-sanctioned and often state-implemented exploitation of Black Americans, Latinos, Native Americans and other minority populations. *The Color of God: America, The Church and The Politics of Race* provides a helpful framework to all who desire a deeper perspective on this significant subject and helps in understanding racially polarized America, while reestablishing the moral and ethical foundations associated with it. This well-researched book helps the entire body-politic and the Church in its global witness. It is a must read for everyone disturbed by the incongruity of race, religion and politics in America and seeks answers. It comes highly recommended.

—Rev. Dr. Appianda Arthur is a seasoned Christian leader with more than thirty-eight years' experience in ministry, government and NGO's. He holds a PhD from Wesleyan University, Connecticut, and a post-doctoral degree from Duke University, both in USA.

Rick Donkor's *The Color of God: America, The Church and the Politics of Race* is a timely book, considering the racial tensions our world has witnessed in the past couple of centuries, not only in America, but also in other parts of the world. Exploring how somber the politics of race can be, particularly in America, Rick Donkor takes us on a thought-provoking journey that illumines even the brightest of readers about this often-misunderstood topic. Among other things, he makes it clear that the required solution to this centuries-old problem is more spiritual, than cultural or economic. In the end, after the exploration, investigation and conversation, one can only appreciate the author's unique style. I believe that this thoroughly researched, and beautifully written primer must be read by all. This is a serious work, a significant contribution and addition to the extant literature on race relations, and a definite must-read!

—Dr. Charles Agyinasare, Presiding Bishop, Perez Chapel International; Chancellor, Perez University College

DEDICATION

This book is dedicated to Sharon, Jude, and Chantel, my three children, and to their posterity, born and/or raised in the diaspora, and to the next generation of ICGC kids, our future missionaries, leaders, church planters and educators, particularly, in the diaspora. May you be the generation that brings America's "unfinished business"—racial healing and reconciliation—to its logical conclusion. May you live in a society and in a world bereft of racism, where racial equality is the norm, and the color of an individual's skin is of no more significance than the color of his or her eyes.

CONTENTS

Foreword 25

Acknowledgments 31

Prologue—The Inspiration behind *The Color of God* ..37

My American Odyssey —The Evolution of a

Multiracial Paradigm 49

    From Black Power to a Multiracial Paradigm 59

    Victory Outreach Ministries International 63

    The Los Angeles Riots 66

    The Trigger 67

    Cumulative Impact 69

Part One: The Problem 75

    "Black Like Me": The John Howard Griffin Story 75

Chapter 1: A Limited, Nuanced Definition of Racism ... 81

    Personal vs. Institutionalized (or Systemic) Racism ... 82

    It's Not Just A Black Or White Thing:

    Spiritual Undertones of Racism 86

    America: The Subjective Construction of Race 88

    One-Drop Rule 96

Chapter 2: Is America Post-Racial or Still a

            House Divided? 103

    A Black Man in the White House 104

    Reaction to Obama Victory 111

    "Post-Racial" Defined 113

    Can America Ignore Race? 114

Cultural Pluralism 119
Cultural Pluralism and America Today:
From Homogeneity to Heterogeneity 120
America: A Melting Pot or Salad Bowl? 123
Will the Center Hold? 126
Chapter 3: The Roots of American Racism.................129
Historical Precedents of a Warped Logic 131
The Ideology of White Supremacy 133
Manifest Destiny: Divine Rationale for
Expansion 140
Scientific Racism: Hottentot Venus and the
Purveyors of a Pseudo-Science 141
Scientific Racism: Purveyors of a Pseudo-Science... 143
Conclusion.. 145
Chapter 4: The Morbid Tentacles of Racism..............147
The Politics of Race....................................... 149
Professors Henry Louis Gates, Allen
Counter, and Cornel West 150
Amadou Diallo, Sean Bell, Abner Louima,
and Trayvon Martin 152
The Politics of Race: The Demagoguery of
the Birther Movement.................................... 153
Eugenics: Racial Hygiene and the Creation
of a Super Race... 159
Lebensborn.. 159
America and the Roots of Germany's
Reproductive Persecution................................ 163
Eugenics 164
America's Eugenics Industrial Complex................ 165
Murder in the Name of God: America's
Culture Wars.. 167
Christian Identity... 173

Chapter 5: **Racism and the Silence and**
             Complicity of the Church 177
   Genocide.. 179
   The Jewish Holocaust.. 181
   Ethnic Cleansing and Genocide in Rwanda........... 182
   A Racist Church: A Historical Perspective............. 184
   Pentecostal Leanings and Tradition 187
   Racism and the Pentecostal Movement:
   Charles Parham's Dubious Legacy......................... 189
   The Church's Shameless Support for Eugenics....... 192

Part Two: The Solution..197
Chapter 6: **The Ministry of Reconciliation**................199
   Reconciliation: The Essence of God's Mission....... 201
   Racial Healing and Reconciliation: The
   Preeminent Mission of the American Church....... 203
   Change in the Church: A Divine Imperative......... 206
   Reconciliation and the Imago Dei......................... 210
   Imago Dei and Implications for Racial
   Healing and Reconciliation 212
   Healing and Reconciliation: The Place of
   Restorative Justice... 216
   Reconciliation: Satisfying the Demands of
   Divine Justice 221
   Developing a Cross-Cultural and
   Multiracial Paradigm (The Principle of
   Incarnation).. 224
   Monocultural Perspective..................................... 225
   The Master's (Jesus) Example: The
   Principle of Incarnation....................................... 229
Chapter 7: **The Origin of the Races: A Biblical**
             Genealogy 231
   What is the Origin of the Races, Cultures,
   and Ethnicities of the World?................................ 237

The Descendants of Shem, Japheth, and Ham....... 239
Was Ham Cursed to Be Black?................................. 242
Ham and the Chinese or Mongoloid Connection... 247

Chapter 8: The Purpose and Contributions of Shem, Ham, and Japheth (Divine Election and Ordination) 255
The Contribution of Shem, Ham, and Japheth...... 257
Descendants of Ham: The Sumerian Culture and Civilization 259
The Phoenicians: Carthaginians............................ 261
The Etruscans... 263

Chapter 9: Racial Healing and Reconciliation: An Ideal Whose Time Has Come 267
White Sensitivity: Black Empowerment.................. 269
Mutual Respect and Equality: White Man's Burden.. 271
Mutual Respect and Equality: A Biblical Paradigm... 273
Racial Healing and Reconciliation: Is It Realistic?... 282

Chapter 10: Black America Today: A Dream Ambushed 289
The American Dream.. 290
Black America before Integration........................... 293
Impact of Integration on Black America 295
Black America: A Dream Ambushed...................... 298
Black America Today 301

Chapter 11: Black Redemption and Lift 309
Change: Toward a Paradigm of Personal Responsibility... 311
Eyes in the Wilderness.. 313
Change: Requirement for Success and Leadership in Black America 317
The God Factor: A Platform of Faith (The Supreme Being or Supreme Court) 330

Secular Humanism: The Anti-God Campaign 333
God Rules in the Affairs of Men: The Rise
and Fall of Nations in Bible Prophecy..................... 336
The Babylonian, Medo-Persian, Greek, and
Roman Empires.. 338
Benefits of Religion..................................... 342
Family Matters: Setting the House in
Order, the Black Family 343
A Theology of Restoration for the Black Family.... 349
Absentee Fathers: A National Epidemic 352
The Black Man: An Emasculated and
Endangered Species..................................... 356
From Male Domination to a Legacy of
Matriarchy 356
Restoration of the Family: Hope for America........ 359
Boys to Men: Black Males—a Return to
Biblical Fatherhood 359
Fatherhood: A Biblical Paradigm 360
Biblical Role of Fathers: Priest, Prophet,
Role Model, and King 361
Fathers as Prophets: "Thus Says the Lord" 362
Fathers as Role Models................................... 363
Fathers as Kings: Revelation 5:9–10 364
A Couple of Points to Note................................ 366
Emancipation Proclamation: Let My People Go ... 367
Cry Freedom: Let My People Go 369
Breaking the Mental Shackles: Education,
the Great Equalizer...................................... 372
Mental Shackles 373
The Prison Door Is Open; Why Stay In?:
Living a Life without Limitations 378
Education: The Great Equalizer............................ 380

**Chapter 12: The Multiracial and Cultural
         Church Christ's Agent of Racial
         Healing and Reconciliation**......................383
  Change in the Church: An Urgent, Divine
  Imperative... 387
  The Multiracial Church Vis a Vis
  the Homogenous Unit Principle In a
  Pluralistic, Multiracial and Ethnic Context............ 391
  Multiracial and Cultural Churches: A
  Panacea to America's Race Problem
  Multiracial and Cultural Church Defined.............. 397
Conclusion...403
References 409
Thank you...444

FOREWORD

By Dr. Mensa Otabil

In *The Color of God—America, the Church and the Politics of Race,* Rick Donkor issues a clarion call for racial healing and reconciliation, in what he refers to as America's "unfinished business"; its "last hurdle," perhaps, toward building "a more perfect union." With prophetic zeal and the fervor of an evangelist, Rick takes the Church, the moral vanguard of our society, to task for its complicity in helping create a racially fragmented society.

The Church's complicity, Rick asserts, is seen in its historical manipulation and employment of heinous and contrived theological assumptions to perpetrate various atrocities, the impact of which is manifested in modern times, in its corporate silence over matters of race and ethnicity, similar to its silence during the Jewish Holocaust, ethnic cleansing in Bosnia, the genocide in Rwanda and currently in the Sudan and the Congo. It is these same hideous assumptions, he emphasizes, that provided the rationale for European colonialist expansion, the institution of slavery, Jim Crow, the apartheid system of government in South Africa and the Eugenics movement, which later inflamed Hitler's fury against minorities, resulting in the Jewish holocaust.

Rick Donkor exposes the problem of race, particularly in America, with surgical precision, but yet asserts his conviction most importantly, that racial healing and reconciliation, not superficial, but rather at a deep and real level, is still possible, even probable, if Africans in the Diaspora will take their destinies into their own hands and initiate certain cultural reforms. He issues a challenge to Black America, therefore, to recognize its divine destiny in God, rise, despite the mammoth spiritual, psychological, social and economic challenges confronting it and fulfill its destiny.

America's racial, cultural, and political polarization is complicated by the ever-increasing tide of immigration of various people-groups into the country, some of whom have no interest whatsoever in acculturating into mainstream society. Rick poses certain questions about this enduring American division—race and emphasizes historical migration patterns and how new arrivals are caught in the cross-fire (between whites and blacks) and sometimes forced by existing sociocultural patterns, to choose which side of the divide to belong to. He examines the metaphor of the melting pot and America's designation by some as a post-racial society, particularly with the election of the first Black man to the White House. Using various rulings by the Supreme Court, he sheds light on the issue of Race as a sociological, economic, legal and political construct, aimed at dominance—that is one ethnic group exercising and perpetuating its dominance over another. Above all, he explores the spiritual, sociological, and missiological implications of these trends for the Church and the nation:

- Is God amid these mass migrations of various cultures and people groups to the United States?

- Does the bible provide any clues as to the origin of the various races and cultures of the world?

- Is there a place and purpose for each "race," culture, or people-group in God's grand design or scheme of things in this "boiling" multicultural cauldron? What is each nation's contribution supposed to be?

- How relevant is Dr. King's Dream and call for racial equality, harmony and economic justice for America's poor, minority communities, Black America, and for that matter all America, today?

- How should the Church and the Nation respond to the racial and cultural dynamics reshaping the national landscape today? (what CNN and others have dubbed, "The Browning of America").

- Is the Church, and Nation ready for a possible escalation in racial tensions in the wake of evidence pointing to a resurgence of neo-Nazi groups, hate groups and crimes, vis a vis the rise again to prominence of Islamic extremism?

Rick likens America's racial malaise to a dormant volcano, or a malignant cancer in remission; though latent, time is the only gratuitous element standing between it and its ultimate and fatal eruption. The Watts and Los Angeles riots of the sixties and nineties respectively, the racial polarization and mayhem in America in the aftermath of the Rodney King beating trial, the OJ Simpson verdict, the Jena Six trial, the Jeremiah Wright–Obama flap, the Sheryl Sherrod incident, the advent and racial politics of the Tea Party, the demagoguery of the "Birther" Movement, not to mention the recent polarization brought about by the murder of Trayvon Martin, and other young, unarmed, Black men, are all typical of how volatile and polarizing the race issue is, and can be.

Rick posits that this cancer is NOT a Black thing or White thing; nor is it just an economic, social, or political problem, but at its core, a spiritual condition, with obvious physical, cultural, and economic manifestations and implications. Consequently, the Church, he contends, is the foremost, if not the only entity on earth, with the divine ability or wherewithal to initiate, if not orchestrate real change and healing in this sphere.

He calls on the Church to champion the cause of racial healing and reconciliation with more intentionality, and suggests several ways to heal the divide, including and perhaps most importantly, a massive agenda of Black economic and social upward mobility, initiated by the Black body-politic itself, the planting of multiracial and cultural churches, and the discovery and fulfillment of each culture or nation's purpose and destiny in God. Without an over-arching sense of destiny or purpose, he asserts, a nation, race, culture or people will float on the vast ocean of mediocrity, with huge deposits of God-given potential, but without the requisite direction, focus and passion to fulfill it. The Church, Rick proposes, must also be counter-cultural, a prophetic prototype of what the heavenly Jerusalem will look like, a kingdom consisting of "every kindred, tongue, people and nation" (Rev. 5:9–10).

To the degree that the Church is able to break down its own racial and ethnic barriers, be the voice of justice for the oppressed and marginalized, Rick asserts, God's mission of "healing the nations" (panta te ethne) first in the US and in the "uttermost parts of the earth," will be seriously initiated. Until that day, when ALL of God's creation: Black, White, Brown, Yellow, and Red, particularly in America, are able to stand together as partners on an equal and level spiritual, social, and economic playing field, *One Nation, Under God—Indivisible, with Liberty and Justice for All,* the quest for racial healing and reconciliation in a more "perfect union," and justice for all oppressed and marginalized people, the world over, will continue to escape us.

Dr. Mensa Otabil
International Central Gospel Churches
Founder and General Overseer

ACKNOWLEDGMENTS

This book has been over twenty years in the making, the seeds of it having been sown in my heart for even longer. As a ghetto-stricken and economically disadvantaged teenager raised in the ghettoes of Nima, a suburb of Accra, Ghana, I found that the claims of Christ and the tenets of Christianity, as revealed in the Bible and studied in my religious studies class in high school, seemed right. The *practice* of that same religion by its emissaries from the West and their local surrogates, church folks, however, seemed abysmal, and a far cry from what Jesus taught and modeled.

It is against that backdrop that I cannot help but thank, first and foremost, my parents, Herbert and Emma Dorothy Donkor (both deceased), for instilling the fear of God in me; for shaping my earliest impressions of what it meant to be a Christian through character and dedicated service to His cause; and for inculcating in me, as teachers, the value of intellectual curiosity and rigor.

A big thank-you to my wife, Felicia, my better half and the love of my life, for her indefatigable spirit and support, demonstrated through countless nights and hours of proofreading, critiquing, and editing the manuscript. There is nothing more reassuring than knowing I can always count on you, honey. Thank you again.

Thanks to my three children for the invaluable life lessons I learned from them that no classroom could ever teach: Sharon, my oldest, and the (main) inspiration behind this book; Jude, my "only begotten son," for taking me through those episodes at Horace Mann Elementary School, where he, as one of the only two Black kids in the entire school (together with his sister Sharon), attempted to look White one day by putting talcum powder in his black hair; and to Chantel, my bilingual baby girl, for exposing me to another dimension of cross-cultural engagement by being a Black kid learning Spanish in a dual-immersion school.

A special thank you to Dr. Mensa Otabil, the Founder and General Overseer of International Central Gospel Churches (ICGC), my pastor and mentor, whose strength of character and leadership have always been an example and inspiration to me.

Thank you to my ministerial colleagues in ICGC. My older brother, Reverend Edwin Donkor, Senior Pastor of ICGC, Kings Temple, London, and former General Secretary of ICGC (1995–2015), who had a divine encounter with Jesus through Dr. Otabil's intercession and witness and subsequently introduced me, our family, and most of our extended family to Christ. Prophet Christopher Annor, my brother-in-law, Senior Pastor of Holy Ghost Temple, Accra, Ghana, whose inspired prophetic words have sustained me for years on the frontlines of missions and ministry. Pastor Gracious Awoye, Pastor of ICGC, Treasure House, Greater London, UK, my friend, brother, and comrade in ministry from ICGC's very inception, starting with our partnership in the Evangelistic Team. And Pastor Morris Appiah, current General Secretary of ICGC, a pillar and a trustworthy friend and brother. You have all inspired me and always stood by me, even on the bed of affliction and when all hope seemed to be lost. May heaven bless and reward you immeasurably.

To all the members of ICGC's Presbytery—pastors, ministers, elders, deacons, and membership of the entire ICGC organization, in Africa, Europe, and the United States, ICGC, where my "umbilical cord" was cut, providing the perfect spiritual nursery for my evangelistic, teaching, leadership, and missionary gifts to emerge and be nurtured, I say a big thank-you.

To Pastor Ralph Osabutey, my bosom friend (and brother from another mother), who was the first to read this manuscript before his untimely death. I thought we would be combing the last bit of gray hair on our mostly bald heads together; it was not meant to be, but I know you are smiling on me today as part of the cloud of witnesses. Continue to rest in peace, Ralph J.

A big thank-you goes to my sister, Beatrice, for her unwavering faith and tireless efforts toward helping me to migrate to the United States after the death of our parents. She must have seen this book being written, with the eyes of faith, long before I ever stepped foot on American soil. To Pastor Augie Barajas, of Victory Outreach Ministries International, the largely Hispanic church with global reach, who quickly discerned my gifting and embraced my ministry in the US, I say: *Muchas gracias, mi hermano. Dios te bendiga.* To Dr. Cephas Narh, who edited the first manuscript when this book was in its formative stages of writing: thank you, sir. More grace to you. May He multiply your time and seed sown into my life and this project. Thank you also to Dr. Frank Opoku-Amoako and Mr. Francis Bondzie-Simpson for their intense scrutiny and critique of this work. A big thank you to my nephew, Albert Amoani Jr., for your support in making this a reality.

To the entire membership and leadership of the first ICGC planted in the United States, the beautiful, multiracial, rainbow church birthed in Eaglerock, and later in Van Nuys, California, in 1995; to Bishop Joe and Lady Vicky Kwapong, Pastor and radio host Mrs. Marilyn Allen; Pastors Casey and Sana Diaz; Evangelist Liz Grant and Elder Goddy Erhahon; Pastors Osas and Gershen Busum; Matthew (RVP) and Mark Darling; Benjamin Onyango (actor); Sisters Gloria Perez, Charlotte Vincent, Lizet Simien, Sonja Busum, and Elizabeth Onyango—I say a special thank-you. You all served as my family, the essential multiracial and cultural matrix that God placed me in, to school me in cross-cultural missionary engagement and praxis. To you all, I will be forever indebted.

And last but not least, to Jehovah God, the Great I AM, my Savior and Deliverer, the God who formed me in my mother's womb and called me to reveal His Son, Jesus Christ, in and through me, that I may be a witness to His love, mercy, and grace, I ascribe all praise, glory, and honor, for the knowledge and wisdom embedded in the pages of this book, and for the grace and resilience to complete this worthy project.

Shalom in Christ.

"Racism is a blight on the human conscience. The idea that any people can be inferior to another, to the point where those who consider themselves superior, define and treat the rest as sub-human, denies the humanity even of those who elevate themselves to the status of gods."
—Nelson Mandela (1996)

The Inspiration behind The Color of God

It was a beautiful Saturday morning, and the lingering cold, winter temperatures had become a faded memory. The April showers had finally ushered in the spring season, adorned in all its magnificent splendor. Lawns were lush and green, punctuated by budding daffodils. Around them, industrious bees hovered and circled feverishly in an apparent rush for nectar, buzzing incessantly and cross pollinating, as they moved from flower to flower. A morning breeze leisurely blew over the city. The rising sun had shone through the bedroom blinds and woken me up to the symphony of buzzing bees, chirping robins and to the morning humdrum. It occurred to me that it was time for my customary Saturday walk with my kids.

That day, I went with Sharon, my oldest daughter, who was seven at the time. Our pace was more casual than brisk. The city was already bustling with Saturday morning activities. The genres of music blaring and the unique smells, flavor, and aromas of meals being prepared by the various ethnic groups blended and hung thick over the city, in all its multicultural glory.

The city of Glendale, California, was a unique place, with a lot of history. Not only was it the original home of Bob's Big Boy hamburger chain of restaurants started in 1936, but also the Baskin Robbins chain of ice-cream joints started there in 1945. In 1964, Glendale became the headquarters of the American Nazi Party, founded by George Lincoln Rockwell in February of 1957. In the mid- to late-nineties, Glendale recorded a population of about 190,000 to 195,000, comprised of about 35% Whites, 20 % Latinos, 16% Asians, and a large Middle Eastern population comprised predominantly of Persian-born Armenians who had fled from Iran after the fall of the Shah, for fear of religious reprisals from the Ayatollah Khomeini's Islamic revolutionary regime. They constituted about 30% of Glendale's population. The Black population in the city was only 1.0 to 1.6%.

As Sharon and I walked through this complex multicultural milieu she was definitely excited. She chatted and battered me repeatedly with questions, totally relishing the moment, especially the attention she was getting and the treat she knew was to follow donuts and a cold chocolate shake at Winchell's. When her banter had subsided, I popped the tantalizing question, "What is the color of God?"

Sharon turned to look at me, no doubt, surprised by my question. It was not a subject she had ever thought about or heard discussed at Sunday school, but then, neither had I. I asked the question off the top of my head. The subject of color and race had always held a fascination for me, but its correlation with God? The color of God? I hadn't explored that before.

She pondered awhile, still wearing that quizzical look on her face. Was it a trick question? It was easy to read on her face the mental contortions her tender intellect was being subjected to. Her struggle to answer was so real it hurt, but I also enjoyed her sense of bewilderment, the stretching of her intellect. I kept smiling and walking, looking straight ahead, ostensibly trying not to make a big deal of the question, as I observed her reaction from the corner of my eye. Her face mirrored the battle raging within. She finally turned to me, after what seemed like eternity, still struggling and still bearing the uncertain look on her face, and blurted out, "White." It was partly a question and partly an answer, like she was hoping that her uneducated guess was right. Her response eased the mild tension and suspense that hung in the air.

That response from Sharon was not surprising. She reminded me of me. I had grown up subconsciously thinking that God was White. And why not? I had read the Bible in grade school in Ghana, where I grew up, and subliminally formed the impression that every character in its pages was White. After all, every artistic image and impression of Jesus I had seen portrayed him as the blonde, blue-eyed Savior. If Jesus was White, then the Holy Spirit, often symbolized by a *white* dove, I reasoned, must also be White. Thus, God, the Father, Jesus Christ His Son, the Holy Spirit, Angels, all the Apostles and disciples, as well as the patriarchs and prophets of old, Abraham, Moses, Isaiah and Jeremiah, must all have been White. Even Santa Claus, or "Father Christmas," as we called him, who brought goodies during Christmastime, Jesus's birthday, was a jolly old White man.

The only personalities I figured were not White were the devil and his demons and witches. I also got that from artistic impressions. They were Black, like me.

The White man brought the Bible and Christianity to us. Christianity, I further assumed and concluded, was the White man's religion. It was little wonder that people dressed up in suits and ties, just like the White man, when they went to church, even in the intolerably humid and agonizingly hot temperatures of the place where I grew up. That was a strong, reinforcing thought, one that sealed all the assumptions made by my young and analytical mind.

My initial encounter with "the White man" remains a memorable childhood experience. I was a five-year-old boy growing up in Ghana, on the West coast of Africa. My "homies" and I had fun when we saw the man with a light pigmentation. He was not exactly white, but I later learned that he was "the White man." Anyone who was not dark like us, we automatically considered White anyway—Syrians, Indians, Chinese, British or Europeans, Lebanese, Egyptians were all lumped together as one. Often, we would yell out to White folks in excitement and from a distance, just to get their attention and see their reactions. Other times we would muster up courage and approach him. Though not quite sure why we did so, we would often ask him for a penny or pennies so we could buy candy or acquire some childhood fancy. We would also mimic his way of talking. That was a practice we relished. These were times of real amusement and sheer delight, not only for us but for him as well, it seemed, as we displayed our utter vulnerability and childish innocence.

Later, in elementary and secondary school, I read and learned about the Transatlantic slave trade, Colonialism, Apartheid in South Africa, and White control—not only of South Africa and Southwest Africa (now independent Namibia), but about the racist Ian Smith government in power in Rhodesia (now Zimbabwe). I learned about the numerous atrocities that had been perpetrated and were still being perpetrated by "the White man" against my people in regions of the African continent, as they plundered the continent of its rich mineral resources, gold, diamonds, and various precious metals.

When I learned how missionaries from Europe came to Africa to spread the Gospel, in the wake of what later became known as the Scramble for Africa that, particularly, caught my attention. I learned stories about Nelson Mandela, his incarceration on Robben Island, the cold-blooded murder of student leader and political activist Steve Biko while he was in police custody, and the steady elimination, often by assassination, of other African leaders, such as Amilcar Cabral and Patrice Lumumba. There was also "the White Man's" constant meddling in and manipulation of the politics and economics of the countries on the African continent.

All of that became indelibly printed on my memory. It provided the rationale for why so many civil and tribal wars occurred on the continent. Military coup d'états and the installation of puppet regimes seemed to be woven into the very fabric of African political life.

The rule of leaders of Africa's independence movements—such as Dr. Kwame Nkrumah of Ghana, Sekou Toure of Guinea, Nnamdi Azikiwe of Nigeria, and Jomo Kenyatta of Kenya, marked the era and generation in which I was born and grew up. Several African leaders of that era were similarly and summarily deposed and replaced, by either Western-educated intellectuals or military men with a socialist and revolutionary bent, most of whom, it soon became apparent, were themselves pawns and puppets, caught in the geopolitics of the East-West superpower rivalries, led by the United States and the Soviet Union.

I had been raised a Methodist, first baptized as a baby and confirmed, without being given the opportunity to "repent and believe." My parents were faithful Christians. Upon marriage, my mother left the Presbyterian Church and converted to my father's denomination of Methodist. Papa was a lay preacher in the local Methodist church, and Mama was a devoted prayer warrior. Her concern for the security and well-being of her children sometimes drove her to seek extra spiritual protection and cures from the local spiritualist, or herbalist. There was no distinction made between those belief systems. After all, it was the same God we all sought and called on, in times of trouble or need.

My innocence was shattered in my early teenage years, when I became aware that being White was supposed to be superior, and being Black was, therefore, considered inferior. To say that I was disappointed would be an understatement. I realized as I gave thought to those matters that every word in the English language that included the word "black" had a negative and derogatory connotation to it: *blackmail, black market, black magic, black sheep, blacklist, black comedy*. The list went on. My initial childhood excitement upon encountering a White person turned into a rude awakening as I read about world events and became more acquainted with the implications of being White or Black.

Am I an accident in creation? Did I have any part in determining which region of the world I was to be born in, or what skin color I came to this world with? Did I deserve an inferior designation and treatment just because of my skin color? I pondered: Why does the African treat "the White man" with so much respect, even reverence and awe, when "the White man," in contrast, treats us so terribly?

Confusion and rebellion toward anything and everything having a semblance of Christianity was the result of my learning and pondering. The more I read—particularly the Bible, which was used as a textbook in my religion class in secondary school—the more confused and enraged I became. Reconciling the tenets of the Christian faith with what its emissaries, missionaries, multinational companies, etc. did to my people, created within me a turmoil that my young, naïve, and pure heart could not understand. It was too painful and outrageous to comprehend.

Religion during my teenage years became exactly as Karl Marx described it: "the opium of the people" (1844), a most effective and lethal weapon in the hands of the oppressor, used to sedate the sensibilities of the oppressed, for the purpose of exploitation. "The White man" had taught us Africans to "look up" to heaven for our sustenance; as we did, he "looked down," dug up all the gold, diamonds, and other resources from under our feet, finally enslaving and colonizing us. That became my perspective. "How so stupid and ignorant of us. And how deceptive and treacherous of him," I thought.

Everything I knew about racism, racial segregation, and atrocities around the globe—such as Apartheid in South Africa, Nazism in Hitler's Germany, and Zionism in the Middle East, came at that stage in my life, from accounts I read in books, newspaper reports, or from watching the news on television. I had never personally experienced racism firsthand, having been born in post-colonial Ghana. Los Angeles was to be my baptism into the hostile fires of the race dynamic. It was literally a baptism of fire, as I will explain.

In **part 1** of this book, I discuss the problem of race in America and how recent developments such as the cold-blooded murder of parishioners at the African Methodist Episcopal church in Charleston, South Carolina, and incidents of police brutality against young, unarmed Black men by (mostly) White police officers, have once again brought to the fore the issue of race and the ethnic polarization still festering beneath the apparent air of tranquility. Instead of America being a melting pot, as Israel Zangwill so eloquently dramatized in his epic play in 1908 (Mantle et al., 1933) and a bastion of cultural integration, the contrary appears to be true: America, to all intents and purposes, is still a boiling cauldron of racial and ethnic tension—what Andrew Hacker describes as *two nations, Black and White, separate, hostile and unequal.*

The complicity of the Church in America's racial fragmentation is highlighted in this book. As "the light of the world" and "the salt of the earth" (Matthew 5:14), the Church has been the moral vanguard of our society. However, by employing theologically contrived suppositions, the Church buttressed the ideology of White supremacy, which spoke to the genetic inferiority of all people of color, especially those of African descent, thereby providing divine sanction for White supremacy—and, by extension, Black inferiority. The assertion that Sunday morning, 11:00 a.m. is the most segregated hour of the week is, sadly, a manifestation in contemporary America of an ideology which was formulated centuries ago to segregate its Black and White races.

Further widening this racial and cultural chasm between Black and White America is the ever-multiplying tide of immigration into the United States, turning this country, particularly its major cities, such as Los Angeles, into microcosms of the world. The pluralism noted in Los Angeles is a reflection of the trajectory of the American cultural landscape, one that Ronald Sundstrom captures in the title of his seminal work, *The Browning of America and the Evasion of Social Justice* (2008).

Within the beautiful mosaic of ethnic and cultural groups gathered in America, however, fault lines remain and are often volatile. A "salad bowl," metaphor as opposed to the melting pot metaphor, has been touted by sociologists and scholars—like Amy Chua in *Day of Empire: How Hyper-*

powers Rise to Global Dominance and Why They Fall (Chua 2009)—as the over-arching motif of this increasingly multicultural milieu. The salad bowl motif alludes to each ethnic group remaining a separate entity, an un-melted piece in the American pot, essentially retaining cultural identity and distinctives, in what Arthur Schlesinger in *The Disuniting of America: Reflections on a Multicultural Society* (1991), refers to as the "cult of ethnicity" and a "separatist impulse." An article in *Charisma Magazine* titled "Is Racial Reconciliation a Top Priority for Your Church?" captures the racial and ethnic mood in America today: "Everybody is fed up. White folks are tired of Black folks playing the race card. Black folks are tired of waiting for White folks to 'get it.' American-born Latinos are tired of being judged and treated as if they were illegal" (Gilbreath 2015).

The paradox is that amid this racial morass and polarization is a marked increase in interracial marriages and relationships, which, in turn, is giving rise to a new generation of biracial or mixed-race children in increasing numbers. This group is growing three times as fast as the American population, according to a Pew Research Center report (Pew 2008). Since 1980, interracial marriages have increased almost fourfold, from 1.6% to 6.3 in 2013. The US Census Bureau in 2013, according to the Pew report, emphasized that nine million Americans chose two or more racial categories when asked about their race. Between 2000 and 2010, the number of Black and White biracial children more than doubled, while adults with a White and Asian heritage rose by 87%.

I posit that the cancer of racism, including its nuances and morbid tentacles, is neither a Black nor a White thing, i.e., a skin thing, nor is it simply an economic, social, or political problem, but is, at its core, a spiritual condition, a "sin" thing. Consequently, I contend that the Church is the foremost, if not the only, entity with the credibility and divine ability to facilitate real rather than superficial healing and reconciliation in this sphere.

The question this raises is; what if the Church, the paragon of virtue, is itself complicit in the creation of a racially-fragmented society, through its historical and contemporary praxis? How does a divided and racially-polarized American Church fulfill its moral and divine responsibility to our nation, with respect to fostering racial healing and reconciliation and creating a racially-friendly and egalitarian society for all its people?

In such a multiracial and cultural milieu, where all races, cultures and ethnicities are validated, affirmed, and celebrated, biracial kids do not have to be forced to choose which side of the family they should identify with. The Church in America needs to seriously examine its contemporary praxis, particularly, its apparent embrace of the Homogenous Unit Principle as a key to church growth. This principle, invariably, feeds the racist and "separatist impulse" (Schlesinger) within us. For the Church to become a voice of hope for the oppressed and marginalized, a prophetic prototype of what the heavenly Jerusalem will look like (Rev. 5:9), earnest introspection is necessary. In this regard, I posit that the multiracial or multicultural church is the panacea to America's festering, racial wounds, and the answer to its increasingly pluralistic makeup.

Part 2 of this book focuses on the solution to the problem, with the theme of racial healing and reconciliation as the overarching quest, motif, and answer to America's racial divide. Of critical importance to this theme is not only the subject of interracial marriages, but also how the progeny of such relationships is a key to bridging the complex chasm between America's races.

Also, of importance is the place of Blacks, or African-Americans, in contemporary American society. Having borne the brunt of America's centuries-old racial malaise, resulting in much internalized oppression and nihilism (Cornel West 1994), what is the place and role of Black America in the future development of this great country? What racial climate will characterize the America that our Black, White, Latino, Asian, Native American, and, of course, mixed race children, inherit from us? What kind of nation are we willing to bequeath to posterity? Will it remain beholden to its ugly racist past, whose ghosts continue to haunt us, or will America transcend the issue of race, thereby creating a truly multicultural society, one whose people embrace, validate, and celebrate each other, and whose economic, academic, political, and legal resources and systems are accessible to all, regardless of color, culture, or creed?

I argue in this book that it is time for Black America to rise from the ashes and fulfill its destiny in this land. This requires a serious overhaul of nihilistic attitudes or tendencies which have been counterproductive and detrimental to progress. Embracing and applying the keys of Black upward mobility that are highlighted in this book—most of them not new, but nevertheless vital—will mark the resurgence of a new Black culture and people. The removal of debilitating and self-defeating tendencies will close the achievement gap and, ultimately, move us closer to achieving greater social and economic parity with all other groups in the American milieu. Black America's role and contribution in fostering racial healing and reconciliation, and in creating a just, equitable, and egalitarian society, one we can proudly bequeath to our children—to all our children—is indispensable.

The words of Marcus Garvey are instructive and poignant in this regard: "The character of a man," he said, "is defined by never depending upon others to do for him what he ought to do for himself" (Garvey 2013).

This is a call to personal responsibility, one we must all pay heed to and give our due diligence. Outsourcing responsibilities that fall within our purview to another group or race will sadly lead to much disappointment. The onus, in many respects, is on us. Social and economic parity, eventually achieved, will promote not superficial but real, healthy, and substantive healing and reconciliation in race relations.

I eagerly look forward to that day when, in the words of Dr. Martin Luther King Jr., "all of God's children," Black, White, Latino, Asian, Native American and Mixed race, "will be able to sing with a new meaning," Samuel Francis Smith's song presented in 1832 'My country, 'tis of thee, sweet land of liberty, of thee I sing…" if America is to be a great nation this must become true'" (MLK 1963).

The Evolution of a Multiracial Paradigm

I arrived in the United States on the afternoon of October 24, 1990. Except for the few hours of respite at Gatwick Airport, London, the almost seventeen-hour flight was excruciatingly long, exhausting, and frequently scary. It was not bad enough, however, to deny me the sense of destiny and anticipation I felt as the plane circled above the city of Los Angeles in preparation for landing.

I had fallen asleep countless times during the long flight, out of sheer drudgery and boredom, until the force of the turbulence repeatedly woke me up to find myself still hanging in the air. The silent prayers and vows made during those moments were many, as we buckled up time and time again upon the orders of the crew, waiting for the turbulence to pass. Those were really pensive moments, and the silence on the plane was almost deafening.

I was more relieved than excited when finally, the pilot's voice, crisp and clear, came through the loud speakers asking us to buckle up and prepare for landing.

49

Our descent was smooth and exhilarating. That was my first ever flight. As the plane touched down and taxied to a stop, I muttered a prayer to the Lord for His traveling mercies.

At that point in my life, His purpose for me and my calling were still unclear, but that didn't matter at that moment. "Welcome to Los Angeles," the pilot bellowed for the last time. That was a huge moment in my life. I had finally landed in Los Angeles, the entertainment capital of the world. I savored the moment.

My first few days in Los Angeles were quite eventful. We went to meet and greet family and friends of my hosts, my sister Beatrice and her family. There were sight-seeing tours, visits to LA's commercial district, rides through Beverly Hills, stops at the Golden Arches for Big Mac combos, and at Carl's Junior for Double-Western bacon cheese burgers. And more.

A week had not passed though when the novelty began to wear off and I started feeling homesick, a sense of loss and separation from my wife, Felicia, and our kids, who were still in Ghana. The kids were still toddlers and babies when I left. Sharon was a year and nine months old, and Jude was only seven months and still crawling. Our idea and plan was that I would come over to Los Angeles, settle down, and then have them join me. Though it seemed a very safe and sound plan, it did not resolve the uncertainty that was beginning to eat me up regarding when that would be.

Stories about craziness in the streets, drugs and gang violence, drive-by shootings—even of kids, and particularly in the "hood"—were drummed into me by my hosts. With my sensors up and ready to pick up on any potential problems, I made every move with caution, evaluating every individual I passed by on the streets through heightened street instincts acquired from years of growing up in the ghettos and alleys of Nima, in Ghana. Though I was in a different context, the vibes were very similar.

My accent never failed to betray me, despite all efforts to remain incommunicado, keep a low profile, and not attract attention. "Hey, where you from, Jamaica?" was often the question I heard, the ice-breaker. "No," I would answer, "I'm from the motherland."

I knew that any attempt on my part to match the slang of my Black "brothas" and "sistas" in the Crenshaw district of LA was going to be ineffective. I dared not attempt that feat prematurely and make a fool of myself. I would sound unintelligible and ridiculous, and I was not prepared for that. I tried, therefore, when confronted with questions about where I was from, to come across as an educated, Black African brotha—different, yes, but smooth, nevertheless. It worked, for the most part, often drawing favorable reactions from my interviewer. Interest would often soar, followed by more questions, especially when I intentionally put my Afro-British English accent on exhibition, emphasizing the Ts and eliminating the Rs in my elocution.

"Which part of Africa? South Africa?" the more educated brothers and sisters, the ones with some knowledge of Africa, its history, or its geography, would ask. "So did you see lions, zebras, giraffes, and stuff?" others would ask. "Did I see lions and giraffes? Yeah, when I visited the zoo as a kid," I would respond.

Occasionally, strange questions would come up, like whether people still lived on trees in Africa. I had no clue what the motivations were behind those particular questions, but I heard them too many times not to be bothered by them eventually. In time, I realized that they were simply genuine questions asked out of sheer curiosity.

Conversations would sometimes carry over into issues of racism, particularly, in America, how wrong and despicable it was for Africans to sell their fellow African brothers and sisters into slavery, the continued oppression of the Black man in America, issues of emancipation, and which Black leader was more effective for Black America, Dr. King or Malcolm X. Occasionally, these discussions would end with my interrogator expressing a much-cherished, life-long dream of visiting the motherland, possibly even living there someday, permanently or temporarily, like Maya Angelou, or like W. E. B. Du Bois, who died in Ghana and was buried on African soil. Some, sadly, harbored a disdain for Africa and Africans.

Explaining issues about Africa to my Black American "brothers" who, invariably, were physically just like me but culturally very different, was not always an easy undertaking. The cultural and linguistic barriers were, more often than not, quite formidable, disabling them from making sense of some of the topics we talked about. Sharing information and providing perspectives on African culture, life, and history were, nevertheless, always enriching and fulfilling experiences, and the sense of the general American ignorance about Africa and things African, struck me frequently as quite remarkable. Africans, generally, seemed to know a lot about America, but Americans, even Black Americans, seemed to know so little about Africa, or the rest of the world, for that matter.

Los Angeles's Crenshaw district, thus, served as my initial exposure to American society, particularly the Black culture. Church attendance at Bishop Charles Blake's West Angeles Church of God in Christ, located within walking distance of where I lived, and Dr. K. C. Price's Crenshaw Christian Center, added to my fledgling life and experiences in America. Getting to see, in person, at a Fred Price meeting, and the "Third World"—affected me more than words could describe; it was simply incredible.

Navigating these encounters and experiences in Los Angeles, the bulk of them cultural, helped prepare me for the long journey that lay ahead.

In May of 1991, seven months after my arrival in the US, I relocated to an apartment in Glendale. Moving was, I surmised, part of the normal evolution of life in America. Change was inevitable and unpredictable, but when it knocked at one's door, one simply embraced it and went with the flow. I still had no job, after almost seven months in the country. I'd arrived amid the terrible recession of the George Bush Sr. era. A four-month banking course at the Wilshire Banking Institute had not helped the situation, as I had hoped. That my right arm was still in a cast from a car accident sustained about a year prior to leaving my home country was not helpful to my job prospects either.

I moved in with the few belongings I had brought with me from Ghana, having given away everything else. I had no money in my pocket, no job, and was not sure how I was going to pay the rent or the utility bills, soon due. I had a pillow, a comforter, but no bed, no furniture for the living room, no television, no means of transportation—I didn't have what I considered the basic amenities and conveniences I'd had back home in Ghana as pastor of a sizable church. Those things were now luxuries I could only dream of. The only belongings I had to show for my seven-month sojourn in America were some winter clothing and gear, and a small tape player/radio I had picked up from a garage sale. America was not the land flowing with milk and honey that I thought; at least, not yet.

It was not all bad and grim, however; I had bought a big bag of rice and a gallon of cooking oil. I had a few cooking utensils donated per the kind care of my sister, also. Most importantly, I had my health and God's divine favor and grace upon my life. Those ingredients were going to be the difference-makers. They were the intangible, yet powerful and gracious endowments bestowed by the God of Abraham, who called him (Abraham), out of his motherland (just like me), and commissioned him to go to a land that he would show him. It was this same God who had, through various means, orchestrated my migration to the United States. That was my belief and conviction.

I plunged ahead, armed with that conviction, undaunted but nevertheless a little nervous about how my life in Glendale was going to unfold. The honeymoon was really over; my real life in America was about to begin. I had not called or written to Felicia and the kids in a while; that would be my first order of business once I settled into my new life, in my own apartment.

As I lay on the carpeted floor in my bedroom that first evening in the new place, half of the king-sized comforter my bedding and the other half my cover sheet, I was overcome by an overwhelming sense of isolation, loneliness, and fear. The solitude was acute and unsparingly depressing. It was as if hell had released hordes of demons to invade my mind and space. I tried to pray, but stopped. For some reason, I just couldn't. I felt very low and extremely discouraged.

Was I really in America on a divine assignment, as I had previously thought and believed? Did God really send me or did I make a mistake in coming over? Should I have simply stayed on in my last pastorate in Cape Coast, in Ghana? How was I going to pay the bills, rent, and utilities? Would I, too, be rendered homeless—on the streets, like the many homeless people I had seen in Los Angeles, on Skid Row? Negative thoughts and questions raced through my mind as I drifted off into a restless sleep.

I woke up in the morning a bit refreshed. I had definitely needed the rest. I began to replay the events of the previous day in my mind: the move from Los Angeles to Glendale, the pressing issues on my plate, the rent and bills, the family back home, how and when I could bring them over to join me, my options, how to resolve all these issues...and on and on; the list seemed endless. The sense of foreboding from the night before still hung in the air; like a ton of bricks, it weighed heavily on me.

I turned on the little tape player/radio that sat on the carpet next to me, hoping to hear something, just some-thing...anything that would serve as a distraction to the hounding psychological onslaught, the emotional siege and mental bombardment I was going through; perhaps the news, maybe a funny commercial, gospel music, soul music, any music, anything, just anything.

I tuned in to NPR but could not relate to anything being discussed, except perhaps, excerpts and commentary on the Gulf War, the Iraqi War, news I had been following in Ghana before migrating. I listened for a while, gaining tem-porary relief, but the din in my head persisted.

I shut the radio off, rather abruptly, closed my eyes, and just lay there. I opened my eyes, seconds later, and slowly looked up at the ceiling. In a weird way, I could picture the faces of Felicia and our kids, Sharon and Jude, on the ceiling. I could not separate imagination from reality. There was no need to. The sight was lovely, heart-warming. My face lit up with a smile, the tension in my facial muscles eased a bit. I beamed at them with a bigger smile, as if to assure them I was okay. It was a comforting feeling, and for them as well, I thought. Without any premeditation, I found myself repeating the baby sounds and noises they used to make when I was with them in Ghana, noises I always found amusing. I had often repeated their sounds back to them, which would make them break out into radiant smiles, sometimes even chuckles. That special bond I felt back home in Ghana when I did that with them filled my heart. Tears welled up in my eyes. I felt like they were with me, as I muttered things at them and made silly jokes, still lying on the carpet. All that lasted a couple of minutes, I suppose.

I slapped myself back into reality. I had been caught in an awkward moment, very difficult to explain, yet very reassuring. Then I felt an urge to play one of several tapes I had brought with me from Ghana. It was a recording of Okasa Lamptey, the celebrated reggae musician in my church back home. I slotted it in and waited for it to begin doling out its repertoire of mostly reggae music.

"*I got Zoe,*" my favorite number on the tape, began to play. I immediately connected with the rhythm, singing along as I began to get up lazily from the makeshift bedding on the carpet. I began to do a little dance, as well, snapping my fingers in sympathy with the reggae beat. As I did, I felt a strange but nice breeze blow over me, from the window, it seemed. But the window was still shut, so it couldn't have been from there. The next song was a fast-paced one with roots-rock, reggae-like rhythm, a Ghanaian highlife beat, with English and Ewe lyrics: "When the roll is called up yonder, yonder over there…I'll be there."

What happened next was almost inexplicable. It was as if "something" just came over me, suddenly hit me and moved me. My little dance moves in my bedroom took on a new turn. I picked up the pace in sync with the music and began dancing and praising the Lord, unabashedly, like a drunk or a raving maniac. Something had taken over my faculties. I twirled, twisted, hollered a bit, doing my thing, and seriously getting my boogie on without any reservations, all while being conscious of an intangible, but powerful presence. Whatever that breeze was that blew over me, it was a good one. I knew, unmistakably, that it was the presence of the Lord; it had to be. And it propelled me to another level.

I was reminded of how despicable King David had looked in the eyes of his wife, Michal, as he shouted, leaped, and danced before the Lord with all his might (2 Samuel 6:12–16). As maniacal as my "boogie" also was, set off and inspired initially by Okasa's music, I knew it had been divinely orchestrated to be an expression of praise to my God, the God who had brought me thus far, and was going to deliver and see me through all my tribulations.

I felt instant relief. I was sweating and panting, trying to regain my breath as the music ended. The evidence of this "wild," frenzied praise was almost immediate. Indeed, I felt much lighter. The heavy burdens I had been carrying were lifted; the "yoke" was broken. Instead of tremendous fear and hopelessness, I felt a new surge of faith and hope rising within me. That God had indeed "given me the oil of joy for mourning and the garment of praise for the spirit of heaviness" (Isaiah 61:3) was undeniable. My expression of trust in the goodness of God, through my praise and dance (Psalm 100:1–5/150:4) had moved the hand of God and activated the forces of heaven on my behalf. It was pure Spirit, apparently supernatural, the manifestation of a burden-lifting God, who said, "Come unto me all ye that labor, and I will give you rest" (Matthew 11:28).

The bills had still not been paid, and the issues that brought on the atmosphere of doom and gloom had not resolved physically, yet I was a different man with a new and different attitude. Somehow, I knew intuitively and by faith (Hebrews 11:1) that my problems were taken care of, for "He calls the things that be not, as though they were" (Romans 4:17). There was no denying the spiritual and physical breakthrough—"the Lord had indeed turned my captivity" (Psalm 126:1). He would soon, additionally, and in accordance with His word, "fill my mouth with laughter" (Psalm 126:2). The developments in the days, weeks, and months ahead proved that to be exactly so.

With that invigorating sense of hope, I picked up the yellow pages and got on the phone. I started making calls, hoping to locate a church within walking distance of my apartment, because the next day was Sunday. I needed to plug in to a local church quickly. I found a couple of churches in the neighborhood, found out their service times and picked one I felt comfortable with.

The next day, I was there on time for service. It was a small church called Neighborhood Christian Fellowship. On that particular Sunday, there were thirty or fewer people in attendance, mainly Caucasians, with a very small sprinkling of Blacks—perhaps three or four. I learned that actual membership was around a couple of hundred. I wondered where the rest of the members were. The service was pretty nice—not as exuberant and charismatic as we did it back home, but still nice. The Word was sound doctrinally, and the people were friendly enough to make me want to return. I met with the associate pastor, Jim, after the service, and also made some other acquaintances.

An Armenian gentleman, Emmanuel, and his fiancée, Beth, a white lady, learned that I had walked to church and offered to give me a ride home in their two-seater, red sports car. It was a nice gesture, which I appreciated and readily accepted. The ride home was uncomfortable: three people stuck in a two-seater. For some reason that I don't remember and can't explain, I had on me a copy of the last message I had preached at ICGC's mother church, Christ Temple, the week of my departure from Ghana. Emanuel and Beth asked to borrow it, and I let them. Little did I know the impact that seemingly insignificant act was to have on my entire life, vision, mission, and ministry in America. My life was about to undergo a seismic transition, never to be the same again.

From Black Power to a Multiracial Paradigm

Michael heard my last message preached at ICGC-Baden-Powell Memorial Hall, on tape, at Emmanuel and Beth's house, and decided he needed to meet the fiery African preacher. He managed to get my contact number, and called me up to set up a meeting. We hit it off really well upon our first meeting, and Michael expressed his desire of wanting me to "disciple" him.

Michael was a Caucasian gentleman about my age, perhaps a few months younger. He was self-employed, worked in construction as a contractor, and made quite a decent income. The nature of his business allowed him much liberty with his time; he worked whenever he chose to and kicked back as he pleased. Michael was single, but had a daughter. To all intents and purposes, he was a decent fellow. He was friendly and likable, he loved Jesus, and was committed to winning souls and to the establishment of Christ's kingdom and work on earth. Mike, as I came to call him, however, had a serious flaw in his character, a chip in his armor, a condition that had hounded him for years, up until I met him: he was a drug addict.

Michael used cocaine frequently. He had struggled with his addiction since his teenage years, having been exposed to the drug culture in high school. Like many kids do, he had experimented with it and had gradually gotten sucked in. It had been the craze of the day and the *hip* thing to do. The separation and subsequent divorce of his parents drove him deeper into the vices of the streets and into the grip of dealers who peddled those vices.

Mike's ability to make serious money did not help his situation. As a good negotiator, he could and would sell you a business deal at the drop of a hat. He would secure and sign a contract, complete the job ahead of schedule, and, in the process, do such an excellent job that one would waste no time in giving him referrals. He was that good when it came to his business acumen. The drawback was always the same: having made the money, Michael would rent a motel room, go on a coke binge, and simply squander everything he had made, to the very last cent. He would feed that expensive habit of his until he hit rock bottom and had no more to spend, at which time he would come back to reality and the cycle would then begin all over again. His drug addiction had, over the years, made him a regular at Narcotics Anonymous meetings, and in programs in their numerous rehabs and group homes.

It was not long before Michael and I bonded and became good friends. We started prayer and Bible study sessions in my apartment. Since I had little furniture, we simply sat on the carpet and did our thing. Michael was not a total ignoramus, a "baby" Christian, so to speak; he had been around, and in the "Body of Christ" for a quite a while. He knew what was up in the church world and where it was happening. Michael would later provide me with much insight into Christianity, American style. Also, he knew the word of God to an appreciable degree. However, he needed someone to stand with him, to hold him accountable, and to reinforce some missing but critical ingredients, such as prayer, consistency, holiness, and general spiritual discipline. Those were values I soon came to realize were seriously lacking in the American Christianity I was being exposed to—values that most Christians in the two-thirds world took for granted. I often joked that the American Church and American Christians needed to give the African Church some of their wealth and financial prosperity in exchange for the passion, holiness, and spiritual discipline of the African Church.

Michael knew I was genuine. Obviously, the peace I displayed under the very humbling circumstances in my apartment made some impression on him. He needed someone he could trust, because he hadn't had many people of such caliber or disposition in his life. I identified with Michael. I understood and appreciated his struggles; he was where I had been years before my conversion. Our friendship grew.

Michael would pick me up from my apartment and we would drive to church together. He also arranged for me to meet his mom and stepdad. For some reason, his mother was not particularly enthused about meeting me, it seemed. As Michael later explained, she "was not too comfortable with Blacks." I was not offended by it; it simply made me conscious of the need to stay away or not intrude too much into her space. I was friends with her adult son, not her, and that was enough. I would often wait in the car when Michael and I were together, and he decided to stop by to say hello to his family.

A few weeks after meeting Michael, Bernard Cooper, the owner of my apartment complex and an attorney and a business man, by a strange turn of events, decided to appoint me the manager of the entire complex. That was about three weeks after my "crazy" *American Idol* moment as a praise dancer, alone in my bedroom. Call it whatever, but that had been no joke. It was a breakthrough of godly proportions; a divine intervention, to say the least.

I welcomed Bernard Cooper's decision with some degree of trepidation. My job was to collect rent from tenants, issue them receipts, ensure that tenants kept the neighborhood clean, be responsible for calling on the maintenance crew to fix any structural damage or problems in the apartments when they occurred; in essence, supervise the entire place. The best part about all of that was that as the manager my rent was greatly reduced. I had to pay perhaps a third or a quarter of what would normally be due. Was that God, or what?

As if that was not enough, within a month of being appointed manager, Michael had furnished my living room, providing me with a TV and other accessories to boot. The lengths he went to procure those things were rather astounding. He was my buddy, alright, but I hadn't expected him to go out of his way to do that. I still shudder at the thought of tenants coming to the manager's apartment and finding it empty, so I was grateful to Michael for his help.

Around that time, I got my first job at Bank of America, as a microfilm operator, through Apple One, an employment agency. Man, I was on a roll. God was most certainly on the move. Glory!

I worshipped with Neighborhood Christian Fellowship until December 1991. During my tenure, here, though not in an official ministerial capacity, I galvanized and organized the church for evangelistic activities in the city, a mission the church seemed to have completely lost at this time. The success of that effort was minimal, but nevertheless vital in stirring the entire congregation's faith toward bigger and better things. Unknown to me at the time, my close association and friendship with Michael, as well as my fellowship with a predominantly Caucasian church, was gradually removing my deeply rooted Afro-centricities and perceptions of people of other races and cultures.

Victory Outreach Ministries International

On December 31, 1991, I found myself at the Crossover/Watch night service of Victory Outreach Ministries International, Glendale branch. I had no idea what that ministry was about, except that someone at a Bible study I attended mentioned it as an outreach and missions-oriented ministry.

In the pulpit that night was a Mexican guy. His message revealed a man bigger on the inside, in his heart, than his diminutive physique. He was pretty fired up that evening, and conveyed his New Year's message with fervor, but also in the strongest accent I had ever heard behind a pulpit. His accent, in fact, gave me hope—if that guy could do the great work he was doing, I rationalized that I could as well; my own African accent strong as it was, would not be a hindrance. I later found out that the Mexican brotha was Augie Barajas, the senior pastor of that approximately two hundred–member, largely Hispanic church I visited on New Year's Eve.

Augie and I soon connected. It wasn't long before he also fully embraced my ministry, and he was the first pastor in the United States to do so. He put me to work and appointed me Pastoral Advisor of his church. Augie had me involved in church leadership meetings at the highest levels, picked my brain on several issues, and had me fill in for him in the pulpit whenever he had invitations to preach in other churches or was off on vacation with his family. There was no financial remuneration—everything I did was more or less on a volunteer basis. I appreciated and enjoyed the opportunity, however, having gone without any serious ministry activities or speaking engagements since my arrival in the US over a year ago.

Augie also blessed me with my first car, a 1996 Buick. A jalopy it, certainly, was rickety on the outside, yet road-worthy enough to get me around. I nicknamed it the *Spaceship*, for its sheer length and size. Augie also began championing, from the pulpit, the drive to bring Felicia and the kids over to the United States, and he would, on occasion, raise an offering toward that goal.

With Augie Barajas, I soon came to know the global reach of Victory Outreach Ministries International. Born in 1967 under the leadership of the founding pastors, Sonny and Julie Arguinzoni, the outreach had hundreds of branches worldwide, with footprints on almost every continent. It stretched from Los Angeles to London to the Netherlands, from Manila to Mexicali to Rio de Janeiro, as well as to Africa, Australia, and New Zealand.

Because the church had a predominantly and distinctly Latino/Hispanic membership, I was soon thrust into another cultural cauldron, one totally foreign to me. The warmth and embrace of the people in that church enabled me to more easily navigate the contours of the culture of my new church family. I gained visibility and prominence rather quickly, the Lord obviously making a way for me through my gifts in ministry. Not only did I get to meet Sonny Arguinzoni, the church's founder, personally—a rare occurrence for someone of my station and so new in the organization—I also became an instructor at VOSOM, the organization's eight- to ten-week ministerial training program for pastors, leaders, and members, organized at the mother church's facilities in La Puente, California.

The critical test for me in Victory Outreach came when Pastor Augie asked me to direct the church's reentry program. That was the next phase after rehabilitation, designed for inmates: drug addicts, alcoholics, ex-gang-bangers, and plain street folk, helping them to reenter mainstream society. By the time I moved in to the reentry facility to live among those guys, I was with Felicia, who had joined me in the United States, but without the babies. That it was a challenging ministry undertaking is an understatement. The patience, the test of wills, the skills required to manage such a bunch of hard-core men from such anti-social backgrounds, was often daunting.

I organized and supervised the smooth running of the facility and held Bible studies for the inmates. The relapses were very frequent, not to mention the physical altercations between a bunch of men, most of them ex-convicts and victims of America's justice and penitentiary systems. They were separated from their wives and families, and still reeling from the devastating effects of drug and alcohol abuse. On occasion, fights with stiletto knives and base-ball bats would break out among the biggest of the guys, as they jostled for leadership and position through sheer brawn, machismo attitudes, and street instincts. Those were the only ways they knew to survive in LA's mean and tough streets. That some of them were fully delivered and rehabilitated, going on to become ministers of the gospel and pastors, is a testament to the power of the gospel and to the work Felicia and I did in that program.

Unknown to me then, my tenure in the Latino culture, eating Mexican food, listening to Mexican music, and sharing fellowship with Augie and his church members, and then ministry with Felicia in the reentry and subculture of Victory Outreach, were all part of my orientation to ministry in America, a preparation for cross-cultural ministry and missions that only the Lord could have designed and orchestrated.

The Los Angeles Riots

"Riots are massive temper tantrums from
a neglected and voiceless people."
—Martin Luther King Jr., *The Autobiography*
of Martin Luther King Jr.

Suddenly, all hell broke loose. Violence erupted as the verdicts were read; indiscriminate mayhem everywhere. The date was April 29, 1992. The entire nation had been waiting, in nervous anticipation, to hear what verdicts the jury had reached in the epic case. Americans had been horrified by the footage repeatedly broadcast on every news channel in the country. Four baton-wielding White police officers were videotaped beating a seemingly helpless Black man to a pulp, after a botched traffic stop spiraled into a high-speed pursuit through the streets of Los Angeles. The Black man's name was Rodney King.

Newspapers, magazines, radio stations, and various television outlets captured the ongoing riots in the streets. Los Angeles was burning, shops were being ransacked and looted, police cars car-jacked, overturned and set ablaze.

The Trigger

Koon, Briseno, Wind, and Powell, the four police offi-cers charged in the Rodney King incident, were acquitted by a jury comprised of ten Whites, one Latino, and one Asian—no Black person. In 2012, that is, twenty years later, one of the apparent "White jurors," Henry King Jr., revealed that his father was Black. The acquittal of the four police offi-cers by a jury that had no obvious Black representation was, nonetheless, the immediate trigger for the Los Angeles riots. On the third day of the riots, a visibly shaken, physically battered, and emotionally distraught Rodney King appeared on television. Stammering nervously through heavily halted speech, he appealed for calm in the city: "People, I just want to say…can we all get along? Can we get along? Please, we can get along here. We all can get along. I mean, we're all stuck here for a while. Let's try to work it out" (King 1992).

"Please, can, can we all get along? We are all stuck here for a while." Those few words from a man vilified by the news media as a drunk, pot-smoking scallywag clung to my mind in the weirdest way, like a blood-sucking leech would stick to its victim. His words cut deep, to the very core of my soul and I could not shake them off. I felt like his words were prophetic, aimed at and spoken to the conscience of a captive nation, a nation still struggling with the vestiges of its racist past. It was an overtly racist past, a past that was being showcased through the current incredible and painful national drama.

As Rodney King spoke before the TV cameras, it struck me that God, true to His word, was using "the foolish things of this world to confound the wise" (1 Cor. 1:26–28). If He could use a donkey to speak to His prophet, Balaam (Numbers 22:28), He could most certainly choose to use a broken, dented, and vilified man, Mr. Rodney King, to speak to the conscience of a nation.

I heard the voice within his voice. The message was right, truthful, pure, and moral—"Can we all get along?"—even though the messenger was flawed, seriously flawed, his face disfigured, his character in question, literally and figuratively battered and shred to smithereens. Consequently, to most, he was no messenger at all; perhaps to some, he was the wrong one to convey a message of any kind, much more a message of racial healing and reconciliation.

"Can, can we all get along?" So many people heard it amidst the glare of the TV cameras yet did not hear it—"for many have ears, but cannot hear" (Mark 8:18). It was a question of great national significance and import, and with vast implications; a question that every American, regardless of race, creed, or class needed to answer for themselves. It was the kind of question I wished all would hear along with me. But I remembered that Moses saw the burning bush all alone, and by himself. The only verification and validation Moses could hope to get for his experience would have to come from the very God that showed him that fiery bush that burned not and mysteriously spoke to him from its flames. That encounter was to be Moses's only point of reference, and Almighty God, was to be the sole arbiter and voucher for his credentials and testimony.

If the racial upheaval I was witnessing in Los Angeles was not debunking my racial biases and prejudices and driving home the need for some sense of justice and decorum between America's polarized races, Rodney King's call to racial healing and harmony surely was. His words tugged at my heart every waking minute from then on.

I was conscious of the fact that I was undergoing a major shift in my thinking, perceptions, and perspectives; a total overhauling and transitioning of my paradigm. I felt a sense of responsibility—not for having created the problem, but to heed the call as a co-laborer with God in helping find a panacea. I had no illusions about solving a centuries-old malady, but I strongly felt that I needed to make a dent, a difference in the problem, wherever and whenever I could. Those thoughts coalesced, gradually grew, and crystallized into a missionary zeal.

Cumulative Impact

My newfound zeal sparked by the riots and the previous encounters that I have mentioned in this chapter, drove me into research mode. I had a compulsion to search and study the scriptures. I wasn't sure what exactly I was looking for, initially, but as I devoured the scriptures, I felt drawn to the parts relating to race, color, culture, ethnicity, healing, and reconciliation—those started coming alive. It was as if someone had suddenly lit a light bulb in my head. Scriptures that, hitherto, held relatively little or no significance for me suddenly took on a new and fresh meaning and significance. Revelation knowledge began to pour into my spirit. God had obviously turned on the light, and the darkness—my racial and ethnic prejudices formed since my youthful days in Ghana, Africa—were being dispelled.

Having grown up thinking that everyone in the Bible was White, I began to wonder if there was ever a Black presence in the Bible, and, if so, to what extent. All of a sudden, I saw scriptures like "I'm black and beautiful" (Song of Solomon 1:5) and "Can the Ethiopian change his skin?" (Jer. 13:23). Questions about the origin of the races began to fill my mind. God's call to the nations took on much more importance. Peter's vision in Acts chapter 10, the progressive revelation of the mystery of Christ to the nations, starting with the Jews in Jerusalem on the day of Pentecost, and going on to the Samaritans, half-breeds, the Ethiopian eunuch who became an emissary of the gospel to Abyssinia, and the African continent, and further down to the Gentile nations—all became matters of keen interest to me.

Scripture began to take on meaning such as I had never known it. I realized that God was, primarily, a reconciler, that it was His utmost desire that the nations, *all* nations, be reconciled to Him through Christ, and to each other. This was the essence of my call to the gospel ministry. My understanding and paradigm of my mission and ministry totally shifted.

My passion for missions, particularly church-planting was still intact, but my understanding of it, the details and specifics of it, changed. I knew I had come to America not just to plant a Ghanaian or African church, but a truly international church, a church whose make up would be truly reflective of the broader culture God had placed me in. I realized that if God wanted me to plant another Ghanaian church, as I had done before, He would probably have kept me in Ghana, since there were more Ghanaians in Ghana than in America. I also reasoned that, God did not send the European missionaries, like Mungo Park or David Livingstone, to Africa to reach the few Europeans that were in Africa, but rather to reach the indigenous Africans for Christ. Why, then, wouldn't he send me as a missionary from Africa to America to do the same?

Unbeknownst to me just yet, the vision of multiracial, cultural, and ethnic church-planting and mission was being birthed within me. My previous vision of emancipation of the African from the vestiges of colonialism, a vision infused with quite a bit of prejudice and racial bigotry for what the

White man had done to my people, evolved into a love for all humanity, regardless of color or race, and led to the birth of a multiracial and ethnic church plant, with a cardinal goal of fostering racial healing and reconciliation through the power of the gospel.

My friendship with Michael, my exposure to the predominantly White Neighborhood Christian Fellowship, to the Victory Outreach Ministry International's largely Latino/Hispanic outreach ministry, to the Los Angeles riots of 1992, to Rodney King's remarks in the heat of the worst race-inspired riots I had personally witnessed, and to God's revelation of the Holy scriptures to me personally, had brought me far in the shaping of my vision and paradigm. My admission to Fuller Theological Seminary's School of World Mission in 1994 to get a master's degree, and my subsequent study of the issue of multiculturalism in America (the results of which I comment on later in this book) sealed my conviction.

The founding of the International Central Gospel Church, a multiracial, multiethnic and multicultural church, in Los Angeles, in April of 1995, was the culmination of those experiences. It was the first official branch of ICGC in the United States, with a cardinal vision of planting multiracial and multicultural churches for the purposes of fostering racial healing and reconciliation by the power of the gospel. By the third year of its inception, ICGC had grown to an approximate numerical strength of about two hundred, in the process, exhibiting a beautiful mosaic of cultures, truly reflective of the American racial, cultural and ethnic landscape—a rainbow church, it was, indeed.

It is my conviction that, first, God allowed me to have those encounters to help me better understand and appreciate the issues of race and racism as they relate to America, in particular. I had only read about racial hotspots around the world and had seen much upheaval in this arena on television when I was growing up. My entry into Los Angeles served as my baptism into the realities of racism, and America's racial dynamics.

My journey was also to acquaint me with the sensibilities of the various races, cultures, and ethnic groups represented in the American milieu. That most of my cross-cultural encounters occurred in the context of the church, notably the West Angeles Church of God in Christ, Dr. K. C. Price's Crenshaw Christian Center, a predominantly White Neighborhood Christian Fellowship, and the Latino Victory Outreach Ministries, was part of the divine plan orchestrated by the Divine Architect. Secular solutions cannot undo spiritual problems, because racism, at its core, is a spiritual disease, requiring divine intervention and solutions. My path was set.

The Los Angeles riots of 1992 exposed me to the extreme racial polarizing submerged under the façade of apparent calm. It was necessary for me to be at the epicenter of where the Rodney King riots had happened, for maximum exposure to this racial volatility.

Complicating that volatility further, was the increasing numbers of mixed-race children being born into this boiling racial and ethnic cauldron. In an increasingly multicultural American matrix, how do we foster racial healing and reconciliation among America's polarized racial groups and ethnicities, thereby bequeathing to our children a better world, one that is just, equitable, and egalitarian? How does our cultural pluralism become a strength, an asset instead of a liability? How does America transcend race and racism, achieve racial unity and harmony amid increasing diversity, and thus relieve mixed-race children of the Herculean burden of having to choose which side of the divide to belong to?

It is interesting to note that, that despite our continuing racial imbroglio, there are some people who, in typical ostrich fashion, believe that racism and discussions about it have no contemporaneous relevance. To them, racism is simply a historical fact, consigned to the archives of America's national experience, and better left alone than dug up. Any discussion of it, seem to them to amount to reliving our unwholesome past. But racism is not fiction. It is real and is a fact of American life.

In *Beyond Black and White*, Yancey points out that "we cannot change a reality unless we are willing to acknowledge the presence of that reality" (Yancey 1996). Haney-Lopez, asserts that, "In order to get beyond racism, we must first take account of race. There is no other way" (Haney-Lopez 1996). I am convinced that until America is willing to address these issues of race with equal candor from all sides, racial healing and reconciliation will remain but a fleeting illusion.

Part One: The Problem

*"At the heart of racism is the religious assertion
that God made a creative mistake when
He brought some people into being."*
                                        —Friedrich Otto Hertz

"Black Like Me": The John Howard Griffin Story

"The transformation was total and shocking... I was imprisoned in the flesh of an utter stranger, an unsympathetic one with whom I felt no kinship... I looked into the mirror and saw reflected nothing of the white John Griffin's past." (Griffin 1961)

The above quote captures the saga of a White man with deep religious convictions who is troubled by the racism in America, particularly in the Deep South. The issue at stake, and which for years had constantly pressed on Griffin's mind and conscience was this: "If a white man became a Negro in the Deep South, what kind of adjustments does he have to make? What is it like to experience discrimination based on the pigmentation of one's skin, over which one has no control? His name was John Howard Griffin. The year was 1959.

Using an unorthodox method, John Griffin set out on an expedition in search of answers to the questions above. "How else except by becoming a Negro could a white man hope to learn the truth? Though we lived side by side throughout the South, communication between the two races had simply ceased to exist." Eliciting the help of a dermatologist, Griffin chemically altered his skin color, using Oxsoralen, a drug used for combating vitiligo, and through exposure to ultraviolet rays from a sun lamp. Lest his straight hair give him away, he shaves his head completely, and—with a little touch-up with black-dye—Griffin turned into what he himself described as "a fierce, bald, very dark Negro." He was ready to embark on his quest.

Enormously self-conscious, he set out in the dark of night on his expedition through Dixieland with the goal of discovering for himself the bigotry that Blacks had to endure daily in that part of the world.

"I was a newly created Negro, who must go out that door and live in a world unfamiliar to me." Griffin said. By tampering with his own existence, he had lost a sense of his own being. Devastated, he must be this aging and bald Negro; "I must walk through a land hostile to my color, hostile to my skin," Griffin added.

For six weeks, his odyssey took him through four Southern states: Louisiana, Mississippi, Alabama and Georgia.

Griffin's perception and depiction of the South is dark and hostile and exceedingly ominous. Through his book

Black Like Me, published in 1961, he provides the reader with a chilling account of this grim outlook, as shaped by his experiences.

That area of America was shown to be a cold and heartless region with respect to its treatment of Blacks. "The criterion," Griffin recounts, "is nothing but color of skin." He said that Whites, judged him "by no other quality." He concludes: "That was sufficient reason for them to deny me those rights and freedoms without which life loses its significance and becomes a matter of little more than animal survival" (Griffin).

John Griffin notes the "morbid curiosity" of Whites, "about the sexual life of the Negro." He emphasizes that almost all the Whites he encountered as he hitchhiked "had, at base, the same stereotyped image of the Negro as an inexhaustible sex machine, with oversized genitals and a vast store of experiences...," some even going as far as wanting to know if his wife had ever been with a White man sexually. "We figure we're doing you people a favor to get some White blood in your kids," they would add, flagrantly disregarding all sensibilities and any aversion he might have had to such an indecent subject. After all, he was Black.

All that was at a time in the South when miscegenation was seriously frowned upon and there were laws forbidding it. Ogling and "eyeballing" laws were also in force. Those were essentially used in the pre-civil rights era to intimidate, punish, imprison, and sometimes lynch Black men for reasons as trivial as looking at a White woman "inappropriately," and they represented the inordinate and complex confluence of power and gender politics.

Griffin's book about his race experiment and its results hit the bestseller list. Though heralded as historic, a work of pure genius, and a landmark achievement in stirring up the conscience of a White nation, the backlash against Griffin from other segments of the White population was equally fierce and immediate. Effigies of him were publicly burned in various parts of the South, and he was alleged to have been seriously beaten on one occasion. Fearing for his own safety and that of his family, he relocated to Mexico and lived there for a while, until tensions in America abated. For the rest of his life, Griffin remained a passionate and compelling voice for civil rights, until his untimely death in 1980, at the age of sixty.

Although *Black like Me*, it would seem, pointed out the warped and racist logic of a distant era, that same logic, unfortunately, appears to still exist in contemporary American society. The John Howard Griffin story underscores my contention that without a thorough understanding and appreciation of the problem and reality of racism in American society, any prescribed panacea for racial healing and reconciliation will fall woefully short of remedying this entrenched, centuries-old malady. Yancey's words in *Beyond Black and White*, are still instructive in this regard: "we cannot change a reality unless we are willing to acknowledge the presence of that reality" (Yancey 1996).

This section of the book—part 1—highlights the theory and practice of racism in America, in the context of our quest for racial healing and reconciliation.

Racial healing and reconciliation is defined by Yancey as "the process by which we overcome the previous dysfunctional, unequal relationship between the races and develop an egalitarian, healthy relationship" (Yancey 1996). W. E. B Du Bois stated in *The Souls of Black Folk* that the problem of the twentieth century is the problem of race (Du Bois 1903). It appears that the problem of the twenty-first century is America's persistent flirtation and marriage with race and racism.

It is noteworthy that America's only civil war was about racial politics—specifically, the place of the Negro in American society. The genocide of Native Americans, the institution of slavery, the incarceration of thousands of Japanese during World War II, the Chinese Exclusionary Act of 1882, the Emancipation Proclamation and the Jim Crow laws promulgated in its aftermath, and the Civil Rights Movement all attest to the profound significance of race in American life.

Although *Black Like Me* and John Howard Griffin's story points out the warped and racist logic of a specific era, it seems to have been the pervasive logic of centuries of American history and life...and unfortunately still is.

CHAPTER 1

A Limited, Nuanced Definition of Racism

Carlos Hoyt Jr. in *The Pedagogy of the Meaning of Racism: Reconciling a Discordant Discourse*, defines racism as "the belief that all members of a purported race possess characteristics, abilities, or qualities specific to that race, especially so as to distinguish it as inferior or superior to another race or other races" (Hoyt 2012). He presents three concepts critical to the understanding of racism. They are *prejudice*, a preconceived opinion not based on reason or actual experience, but bias and partiality, *power*, the capacity to exert force on or over something or someone, and *oppression*, the exercise of authority or power in a burdensome, cruel, or unjust manner; the three corollaries of racism (Hoyt 2012).

In further noting the discordant perspectives on racism, Carlos Hoyt Jr. draws on definitions by several notable figures, among them Adams, Bell and Griffin, who, in *Teaching for Diversity and Social Justice*, concur with the view of racism that lays the charge of racism exclusively at the feet of the powerful (Adams 1997). The trio above define racism as the "systematic subordination of members of targeted racial groups who have relatively little social power in the United States (Blacks, Latino/as, Native Americans, and Asians), by the members of the agent racial group who have relatively more social power (Whites)" (Hoyt 1997).

DorothyVan Soest and Betty Garcia, according to Hoyt Jr.'s pedagogy are of the same persuasion. In an article titled *Teaching About Diversity and Oppression,* racism, in their view, is a sociopolitical phenomenon undergirded by social power. It is the power behind discrimination that turns it into racism and oppression. Without this power, any behavior that smacks of prejudice is simply an individual discriminatory action (2003).

The third authority Hoyt Jr draws insights from on the subject of racism is Elaine Pinderhughes. In *Understanding Race, Ethnicity, & Power*, Pinderhughes emphasizes the same thesis about the nexus between racism and power, but with a little more reservation, while asserting, nevertheless, that while both Whites and people of color may harbor prejudice or bias, the bias of people of color can usually not be used to reinforce advantage, since they usually lack such power (1989). That the arrogation of power is fundamental to the exercise of racism is amply demonstrated in all these perspectives.

Personal vs. Institutionalized (or Systemic) Racism

Emerson and Smith, in *Divided by Faith*, add a fascinating twist to the discussion on race. Underscoring the almost inextricable nexus of race to the American experience, in what Swedish researcher Gunnar Myrdal called an

American dilemma, they explain that only a few issues may be compared to race, with respect to the volatility associated with the subject, in America. They label the United States a "racialized society," which they define as one in which "race matters profoundly for differences in life experiences, life opportunities and social relationships…a racialized society is also one where different economic, political, social, and even psychological rewards are allocated to groups along racial lines" (2001).

To explain this concept of racialization further, Emerson proposes a framework for its proper understanding by making a distinction between racism under Jim Crow, or legal segregation, and the brand of racism that currently exists in America, that is, from post-Civil Rights Movement up to now. He observes, for the sake of this distinction, that contemporary racism and racial practices in America today are increasingly covert, embedded in normal operations of institutions, avoid direct racial terminology, and are, lastly, invisible to most Whites (Emerson 2001). The racism of today, Emerson further explains, is thus not necessarily individualized, but institutionalized. In such a racialized environment, one need not be personally racist. In fact, one could be unprejudiced but still be participating in racism, because to reproduce racism, one only need defer to societal structures and systems to do the dirty work. The methods may differ, Emerson contends, but the results are the same.

In *Facing Racism: A Vision of the Beloved Community*, a manifesto written by The Initiative Team on Racism and Racial Violence of the Presbyterian Church, Emerson's scenario is explained even better. That racism is nurtured and sustained by systemic power is well noted. Such power, however, must be understood in social, not individual, terms. A climate of support, acceptance, and participation by large numbers of people is what creates racism's power base, the manifesto notes. Institutions do not function in isolation. The social dimension of racism is thus highlighted again. When several institutions come together, they form a system. These institutions and systems are the repositories of social power (PCUSA 1999).

The manifesto states that, "In the context of the United States, racist institutions preserve power and privilege for White society. Rewards are based on group membership not personal attitude" (1999).

In making this case, the Initiative Team on Racism and Racial Violence defer to Jim Wallis, who captures the institutionalized and social dimension of racism so well in *Facing Racism*. Wallis observes, in *The Legacy of White Racism* that, because of the prevailing institutionalized and systemic nature of racism, Whites benefit from racism…whether or not they have ever committed a racist act, uttered a racist word, or had a racist thought…" (2007).

Thus, in differentiating between prejudice and racism, Hoyt, in particular, and in concert with the above theories, emphasizes the conventional notion largely held that to be guilty of racism, a person or group must have power and, through that power, be able to exercise their bias or prejudice at a macro, systemic, or institutional level to maintain their privilege. This perspective presupposes that, in a country such as America, only the dominant White culture can be racist since Whites wield the social, economic, and political power, which is also institutionalized. Does that mean, therefore, that Blacks and other minorities are immune to the infection of racism?

It is my contention that Blacks and other minority groups and individuals can also be racist, inasmuch as "holding irrational unjust beliefs and acting on them is an equal-opportunity peril" (Hoyt 2012). Black and minority groups may not be able to employ these "irrational and unjust beliefs" in so far as acting on them to the degree that the dominant White culture can, to cause mass oppression of other racial groups. In no way does this completely erase or negate the presence or reality of bias or prejudice, however. Yancey, in also disagreeing with the premise that only Whites can be racist, highlights the uniquely disproportionate benefits that power and privilege have accrued to Whites in America, as a result of institutionalized racism, a creation of Whites for Whites. He emphasizes, nonetheless, that although members of other races in America do not have this facility, they may exhibit what he calls "personal racism" (Yancey 1996). As Thomas Sowell so eloquently explains in *Race and Culture: A World View*, "if this kind of reasoning were followed consistently," that is, the assertion that only the powerful can be racist, "then Hitler could not have been considered a racist when he was an isolated street corner rabble-rouser, but only after he became chancellor of Germany" (Sowell 1994). This is the idea that any individual, White or Black, powerful or powerless, is or can be susceptible to the power and influence of racism. Expressed another way, the sin of racism is not exclusive to any particular race, culture, ethnicity, or individual. Any individual or group with a degree of power can exercise their power cruelly or abusively over another individual or group. Thus, institutional and personal racism are the two evil faces of the same coin, as Yancey explains further (1996).

What distinguishes White racism in America is, perhaps, the degree and duration of systemic or institutionalized race-based oppression. To think that such oppression has thrived primarily because of physical differences, along with other contrived and nuanced factors, inuring to one group benefits and privileges, and to the others deprivation and degradation, is not only what makes American racism quite unique, but also what fuels the historical chasm between Blacks and Whites and causes the wounds to continue festering till this day.

For racial healing and reconciliation to become a real achievable proposition, the larger and White-inspired institutional and societal racism has to be dismantled, perhaps, by government or legislative action and intervention, without negating or minimizing the power of the personal, which may require hearts to be touched or transformed on a more personal level.

It's Not Just A Black Or White Thing: Spiritual Undertones of Racism

From a Christian (worldview) perspective, racism is not simply a structural issue or mental orientation, but a spiritual malaise, emanating from the heart of man. In *Facing Racism: A Vision of the Beloved Community*, the General Assembly of the Presbyterian Church again observes that "Racism is fundamentally a spiritual problem because it denies our true identity as children of God" (PCUSA 1999). The Assembly further notes, from an article in *Sojourners*, titled *Crossing the Racial Divide, America's Struggle for Justice and Reconciliation*, that "racism is a spiritual issue. Neither its solutions or causes will be found (solely) through government programs, social ministries or our own best intentions... The forces that perpetuate racism through our society are rooted in spiritual realities that require us to call out God for spiritual solutions" (PCUSA 1999). Yancey, in turn, observes in *Beyond Black and White* that "racism and discrimination are not simply secular issues but have important spiritual dimensions that must be addressed (Yancey 1996).

The scripture is amply clear that the Creator, God, created all humanity in His own image (Gen. 1:26–27). Racism is a deviation from divine order, since it suppresses and devalues God's image in humanity. Everything God created prior to the Fall was in a state of perfection; He saw that all he had created was very good and nothing to be rejected (1 Tim. 4:4). Any orientation to the contrary, therefore, of the created order—such as a perception of a group or individual as inferior or subhuman because of racism—is anathema to divine order, and a consequence of the Fall.

At the heart of evil, hatred, prejudice, racism, and oppression is the depraved heart of mankind. Scripture declares all humanity to be sinful, corrupted by the willful disobedience of its progenitor, Adam. "By one man sin entered the world, and death by sin and so death passed on all men, for all had sinned" (Rom. 5:12). Consequently, all humanity bears the corrupted DNA of Adam, which is embedded in the heart, the core of mankind's being. Jeremiah 17:9 reveals that "the heart" of man is the crucible from which racism and all evil spring. "It is deceitful above all things and desperately wicked." Jesus concurred with this, adding that from the heart issues all evil thoughts—such as murders, adultery, fornication, theft, slander and false witness (Matt. 15:19).

Rick Joyner, in *Overcoming Racism Combating Spiritual Strongholds*, refers to racism as a demonic stronghold (2001). Thus, we may conclude that racism is, at its core, a spiritual problem rooted in sin in the heart of humanity, driven and influenced by satanic or demonic impulses. The Apostle Paul's words to the Ephesian church are instructive here. He admonishes the believers here to equip themselves for battle, emphasizing the cosmic dimension of the battle and who the real enemy is, in the process. The real culprit is Satan: "Put on the whole armor of God that you may be able to stand against the wiles of the devil. We wrestle not against flesh and blood, but against principalities, against powers, against the rulers of the darkness of this world, against spiritual wickedness in high place" (Ephesians 6:11–12).

Racism's overt manifestations in the physical, then, may be political, social, legal, or economic oppression of one by another. However, at its core, it is a demonic structure and stronghold, one that no legal or legislative apparatus alone can completely and permanently cure. It is only renewed hearts and transformed minds that can effect change in this sphere. This spiritual understanding of racism in America is critical to our overall appreciation of the cancer of racism. Such understanding is also vital for the role of the Church, particularly the role of the multicultural church, in fostering racial healing and reconciliation in contemporary urban settings.

America: The Subjective Construction of Race

*"Race is not based on biology, but race is rather
an idea that we ascribe to biology."*
—Alan Goodman, *Biological Anthropologist*

"Every single one of us is a mongrel."
—Student

"It is all around us. It is an illusion and yet profoundly real. What we perceive as race is one of the first things, we notice about each other. Skin: darker or lighter. Eyes: round or almond, blue, black, brown. Hair: curly, straight, blond, or dark. And attached to these characteristics is a mosaic of values, assumptions, and historical meanings." (RACE-Power of an Illusion 1968)

Long before Ota Benga, the Congolese Pygmy was displayed alongside an orangutan in the Monkey House at the Bronx Zoo in 1906, men like the French philosopher Voltaire had ridiculed the very notion that Blacks, like Whites, were created in the image of God. In The French encounter with Africans: White response to Blacks, 1530–1880, Voltaire is quoted by Cohen as saying "Now here is a lovely image of the Divine Maker…a flat and black nose with little or hardly any intelligence…" (2003). Voltaire questioned whether Africans descended from monkeys or if monkeys descended from Africans.

In IQ and the Wealth of Nations, published in 2002, Richard Lynn and Tatu Vanhanen, both professors emeritus of Psychology and Political Science, respectively, propounded a theory establishing a nexus between the Intelligence Quotient of nations and their development or underdevelopment. They attribute the gap between rich and poor nations to both genetics and environmental factors. The implication of this is obvious; since the world's least developed nations are south of the equator, within which zone lies sub-Saharan Africa and most of the world's people-groups, the Intelligence Quotients of these people must be defective and not up to par.

In "An Essay on the Inequality of the Human Races," Arthur de Gobineau, who is considered one of the foremost advocates of scientific racism divides the human race into White, Yellow and Black races, attributing various genetic particularities to each group. He postulates that only the White races are the descendants of Adam and are the only race with the capacity for intellectual exercise. The Black race is much more equipped for physical enterprises as "hewers of stone and drawers of water." Miscegenation among the races, according to Gobineau, would be the key to the decline of civilization (1967).

The modern version of this theory that alludes to the genetic intellectual inferiority of Blacks as the rationale for their dismal life conditions in America is what Charles Murray and Richard Herrnstein argue in the Bell Curve. The publication of the Bell Curve: Intelligence and Class Structure in America in 1994 suggested a link between academic achievement, economic and social outcomes (among others), and an individual's or racial group's genetically inherited intelligence quotient (IQ). The book was a classic example of scientific racism. The code word here is "genes," because social, economic, and academic achievement was, thus, biologically or genetically determined, with the inferior gene pool obviously producing inferior socioeconomic and academic outcomes. The backlash and furor generated over the book's assertions about race and ethnicity was once again, a testament to how volatile the issue of race is and can be in our society.

For centuries, craniologists, evolutionists, and scientific racists in the fashion of Voltaire, Gobineau, and, in more modern times, Murray, Herrnstein, Lynn and Vanhanen, have propounded various theories about the Negro race, ranging from the bigger size of the Negro skull to the smallness of his brain, to his darker hue, the darker hue attributed by men like Rush, to an incurable, hereditary, skin disease called "negroidism" (Rush 1799).

Despite the often ridiculous and speculative postulates introduced about race and racial differences in the name of science, a true definition and genuine scientific basis for race has proved to be an arbitrary and elusive undertaking. Amid a racialized American society, the lack of a scientific definition and basis for racial categories still haunts us and begs answers, lending credence to Goodman's assertion in a PBS documentary, that "Race is not based on biology, but race is rather an idea that we ascribe to biology" (2003). Is the concept of race simply a hyped-up, nonexistent theory, an illusion, a mere subjective and speculative proposition? Is race real, or is it just a social construct? The implications of this, either way, are vast.

Calling race a "myth," a group of academics in a provocative PBS documentary argued against the construction of race on the basis of biology or physical traits and differences, emphasizing that genetic variations in the human species, even among those of the same race, are as vast and different as between other human racial species. In other words, our differences are not biological or genetic. What we perceive as race is one of the first things we notice about each other. Skin, eyes, and hair—we attach to these characteristics a mosaic of values, assumptions, and historical meanings. Race, contrary to Voltaire, Murray or Herrnstein, these academics therefore contend, is an illusion, a sociological, political, and legal construct. Race is a creation of mankind to perpetuate privileges accorded one race—in this case, the White race—and the dominance such privileges affords them over other races.

Yancey believes that race is a social construct. "It is defined sociologically rather than biologically," he says. "In short," he adds, "we made it up." Yancey further explains that "We developed rules of segregation to control the mixing of the races. Eventually, we actually began to believe that this separation is part of the natural order of things. Some of us Christians may even believe that God ordered this separation. All the while we forget that this is something we have made up" (1996).

In *White by Law: The Legal Construction of Race*, Haney-Lopez reiterates similar sentiments, noting White America's need to invent a plausible definition of "Whiteness," as a means of determining status. Haney-Lopez stresses that Whiteness was key to citizenship in America, according all White immigrants the full benefits of American citizenship, which included access to better jobs, the voting booth, jury work, and public office and service. Although after the Civil War the privilege was extended to persons of African descent, in reality, it was the status of Whiteness, he contends, that was much sought after, since it ensured benefits that Black citizens could only dream of. Social, political, legal, and economic necessities in American history, thus, made the classification of the races an absolute strategic imperative. Such classification was based purely on expediency and subjectivity, however. The laws were manipulated and subsequently constructed, subject to the whims and caprices of the prevailing power structure, with the Supreme Court at the helm.

Highlighting the extent of this subjective interpretation of the laws, historian James Horton observes in Race—the Power of an Illusion that the law in Virginia, for instance, defined a Black person as a person with one-sixteenth African ancestry. Florida, on the other hand, defined a Black person as a person with one-eighth African ancestry, while the State of Alabama conferred the designation of Black on anyone with any Black or African ancestry at all.

The inference, he states, is that one could walk across a state line and literally, legally change race. What race means under these circumstances, thus, is anybody's guess. The one with the power, Horton concludes, can make you any race he or she chooses. With racial distinctions, roles, and rights clearly delineated, and laws enacted to secure and ensure White privilege and dominance, White America was ready to ease itself into an uncomfortable, yet tolerable and, hopefully, peaceful co-existence with its minority racial groups.

To further explain such an arbitrary construction of race and racial designations, let us take a look at the cases of Takao Ozawa, a Japanese businessman, in OZAWA v. US, and Bhagat Singh Thind, a United States Army veteran and an immigrant of South Asian Descent, in US vs THIND. The two were applicants for American citizenship. Takao Ozawa, in 1922, petitioned the US Supreme court for American citizenship. Ozawa submitted his case after Armenians, who are usually regarded as Asiatic Turks were accorded the designation of "White" by the US Appeals Court in Massachusetts. Other Asiatic races, among them Japanese, Ozawa was convinced, would or could gain citizenship as well. According to the account, Ozawa migrated from Japan, attended University of California, Berkeley, for a few years, and relocated to Hawaii, where he settled down and started a family. According to his daughter, Edith Takeya, who was also interviewed on the PBS documentary, Race: The Power of an Illusion, her father "did everything right." Mae Ngai, a historian on the same documentary reports that Ozawa "learned English...had a lifestyle that was American...went to a Christian church on Sunday...dressed as a Westerner... brought up his children as Americans."

Ozawa had been living in the United States for approximately twenty-eight years when his case reached the United States Supreme Court, after eight earlier rejections of his application for citizenship in lesser courts. No doubt, he believed in the rightness of his cause and was determined to bring it to its logical conclusion: American citizenship for himself and his family.

Unable to own land, due to various acts pertaining to alien land ownership, the Japanese (farming) community followed Ozawa's case with keen interest. A designation of "Whiteness" was necessary to guarantee that community the full protection of American law. Ozawa argued that his skin was as white as any so-called Caucasians, if not whiter. As if this argument was not potent enough, the second, without question, was as Ozawa argued: that one's beliefs, not race, should be the basis for citizenship. With these words, he pressed his case before the United States Supreme Court: "My honesty and industriousness are well-known among my Japanese and American friends. In name Benedict Arnold was an American, but at heart he was a traitor. In name, I'm not an American, but at heart I am a true American" (Ozawa v. United States 1922).

Verdict: The Supreme Court ruled against Ozawa, stating that, according to the "best known science," he was of the Mongolian race, not Caucasian.

The court's decision in the Ozawa case was to be put to the test barely three months after the Ozawa verdict. Ironically, the court would not be "bound by science in policing the boundaries of whiteness" in the case of Bhagat Singh Thind, a United States Army veteran and an immigrant of South Asian Descent. Thind's petition for citizenship was predicated on the scientific premise of the Supreme Court in its ruling in the Ozawa case saying that Indians were of the Aryan or Caucasian race and, therefore, White, unlike the Mongoloid Japanese. The court's subjectivity in the determination of racial identities was demonstrably clear, with no deference whatsoever to science. The ruling in Thind's case is stated in Haney-Lopez's White by Law, The Legal Construction of Race: "It may be true…that the blond Scandinavian and the brown Hindu have a common ancestor in the dim reaches of antiquity, but the average man knows perfectly well that there are unmistakable and profound differences between them today."

Thus, in a ruling contrary to the Ozawa case, it was the "average man's" knowledge of what "Whiteness" meant that prevailed; not science. This was the basis for denying Thind American citizenship.

The consequences of those two cases were understandably devastating to the Indian and Japanese communities. For the Japanese community, not only were many unable to buy or lease land to continue in business, but many lost their lands when they were forcibly taken from them by the government and sold to White farmers. Takao Ozawa himself passed away before changes in the racial designations were made, in 1952.

The case of Thind was equally terrible for the Indian community. Some Indians, like Vaishno das Bagai, a successful businessman who had fled British rule and tyranny to raise his children in a free America, committed suicide, choosing to die rather than suffer the humiliation of bridges burnt back home and the hope of a better life in America being taken from them, as he wrote in a suicide note. Many Indians who had their naturalization before the verdict had their citizenships revoked, while others had their property seized (Haney-Lopez 1996).

In summary, we may be able to lean on the supposition that race is more speculative, arbitrary or subjective than objective or real. As the PBS documentary highlighted, our differences do not determine race; it is the laws and practices that affect life chances and opportunities that determine race.

RICHARD D. DONKOR

One-Drop Rule

As the custody battle between Halle Berry and French-Canadian ex-boyfriend, Gabriel Aubry, over their daughter Nahla heated up, Berry, an Oscar-winner and former fashion model, highlighted the "one-drop rule," bringing the concept into contemporary American discourse on race. Halle Berry is biracial. Her father is Black or African-American, a hospital attendant; her mother is White, and a psychiatric nurse at the same hospital where her dad worked. "I feel she's black. I'm black and I'm her mother, and I believe in the one-drop theory," the celebrated actress is purported to have stated about her daughter in an interview with *Ebony* magazine.

Don Lemon of CNN fame commented on the one-drop rule as it relates to his family heritage. He's the descendant of generations of mixed or biracial Black Americans who could easily pass for White. He recalls asking as a kid: "Is Aunt-ee Lacy White?" To which an adult in the vicinity would respond, amid laughter, "Lacy's Black," followed by the phrase, "it only takes one drop." In essence, Lemon adds, it only takes one drop of Negro blood to make one Black. Aunt Lacy, allegedly, was the product of his grandmother's rape at the hands of the White man she worked for, who, ironically, happened to be the town Sheriff also.

President Barack Obama, the son of a White mother and a Black African father, surprised some when he identified himself as being only Black, during the 2010 US census.

Other famous Americans with a racially-mixed heritage include Frederick Douglas, W. E. B. Du Bois, Booker T. Washington, Malcolm X, Jimi Hendrix, Mariah Carey, Beyoncé Knowles, Tiger Woods, and Dwayne Johnson (a.k.a. The Rock).

The theory of the one-drop rule buttresses the subjectivity surrounding the construction of race in America. This theory, named from a colloquial term used during slavery and Jim Crow, undergirds the nuances surrounding the issue of race in America. David Hollinger captures the invidiousness of the one-drop rule, as so eloquently encapsulated in Barbara Fields words in *Cosmopolitanism and Solidarity: Studies in Ethnoracial, Religious, and Professional affiliation in the United States*. He asserts that in America we have a convention that considers "a white woman capable of giving birth to a black child but denies that a black woman can give birth to a white child." In *Sociology for the Twenty-First Century: Continuities and Cutting Edges*, Abu-Lughod states that "more than any other racial group...the racial line drawn around African-Americans has been the most rigid. From the mid-nineteenth century to the present, Blacks have been subject to what Marvin Harris (in 1964) has termed, more informally the One-Drop rule" (Hollinger).

Paula Rothenberg chimes in, in *Race, Class and Gender in the United States,* to emphasize that *in the United States*, the Black/White color line has historically been rigidly defined and enforced. Using Elizabeth Taylor's words in the movie *Raintree County* as illustrative of this theory, she underscores the worst of fates to befall Whites "as having a little Negra blood in ya'—just one little teeny drop and a person's all Negra." According to Rothenberg, the theory originates from Marvin Harris's principle of Hypo-descent, which essentially requires Americans to believe that having a negro ancestor automatically makes one a Negro; nothing more, nothing less. Hypo-descent Rothenberg emphasizes, is a biological association with the subordinate or inferior category, instead of the superior. It is "an invention" made in the United States "in order to keep biological facts from intruding into our collective racist fantasies" (Rothenberg).

Based on the principle of *Hypo-descent*, which also speaks to the contaminating effect of Black or Negro blood on the purity of White blood, the one-drop rule was first instituted by legislation in Tennessee in 1910, and subsequently in Virginia, through the Racial Integrity Act of 1924. It ultimately spread to the other states in the union and became the law of the land.

Blacks, by this law, were designated as "Mulattoes," half (50 percent) Black heritage; "Quadroons" (one-quarter Black); or "Octoroons" (one-eighth Black). The theory of the one-drop rule, at its core, begs the question, "Who is really Black in America and what does Blackness mean?"

In an article in the *Harvard Gazette,* published in December of 2010 under the caption "One-drop rule persists," Steve Bradt discusses research conducted by a group of Harvard University psychologists, the results of which were published in the *Journal of Personality and Social Psychology.* The researchers, according to Bradt, underscored the fact that the centuries-old one-drop rule of assigning minority status or lower status to mixed race individuals or biracials than their parents, still lives on even in our modern-day perception. The group observes from their enquiry that America tends to still "see Biracials not as equal members of both parent groups, but as belonging more to their minority or lower status parent group." They assert that their research challenges the notion that the election of Barack Obama, the first biracial American president, and the growing number of mixed race people, in general, signals the emergence of a colorblind America. "Hypo-descent against blacks (in particular)," they assert, "remains a relatively powerful force within American society." This is a concept that "reflects the cultural entrenchment of America's traditional racial hierarchy" and serves to "reinforce racial boundaries, rather than moving us toward a race-neutral society," they conclude (*Harvard Gazette* 2010).

The confusion surrounding the issue of Blackness in America further underscores the subjective construction of race in this country with regard to Black self-identification. While some biracial or mixed people—like Barack Obama, Halle Berry, and Don Lemon—have identified culturally and ethnically as Black, consistent with the one-drop theory, a multiracial identity movement has evolved whose adherents affirm their dual identity as a basic human and civic right. They highlight the necessity for biracial Americans to be able to freely identify themselves with all their lineage or ancestry.

Tiger Woods is most notable among those who have repudiated the one-drop rule while, simultaneously, laying claim to the right to self-identify as bi- or multiracial, which he did upon winning the much-coveted Masters Golf Championship title in 1997. Woods was asked how he felt about being the first Black man to win such a title. My speculation is that the interviewer was alluding to the one-drop rule in his question. In response, Woods referred to his multicultural roots, calling himself "Cablinasian." He is the son of a Thai mother and lays claim to a multiracial heritage and identity: Thai (1/4), Chinese (1/4), Black (1/4), Native American (1/8), and White (1/8). He checks "Asian" (not "Black") on the census.

The chorus of interracial and multiracial voices calling for biracial and multiracial children to embrace and celebrate their entire cultural, racial, and ethnic heritage is growing, even as the spate of interracial dating and marriages also continues to rise in the United States.

One author questioning Barack Obama's Black racial identity and designation challenges the one-drop rule in these words: "Yeah, I have never liked the one-drop rule," she says. "It is kinda silly if you ask me. For instance, how the heck is Barack Obama 'black,' when he is half-white, was raised by his white folks, and only met his black father once in his life?"

In *White Racial Identity, Racial Mixture, and the One-Drop Rule*, A. D. Powell, writer for Interracial Voices, also makes some very interesting observations. Powell asks why there is "an escape hatch for Hispanics and Arabs when their Anglo and Creole counterparts (who actually have White blood) are condemned as light-skinned blacks?" Is the inferior Negro blood more welcome into the White race "as long as it comes speaking Spanish or Arabic?" he further queries. The rationale for his argument lies in the fact that Hispanics and Arabs within the United States population, show signs of the much-dreaded "inferior" Black blood. Puerto Rico, Cuba, and the Dominican Republic are essentially Mulatto nations, and nearly all Mexicans have some Black ancestry from the African slaves who were brought to colonial Mexico and, subsequently, assimilated into the Indian and Mestizo populations. However, Indians, Arabs, Mexicans, and Latinos, in general, are able to pass as White without problem, despite having Black blood in their ancestry; unlike Blacks, who may even have more recent and closer genetic and color ties to Whites.

Questioning the theory of the one-drop further, Powell points to the contradictions in the theory's application. American Indian blood, he points out, is "harmless and compatible with white ancestry in a way that black blood is not." Explaining this proposition, he observes that an American can easily say, "My grandmother is an Indian but I am white," but that same person cannot say, "My grandmother is Black but I am white," without his right to a White identity being challenged. He buttresses America's subjective construction of race by making reference to famous American personalities, such as Burt Reynolds, Cher, and the late Johnny Cash, who all boldly and proudly made claims to American Indian heritage. That they had Indian blood coursing through their veins did not in any way negate their Whiteness. Their acknowledgment, Powell emphasizes, neither served as a "repudiation of their white ancestry" nor their "right to a white identity," in accordance with the letter of the Virginia Racial Integrity Act, promulgated in 1924.

The nonsense about this theory, Powell further highlights, is evidenced in the cases of Alexander Dumas, the French author of the famous novel *The Three Musketeers*, and Alexander Pushkin, the greatest of all Russian poets, a man who is recognized as the father of Russian literature. These two people are often presented to American school children as being Black. Dumas, Powell explains, was three-quarters White, and not even socially Black. Pushkin, on the other hand, only had a great-grandfather who was Black. Consequently, Powell argues, there are no justifiable reasons, physically or culturally, to label those men "Black," except of course, by the politically, sociologically, and legally constructed, but nonsensical, one-drop rule.

The one-drop Rule became America's yardstick for racial and social classification, a classification that determined who was Black or otherwise. The immediate goal was to prevent light-skinned Blacks, the products of miscegenation, from "passing as White," with the protection of the racial purity of White America as the ultimate motivation. Although racial classification in America, based on that rule, persists in America, the law enacted to give it legal merit was rendered unconstitutional by the US Supreme Court in the anti-miscegenation laws in the case of Loving v. Virginia (Wallenstein 2014) as recently as 1967.

On this subject, bestselling author, Karen Hunter's words are rather instructive. She notes in Connecticut's *Hartford Courant*, that the issue of Barack Obama's racial identity "is forcing conversations about issues that have been easier to ignore for centuries" In the same article, Obama himself is quoted as having said on *60 Minutes*, "I'm not sure I decided it… I think, you know, if you look African-American in this society, you're treated as an African-American." Obama told PBS host Charlie Rose, "If I'm outside your building trying to catch a cab, they're not saying, 'Oh, there's a mixed-race guy'" (Washington Times 2008).

In summing up the subjectivity of race in America, there is no gainsaying that the United States, by virtue of the One-drop rule, is the only country in the world, in which a White woman can give birth to a Black baby, but a Black woman cannot give birth to a White baby As irrational as this is, it is little wonder that a new generation is rising that refuses to be defined by the boundaries of the One-drop rule; it is a generation that instead opts for fluidity in its racial designation, pushing against conventional categorizations and choosing rather to embrace all the ethnic, cultural and racial distinctives that constitute who they are. It is this multicultural generation that represents the emergence, hopes, dreams and aspirations of a new America.

CHAPTER 2

Is America Post-Racial or Still a House Divided?

"The fact is...the issues that have surfaced over the last few weeks reflect the complexities of race in this country that we've never really worked through—a part of our union that we have yet to perfect..."
—**Barack Obama, "A More Perfect Union—Race Speech" (2008)**

"White prejudice and discrimination keep the Negro low in standards of living, health, education, manners and morals... White prejudice and Negro standards...cause each other."
—**Gunnar Myrdal, An American Dilemma: The Negro Problem and Modern Democracy (1944)**

A Black Man in the White House

An air of nervous anticipation overshadowed the eve of the US presidential elections. It had been a *Battle Royale* up until now. The two years of campaigning, first in the primaries and later the presidential elections, were a slugfest of titanic proportions and the longest in recent American political history. The numerous gaffes, mudslinging, and scurrilous innuendos all added to the excitement of an unprecedented political season.

The signs of things to come were written on the wall when Barack Obama trumped Hillary Clinton, the presumptive Democratic Party frontrunner, to win the caucuses in Iowa, a state that is demographically 95 percent Caucasian. Former Senator John Edwards of North Carolina came in third. The *National Enquirer* had published an article on October 10, 2007, detailing an alleged Edwards affair with Rielle Hunter, a campaign staffer, with hints of a resultant "love child." The ensuing scandal would dog the former Democratic senator from North Carolina until his admission of culpability—an admission that ultimately derailed what once was a very promising presidential candidacy and political career.

Hillary Clinton "teared up" after her defeat in the Iowa primary, in a public display of emotion, revealing her softer, gentler side. With that, her poll numbers soared as she "connected" on a more personal level with the electorate, which showed its approval for her transparency and gravitated to the sensitive and tender Hillary. It was a side of her never before known or seen. Her beer-drinking—knocking down shots with the guys in working-class bars on the campaign trail, and the provocative 3:00 a.m. red-phone call before the Texas primary showcased (or was at least intended to showcase) her steadiness in the face of a national crisis, and experience with respect to foreign policy. These were designed to contrast Obama's relative inexperience.

The petulance of Hillary's husband, Bill Clinton (dubbed by Nobel Prize-winning author Toni Morrison "the first black president") in response to questions about race, unfortunately, created a backlash from the Black body-politic, adding to the political furor before the South Carolina primary. Previously solidly for Hillary, Black voters switched, en masse, to Obama, in reaction to Bill Clinton's comments, helping Obama win the South Carolina primary handily, and by a rather huge margin. These highlights added, in no small way, to a frenzied and intriguing presidential campaign.

Questions about Obama's "true" faith and American citizenship also surfaced and were trending on the blogosphere. Despite his insistence on being a Christian, questions persisted about his alleged Muslim faith. Pictures of him dressed in traditional Somali attire, with captions labeling Obama's "native clothes," appeared in the *Drudge Report*. Those unsubstantiated and disparaging rumors, very much akin to the ones about John McCain fathering an illegitimate child with a Black woman in the previous election against Bush Jr., were obviously intended to stamp negative and stereotypical notions about Obama in the American psyche. They portrayed him as an Arab Bedouin herdsman or a Tuareg, a weird blend of Muslim and African, and, therefore, of alien stock or dubious heritage.

In the minds of some, that exotic heritage was quite new, perhaps different, and definitely atypical. It rendered him unfit for the presidency. His middle name, Hussein, did little to help, and added fuel to the fire. Even his finesse or skill in bowling, or rather the lack of it, was not off-limits to the other side's attack machine. In so many subtle ways, the code phrase and message was: "He's not one of us."

Obama's wife, Michelle, who had stayed out of the foray or been spared the vitriol of presidential politics, would get a taste of the "slash and burn" style characteristic of American political campaigns. If going after a candidate personally instead of his politics was bad, going after his wife was definitely a new low. Michelle Obama would soon be repackaged by conservative campaign hatchet men and commentators. Draped in figurative Angela Davis apparel, using her "for the first time in my adult life, I'm really proud of my country" statement in Milwaukee as fodder, she would be branded and reintroduced to the American electorate as the proverbial "angry Black woman," in the likes of Maxine Waters and Cynthia McKinney: Michelle LaVaughn Robinson Obama, the radical wife of Barack Hussein Obama, himself a radical Black, African, Muslim extremist.

The "blunders" committed by both Hillary and Obama did little to quell the crossfire between the two camps. Obama referred to some working-class folk in Pennsylvania as "bitter," clinging to religion and guns in the very heart and bastion of liberalism, San Francisco, and in the process fulfilling the age-old "out of touch, elitist" charge. Hillary Clinton on the other hand bumbles along with exaggerated comments of "ducking for cover under sniper fire in the Balkans."

Despite the blundering and negative press that follows, the quest continues on both sides, to "max out" the super-delegate count. Obama's connection with the Reverend Jeremiah Wright, his spiritual mentor; his business dealings with Tony Rezko, the Lebanese Chicago realtor convicted of extortion and bribery; and his alleged ties to radical and terrorist elements, like Bill Ayers and his Weather Underground organization, again, provided fodder for the political machinery of the other side, looking for any opportunity to pounce and make a case for his un-electability.

The political pendulum, however, swung dramatically, and perhaps irreversibly, when stalwarts in the Democratic Party establishment, such as Caroline Kennedy, the daughter of JFK, her uncle Ted, Congressman John Lewis, a pillar in the Civil Rights Movement, and Governor Bill Richardson of New Mexico, former Energy Secretary in the Clinton administration, all staunch Hillary allies, at least initially, shifted their allegiance from her and threw their political muscle behind Obama. Oprah Winfrey's public endorsement of Obama, as well as Maria Shriver's (also a Kennedy, and ex-wife of the "Terminator," and former governor of California, Arnold Schwarzenegger), demonstrably added to the shift in public opinion and momentum, and coalesced, to a large degree, the women's vote around the young senator.

On the Republican side, what started out initially as an audacious attempt by the maverick to rock the boat, and by extension the vote, by choosing for a vice-presidential candidate a lady, a virtual unknown, turned out to be the biggest blunder of the McCain campaign. The choice of Sarah Palin, the Governor of Alaska, later appeared reckless, especially when her inexperience and ignorance of basic foreign policy matters became apparent. Republican hopes of her appealing to previous Hillary supporters fell miserably flat soon after her introduction to the American public. Although the darling of the religious right conservative hardliners, who were very uncomfortable with McCain's moderate stance on social issues, Palin's bumbling in various interviews gradually revealed the depth of her ineptitude, and thus her unpreparedness for the job.

Many in the party apparatus and across the wider political spectrum, in time, became very uncomfortable with Sarah Palin. Her alleged meeting with the British Ambassador, Sir Nigel Sheinwald, turned out to be a farce. Her inability to explain the Bush Doctrine, her comments about Alaska's proximity to Russia ("Putin rearing his head in America's airspace")—translated and reenacted by Tina Fey to mean a unique and literal ability to see "Russia from her house"—made her an object of derision; her character and misstatements becoming parodies for *Saturday Night Live*. For a prospective vice-presidential candidate, a position just a heart-beat away from the Presidency, a realistic prospect considering McCain's age of seventy-two, the public's concerns over Palin's lack of grasp of the issues, seemed justified.

The *coup de grace* for the McCain campaign came when the maverick announced he was suspending his presidential campaign in order to help with negotiations in congress regarding the Wall Street bailouts. Americans looked on in disbelief, virtually stunned, while John McCain, in wanting to carve for himself an image of patriotism, of putting country above self, instead looked risky and reckless. Such missteps pushed the nail further into the coffin for the maverick of the US Senate.

All the robo calls, political flyers, advertisements, gotchas, innuendos, and intrigue finally came to an end, to the relief of a campaign-weary nation. America stood on the brink of a momentous event—the dawning of a new day. Change was at the door, beckoning to make its entrance unto the American political stage.

Was America going to elect Senator John McCain, the decorated Vietnam war hero with the classy, multimillionaire philanthropist of a wife, Cindy Lou McCain, to the presidency, and thereby reenact another four years of the last eight, or was America going to elect Barack Obama, a Black man of brilliant pedigree, a Harvard- and Columbia-educated community organizer and activist, with a wife who was of equal social and academic standing, a lawyer, and product of Princeton and Harvard Law School? It is ironic and noteworthy that before that election, Barack Obama was the only Black member of the entire US Senate.

Although I felt exceedingly thrilled that my precinct supervisory job was, in some minute but unique way, contributing to making history on that auspicious occasion, I still could not stand the thought of missing the extended CNN coverage of the results, and the fascinating punditry that was to follow, by such notable commentators as John King, Ed Rollins, Roland Martin, David Gergen, Wolf Blitzer, and Gloria Borger.

The crowd was thicker than ever on the November morning of voting day. The lines, spectacularly long, snaked around the Mesquite Elementary School building, which had been turned into a polling center. I could not help but have my eleven-year-old daughter at home texting me the results from CNN as the polls closed on the East Coast and the counting began. She was no doubt fired up about her "news anchor role," being the only conduit for getting the latest breaking news to me.

Results from some of the battleground states, like Virginia, South Carolina, Ohio, Indiana and Florida were still pending when I finally arrived home, besides those from the West Coast states, like California, whose polls had just closed. Being a near political junkie, I was excited beyond measure to be home to get the coverage and raw data myself, directly from the TV networks.

The talk of Barack Obama being a transformative figure had been touted in the media during the campaign. The concept of a post-racial America became synonymous with Obama's candidacy, as well. It seemed that Americans of all shades and stripes had, for once, been exposed, and on the national stage, to a quality, organized, good-looking and charming Black American. Being at the helm of such a disciplined, and superbly-run political machinery, Obama and his campaign, most notably, did not make the issue of race its centerpiece, unlike others in the past. That was new, innovative, and definitely refreshing.

At the defining hour, with Obama ahead in the national polls and also in several key battleground states, history seemed to be on the verge of being made. North Carolina and Virginia had been historically and traditionally solid "red" or Republican States (the red and blue regional designations depicting the "culture wars" present in American political discourse). North Carolina in particular had not voted for a democratic presidential candidate in over thirty years. Similarly, Virginia, also a Republican bastion, had not voted for a Democrat since Lyndon Johnson in 1964, forty-four years ago. With victories in those two southern states for Barack Obama, a marginal victory in Florida (a state with a demographic that did not really favor him), and a victory in electoral college-rich California, CNN, Fox News, and MSNBC were ready to project a winner in the 2008 United States Presidential elections.

At exactly 11:06 p.m. on the East Coast, right on the heels of the polls closing in three western states—Oregon, Washington, and California, CNN was about to make what was, perhaps, the biggest projection of the evening.

The News Network's signature tune began to play, heralding the long-awaited breaking news. Wolf Blitzer, veteran news anchor and leader of the "Best Political Team on Television" appeared, wearing his characteristic serious demeanor, as the music gradually wound down: "CNN can now make a projection." I remember him saying: "Senator

Barack Obama will become the president-elect of the United States of America... Barack Obama, the forty-seven-year-old senator, will be the first African-American President of..."

Chills went down my spine as I stared blankly at the television set, overcome with emotion—sheer ecstasy. The moment I dreamed of had finally come. Fears and doubts overcome, hopes and aspirations fulfilled. Sweet, palpable victory. The heavens had heard our silent prayers and showered on us its blessings. There was a sense of vindication, incredible affirmation, relief, and joy unspeakable—indescribable emotions all around; they crowned my day. The news was posted on CNN's website as well: "Democrat Barack Obama wins the 2008 Presidential election over John McCain, CNN projects, setting him up to become the first African-American to hold the nation's highest office..."

Reaction to Obama Victory

As the Obama electoral victory hit the airwaves in America, it reverberated across the globe. The news was met with euphoria not only in America, but on every continent. From Nairobi, Kenya in East Africa—a country that deemed him their native son (even naming a beer and a high school after him), and Sierra Leone, West Africa (where six newborn babies were named after him), to the capital cities of Europe, Asia, Latin and South America, reactions poured in through the television screens and newspapers. Men and women, old and young, black, brown, yellow, red and white cried freely, tears streaming down the faces of jubilant crowds, as they gathered in front of TV screens wherever they could find one. The world welcomed America's first Black president to the world stage. The moment could not be more surreal. It was as electrifying as it was incredible.

Newspapers, both in America and around the world, captured this historic moment. *The Progressive* called it "A Historic Vote, Defying Racism." *The New York Times*, stated: "Obama: Racial Barrier Falls as Voters Embrace Calls for Change." *The Daily Mirror* (London) "IT'S THE BLACK HOUSE: Obama is new President" (2008). Hamid Karzai, the president of Afghanistan, described Obama's victory as the ushering in of a "new era," an era "where race, colour and ethnicity, both in politics and in the world will hopefully disappear..." Times Magazine's Election Day comments were the most telling and incisive of all the post-racial assertions, however. Under the caption, "Obama's Victory ushers in a New America," *Time* magazine's Joe Klein sounded the most optimistic tone of all the commentaries:

Obama's victory, Klein observed, had created the prospect of a new, heterogeneous America, one whose contours were yet to be fully defined or determined. Though, still majority White, it could no longer be called a White country, especially, in the face of the increasingly pluralistic racial and cultural landscape of the nation. America, in Klein's purview, had become a country where pluralism and "cross-racial synergy" had taken precedence over racial identity, and "where the content of our President's character is more important than the color of his skin" (*Time* Magazine 2008).

The exhilarating choruses of a post-racial America were joined, shared, and loudly proclaimed around the globe by newspapers, world leaders and common folk alike. Never in history, it seemed, had one person's victory had such a resounding impact on the world. It was unprecedented. The significance of Obama's color and race in the post-election editorials and commentaries was hard to ignore.

"Post-Racial" Defined

Some have argued, perhaps rightly so, that with the advent of the Obama presidency America has finally transcended its bifurcation and social stratification based on race. Juxtaposing the world's designation of America as a post-racial society with Andrew Hacker and the Kerner Commission's characterization of her as "Two nations, Black and White, separate, hostile, unequal," seemed to render the latter obsolete. The question, however, still remains: Is America a post-racial society today? Has she finally transcended the national cancer of racism through the election of a Black man to the White house? Was Barack Obama's election the beginning of a golden age of race relations in the United States of America, as some have touted?

The phrase "post-racial," from my perspective, suggests an era bereft of any racial animus, one in which each race, ethnic group, culture, and citizen is granted a seat at the table and accorded an equal amount of dignity, respect, cordiality, and, above all, access to resources with which to better themselves and their dependents. Post-racialism may refer to a new ethos in American history and life, a golden era where race no longer holds sway over the American social, political, economic, and cultural landscape. Race ceases, under this definition, to be the defining motif and overarching factor in determining national character, social interactions, and discourse—the yardsticks by which American society's merits and demerits are judged or determined.

RICHARD D. DONKOR

Can America Ignore Race?

*"But race is an issue that I believe this nation cannot
afford to ignore right now. We would be making
the same mistake that Reverend Wright made in
his offending sermons about America..."*

—**Barack Obama,**
Speech: *A More Perfect Union* (2008)

A cursory look at American society today reveals serious and persistent ethnic and cultural polarization. Obama's presidency, initially touted as the start of an era of post-racialism, seems to have instead, unleashed hordes of racial demons upon the country. The vitriol initially spewed by the Tea Party upon Obama's assumption of the presidency, and the demagoguery of the Birther movement toward him are enough to invalidate any assertions to a post-racial ethos, even if those two movements can be called fringe or outside the mainstream. For example, Tea Partyers and Birthers are constantly crying out "We want our country back" (MacMillan 2012), in apparent displays of nostalgia for a return to a previously "White" country and lifestyle, in a land they once knew, which is rapidly disappearing in the face of increasing demographic change. Added to this, are the stereotyping and the persistent vilification Obama constantly receives in the media from the conservative right. "Barack, the Black Magic Negro," for instance, became Rush Limbaugh's radio theme song during the 2008 election, thus highlighting Obama's race and multicultural background, giving powerful fodder for hate-mongers and others who were already so predisposed.

Dinesh D'Souza, a conservative writer, consistent with the right wing conservative credo, described the United States in *The Obama Question: A Progressive Perspective* by

Gary Dorrien, as a country "being ruled according to the dreams of a Luo tribesman," in reference to Obama's paternal heritage. His dad is further disparagingly described as a "philandering, inebriated African socialist, who raged against the world for denying him the realization of his anti-colonial ambitions." Barack Obama's father, according to D'Souza, is "now setting the nation's agenda through the reincarnation of his dreams in his son" (2012). Whether in statements of the kind above or designations of the president as "Obama bin Laden," it is thoughtless and incendiary comments of that kind that defy the basic rules of common sense and decency and end up inflaming the passions of many people on the fringes.

Tim Wise explained, in an interview with Liliana Segura, the issue of what fuels such racial animosity and rage, as exhibited by groups such as the Birthers or individuals like Limbaugh and D'Souza. He attributes the Birther conspiratorial theories about Obama's faith and place of birth, in particular, to a "narcissistic breakdown...of centuries of ingrained privilege and hegemonic control." He explained further that, if one is used to seeing people who look like one's self in almost every position of authority, waking up every day and seeing a man of color basically running the country "is psychologically debilitating to white folks who all their lives weren't necessarily bigots or racists in any overt sense, but had simply gotten complacent with the way things were. They had internalized these notions of entitlement and superiority" (Segura 2009). Given the depths of these notions of entitlement and superiority, he wonders whether the Birthers are even aware or "fully conscious of the racist impulses behind their crazy allegations..." (Segura 2009).

The attitudes described above have allowed some to call into question the designation of America as post-racial. While some in this category have called post-racialism a myth, others have labeled its connoisseurs delusional. Christopher Metzler of Georgetown University called post-racialism "a problematic conclusion." He explained that Barack Obama's election is a "sea change" event, comparable to the Supreme Court decision on Brown vs Board of Education in 1954 that desegregated American schools. He argues that the sea-change can and should provide us with the right environment within which to discuss the larger issue of race. Hitherto, we have squandered these opportunities instead of appropriating them for "sustained, substantive" or "durable change" (Metzler 2008).

In his article, "Youth and the Myth of a Post-Racial Society, published in *Truthout* in April 2009, Henry Giroux also discusses the issue of post-racialism. He contends that "while post-racialism may mean less overt racism," the notion of post-racialism is premature. "It is an act of willful denial and ignorance," he notes. Against the backdrop of Barack Obama's election, "Racism," Giroux asserts, "has been relegated to an anachronistic vestige of the past."

Charles Ogletree of Harvard Law School reiterates very similar sentiments, with regard to the United States being a post-racial society. He states, emphatically, in response to a question regarding the issue in *Black Star News* that, "we are not in a post racial era. Arguing that race still matters, Ogletree explains that "We may have one black man in the White House, but we have one million Black men in prison." Even though he concedes that a seismic shift in the politics of our nation has occurred with the election of an African-American president, the creation of a post-racial ethos is something we must persistently contend for (Ogletree 2010).

This discussion of America's post-racial ethos with the election of Barack Obama as the first Black president of the

United States will be remiss if author and Professor Rachelle Winkle-Wagner's perspectives on the issue are not mentioned. As a scholar of the influence of race and gender on higher education, she provides a unique and valuable insight into post-racialism as it relates to the education of African Americans in particular. Winkle-Wagner categorically rejects the notion of a post-racial ethos in America. In her article titled "The Educational Consequences of the Post-racial Myth," published on November 15, 2010, she decries the ongoing discourse in the public square about the disappearance or decreasing significance of race, which, she asserts, is not a new theme, but one that has been with us since William Julius Wilson's 1978 ground-breaking best-seller, *The Declining Significance of Race*. It is this same theme, she implies, that is being regurgitated, recycled, or repackaged, and sold in our current discourse.

Winkle-Wagner expresses concern over the erroneous assumption that "all students, regardless of race, class, or gender have equal chances to attend and be successful in college when the numbers indicate that's just not so." She highlights the obvious social, political, and financial inequities between Whites and communities of color—disparities she blames on "the wounds of slavery, racism, and Jim Crow era policies." The "myth" of post-racialism, however, makes it increasingly difficult, though not impossible, to "stimulate new dialogues about the current realities of race in our country, and particularly, in our educational system." Winkle-Wagner, thus, advocates the debunking of the post-racial "myth" as a critical first step in initiating this conversation. The notion generated by post-racialism that issues regarding race will just disappear if we simply stop talking about them has no evidentiary basis, whether empirically or anecdotally, she emphasizes (Winkle-Wagner 2010).

In summarizing, it is my contention that if "post-racial" simply means the election of a Black man to the presidency of the United States by a majority White society, then perhaps America has arrived at this utopian ideal. But the gospel of post-racialism cannot be reduced to such a simplistic purview. Obama's election, even if indicative of a golden age of post-racialism, begs the greater question: would America have, similarly, elected a darker-skinned black man or a woman without any Caucasian heritage, or were Americans more receptive to Obama's candidacy because, being biracial, he symbolized our deepest and noblest ideals and aspiration to be one people, united in our belief in the greatness of this country and its transcendent dream of living in a colorblind society, one in which a person's complexion is negligible and each man is his brother's keeper?

America is not post-racial, at least not yet. Though racialized and still divided in many respects, the sheer symbolism and significance of Barack Obama's election to the highest and most powerful office in the land cannot be discounted as the whimsical caprice of a few excited people. Blacks, and many Whites, for that matter, could not have presaged such a seismic occurrence happening in their lifetime. Though not yet post-racial, we are most certainly and progressively marching forward. America is not stuck in the rut, as the Rev. Jeremiah Wright rant and diatribe indicated in 2008.

It is my contention that a race-less future, one still not fully imaginable, but yearning to be born, awaits America. Thus, Obama's African/Kenyan ancestry, his swarthy, melanin-tanned complexion, and his black lips, set alongside a keen intellect, an often-encyclopedic grasp of issues, and extraordinary calm in the face of pressure, come together in a critical mass to usher us into the dawning of a new, post-racial milieu.

Cultural Pluralism

Further widening America's racial divide is the ever-multiplying tide of immigration to the United States. According to a Center for Immigration Studies report from August 2007, if current immigration trends continue, "the nation's population will increase from 301 million today to 468 million in 2060, a 167 million or 56% increase" (Camarota 2007). The total projected growth of 167 million, the Center further asserts, is equal to the combined populations of Great Britain, France, and Spain. Six states in the union currently serve as the primary ports of entry and ultimate residence: California, New York, Texas, Florida, New Jersey, and Illinois, which are home to 63 percent of all legal immigrants.

Peter Viles, CNN correspondent, reported on how the westward trend of Hispanic migration seems to have abated and shifted. California, the largest state in the union and the historic home of most Hispanic immigrants, seems to be now lagging behind other states with regard to its legal Hispanic population. The Hispanic population in that state grew by only 37 percent from 1990 to 2000, compared to the growth of Hispanics in the Southeast—in states such as Arkansas, which grew by 196 percent; Georgia, which grew by 233 percent; and North Carolina, which grew by 274 percent (Viles 2009).

I will be remiss if I fail to mention the impact of undocumented immigrants in the creation of the American mosaic. According to Elizabeth Grieco for the Migration Policy Institute, the undocumented immigrant population in the United States is probably about nine million people. The illegal or undocumented immigrant population grew by 350,000 per year, particularly in the 1990s, with the states with the largest unauthorized populations of "illegals" being California and Texas.

According to the Institute, one-third of all undocumented immigrants live in California. Three states are particularly highlighted in their report (and corroborated by the US Immigration and Naturalization Service) for their rapid growth in their illegal alien populations; they are Georgia, North Carolina, and Colorado.

There is no evidence, they emphasize, that seismic demographic patterns and phenomena have ceased or changed since 2000.

It is noteworthy that the five countries supplying the bulk of these undocumented migrant populations are Mexico, El Salvador, Guatemala, Colombia, and Honduras (Grieco 2003).

The sum total of these intriguing, sometimes bizarre migratory patterns is the creation of a racially, culturally, and ethnically diverse and pluralistic society, one without any parallel, never before experienced in human history. It is cultural pluralism, at its best...or perhaps at its worst, some would argue.

Cultural Pluralism and America Today: From Homogeneity to Heterogeneity

Cultural pluralism may be generally described as the ability of various and multiple races, cultures, and ethnic groups to peacefully and harmoniously co-exist with each other, especially smaller groups alongside a dominant group, in a context where the distinct identity, values, and culture of each group are validated and respected. Leslie Newbigin defines it as "the attitude, which welcomes a variety of different cultures and lifestyles within one society and believes that this is an enrichment of human life" (Newbigin 1989). The arguments in favor of and against cultural pluralism, just like for and against the multitudinous cultures and people groups represented in the American milieu, are numerous and varied.

As laudable as the concept may be to some as a key to enriching human life, cultural pluralism can also spawn challenges. The two world wars stand on their own as a testament to the inherent challenges involved in forging a single European society and identity out of a diversity of European nations, as Germany tried to do on two separate occasions during World Wars I and II.

The American experiment is very similar, in that the country began with a collection and meshing of White Anglo-Saxon immigrants from Europe into one nation—though not by force or military might, as the Germans tried to do. Throw into that mix, the arrival of millions of immigrants, this time not of European or Anglo stock, but brown, yellow, and black, many of whom harbor ancient resentments and raw hatred toward America and Europe, or toward each other, due to racism, genocide (e.g., Turks and Armenians), slavery, Western colonialism, neo-colonialism and capitalist exploitation of homelands, and the result is the compounding of an already hydra-headed problem.

The United States of America, it must be noted, has been multiracial and pluralistic since its very beginning. Its multicultural and pluralistic composition has increased rapidly with the arrival of new groups of immigrant populations not of European descent. Arthur Schlesinger, in his 1998 book, *The Disuniting of America*, traces the development of America's multicultural makeup. He contends that the language, laws, institutions, customs, and political ideas in America from its very beginning had an "Anglo centric flavor" because of ties with Britain. Non-Anglo immigration, principally from Western and Northern Europe, gathered speed as the nineteenth century progressed, bringing in Germans, Scandinavians, Irish, etc. After the American Civil War came new immigrants from Southern and Eastern Europe: Italians, Poles, Hungarians, and Russians, etc. True to the spirit of the "melting-pot," all those immigrants were gradually assimilated into mainstream America, which has been dominated by British culture and values.

Israel Zangwill's 2007 designation of America as the great melting pot where all the races of Europe are melting, underscored a socializing process whereby an individual, upon migrating to the United States, would automatically be immersed in the "Americanizing" cauldron. Once submerged, a process of cultural sifting would begin as the elements were heated to a boiling point. Like a chemical reaction, the individual pieces in the cauldron would melt, undergo various changes, and produce as a by-product the "ethnic" dross from their culture of origin, to be discarded, while primarily producing an entirely new final product: a pure, fully blended, culturally assimilated individual, one who was no longer a "foreigner" by any means, but American through and through. The "old" culture and value system is thus extinguished, and replaced by a reoriented product, completely different, with a new set of values that are uniquely American.

This amalgam of races, cultures and ethnics into a "melting pot" continued faithfully until the end of the nineteenth century. American multiculturalism or pluralism, however, received a further but somewhat different endorsement and boost at the dawn of the twentieth century, when laws were promulgated making it easier for immigrants from

South America, Asia, and Africa to enter the United States, Schlesinger explains. The triangular and trans-Atlantic slave trade, it must be mentioned, had long preceded these laws, and through it ten to twelve million Africans had been forcibly brought to America and the "New World," with many more dying in the process of their capture and transportation across the ocean.

The forging of the American milieu through the mass migration of various people-groups to her shores, thus, began with the Brits, followed by the Scandinavians, Germans, and Irish, from Western and Northern Europe. They were, in turn, followed by Southern and Eastern Europeans, such as the Italians, Poles, Hungarians and Russians, and then Africans, Asians, Latin and South Americans, and Middle Easterners, at the turn of the twentieth century.

America: A Melting Pot or Salad Bowl?

Today, the arrival of immigrants from virtually every corner of the earth has created an American nation that, according to Oscar Romo, is composed of more than 500 ethnic groups and communicates in 636 languages and dialects (Romo 1993). Immigration, singularly, was responsible for a third of population growth in the 1980s. Most of these recent immigrants were again, not of European origin.

Whereas 90% of all immigrants were of European descent in 1910, Schlesinger notes, in the 1980s, more than 80% came from Asia and Latin America, a great percentage of them settling in big cities or states as New York and Los Angeles, California.

C. Peter Wagner, commenting on America's multicultural makeup, emphasizes that there are more Jews in New

York than in Tel Aviv (1989). Highlighting the same issue, particularly the cosmopolitan identity of Los Angeles, the *U.S. News and World Report*, back in 1983 reported that, "Los Angeles has become the Mecca for people from so many lands that the police speak forty-two languages." Los Angeles, in fact, has been referred to as "the third world capital of the world." Elliot Barkan, in *Freedom's Doors*, describes Los Angeles as a "spell-binding diversity, most truly representative of what the United States of America is today and will become tomorrow" (Barkan 1986).

According to Zena Pearlstone, Los Angeles's population consists of people from over 140 countries. The city is home to the second largest populations of Koreans, Filipinos, Armenians, Mexicans, and Salvadorians (second only to their native lands). It has more Samoans in it than American Samoa itself. It also has the largest Japanese, Iranian, Cambodian, and Gypsy communities in the US (Pearlstone 1990).

Commenting on LA's cultural diversity, Bill Pannell writes, rather humorously that; "L.A. is the place where you can buy a burrito stuffed with sushi" (Pannell 1993). Dinnerstein and Reimers (1999) corroborate these resounding comments about America's diversity in their ground-breaking work. "Never before—and in no other country," they say, "have as many varied ethnic groups congregated and amalgamated as they have in the United States."

As the world moves toward globalization, it is also conversely and paradoxically moving toward fragmentation and polarization. The inclusion of these incredible amounts of varied cultures in an already polarized, multiracial, and ethnic social matrix, characterized by simmering and frequent outbursts of racial and ethnic resentment, tensions and hostility, leads some to contend that Israel Zangwill's metaphor of the melting pot has been rendered obsolete in today's pluralistic America. The concept of the melting pot was, in Schlesinger's purview, the "brilliant solution for the inherent fragility of a multicultural society" where societal norms and cultural traditions are either apparently eroded or compromised through an invasion and influx of ethnics, a trend which, he stresses, ultimately threatens the very fabric, cohesion, or unity of society.

As immigration patterns have changed, tipping America's homogenous scale and balance and, thereby, creating greater heterogeneity, the concept of the melting pot has been questioned, challenged, and denounced by some as indefensible, particularly in its contemporaneous usage. It is a "conspiracy to homogenize America," they claim. Oscar Romo has been notably critical of this homogenizing "conspiracy." An obvious contrarian to Schlesinger's melting pot-unifying philosophy, Romo declares, in the spirit of cultural pluralism, that those ethnics who refuse to acculturate and instead opt to keep their cultural and linguistic distinctive are "equally as American as any Anglo from London" (Romo 1993).

Advocates of multiculturalism describe the current American ethos not as a melting pot but as a "salad bowl." America consists, from this perspective, of several pieces in the bowl; it is a mixture of numerous pieces, which do not necessarily melt together or blend to form an exclusive American identity or personality, as the case may be in the melting pot. Here, each piece maintains its own cultural and ethnic distinctive and value system, while maintaining a peaceful and harmonious co-existence and interdependence with the other pieces in the bowl. Complete assimilation into the American mainstream is one of choice, and not a requirement for acceptance, success or survival.

Eduardo-Bonilla Silva expressed these sentiments best in Race: *The Power of an Illusion* when he stated that, the concept of the Melting Pot, "was a notion that was extended exclusively to White immigrants. That pot never included people of color: Blacks, Chinese, Puerto Ricans, etcetera, could not melt into the pot. They could be used as Wood to produce the fire for the pot, but they could not be used as material to be melted into the pot" (Silva 2003).

It is important to emphasize, yet again, that much of the polarization and fragmentation under discussion here has been and still is along racial, cultural and ethnic lines.

Will the Center Hold?

Amidst the racial, cultural, and ethnic fragmentation and polarization, Arthur Schlesinger asks if "the center will hold or give way to the tower of Babel." Countries break up, he contends, when they fail to give ethnically diverse peoples compelling reasons to see themselves as part of the same nation. The former Soviet Union is a case in point. The "cult of ethnicity," a separatist impulse, Schlesinger suggests, gnaws at the core of our national identity. Discussing the theological implications of pluralism, Romo points to "the manifold pluralism in the Creator's purpose" in the biblical story of the Towel of Babel. "It is God," he says, "who disperses them, into linguistic, spatial and ethnic diversity," as they strive to maintain a primeval unity based, on one language and a single goal (Romo 1993).

It is important to reiterate that God's promise of blessing to Abraham was not meant to end with him; God indicated that through him "all the families of the earth," the ethnically and linguistically diverse nations and cultures of the world mentioned in this chapter, would be blessed (Gen. 12:3). From one man (blood), Adam, then through Noah after the flood, "God has made *all nations* of men to dwell on the face of the earth" (Acts 17:26). God's heart reaches out to "all the sons of Noah, who went out from the ark," Ham, Shem, and Japheth, "of them was the whole earth overspread" or populated, creating the nations (Gen. 9:18–19).

The prophets, particularly Isaiah and Micah, were very eloquent in their declarations of God's intent for the nations: "In the last days," they declared, "the Lord's house shall be established…and all nations shall flow into it" (Isaiah 2:2–3/ Micah 4:1–2).

Jesus commissioned His disciples to go to "all nations" (Matt. 28:18) with the gospel, indicating that the fulfillment of this would be one of the significant pointers to His return (Matt. 24:14). He mentioned that "His House" should be called a "house of prayer for all nations" (Mark 11:17).

Against this backdrop, I reiterate the main themes of this treatise, in the form of questions:

- Could the mass migrations of various people groups (i.e., the nations) to America be divinely orchestrated?
- Could the nations be coming to America perhaps because America is no longer going to the nations, as it has and should?

Undoubtedly, a golden opportunity for global missions has been created with the arrival of these migrant populations. The prospect of seeing biblical prophecy fulfilled is right before us. It is vital that the Church stay sensitive to this development. Ancient resentments and hostilities lie dormant, and still remain potentially volatile (Armenians and Turks). The addition of migrant populations to the equation does not make progress toward healing and reconciliation any easier.

CHAPTER 3

The Roots of American Racism

Scripture is replete with stories with racial undertones. Moses's marriage to Zipporah, an Ethiopian (Black) woman, and the apparent display of displeasure by his sister Miriam and Aaron the High Priest, is a typical case in point (Numbers 12). That God responded with a quick censure of Miriam, Moses sister, by afflicting her with leprosy is, perhaps, indicative of the fact that, not only will He stand up for His servants who walk uprightly before Him, but also that He will not tolerate an unjust criticism of them based on a warped logic or such trivial grounds as marrying a person of color, in this case a Cushite, Ethiopian, or Black woman, Zipporah.

The Jews, with their purist ethnocentric views, would have no dealings with the Samaritans. The Samaritans were half-breeds, what we would call today biracial, mixed race, mulattos or mestizo—products of Jewish and Assyrian intermarriage (John 4:9).

Peter, the Apostle and Pontiff of the early Church, needed a special visitation from the Lord in order to be cleansed of his racial and ethnic prejudices (Acts 10). That even that visitation did not completely "cleanse" him of his ethnocentricity and superiority complex is manifested in his subsequent actions: he refused to eat with the Gentile brethren when Jewish disciples opposed to any interracial or ethnic "bash" with unclean and inferior Gentiles—supposed heathens given to unclean foods or dietary patterns and other ungodly practices—arrived from Jerusalem (Galatians 2:11–13). For that, he received an immediate censure from the Apostle Paul, God's messenger to the Gentile nations. Paul's instructions to the Ephesian church soliciting the whole-hearted obedience of the slave to the slave master (Eph. 6:5) and also to Titus (Eph. 2:9) about teaching slaves to be sub-servient to their masters have been sources of great conten-tion as to their meaning and interpretation to activists on both sides of the racial divide.

By far, the one contrived source of biblical authority for racism is what has come to be known as the Doctrine of the Curse of Ham or the Biblical Hamitic Hypothesis. The narrative is about how Noah, waking up from his alcohol binge, cursed his son Ham, supposedly, with Blackness. To be discussed in more detail in chapter 5, this biblical narra-tive has been the bane of many people of color, whose genetic inferiority is allegedly ordained and sanctioned by God, through Noah. This interpretation of scripture by White rac-ists has lent credence to the warped logic and ideology of White supremacy. It has spawned Western Imperialism, colo-nial expansions in Africa (The Scramble for Africa), North and South America, as well as in Asia. Slavery, Jim Crow, Apartheid, and all manner of devious racist theories have also issued out of this same hypothesis and its corollaries, some of which we will discuss in later chapters.

Historical Precedents of a Warped Logic

Further illustrative of this warped racist logic and the centrality of race and racism in American life are comments made by some of its most prominent personalities. Thomas Jefferson, co-author of the Declaration of Independence, co-founder of the Democratic Party, and third President of the United States, referred to Blacks in *Notes on the State of Virginia* (1853) as "inferior to whites in the endowments of both body and mind."

Highlighting the nuances of race in America is the well-established fact that, Jefferson, who owned about two hundred black slaves, probably also fathered anywhere from one to six children with one of his slaves, Sally Hemmings. Obviously, her inferior designation was not enough to render her sexually unattractive or resistible. Although refuted by some historians, two of Sally Hemmings's children, Eston and Madison, had indicated that Jefferson was their father. In *Wrong on Race: The Democratic Party's Buried Past* by Bruce Bartlett, he states that this was later corroborated by DNA tests and evidence in 1998 by a team of geneticists, led by Dr. Eugene Foster.

Consistent with Jefferson's sentiments, Chief Justice Roger Taney (later appointed Attorney General and, later still, secretary of the Treasury by President Andrew Jackson) in *Freedom: A History of the US*, by Joy Hakim, stated in the famous Dred Scott vs Sanford ruling in 1856, that Blacks "are a subordinate and inferior class of beings who have been subjugated by the dominant race" (Hakim). In *A New Birth of Freedom: Abraham Lincoln and the Coming of the Civil War*, Harry V Jaffa highlights the court's majority opinion on the same case, where Taney states that the framers of the United States Constitution believed that "blacks had no rights which the white man was bound to respect, and that the Negro might justly and lawfully be reduced to slavery for his benefit" (Jaffa 3000). Responding to the statement in the Declaration of Independence that "all men were created equal…," the Chief Justice further states (in Paula S. Rothenburg's *Race, Class, and Gender in the United States*) that "it is too clear for dispute, that the enslaved African race were not intended to be included, and formed no part of the people who framed and adopted this declaration…" (Rothenburg 1998, 552).

Senator Stephen A. Douglas, presidential nominee of the Democratic Party in 1858, held and declared the view, as told in *The Lincoln-Douglas Debates: The Lincoln Studies Center Edition* edited by Rodney O. Davis and Douglas L. Wilson that "a Negro is not and never ought to be a citizen of the United States." He declares, "I hold that this government was made on the white basis; made by the white men, for the benefit of white men and their posterity forever, and should be administered by white men and none other" (Davis and Wilson 2008).

Mayor Fernando Wood, Mayor of New York in 1865, added his voice to the chorus of racist remarks from the corridors of power. His comments, noted in *African or American? Black Identity and Political Activism in New York City 1784-1861* by Leslie Alexander, stated, "The Almighty has fixed the distinction of the races, the Almighty has made the black man inferior, and sir, by no legislation, by no military power, can you wipe out this distinction" (Alexander 2012, 171). As further noted by Bartlett in *Wrong on Race: The Democratic Party's Buried Past* (2009), Senator James Vardaman, once Chairman of the Committee for Natural Resources in the US, declared that "The Negro as a race, in all the ages of the world has never shown sustained power of self-development. He is not endowed with the creative faculty. He has never created for himself any civilization... He has never had any civilization except that which has been inculcated by a superior race. And it is a lamentable fact that his civilization lasts only as long as he is in the hands of the white man who inculcates it. When left to himself he has universally gone back to the barbarism of the jungle" (Bartlett 2009, 83).

The Ideology of White Supremacy

At the core of these statements is an American nation steeped in a culture and ideology of White supremacy from its very beginnings. In a workshop on *What is White Supremacy, Challenging White Supremacy*, Elizabeth Martinez defines White Supremacy as a "historically-based, institutionally-perpetuated system of exploitation and oppression of continents, nations, and peoples of color by white people and nations of the European continent, for the purpose of maintaining and defending a system of wealth, power and privilege" (Martinez n.d.). Robert Jenson, in turn, defines White Supremacist society in *The Heart of Whiteness: Confronting Race, Racism and White Privilege*, as one "whose founding is based in an ideology of the inherent superiority of white Europeans over non-whites..." According to Jenson, the ideology of White Supremacy has served as the justification for all kinds of atrocities against Native Americans, Africans, and non-white people groups in American society. In this racialized context dominated by White Supremacy, Jenson notes that top positions in powerful institutions are occupied by Whites, with similar but lesser privileges extended to non-Whites, who assimilate into the dominant White culture (Jenson 2005).

A by-product of White Supremacy is White privilege. This refers to the advantages or benefits that accrue to people of Caucasian or White heritage by virtue of their skin. White skin confers remarkable dividends in America and Western society. White privilege becomes more obvious when juxtaposed with the disparities non-Whites have to live with, either politically, socially or economically, in the same context and under the same system. Often taken for granted by Whites, White privilege may be regarded by Whites as the normal state of affairs for everyone, including minorities, and may not even be conscious of its existence and implications until such privilege begins to be curtailed. It often desensitizes Whites to Black and minority protests about racism and various forms of inequality. Such insensitivity may be understandable since inequality, where Whites are at the mercy or receiving end of societal hardships, political disenfranchisement or economic injustice are not the systems or world that most White Americans are born into, or grow up in.

In *Race and Prejudice in America Today: A Series—White Supremacy and White Privilege*, Will Smith claims that "White privilege is a complex issue for both whites and non-whites." It is major issue for Whites because for most Whites, they did nothing to earn it, he observes. Non-Whites, according to Smith, on the other hand, do not have the luxury to bring up this issue, because questioning their oppression oftentimes comes across as using race or racism as an excuse (Smith 2012).

Martinez asserts that the United States is the first nation in the world to be born racist and capitalist, simultaneously. She establishes a correlation between White supremacy and the quest and attainment of American economic power and posits these as the two sides of the same coin.

She argues that, contrary to the almost enchanting story of America's origin and birth beginning with its alleged "discovery" by Columbus, the search for political and religious freedom by pilgrims from England, the winning of independence from an imperial Britain through the American revolution followed by a Westward push and expansion across wild and virgin terrain, a fairy tale portrayal, Martinez calls mythical, this story excludes, she emphasizes, three critical facts about America's growth and expansion. These facts point to a White Supremacist ideology being at the core of America's founding, expansion and development. They are (1) The creation of America through military conquest, (2) the use of African slave labor as a key, if not, the primary engine of its economic development, and (3) its expansion to the Pacific by the annexation of much of Mexican territory. That White supremacy is a system of exploitation, Martinez observes, is borne out by the acts of exploitation stated above, which acts are then, subsequently, justified by "institutionalizing the inferiority of its victims" (Martinez).

In *Reflections on The History of White Supremacy in the United Sates*, William Gardiner observes that in the wake of the European quest to conquer and colonize various regions of the world during the sixteenth century, four countries, in particular, competed for hegemony over what later became the United States. They were France, Spain, Holland and England. After several wars between the French and English, the latter assumed domination of the Eastern coast of the United States. Drawing from Malcomson, Gardiner highlights that the Portuguese were the first to begin transporting slaves from Africa in what later became the full-fledged Transatlantic Slave Trade, as we know it today. By the end of the fifteenth century, slavery of Africans had become justifiable based on skin color. Blackness, thus, became the reason for the enslavement of Africans. Out of the creation of a rationale of Blackness for slavery grew the ideology of Whiteness. In other words, until slavery became synonymous with Blackness, the concept of Whiteness was non-existent, with European nations alluding to themselves primarily based on ethnicity or country of origin, such as Italian, German, Irish, or English (Gardiner 2009).

The concept of White superiority was already established in the European mind, however. "Europeans," Gardiner observes, "saw themselves as superior to people of color...this belief forms the basis for the attitude of white superiority and the culture of white supremacy," of which the English, he emphasizes, were the worst culprits. With the English self-perception of moral and cultural superiority to all others, including others of European stock, racist notions of Blacks, Indians and Whites had, more or less, crystallized by the time of the English encounter with the New World. Regarding the English mind-set about Blacks and Whites, Gardiner defers to Ronald Takaki and emphasizes that, "In the English mind, the color black was freighted with an array of negative images: 'deeply stained with dirt,' 'foul,' 'dark or deadly' in purpose, 'malignant,' while the color white on the other hand signified purity, innocence, and goodness" (Gardiner 2009).

White superiority, and the inferiority of other peoples, Gardiner further observes, were already in place when the English colonist arrived in North America; and strategies for social control had already been developed in Ireland, when the English conquered the Irish; these would be used in the Americas. The belief in White superiority was strengthened and reinforced during the colonization of the Americas and the encounter with Native Americans and African peoples (Gardiner 2009).

Martinez and Gardiner agree that it is this ideology of White supremacy that drove the Europeans to annihilate the Native American populations and to annex their lands. It is the same ideology that served not only as the rationale or justification for African slavery, but also as the reinforcement for White Superiority in the Americas. Gardiner highlights the intent of Whites on taking the land of the Native Americans upon arriving in North America. There were approximately seven million people divided into approximately six hundred distinct Native American communities when Europeans first arrived on the continent. Martinez quoting James suggests that the numbers of indigenous people in North America was between 9 million and 18 million. There were about 250,000 and 123,000 in the United States and Canada, respectively, by the end of the Indian Wars (James 1992).

Through a process of conquest, war, disease, and broken treaties, Native Americans were decimated and reduced to about twenty-five thousand by the end of the nineteenth century. "The conquest of Native Americans and the taking of their land, Gardiner adds, was an essential part of forming white supremacy" (Gardiner 2009). The unity of Whites was critical to their ability to conquer the natives and take over the land. To ensure victory in wars with Native Americans, Whites had to close their ranks and unite under a common motif. That motif was the White racial identity. The designation of Native Americans as devils, barbarians, uncivilized, illiterate or inhuman, reinforced the notion of a superior White racial identity (Gardiner).

The enslavement of Africans also reinforced the construction and notion of White supremacy. Economics, specifically, the need for cheap labor, drove the acquisition of Black African slaves. The earliest Black Africans in North America were not categorized as slaves; they were an indentured class who served their White Masters for five to seven years to ultimately earn their freedom, just like their European counterparts who were also indentured servants. All that changed in 1661, when the Virginia Assembly changed *de jure* slavery into *de facto* slavery, with economics as the basis. Bacon's rebellion, where African slaves joined indentured White laborers to revolt and burn down Jamestown in Virginia, served as a wake-up call and rallying cry to the White elite to reconfigure the social stratification of the society with the aim of ensuring the social control of the White underclass and labor force. Through various incentives offered both politically and economically, as well as through duress, in some cases, the indentured lower classes of whites were elevated and made to identify with the ruling White class.

Their newfound elevation and identification with the elite caste system was to avert future insurrections among them, such as occurred in Bacon's rebellion. Martinez states that the main fear of elite Whites was a class fear, the prospect of "discontented whites—servants, tenant farmers, the urban poor, the property-less, soldiers and sailors," joining "Black slaves to overthrow the existing order" (Martinez). The solution was divide and conquer, or control. Thus, indentured Whites were allowed to join militias, carry guns, acquire land, and have other legal rights not allowed to slaves" (Martinez). With that elevation also came a massive increase in slave importation to offset the decrease in the dependence on indentured White labor. Black slaves and indentured Whites were until then, regarded as socially equal. Intermarriage and romantic liaisons occurred freely among them, making it easy for them to unite in Bacon's rebellion. With a superior status conferred upon the indentured White class, followed by assimilation into a new caste system where White supremacy was the overriding motif, Blacks slaves were left confined to the bottom of the totem pole, with any future alignment of the two factions against the ruling class now potentially severed. Patrol groups or militias, consisting mainly of the ruling class and former indentured slaves now more conscious of their Whiteness and, therefore, elevation in status ensured that Black Slaves would not have the capacity for any future insurrection.

Martinez further asserts that with the privileges conferred upon them, the White indentured underclass was legally declared White on the basis of skin color and continental origin. This made them superior to Blacks and Indians (or Native Americans). "Whiteness was born as a racist concept to prevent lower-class whites from joining people of color, especially Blacks against their class enemies" (Martinez). The concept of Whiteness, thus, became a source of unity and strength for European Americans who were vastly outnumbered.

The earliest Europeans who settled in America, it must be emphasized, never called themselves White. Instead, they referred to themselves by their ethnicity or country of origin, whether English, German, Dutch French, Irish, or Italian. Gardiner observes that "White" as a social construct was first used in 1691 when the Virginia Legislature used the terms "white man or woman" (Gardiner).

Just as there were no Whites but Europeans, there were also no Indians, Blacks, Negroes, or slaves, those racial descriptions being non-existent in the nomenclature of the times. Native Americans, upon being conquered, were racialized, and so were Africans upon being enslaved. It was the racial designations conferred by Europeans upon the people they conquered and enslaved that fomented Whiteness, or White racial identity, motivated or inspired by White supremacy.

RICHARD D. DONKOR

Manifest Destiny: Divine Rationale for Expansion

The United States formulated the ideology known as "Manifest Destiny" at the dawn of its founding. Manifest Destiny was a nineteenth-century doctrine, coined by John O'Sullivan in 1845, and steeped in race, religion, culture, economic necessity, and, to a lesser degree, science—specifically Darwinism. O'Sullivan contended, in an essay entitled *Annexation*, that it was America's "Manifest Destiny to overspread and to possess the whole of the continent which Providence has given us for the development of the great experiment of liberty and federated self-government entrusted to us" (O'Sullivan 1845).

Manifest Destiny served as the rationale for the expansion of the continental US territory from the Atlantic to the Pacific, that is, "from sea to shining sea." Based on a belief that the United States had been preordained by God to usurp territory from its culturally and racially inferior neighbors, it led to the annexation of Texas, Oregon, New Mexico, Arizona, California, parts of Nevada, Utah, and Colorado. Later incursions into the Caribbean, and Central America were motivated by the same ideology.

In their quest for land and economic power, the colonizers resorted to biblical metaphors for the divine and moral justification for their conquest. Thus, "the White man's burden" and responsibility was a North America—the New Promised Land that needed to be conquered—rid of its Canaanite inhabitants (Hispanics and Indians) and proselytized by the New Israelites, the new European Protestant colonists. In that "holy war," the Atlantic Ocean was parallel with the Red Sea, and British forces were Pharaoh's Egyptian army, with George Washington as the Yankee Moses.

Ironically, it is that same ideology that led to the quest for "Indian Removal," where "savages" who stood in the way of expansion were either removed by force, i.e., through conquest, or made to give up their lands through unfair treaties. Indians, according to Parkman, in his 1851 publication, *Conspiracy of Pontiac*, "were destined to melt and vanish before the advancing waves of Anglo-American power." That was the pervading mentality of the time, and it still persists, some would argue, in American political ideology.

That the concept of Manifest Destiny is infused with much racism goes without saying. While the doctrine assured the economic development and geographic expansion of the United States, it simultaneously reinforced "racist policies and practices," according to Martinez. The doctrine, she further notes, buttressed the ideology of White supremacy as fundamental to America's self-definition as a nation. Regarding the impact and legacy of such a notion of self, one based on nothing else but pure hubris, she maintains that "the arrogance of asserting that God gave white people (primarily men) the right to dominate everything around them still haunts our society and sustains its racist oppression" (Martinez).

Scientific Racism: Hottentot Venus and the Purveyors of a Pseudo-Science

In 1994, acting upon a request from the elders of the Khosa tribe, President Nelson Mandela of the Republic of South Africa officially requested from the French government of President Francois Mitterrand that the remains of Saraatjie (a.k.a. Sarah) Baartman be returned to South Africa. The story of Sarah Baartman highlights the subject of scientific racism, the intersection or marriage of science and racism, one that has reared its head again in recent times through a book titled, *The Bell Curve* (Fraser 2008). Under the guise of making her wealthy, Sarah, an orphaned maidservant born in 1789, was allegedly smuggled from Cape Town, South Africa, to London by Hendrik Cesars, who at the time was working for a British Army medical officer named Alexander Dunlop. Through Dunlop's persuasion, Cesars was convinced of the entertainment potential and scientific value of Sarah as an exhibit in British circles. The reason was that she had steatopygia, which gave her an unusually large buttocks and an enlarged and elongated labium, a characteristic of Khoisan ladies, according to the rumor (Stephen Gould).

For five years, six days a week Sarah was exhibited from a cage to the fancy of British audiences who paid to watch her. From London, Sarah was sent to France, where she was on exhibition for fifteen months, her stage shows managed by an animal trainer. While in France, she posed nude for scientific paintings and was visited by world-renowned naturalists, such as Cuvier (Gould).

Referring to her with the stage name "Hottentot Venus," and with a picture with the caption, "Flesh Made Fantasy," *The Guardian*'s March 31, 2007 edition observed that Saartjie's instant celebrity was attributable to a combination of British fascination, even obsession, with the large size of the derriere, bums, posteriors—and visual satire (Guardian 2007). Calling her exhibition, a freak show, Rachel Holmes underscored that "The Hottentot Venus arose in London as the very apotheosis of Europe's invented Africa, the dark continent of feminized impenetrability and crude potency." To all intents and purposes, Sarah "offered sexual tourism dressed up as education" (Holmes 2007).

If the exploitation of a young African girl's anatomical features during her lifetime sounds bad enough, what followed upon her death was even more appalling. Gould draws attention to Cuvier's fascination, if not obsession with the dissection of Saraatjie's body, and the public's, as well.

A protracted debate existed about the anatomy of that young woman. In response to the question about this morbid curiosity, Gould offered two troubling responses: first, her stage name of "Hottentot." According to Gould, Hottentot Bushmen vied with Australian Aborigines on the racist ladder of human progress for the lowest tier, just above chimpanzees and orangutans. Cuvier's description of Saraatjie was consistent with this perspective of Hottentots. Her flat nose, the monkey-like head and skull, were all typical of the existing narrative. But, by far, the damning fascination about Saraatjie pertained to her anatomy and physical attributes, particularly her posterior and genitalia.

The famed French anthropologist and professor of comparative anatomy, Georges Cuvier, dissected her corpse in what was supposed to be a scientific verification or disavowal of the speculation that had been going on about her body parts, conserving her brain, vulva and anus and making a plaster of her body, which, together with her skeleton, were put on display as exhibits at a department of the National Museum of Natural History in France.

In 2002, after ten years of petitioning the French government, the remains of Hottentot Venus were finally released to the South African government and given a fitting burial.

Scientific Racism: Purveyors of a Pseudo-Science

The story of Hottentot Venus is a typical example of scientific racism. It usually consists of bogus, subjective conclusions about race and/or racial categories, often cloaked in a semblance of objectivity and presented as the results of legitimate scientific enquiry. Often referred to as a pseudo-science, its underlying rationales and techniques are used to buttress the division of either groups or individuals into racial categories based on either physical or intellectual traits. The dictionary defines scientific racism as "propaganda with the veneer of science which was fabricated to support a racist paradigm" (your dictionary).

Scientific racism has two schools of thought. They are monogenism and polygenism. These are the belief in one (mono) original source or ancestry for all humanity (e.g., Adam and Eve) and Polygenism, is that which assumes different sources of origin or ancestry for different categories of humans, respectively. Voltaire (1694–1778) was a typical polygenist. As a French Enlightenment writer, historian and philosopher, he believed that each race had separate origins and found biblical monogenism laughable. "It is a serious question among them whether the Africans are descended from monkeys or whether the monkeys come from them," Voltaire once stated. "Our wise men have said that man was created in the image of God. Now here is a lovely image of the Divine Maker: a flat and black nose with little or hardly any intelligence. A time will doubtless come when these animals will know how to cultivate the land well, beautify their houses and gardens, and know the paths of the stars: one needs time for everything" (Smollett 1901).

When discussing the differences between Caucasians and Negroes, Voltaire compared Negroes to different breeds of dogs: "The Negro race is a species of men different from ours as the breed of spaniels is from that of greyhounds. The mucous membrane, or network, which Nature has spread between the muscles and the skin, is white in us and black or copper-colored in them" (Smollett 1901).

It was a mentality such as Voltaire's, founded on scientific racism, that rendered Hottentot Venus a savage, with beastly properties, in the eyes of a curious English and French public. It was that same mentality that sent Ota Benga, the African Pygmy, to the ape/orangutan cage in the Bronx zoo in New York as an exhibit.

Other scientific racists, such as Ben Rush, a doctor and a founding father of the United States, propounded the theory that the dark skin of the African was due to a hereditary skin disease called Negroidism. Rush believed that the condition could be cured. Samuel Cartwright, a doctor from Louisiana, in 1851 theorized that "drapetomania," the practice of slaves running away from their masters, was a curable mental disease. Several, such as John Hunter, a Scottish surgeon, believed that the Black man was originally White at birth. Buffon believed that Adam and Eve were Caucasian, and that the darker hue of certain people groups was due to deterioration from either poor dieting or environmental factors.

Conclusion

Scientific racism has been employed by White racists to explain pathological behavior among Blacks. Labeled a pseudo-science, in recent times, it has been used to buttress the notion of White Supremacy and, by extension, Black genetic and intellectual inferiority. From theology to biology, false and bogus hypotheses and theories were propounded and presented as the results of scientific enquiry. This has spawned and undergirded Western imperialism, Colonialism, The

Scramble for Africa, Slavery, Apartheid, Manifest Destiny, the annihilation of entire populations in the Americas, and eugenics. It's little wonder that scientific racism was officially and categorically debunked by the United Nations. In its antiracist declaration, titled *The Race Question*, UNESCO, in 1950, declared that: "The biological fact of race and the myth of 'race' should be distinguished. For all practical social purposes' 'race' is not so much a biological phenomenon as a social myth. The myth of 'race' has created an enormous amount of human and social damage. In recent years, it has taken a heavy toll in human lives, and caused untold suffering" (UNESCO).

Though debunked as a science, racism's morbid tentacles are still with us to this day. They are evident in our institutions, such as our criminal justice system, our educational facilities, our politics, economics, housing and residential structures, in our police forces...and sadly, also in the Church, the moral vanguard of our society.

CHAPTER 4

The Morbid Tentacles
of Racism

*"Discrimination is a hellhound that gnaws at Negroes
in every waking moment of their lives to remind
them that the lie of their inferiority is accepted
as truth in the society dominating them."*
—Dr. Martin Luther King

A little White girl of five is asked questions as she observes cartoon-like dolls of varying shades of color, from a lighter to a darker complexion. In response to a question regarding which of the dolls is nice, she points to the one with the lighter complexion; in response to a question regarding which child is the mean one, she points to the doll that looks dark. She points to the doll with the lighter complexion, when further asked to point out which child is the smart one, but to the darker doll when asked who the ugly, dumb, or bad doll is. The little girl associates "goodness" with the light doll because, in her words, "she looks like me." The "other," in contrast, is ugly, because she is "a lot darker."

Such were the results revealed by a recent CNN-backed pilot research study conducted by renowned child psychologist and Professor Margaret Beale Spencer of the University of Chicago. The results, as shown in 2010 on the CNN segment *AC 360*, were as revealing as they were worrisome.

Responding to questions about the results revealed in the research project, Dr. Spencer highlighted the fact that, "although all kids are exposed to the same stereotypes, what is really significant...is that white children are learning those stereotypes much more strongly than the African-American children." As she further reiterated, "the white youngsters are even more stereotypic in their responses concerning attitudes, beliefs and preferences than the African-American children" (Spencer 2010).

That the bias on both sides was higher in favor of Whiteness, with the White kids exhibiting greater stereotypical behavior patterns, was indicative of the fact that "white parents as a whole do not talk to their kids about race as much as black people do" (Spencer 2010). According to the segment on CNN by Spencer, a 2007 study in the *Journal of Marriage and Family* found that 75 percent of White families with kindergartners never, or almost never, talked about race. For Black parents, the number is reversed, with 75 percent addressing race with their children. Dr. Spencer further attributed the difference in parenting attitudes to a certain "level of entitlement" that Whites have. Although she cautioned against making it a definite word on children and race, she nevertheless concluded that, even in the year 2010, Americans "are still living in a society where dark things are devalued, and white things are valued" (Spencer 2010).

The Politics of Race

The swift national reaction and outpourings of indignation at former Republican Majority Leader Trent Lott's remarks on December 5, 2002, the occasion of Strom Thurmond's one hundredth birthday celebration, serves as an interesting illustration of the significance of race and racism in American life, particularly as it relates to those in the corridors of power. In what appeared to be reminiscent of a nostalgic past, when Thurmond stood for president on a segregationist platform, Lott stated that, "We voted for him. We're proud of it, and if the rest of the country had followed our lead, we wouldn't have had all these problems over all these years, either" (Mercurio 2002). Race, as usual, was at the center of this national contention. Strom Thurmond's segregationist platform decades earlier had set the stage for this public outcry. Thurmond was for the segregation of the races. "All the laws of Washington and all the bayonets of the army cannot force the Negro into our homes, our schools, our churches" he is purported to have stated (Seattle Times 2003).

Lott apologized for his comments in the wake of the national outcry that ensued, refuting any impression created by his remarks that he embraced the "discarded policies of the past," to which he responded that "nothing could be far from the truth." That such a thoughtless remark could be repeated by a national figure in this twenty-first century, is not only revealing about real and often hidden feelings about race in America, but also leaves much to be desired. That the reference to a racist past could spark such a national reaction is testament enough also, to the enduring nature of the race problem. This incident, demonstrating a marriage of politics and race, again, represents the warped logic of a distant past, carried over into contemporary American society.

The elevation of Robert C. Byrd, Democratic senator from Virginia, to the coveted position of Senate Majority leader as recently as 1987, and then to Senate President Pro Tempore from 2007 until his death in 2010, is also testament to America's enduring flirtation with racism. Lest we lose the significance of the above, may it be emphasized that Senator Byrd, was a man of enormous power on the political landscape. For several years of his life, he was just a couple of heartbeats away from the presidency of the United States. Byrd, to be specific, was third in line to the presidency of the United States, after the Vice-President, and Speaker of the House. He was the longest-serving member of the United States senate, having served for over fifty years, until his passing on June 28, 2010. Byrd, however, was once also a recruiter for the Klu Klux Klan. In 1946, he had called for the rebirth of the Klan and the promotion of the order immediately and in every state in the union (Bartlett 2009).

Professors Henry Louis Gates, Allen Counter, and Cornel West

One would assume that America's institutionalized racism only affected Blacks and minorities belonging to the lower echelons of society. The experiences of Henry Louis Gates, Allen Counter, and Cornel West prove otherwise. Professor Henry Louis Gates of Harvard University, one of America's preeminent African-American scholars, was arrested on July 16, 2009, by Sgt. James Crowley, a White cop who was responding to a neighbor's call about a robbery in progress. An article by Krissah Thompson in *The*

Washington Post discusses how Professor Gates was arrested for "disorderly conduct" after expressing frustration about the threat of arrest in his own home, despite showing his driver's license and Harvard Identification card, and thrown in jail (Thompson 2009). The spontaneous, unscripted, and heartfelt sentiments expressed by the president, a Black man, sentiments easily understood and shared by most in the black and minority communities, on the one hand, and the ensuing backlash from the dominant white community on the other, were sadly and simply indicative of the gulf that still exists between the two sides. How quickly Black and White Americans become polarized around race, almost always ending on opposing sides, is worth noting

Professor Allen Counter, another African American scholar, a professor of Neurophysiology at Harvard Medical School for over twenty-five years, mentioned in an article of *The Tech*, has also brought up similar allegations of unfair treatment by the Cambridge Police. He recounts a day back in 2004 when he was stopped by two Harvard police officers as he crossed Harvard Yard. He was threatened with arrest after being mistaken for a robbery suspect.

Professor Cornel West's depiction in *Race Matters* of his encounter with the taxi cab drivers in New York also comes to mind. Empty taxi cabs passed him by, a total of ten altogether, some going past him to pick up other clients of "European descent" next to him. Admitting that his experience was minimal in comparison with other more vicious acts of racism, he yet recalls that the "the memories cut like a merciless knife at my soul as I waited on that godforsaken corner" (West 1994). Despite all of them being men of high intellectual pedigree, they were not immune to the egregious act of racial profiling. Were those incidents merely coincidental, occasional blights dotting the American racial landscape? How easy it is to be dismissive of these acts unless one has been through them, in some form or fashion.

Amadou Diallo, Sean Bell, Abner Louima, and Trayvon Martin

And, what do we make of these, equally, unnerving episodes, all of them with racial undertones? Amadou Diallo, the twenty-two-year-old, unarmed, West African immigrant, of Guinean descent, shot by cops from the New York Police Department, an incredible 41 times, while reaching for his wallet. Sean Bell, also unarmed, a victim of police gunfire, fifty shots total, fired as he left a bachelor party on November 25, 2006, killed on the morning before his wedding. Abner Louima, the Haitian immigrant, sexually molested, sodomized with the head of a plunger, after being assaulted and brutalized while in the custody of the NYPD. The less said about the murders of Trayvon Martin in 2012, and Michael Brown, Eric Garner, Freddie Gray, and the twenty plus other young black men at the hands of the police, all of them between 2014 and 2015, the better. *The Washington Post* reported that "unarmed black men are seven times more likely than whites to die by police gunfire" (*Washington Post*).

From the foregoing, we can conclude that whether it is the fatal shooting of young unarmed Black men, or Black kids being kicked out of a suburban swimming pool because, as stated in an NBC article by Vince Lattanzio, it was thought that they "would change the complexion of the club," the intent, motivations, and attitudes appear to be the same (Lattanzio 2009).

Whether it is Susan Smith, the mother who drowned her three kids in her car in a lake back in 1994 and accused a fictitious Black man of carjacking her vehicle and making away with her kids in it, or Sgt. Robert Ralston, the Philadelphia cop who shot himself in the arm on April 5, 2010, and placed the burden of the shooting on an unknown Black assailant, again, the intent, motivations, and attitudes are no different. In the cases of Susan Smith and Robert Ralston, the use of the code words "Black man" in their reports gave their stories instant national credibility and notoriety—until they themselves were exposed as the culprits. Being White, they knew the exact code words to use to make their stories appear credible. They are the words often used by White racists to revive racial stereotypes and inflame passions and tensions.

The Politics of Race: The Demagoguery of the Birther Movement

On Monday, November 29, 2010, the Supreme Court of the United States threw out yet another challenge to President Obama's legitimacy as president of the United States: the case of Kerchner vs Obama (SCOTUS 2010). The highest court of the land rejected a lawsuit by Charles Kerchner Jr. from Pennsylvania, one that sought to force the president of the United States to provide corroborating evidence of his birth and citizenship. In contention was the supposition that the president did not satisfy the requirement of a "natural born citizen," as stated in the Constitution of the United States.

The hot-button issue of President Obama's birth, citizenship, and therefore, legitimacy as President of the United States, is what has spawned the Birther Movement, which, as of December 2008 (that is, soon after his election), had filed almost twenty lawsuits. Many more such lawsuits have followed since. In an age of post-racialism, the question is, "What drives the 'Birther' movement?" "Are the Birthers a part of the mainstream or simply a fringe movement?" Are its claims founded on evidence or simply the skewed rhetoric of a few disgruntled citizens, and therefore unfounded? Is there an element of racism in its motivations?

The contention of the Birther movement and the premise of its discontent is that there is a massive governmental, or other, cover-up of Barack Obama's background or history that disqualifies him from being president. Birthers sincerely believe he is not an American citizen. They dispute his birth in Hawaii and instead claim that he was either born in Kenya or Indonesia. For the most part, they believe that his birth certificate, issued in the wake of the 2008 presidential campaign, is forged. Some also believe that he had dual British and American citizenship, since his father was from Kenya, a former British colony. According to those definitions, Barack Obama does not meet the constitutional eligibility requirement of being a "natural born" citizen, and, therefore, does not qualify to be president of the Unites States.

Obama's birth on August 4, 1961, at the Kapiolani Maternity and Gynecological Hospital was officially posted in two local newspapers: *The Honolulu Advertiser* and *Honolulu Star-Bulletin*. This, according to politiFact.com, was verified and confirmed by "Will Hoover, who wrote a well-researched story for the *Honolulu Advertiser* on November 9, 2008, about Obama's childhood years in the "Aloha State." "In researching the story," PolitiFact.com states, Hoover "went to the microfilm archives and found the birth announcement for Obama," one in the *Honolulu Advertiser* on August 13, 1961, and in the *Honolulu Star-Bulletin* the next day. They both said the same thing: Mr. and Mrs. Barack H. Obama, 6085 Kalanianaole Highway, son, Aug. 4" (PolitiFact 2009).

A certificate of live birth, officially acceptable in Hawaii, was released by his campaign and made available online during the 2008 campaign. Specifically, on August 21, 2008, *FactCheck.org*, a nonpartisan entity published the birth certificate and the number of the certificate, making it available for public access. It released the following statement to validate its findings: "FactCheck.org staffers have now seen, touched, examined and photographed the original birth certificate. We conclude that it meets all of the requirements from the State Department for proving U.S. citizenship. Claims that the document lacks a raised seal, or a signature are false. We have posted high-resolution photographs of the document as 'supporting documents' to this article. Our conclusion: Obama was born in the U.S.A. just as he has always said" (FactCheck 2008).

Politifact.com, a well-known fact-checking project of the *Tampa Bay Times*, dedicated to critically examining statements by the White House, members of congress, lobbyists, and interest groups, also verified it. Furthermore, the Director of Hawaii's Department of Health, Dr. Chiyome Fukino, issued a statement on October 31, 2008, that, together with the State Registrar of Vital Statistics and Chief of the Office of Health Status Monitoring, Alvin Onaka, they had verified President Obama's original birth certificate in person at the Hawaii Department of Health "in accordance with state policies and procedures" (PolitiFact 2009).

The conspiracy theories surrounding President Obama's birth have not abated, despite all efforts at substantiating his American citizenship. While the movement seems to find its most ardent support within conservative ranks, others within the same ranks regard it as a nuisance. Men like Hannity of Fox News, Rush Limbaugh, the conservative radio talk show host, and Lou Dobbs, formerly of CNN, have accorded the Birther theory and its adherents the much-needed profile and support through their media platforms. On the other hand, Michael Steele, chairman of the Republican Party, has labeled the Birther cause an unnecessary distraction, and stated his belief that the president is an American citizen. Senator Lindsey Graham has advocated calling out the behavior of the Birthers for what it is—lunacy.

Speaking at The Atlantic, the Newseum and Aspen Institutes *First Draft of History Conference*, on October 1, 2009, in Washington, DC, Senator Graham said on the subject of the Birthers that: "This is what the Republican Party needs to do: we have to say that's crazy. So I'm here to tell you that those who think the president was born somewhere outside Hawaii, you're crazy..." He said, "Let's knock this crap off and talk about the real differences we have" (Peyronnin 2010). He also chided television anchors, like Glen Beck, who provide them the platform to spew out their "crap" as well.

Perhaps it is worth noting that the volatile impact of the "craziness" Senator Lindsey Graham alluded to among the Birthers. James W. Von Brunn, shot and killed a security guard at the United States Holocaust Museum. Brunn was not only a White supremacist; he was also a Birther (Schapiro and Meek 2009).

But exactly what fuels the fallacious theories of the Birthers, despite all the evidence to the contrary? Is it politics? Is it religion? Is it economics? Is it racism? Or is it a fusion of all four?

Former President Jimmy Carter, who often pulls no punches, pointed to what he believed to be the cause of this hatred and rage in an interview on *NBC Nightly News*: racism. "I think an overwhelming portion of the intensely demonstrated animosity toward President Barack Obama is based on the fact that he is a black man, that he is African-American. Racism still exists and I think it has bubbled up to the surface because of a belief among many white people, not just in the south, but around the country, that African-Americans are not qualified to lead this great country" (Edwards 2008). The former president expressed the hope that in the future, Democratic and Republican leaders will take the initiative to condemn such "racist attitude" against the president of the United States."

Andrew Sullivan, a conservative political analyst, stated in the *Sunday Times* that "the demographics tell the basic story: a black man is president and a large majority of white southerners cannot accept that, even in 2009. They grasp conspiracy theories to wish Obama and the America he represents—away" (Sullivan 2009).

Writing to his supporters about the prime cause for the conspiracy theory regarding Obama's birth certificate, the president of the Southern Poverty Law center, J. Richard Cohen stated that this "conspiracy theory" referring to the Birthers "was concocted by an anti-Semite" and "circulated by racist extremists who cannot accept the fact that a Black man has been elected president" (Cohen 2009).

Writing for the Washington Post in May of 2010 on the Tea Party battling perceptions of racism, Amy Gardner and Krissah Thompson refer to a quote by Herb Neumann, a White Democrat from Tulsa: "I think there is an element of fear that 'our white country' is now being run by a black man. There is a sense that 1950s America is gone," Herb Neumann says. "There is a sense of loss. I grew up in the 1950s, and I don't think that moving on is a bad thing" (Gardner and Thompson 2010).

Tim Wise, on the other hand, attributes the Birther theory, to a "narcissistic breakdown...of centuries of ingrained privilege and hegemonic control." He explains further that if one is used to seeing people who look like one's self in almost every position of authority, waking up every day and seeing a man of color basically running the country "is psychologically debilitating to white folks who all their lives weren't necessarily bigots or racists in any overt sense, but simply gotten complacent with the way things were. They had internalized these notions of entitlement and superiority." Given the depths of these notions of entitlement and superiority, he wonders whether the Birthers are even aware or "fully conscious of the racist impulses behind their crazy allegations…" (Wise 2009).

Drawing from W. E. B. Du Bois's concept of the "psychological wage of whiteness," Wise elaborates further on his thesis of the loss of white hegemonic control: "A lot of white folks don't have much. They're struggling, they're hurting, but they've been able to content themselves with the idea that at least they're not black. So, they get this psychological wage from their whiteness. The problem is, that's a wage which is diminishing in value. If you say to yourself, "Well I may not have much, but at least I'm not black,' and then you look around and say, "Shit, black is the new president!" Now the value of your psychological wage is reduced in real dollar terms. Now you've got nothing" (Wise 2009).

From that perspective, it is little wonder that Tea Partyers and Birthers are constantly crying out "We want our country back" in apparent displays of nostalgia for a return to a previously "White" country and lifestyle, in a land they once knew, which is rapidly disappearing in the face of increasing demographic change. In that Caucasoid world, exotic names like Barack Obama, Nkrumah, Mandela, Ndabaninge, Tutu, Sithole, Ziqueque, Pokou—or Donkor, for that matter— were nonexistent.

Not surprisingly, Obama himself, when asked in August, 2010, in an interview about the fact that about one-fifth of the American population believes that he is not a Christian or American-born, coolly answered: "I can't spend all my time with my birth certificate plastered on my forehead."

"Conspiratorial theorists," governor Abercrombie of Hawaii said, "are never going to be satisfied anyway" (Shahid 2011). I fully concur.

Eugenics: Racial Hygiene and the Creation of a Super Race

"We shall make of eugenics the biggest pillar of the church, and eugenics will become embedded in the religion of the future. It shall happen hereafter that instead of conflicts between science and religion, these two great human interests will be marching together, hand in hand."
—Irving Fisher, 1913

Lebensborn

In November of 2006, forty men and women had a public meeting in the German town of Wernigerode. The meeting was intended to, once and for all, break the silence and secrecy surrounding their births. It was also intended to find out who their real parents were. Most of them were in their sixties, gray-haired, wearing glasses, and a little bent over with age. They told the stories of their horrendous heritage, shrouded for the most part in secrecy for over sixty years. They were the children of the *Lebensborn*, a Nazi breeding or procreation program, which lasted from 1935 to 1945, with locations or camps in Germany and surrounding countries, like Norway, that had been overrun by Hitler's invading forces in World War II (Fold3).

The word *Lebensborn* means "spring" or "fountain of life." Engineered by Hitler and his henchman, Heinrich Himmler, ex-head of the Gestapo and the notoriously feared paramilitary unit, the SS, human farms or nurseries were created, not only to stem Germany's low birth rate, caused by the alarming numbers of abortions, but also to reverse the reduced number of births due to war casualties. Primarily, and most importantly, they were established to produce a pure "Aryan Super Race" or "Master Race" that would lead a German-Aryan/Nordic nation and ensure the one-thousand-year reign of the German Reich over Europe and the world (Fold3).

Thus, SS officers, many of whom already had families, operated as sires. They were instructed to "father" children with women of certain specific Aryan or Nordic qualities, chief among them blond hair, and blue eyes. Tacit approval was given to SS officers to procreate with the women either through love affairs or one-night-stands. Passing a "purity test"—that is, being of "pure Aryan blood"—was a key criterion for entry into the program. To be accorded the designation of such pure racial stock, one had to be able to trace his or her lineage three to four generations back, to at least grandparents on both mother's and father's sides. The father's Aryan heritage was particularly vital, and therefore verified. Both parents were to have no mental or genetic illnesses or defects in their lineage (Fold3).

The christening ceremony for the Lebensborn babies was typical of SS rituals: the baby was placed on an altar with a swastika flag on or by it, while an SS dagger was held over it. The mother paid homage to the Fuhrer, Adolf Hitler, and swore her loyalty to the Nazi dictum (Sharp 2008).

Pregnant, unwed, single mothers carrying babies belonging to those sires were conveniently tucked away at various *Lebensborns,* away from the spotlight and from invading allied bombers. Mothers who did not want to keep their illegitimate babies had them taken away and placed in foster homes under the care and tutelage of special German parents, who raised them under strict Nazi philosophy and indoctrination (Fold3).

In all, about seven to eight countries were known to have housed *Lebensborn* nurseries: Luxembourg, Netherlands, France, Denmark, Austria, Poland, Norway, and, of course, Germany. Germany, followed by Norway and Poland, were believed to have housed more of these locations than all the other countries. Norway, in particular, was believed to have had as many as nine to 15 nurseries, according to one record. If true, that would have made it more than the German locations (Fold3).

About eight thousand Lebensborn babies were believed to have been born in Germany, with approximately the same number born in other parts of Europe. Many kids with apparent Aryan features, and, therefore, considered to be of racial hereditary value, were kidnapped, stolen from neighboring countries, particularly Poland, and brought to Germany to be Germanized. It is estimated that about one hundred thousand of such children were forcibly taken from Poland alone. In 1946, it was estimated that about 250,000 such children were kidnapped and sent to Germany; only 25,000 were eventually retrieved and sent back to their native countries (Fold3).

Hitler's views on racial mixing and purity are well-documented in the historical record. Edwin Black's gripping and chilling account of the eugenics movement notes some of Hitler's views on the subject: "The Germanic inhabitant of the North American continent, who has remained racially pure and unmixed, rose to be the master of the continent; he will remain the master as long as he does not fall a victim to defilement of the blood" (Black 2003). In typical racist tone and fashion, Hitler further wrote, "It is a scarcely conceivable fallacy of thought to believe that a Negro or a Chinese...will turn into a German because he learns German and is willing to speak the German language in the future and perhaps even give his vote to a German political party" (Black 2003). Hitler's aversion to race mixing is furthermore revealed in some of his salient quotes in *Mein Kampf*, which is purported to have sold over 11 million copies: "from time to time illustrated papers bring it to the attention of the German petty bourgeois that in some place or other a negro has for the first time become a lawyer, teacher, even a pastor,...this is positively a sin against all reason; that is criminal lunacy to keep on drilling a born half-ape until people think they have made a lawyer out of him, while millions of members of the highest culture-race must remain in entirely unworthy positions; that it is a sin against the will of the creator if his most gifted beings...are allowed to degenerate in the present proletarian morass, while Hottentots and Zulu Kaffirs are trained for intellectual professions" (Hitler 1925).

Despite its knowledge of Hitler's Nazi and Master-race ideology, the world watched, aghast, in utter disbelief, as he began his systematic purging from German society, of the people he deemed inferior and unfit to belong to his Master Aryan race and nation. Black contends that, upon Hitler's assumption of power, it did not take long for Hitler and his Nazi accomplices to begin implementing its eugenic vision.

The Law for the Prevention of Defective Progeny, a mass sterilization law, was enacted on July 14, 1933, outlining nine categories of unfits to be targeted for sterilization. They included those who were feeble-minded, schizophrenic, manic-depressive, epileptic, blind, deaf, alcoholic, or afflicted with Huntington's chorea or hereditary body deformities. 400,000 Germans were earmarked for immediate sterilization, beginning January 1 of 1934 (Black 2003).

The culmination of that reproductive persecution and the racial hygiene procedures was the annihilation of 600,000,000 Jews who, right from the very beginning, were the prime object of Hitler's racial animosity.

America and the Roots of Germany's Reproductive Persecution

"It is hard for me to accept or understand or even try to figure out why these kinds of atrocious acts could be carried out in this country."

Governor Perdue of North Carolina

"They cut me up like a hog...my heart bleeds every single day. I'm crushed. What can they do for me?"
—Elaine Riddick

Those were the heart-wrenching words of Elaine Riddick, the fifty-seven-year-old Atlanta resident who spoke before the Eugenics Task Force, appointed by Governor Perdue of North Carolina, to determine appropriate compensation for victims of America's and North Carolina's horrific and ignoble eugenics program, which caused many to undergo forced sterilization procedures (Fox News 2011).

The program in North Carolina ended as recently as 1974. Tom Breen of the Associated Press reports that about 7,600 involuntary sterilizations occurred in North Carolina alone. Ten counties in the state accounted for over 1,700 "involuntary sterilizations" between 1946 and 1968. Elaine Riddick was one of the poor victims of this heinous and criminal program. In 1968, at the age of fourteen and pregnant by a rapist, she underwent a surgical procedure that rendered her permanently incapable of having children (Breen and Elder 2011).

Eugenics

The word *eugenics* means "well-born." *Merriam-Webster's Dictionary/Medical Concise Encyclopedia* defines eugenics as "a science that deals with the improvement (as by control of human mating) of hereditary qualities of a race or breed." It was made popular as a science in 1883, by Sir Francis Galton, a British scientist and a half-cousin of Charles Darwin, who introduced the concept through the publication of his book, *Inquiries into Human Faculty and its Development* (Galton 1907). Galton introduced the concept of nature versus nurture, as well. He is known to have written a controversial letter to the *English Times* also, under the caption, *"Africa for the Chinese,"* in which he advocated a take-over of the African continent from the supposedly inferior aboriginal Black Africans, by the highly civilized Chinese, whose progress and development, he believed, had been occasionally stunted by their dynasties (Galton 1873).

The subject of eugenics gained much notoriety particularly in the wake and aftermath of the Holocaust. The word "eugenics" conjures up horrible images. It generates much pain and passion, because of its connection with Christianity and America's racist history.

The advent of Darwin's theory of natural selection, introduced in 1859 in his groundbreaking work *The Origin of Species*, along with the work of Gregor Mendel, the Austrian monk who made inroads in the field of genetics and inheritance, laid the foundation for Galton's eugenics movement and science. Natural selection, posited that the species least suited for its environment would be naturally eliminated, while the one best suited would survive, flourish, and generate offspring. In a competitive naturalistic environment, only the strong survive and continue on. Herein lies Darwin's theory of the survival of the fittest.

With the introduction of those two scientific theories, the idea of selectively breeding humans, just like genetically breeding peas, plants, or livestock, became appealing as a means of eliminating certain categories of people who were deemed unfit for society's betterment. In the United States, it laid the ground work for the purging of not only thousands of racially undesirable and unfit Black folks, Latinos, and some poor White folks, but also paupers, imbeciles, the disabled, blind people, people who were hearing impaired, petty criminals, etc., through a massive governmental sterilization program. Riddick is just one living example of that American holocaust.

America's Eugenics Industrial Complex

Ironically, Hitler's sinister and maniacal intrigues at creating a "Super Master Aryan" race and nation were birthed and largely nurtured by the notable progress made on the

American eugenics front. American eugenics, engineered by Harry Davenport and Charles Laughlin, the two stalwarts of its eugenics complex, became the precursor not only of the German program of racial hygiene, but other eugenics programs that started in other countries, as well.

In exploring the history of eugenics, Edwin Black highlights the nexus between Germany's Nordic supremacist goals, and America's shameless racism, manifested and deployed through the eugenic movement. The "Nazi principle of Nordic superiority," he asserts, "was not hatched in the Third Reich but on Long Island decades earlier, and then actively transported to Germany." He traces America's eugenic industrial complex to "America's finest universities"—from Harvard, Stanford, Princeton, Yale, etc., to its "reputable scientists, most trusted professionals and charitable organizations," its "most revered foundations," including the Rockefeller Foundation and Carnegie Institute, and even to as far as the US State Department (Black 2003).

Adolf Hitler and the Nazi movement's fascination with America's eugenics progress was obvious right after Hitler seized power on January 30, 1933. Black observes that "under Hitler, eugenics careened beyond any American's eugenicist's dream." Through "National Socialism," Hitler's political philosophy and ideology, he "transduced America's quest for a 'superior Nordic race' into Hitler's drive for an Aryan Master race." He further notes that "Hitler recited Social Darwinian imperatives" in *Mein Kampf* and "praised the policies of the United States and its quest for Nordic purity" (Black 2003).

The landmark Supreme Court case of Buck v. Bell, in 1927 not only set the stage for America's eugenic industrial complex by lending it the necessary credence, but also provided the impetus for its speedy development.

Carrie Buck was led like a sheep to the slaughter and steril-
ized, after the highest court of the land found her to be mentally
and genetically defective—in essence, a "moral degenerate,"
socially unfit to reproduce children. Her mother, who had been
accused of prostitution and pauperism, and her newly-born
daughter, who was equally deemed retarded, had already been
consigned to a colony in Virginia, to a home designed to house
unfit women and keep them from procreating.

The Supreme Court decision, a unanimous decision
handed down by the best judges in the country, was written by
the Chief Justice of the United States, Oliver Wendell Holmes
Jr: "It is better" he wrote, "for the world if instead of waiting
to execute degenerate offspring for crime, or to let them starve
for their imbecility, society can prevent those who are mani-
festly unfit from continuing their kind." He concluded with,
"Three generations of imbeciles are enough" (Holmes 1927)

With corporate philanthropy maximized and extended
to the eugenics movement, the nation's best scientists aligned
with the eugenic agenda, a force led by men of unparalleled
missionary zeal, like Davenport, coupled with the necessary
legal framework and protections provided by the highest court
in the land, America was poised to embark on its self-cleans-
ing mission of sterilizing an estimated 14 million of its "unfit"
citizens, and millions more around the world until a nation
comprising only a pure-bred race, with Nordic identity and
features, blond, blue-eyed, was created (Black 2003).

Murder in the Name of God: America's Culture Wars

In recent times, remnants of the church, right-wing
radical Christian extremists have also employed biblical and

theological premises to wage their brand of holy war and crusade against society. Although their religious rationale and tactics differ from Moslem jihadists, the impact of their actions is no less lethal than the havoc wreaked on the West by Islamic fundamentalists. We may justifiably call them "Christian jihadists," or terrorists, since they carry out their "sacred" cause against secularism in the West and multicultural American society in the name of Christ.

An area of interest targeted by these "Christian holy warriors" is the issue of abortion. Reproductive rights, including abortion, along with other thorny issues like gun rights/control, gay unions and/or marriage, race and affirmative action, family values, secularism and multiculturalism, often define America's cultural landscape. Thorny issues in America's ongoing cultural debacle, they are also the cause of the red-state/blue-state divide, with "red states" referring to Conservative Americans, comprising those whose political affiliation or leanings are with the Republican Right, and "blue states" referring to Liberal Americans, consisting mostly of Democrats, usually referred to as "the Left." In the middle are the Independents, whose views and inclinations as they relate to political, economic, and social issues, often tilt and thus determine the outcome of national political elections. The views of Centrists, as Independents are often called, unlike Conservatives or Liberals, are usually pragmatic, as opposed to ideological.

So far, eight people, four of them doctors, have been slain by assassins belonging to the Christian jihadist movement, for providing abortion services in the United States. On May 31, 2009, Dr. George Tiller was gunned down while serving as an usher in his church in Wichita, Kansas. The perpetrator was Scott Roeder. Dr. Tiller had survived an assassination attempt on his life by Shelley Shannon earlier in

1993. On October 23, 1998, Dr. Barnett Slepian, an upstate New York doctor, was assassinated in his home by James Kopp, who was arrested in France in 2001. In 1994, Dr. John Britton and his aide, James Barrett, were both assassinated by Reverend Paul Jennings Hill in Pensacola, Florida. Barrett's wife, June, was wounded in the attack. On March 10, 1993, Dr. David Gunn met his untimely death at the hands of another assassin. The perpetrator was Michael Griffin, a thirty-one-year-old anti-abortion activist, who shot the doctor three times from behind.

Interspersed with those murders were bombings, kidnappings, and various forms of assault and foiled assassination plots. For example, on Christmas day of 1984, four youngsters, Jimmy and Kathy Simmons, Matt Goldsby, and Kaye Wiggins bombed an abortion clinic and two physician's offices in what they claimed were their "gift to Jesus on His birthday." Although no one was killed then, that clinic was later the site of Dr. Britton and his aide's deaths in 1994.

After driving his car into a clinic, John Earl, a Catholic priest, drew an axe to attack the owner of the clinic before he was subdued.

On December 30, 1994, Shannon Lowney and Lee Ann Nichols, receptionists, were killed by John Salvi, in two separate attacks on clinics in Massachusetts.

Of interest in this right-wing extremist religious vendetta against abortion doctors, is the case of Reverend Bray, and several others of his persuasion, like David Duke and Bob Jones. Manifested through their actions, is a rugged confluence of faith and violence, one that has assumed a high level of toxicity in America's culture wars. Race is a common thread among their ranks and the extremist religious groups with which they are affiliated. Whether it is the Hutaree Militia, The Army of God, or the Christian Identity

Movement, their religious fervor and violent actions are often fueled by racist ideologies and steeped in awkward interpretations of scripture. Awkward, because they are usually at odds in both their essence and expression, with mainstream Christian biblical orthodoxy.

Rev. Bray is alleged not only to be the author of the manual used by the Army of God for their terrorist acts; he is also known to have authored and published *A Time to Kill*, another theological manual, justifying the murder of abortion providers. Bray draws heavily from theologians such as Dietrich Bonhoeffer and Reinhold Neibuhr, who advocated through their Just War theology and doctrine that violence by Christians was necessary, to a certain degree, to resist Nazi brutality. Bray extrapolates from Christian Reconstructionist and Dominion theological views that, in turn, have at their core Christian Identity Theology (Bray 1994).

In *Children of a White God, A Study of Racist "Christian" Theologies*, Matthew Ogilvie makes reference to the "gospel of white power" among certain sections of the Christian Right, at a time when many churches are attempting to reform a history of white supremacy. Of much concern, he states, is the issue of "white racists, who call themselves Christian, and who believe in a theology that gives divine justification to their beliefs." He asserts that some of these Christians groups "possess arsenals of high-technology weapons, the likes of which many Middle-east terrorists would be jealous." Not only do these groups preach a White supremacist "gospel" of Black inferiority proven by biblical texts, that is also a main focus (Ogilvie 2001).

Ogilvie specifically mentions the Dutch Reformed Church Minister DL Malan, who later became prime minister and president of South Africa. Ogilvie notes that, as prime minister, Malan asserted, "Apartheid was based upon the Afrikaner's 'divine calling' to convert the heathen to Christianity without obliterating his national identity" (Ogilvie 2001). Thus, Apartheid, which in Malan's view "ensured the racial purity of whites" as "a matter of divine law" became a necessary tool for the actualization of this "Christianization" process (Ogilvie 2001).

Of similar stock was the Christian Fundamentalist Bob Jones, founder of Bob Jones University, who asserted that "intermarriage of the races is a breakdown of the lines of separation which God has set up and, therefore, rebellion against God" (JBHE 2008). That then presidential candidate, and later President, George W. Bush chose to visit that institution during the 2002 campaign signifies the intermarriage between race and politics in American society, in general, and the extent to which candidates will go to authenticate their credentials, whether Conservative or Liberal, in the eyes of the voting public. Blacks were not admitted to this "Christian" institution until 1971, and for the next thirty years, interracial dating was prohibited.

Jones Sr., the founder of the institution, a fundamentalist evangelist, stated that Blacks should be grateful to Whites for bringing their ancestors to America as slaves. They might still be in the jungles of Africa unconverted if that had not happened (JBHE 2008).

In explaining the school's policy against interracial dating and marriage, in 1998, Jonathan Pait, a public relations officer, stated that "God has separated people for his own purposes. He has erected barriers between the nations, not only land and sea barriers, but also ethnic, cultural and language barriers. God has made people different from one another and intends those differences to remain. Bob Jones University is opposed to intermarriage of the races because it breaks down the barriers God has established" (JBHE 2008).

Such a view, according to this theology, was again steeped in Paul's statement to the Athenians, found in Acts 17:26.

The notion of a "New World Order," in Jones's view, was a conspiracy toward race-mixing, the end of Christianity, and the weakening of the United States. Any support of the United Nations he considered an effort in the same direction. Such notions, according to Ogilvie, run amuck within the ranks of the Ku Klux Clan and various Christian militia groups of McVeigh's kind. It is a confluence and "merger of Christian nationalism with white nationalism," according to Leonard Zeskind, president of the Institute for Research and Education on Human Rights, based in Kansas City, Missouri, and a leading analyst of White supremacist groups in the United States (Zeskind 1999).

The resultant violence from this merger of religion (Christian nationalism), race, and politics (White nationalism) is captured in several books. One is Ben Klassen's (1981) *The White Man's Bible*, published by the World Church of the Creator, in which the "the Mud Races" (referring to non-Whites, of course) are denounced, according to Brad Knickerbocker, in an article titled "When the hate comes from 'churches.'" In the article, published by the Christian Science Publishing Society, Knickerbocker stated that what is "bad for the White Race" is presumed to be "the ultimate sin," and what is good for it "the highest virtue" (Knickerbocker 1999).

Another infamous book, a novel spewing and inspiring similar or even more hate and violence, is *The Turner Diaries*, which has been labeled by the Southern Poverty Law Center and FBI as the "Bible of the Racist Right." Published in 1978, the book was written by a physics professor named William Pierce, using the pseudonym Andrew MacDonald. He recounts in chilling detail a fictional but bloody race war in the United States that leads to the overthrow of the federal government and the annihilation of all non-Whites, especially Blacks and Jews (Macdonald 1978). The book has spawned many other hate-filled, extremist novels, and it had a documented impact on Timothy McVeigh, the Oklahoma City bomber.

Christian Identity

Christian Identity is a derivative of the doctrine of British Israelism, which became popular in the nineteenth century. British Israelism postulates that the British were "God's Chosen people" and one of the ten Lost tribes of Israel, which migrated to Northern Europe from Palestine, so the British Monarchy represents the throne of King David, which was prophesied would be an everlasting throne. British Israelism boasted many prominent leaders, from all spheres of life, including leading evangelical and charismatic Christian figures. British Israelism spawned the Christian Identity Movement, especially in the United States and Canada, and its "two-seed" doctrine. In time, its beliefs and doctrines provided the spiritual and moral justification and impetus for British colonialism and empire-building.

In *God's Country: The Patriot Movement and the Pacific Northwest*, David Neiwert identifies Christian Identity philosophy and teaching as the common thread or denominator that unites the various factions of the radical right-wing in America. This includes gun-toting militia groups inclined to employing violence as a means of saving, reclaiming, or restoring faith, the White race, and country (Neiwert 1999). A faith-based organization, The Center for New Community, reports that there are approximately 272 hate groups in the

Midwest of the United States, including those with ties to Christian Identity. Eric Rudolph, the Olympic Park Bomber, who for many years remained on the FBI's most-wanted list, eluding capture, is known to be a Christian Identity adherent, along with prominent evangelical and charismatic leaders such as evangelists Alexander Dowie, F. F. Bosworth, and healing evangelist William Branham (Knickerbocker 1999).

So what is Christian Identity and what do its adherents believe?

The Christian Identity movement is a racist, anti-Semitic, militant organization that subscribes to the religious notion and belief that Whites are God's chosen people. Christian Identity believes that every race has the divine right to "exclusivity, reproductive isolation and geographic separation, to be free, safe and secure, from the racially destructive effects of racial intermixture and replacement" (Ogilvie 2001).

The core of Christian Identity doctrine is its two-creation accounts. The first creation account, as recorded in Genesis, chapter 1, resulted in the creation of a Black pre-Adamic race. The second, recorded in chapter 2 of Genesis, resulted in the creation of the Adamic race, which is White. Cain is born out of a sexual liaison with the serpent. Abel, on the other hand, is the offspring of a sexual union between Adam and Eve. A "serpent seed" is born and proliferates as Cain marries from the Black pre-Adamic race. Adam's posterity, through union with Eve, is blessed, but Cain's is cursed by God. The stage is set, as Satan plots to steal Abel's blessings for his seed (serpent seed). The only way to accomplish this is through intermarriage between Cain's descendants, the Black and mixed races of the earth, and the White, untainted Adamic seed.

According to Christian Identity theology, the pure White, uncontaminated seed or descendants of Adam may be found in these modern times in Western Europe and North America, in the United States and Canada. These are the descendants of the Ten Lost Northern tribes of Israel that were conquered by the Assyrians in 722 BC. They subsequently migrated to the Caucuses of Europe, where they preserved their racial purity. The tribe of Judah and Levi were, in turn, conquered by the Babylonians in 589 BC. These also were taken into Babylonian captivity, where they also preserved their racial purity, until a remnant of them, Jews, returned to Palestine, and in time, rejected Christ, the Messiah, where-upon they were cursed by God. The subsequent judgment that came upon them, by reason of the curse, culminated in their defeat and dispersal throughout the nations at the hands of the Romans. Those Jews became mongrelized, as intermarriage with their conquerors and other ethnic groups and cultures could no longer be resisted. The resultant seed is, thus, contaminated, part of the original serpent seed, with a divine curse upon it. That includes all modern-day Jews, Blacks, Latinos, Indians, Asians, etc. The pure White races are the seed of Adam and Abraham, who inhabit North America, including the United States and Canada.

Christian Identity adherents are post-millenialists, as opposed to pre-millenialist or a-millenialist, which means that, for them, there is no Rapture by which one can "escape" the Great Tribulation. To usher in the millennial Kingdom of Christ, one must be prepared to go through the terror of the Tribulation (war, famine, and disease)—an apocalyptic holy war, a Christian jihad of sorts, a race war, aimed at cleansing this earth of the scum, the serpent seed, in order to usher in the Kingdom of God and his Christ (Barkun 1999).

Jews and Blacks, in particular, stand out in Identity philosophy as the scum of the earth. Ironically, any charge of being anti-Semitic is one that is vehemently refuted by Identity adherents; after all, how could they be if they are the true sons and daughters of Shem, one of the three sons of Noah. Again, and consistent with Identity philosophy, "of the cattle, creeping things and beasts created before Adam, black people were among those beasts," says Ogilvie. "They, like other animals, have no spirits." Furthermore, the word "beast," according to Christian Identity adherents includes all non-White races (Ogilvie 2001).

Whether among the violent elements or the more moderate elements, Christian Identity and its variant, British Israelism, thrive, making the most inroads with suburban White youth today. Time will tell whether they fuel the same religious fervor and inclinations to violence as the kind noted among these Christian jihadist elements mentioned here, or not.

CHAPTER 5

Racism and the Silence and Complicity of the Church

"It is appalling…" that the most segregated hour of Christian America is eleven o'clock on Sunday morning,
—Martin Luther King Jr.

"In the end, we'll remember not the words of our enemies, but the silence of our friends."
—Unknown

"If you're neutral in situations of injustice, you have chosen the side of the oppressor, if an elephant has its foot on the tail of a mouse, and you're neutral, the mouse will not appreciate your neutrality."
—Archbishop Desmond Tutu

The Father's call to the nations, initially extended to all families through the patriarch Abraham, and later finding its extension and consummation through Christ's vicarious sacrifices, is undermined by the bearer of the message, the Church. In the American context, the Framers (Thomas Jefferson, James Madison, and Alexander Hamilton, among others) pointed to what they called, "self-evident truths" in the Declaration of Independence. Salient among those truths was the principle that "all men are created equal…endowed by their Creator with certain inalienable rights," among which are "Life, Liberty and the pursuit of Happiness."

As noble as that pronouncement was, it did not produce a halt to racism, slavery, and segregation; neither did it change the perception that the Black man—or the Native American, for that matter—was genetically inferior to the White man, fit only as chattel and beasts of burden.

As stated earlier, the Doctrine of the Curse of Ham was deeply entrenched in the American psyche, the Church and clergy being at the very forefront of its advocacy. Thus, on the one hand was a White world, puffed up by a complex, intrinsic, and divinely sanctioned genetic superiority, the sign of whose racial purity was the ability to "have blood in the face" or blush, and a Black world on the other hand, stripped of its humanity, victims of stereotypical assumptions and labels of the most heinous kind (intellectual inferiority, sexual prowess, athletic genius and artistic impulses), assumptions rationalized from theology to biology, and presented as the results of scientific enquiry (Lumeya 1988). These warped and severely perverted notions on both sides, the effects of those racist assumptions and labels, are still with us today, though subtle. They are the pathological assumptions that the Church in the West, and Western society as a whole, are beholden to, to this day. They continue to foment negative stereotypes and social attitudes, and shape public and foreign policy with respect to people of color, not only in America and the West in general, but also in nations with darker-skinned people. Who gets America's or Europe's priority attention, or favorable treatment is often dictated by not only economic interests, but also such narrow interests as race and ethnicity.

Genocide

"A Christian's first allegiance is to the City of God. Whether Caesar listens or not, we are to be the conscience of society..."
—Chuck Colson

Edmund Burke, the Irish statesman and political theorist once stated that all it takes for evil to thrive is for good people to do or say nothing in the face of it. That this sentiment is so true is borne out by several precedents in history (Burke 1792).

The late Chuck Colson calls "disturbing" "the almost total silence of the Christian Church" in the wake of the American aerial bombardment of Belgrade, Yugoslavia. For Colson, at issue was the American military intervention policy adopted by the Clinton administration in March of 1999, to halt the ongoing genocide in Kosovo perpetrated by the brutal Serbian dictator Slobodan Milosevic (Colson 1999).

The Church's silence was most disturbing, Colson suggests, in that the expedition into Yugoslavia raised profound moral questions that the Christian Church was "uniquely qualified" to address. The Church's unique qualification stemmed from certain specific moral standards and guidelines established in the Just War Theory, established by St. Augustine, a notable African theologian and respected early Church father. The Just War Theory is a criterion that, Colson states, the West has used to judge the merits and/or demerits of military interventions for over 1,500 years. Against these criteria, Colson sees no moral authority or rightness for military intervention in Belgrade (Colson 1999).

The American Church, faced with the ensuing national debate and outrage, was "strangely silent," Colson further charges. Such silence, he alleged, represented a stark departure from the mass protests a generation ago during the Vietnam War. The number of clerical collars, symbolic of the leadership of the mainline churches, among the thousands upon thousands of anti-war demonstrators, who marched through the haze of marijuana smoke and tear gas to encircle the White House, he reminded us, was quite striking. The question to be asked is quite simple: Why the silence? If the incursion into Kosovo turned into a quagmire, Colson warned that the blame would lie not only at the feet of the President and his administration, but also at the feet of those Christians who said nothing (Colson). Thank God, Colson's worst fears did not materialize; the intervention, fortunately, did not turn into a quagmire.

The justification for American military intervention in the Balkans, although my personal conviction tells me it was necessary, is not the issue here. In my opinion, it was the humane thing to do, and was justified, whether the Kosovars were Christian, Moslem, Buddhist, Heathens, or Atheists. Obviously, I speak not as a politician or an expert in military affairs, but as a regular, normal human being who sees another human being victimized or suffering injustice at the hands of a much stronger adversary—a bully, so to speak—and seeks justice for the bullied. Humanitarian military intervention, where possible, to stop the senseless slaughter of innocent people—civilians, and especially children, is, in my estimation, always justifiable.

The disturbing issue echoed by Colson, is the non-chalant posture and utter silence of the Church in the wake of the national debate prior to the initiation of military action and the hostilities that followed. That the Clinton Administration acted to stop the genocide in the Balkans but did nothing in other hot spots around the world, such as in Africa, where some of the most horrific wars of equal, if not worse, barbarism and brutality were going on, with many more thousands murdered in cold blood, was an unconscionable double standard worth noting. What justified intervention in one theater, but disqualified it in another? What standard or yardstick was used to determine and justify one over the other?

The Jewish Holocaust

On October 1' 1997, CNN World News reported on a story titled "French Catholics apologize for World War II silence on Jews." Bishop Olivier de Berranger, standing before a sealed car similar to the ones used to transport millions of Jews from various locations to Nazi concentration camps, and ultimately to their deaths, read a statement atoning for the silence of the church and its clergy from 1940 to 1942: "We confess that silence in the face of the Nazi's extermination of the Jews was a failure of the French church. We beg God's forgiveness and ask the Jewish people to hear our words of repentance...we recognize that the church of France failed in its mission to educate consciences and thus bears the responsibility of not having offered help immediately, when protest and protection were possible and necessary, even if there were countless acts of courage later on" (Berranger 1997).

It is believed that 76,000 Jews, including 12,000 children, were deported from France alone between 1941 and 1944; only 2,500 are believed to have survived. The laws promulgated in France against Jews were believed to be even stricter than the ones already in force in Germany. Not only were Jews prohibited from working in such professions as medicine, teaching, civil service and law, their right to own property and visit public parks were also taken away, and they were required to wear a yellow Star of David, the symbol of Judaism. Although the Church's apology was supposed to have been motivated, in part, by Pope John Paul II's call to the Roman Catholic church to acknowledge the sins of its members as it enters the new millennium, the Pope and the Vatican still stood in defense of Pope Pius the XII (1939–1958) against charges of silence and indifference in the face of the Holocaust. This bifurcation makes no sense. It is yet again a display of the double standards ever so often exhibited by the Church, when confronted with issues requiring a muscular and united moral posture or voice.

Such silence and passivity are overtly evident not only in the war in the Balkans, but also in the case of the Ogaden desert region wars between Somalia and Ethiopian, and in more recent times in the Darfur region of the Sudan. By far, however, the worst manifestation of indifference, silence, and complicity on the part of the Church was seen in the case of Rwanda.

Ethnic Cleansing and Genocide in Rwanda

"Silence in the face of evil is itself evil: God will not hold us guiltless. Not to speak is to speak; not to act is to act."
—Dietrich Bonhoeffer

"We will have to repent not merely for the vitriolic words and actions of the bad people but for the appalling silence of the good people."

—Martin Luther King Jr.

In 1994, the world watched, aghast, but stood by in silence and disbelief, as ancient resentments erupted into a full-scale blood bath and genocide in Rwanda. In a matter of months—a hundred days, to be precise—over a million Rwandans were slaughtered by marauding, machete-wielding Hutu tribesmen and gangs, who hacked to death Tutsis and moderate Hutus. It was "ethnic cleansing" at its worst. The West and its Church watched daily from the comfort of their television screens, as hundreds of putrefying human corpses were dumped into mass graves. And yet they kept silent.

In April 1998, four years after those massacres, two Rwandan priests, Jean Francois Kayiranga and Edouard Nkurikiye, were found guilty by a war-crimes tribunal and sentenced to death for their part in the killing of two thousand Tutsis. They were specifically accused of encouraging hundreds of parishioners to seek refuge in their church just before Hutu soldiers attacked the building. The priests then, allegedly, summoned or brought in a bulldozer to destroy the building, crushing the people within.

In *Genocide in Rwanda: the Complicity of the Churches*, Dr. Carol Rittner, a Roman Catholic nun and distinguished professor of Holocaust and Genocide Studies, further exposes the shameful and horrific complicity of the churches in Rwanda. Her inquiry and observations are against the backdrop of a country that is believed to be the most Christian in Africa, with about 90% of its nationals professing to be baptized Christians. Sixty-five percent of professing Christians in Rwanda are Roman Catholic and 30 percent are Anglican. Her research findings point to wholesale involvement of the churches in Rwanda's genocide. Her research points not only to the silence and indifference of the Church, as was the case during the Jewish Holocaust, but rather to the active participation of priests and parishioners alike, who were covertly instrumental and complicit in the execution of the mass killings (Rittner 2004).

"All it takes for evil to thrive is for 'good' people to do or say nothing in the face of it. The Church is called to be "the city set on a hill," a lighthouse in the midst of the surrounding darkness, and the salt of the earth. If its light dims and turns into darkness, and as salt, it loses its flavor, as in the Rwandan and Jewish instances, or as the case was in the Balkans or Darfur (Sudan) arenas, what hope is there for the world?

A Racist Church: A Historical Perspective

*"When the missionaries came to Africa, they had
the bible and we had the land. They said, "Let us
pray. We closed our eyes; when we opened them,
we had the bible and they had the land."*
—Archbishop Desmond Tutu

America's racist history is significant to this treatise. In his book *Beyond the Rivers of Ethiopia*, Otabil refers to this history. In 1832, he writes, "the U.S. Senator, Henry Berry made a revealing statement to the Virginia House of Delegates. Concerning the state of the Negro slave, he said, "we have as far as possible closed every avenue by which light may enter the slaves' mind. If we could extinguish this capacity to see the light, our work will be complete. They would then be on the level with the beast of the field and we should be safe" (Otabil 1993).

Otabil contends that, although Senator Berry died long ago, the structures his generation put in place are predominantly still with us and are being used to keep part of God's people and creation subjugated today. The Senator's statement, Otabil adds, "Was not an isolated one, but a fair representation of the logic of the powers that existed in that era" (Otabil 1993). Unfortunately, it still appears to be the logic of this era, though in more covert and subtle ways.

"There would indeed not be much to worry about if such dangerous ideas could simply be ignored as the exclusive notions of unenlightened people and institutions of Senator Berry's kind..." Otabil further states. The reality is that the Church—the moral vanguard of society—has been an accomplice. The Church's complicity is manifested in its employment of one of the most hideous and devastating doctrines ever used to further the cause of racism: the Doctrine of the Curse of Ham (Genesis 9:18–21). Noah recovers from his alcohol-induced stupor and learns of Ham's derision, accompanied by unseemly acts that reveal his perverted potential for unfilial conduct, and subsequently curses him.

Despite the mountain of evidence to the contrary with respect to the true implications of the curse, the Church world persisted in perpetrating that horrible doctrine. Nzash U. Lumeya of Zaire, in his doctoral thesis *The Curse on Ham's Descendants*, does a fascinating expose on the subject. He asserts that the Church and the clergy have interpreted this biblical story over the centuries to demonstrate the superiority of the White races over the Black. (Lumeya 1988) He enlists a host of cases to make the point, as follows.

Lumeya writes that Augustine Calmet, the French Benedictine Abbot who is regarded as the prime proponent of the Western thought, identified all Black Africans with the curse pronounced by Noah. Thomas Newton, an Anglican Bishop, echoed Calmet's theory of Ham's curse. He stated that all Negroes are accursed; "they are the people through whom the curse of servitude is being borne and extended" (Newton). Thus, increasingly, church leaders in the New World adopted and built their views of Black people upon Calmet and Newton's findings.

Most Southern churches and their leaders in post-colonial America favored a separated society. This arose from their adherence to the dogma of White supremacy based on the adoption of the Ham thesis. Frederic A. Ross, a Presbyterian minister from Alabama, interpreted the colonization of Africa and slavery in the South as the fulfillment of Noah's prophecy in Genesis. The Rev. Thomas Thompson, a theologian, endorsed slavery as "consistent with the principles of humanity and laws of revealed religion" (Lumeya 1988).

The Bible, in the hands of European and American theologians, thus provided the divine and moral authorization for all types of oppression: racial segregation, slavery, colonization, and exploitation of Africa. It is disheartening to learn that the Baptist Church in America split up over the issue of whether "the Black man" had a soul worthy of salvation. Also disheartening is the knowledge that the principles of the policy of Apartheid in South Africa were built on the teachings of the Dutch Reformed Church, a policy that was also endorsed by the Apostolic Faith Mission, a mission with its roots in the Azuza Street Revival of 1906, the birthplace of the Pentecostal Movement.

Pentecostal Leanings and Tradition

I trace my personal and present religious experience to the Pentecostal Movement and tradition, with its roots in the Azuza Street Revival in Bonnie Brae, Los Angeles. The Pentecostal movement has had worldwide acclaim since its inception, and has impacted the world at an unprecedented, whirlwind pace. It is a pace only akin to the early Church in Jerusalem, as recorded in the Acts of the Apostles. From Africa to Latin and Central America to Asia, experiences characteristic of the Pentecostal tradition, such as miraculous healings, deliverance from demonic oppression, and speaking in tongues, have been widely reported.

The super-naturalistic worldview and message of Pentecostalism, one of hope not just for tomorrow or a futuristic heaven, but in the "here and now," are very much at home in these regions of the world. The message of prosperity, both spiritual and material, and upward social mobility (redemption and lift) for the poor and marginalized, regardless of race or color, has been uniquely suited for the peoples of the two-thirds world, and warmly embraced by them. Such has been the appeal of Pentecostalism.

As a young man, particularly in my teens, while mired in abject poverty in Ghana, I was angry and frustrated by my family's rather pathetic and marginal circumstances. Growing up in a ghetto with so many deprivations and a lack of any socioeconomic clout, I had immersed myself in the vices that the ghetto offered: drinking, smoking, drugs, gang activity, and prostitution, to mention a few. They were all symptomatic of the subculture in which I grew up. "Partying" was a temporary, but necessary, "numbing balm," a quick way to escape the pains of ghetto life.

Having grown up in a very traditional, nominal, and pseudo-Christian home, I was struck by the novelty, freshness, and vitality that Pentecostalism presented. It was a marked departure from the drudgery of the formal religion I had grown up knowing. Methodism, Anglicanism, Catholicism and Presbyterianism—all mainline Christian denominations, presented me with only a dead religious orthodoxy, "a "form of godliness," but "denying the power thereof" (2 Tim. 3:5). Thus, at a time in my life when my Methodist denomination only presented me with a distant God who demanded my dutiful worship and obeisance, Pentecostalism, in contrast, offered a vivacious and dynamic relationship with a living, ever-present Father, whose worship was not forcibly demanded, but naturally induced by His unfailing love for me. This God was interested in my success, goals, dreams, and daily affairs. Unlike my earthly father, this one was so concerned about my personal well-being, and all of humanity's, that He sent His Son to come and die a vicarious death for me. By that act, He fully paid the penalty for my sins, as sordid as they were, fully satisfying the demands of divine justice—not because I deserved it, but because He loved me unconditionally. Such a Father, I felt, deserved my worship and obedience, plain and simple. I accepted the free offer.

I was alive from the dead, my hopes and my dreams were invigorated. My previous desires and habits began to give way; what had once been pleasurable ceased to be, and the lifestyle I once scorned, I came to fully love and embrace.

The change was dramatic as it was liberating. I was a new kid—the new kid on the block. Soon it became obvious to many around me that something was different. Some friends of mine waited to see how long my temporary religious "high" would last. While some believed, and joined the ranks of the faithful, seeing and hearing the testimony of their transformed buddy, others insisted on waiting it out. I'm sad to say that they have been waiting a long time.

Despite my remarkable transformation, I was soon to discover that I was simply one out of hundreds of thousands of dejected kids who were being touched and impacted in my country and on the entire continent of Africa.

Christianity, to me, was no longer the White man's religion, but a personal and dynamic relationship. That sense of spiritual ownership, of belonging and closeness to God, was inescapable. I belonged to Almighty God, the Creator of the universe. He was my Father and Christ, my personal Savior and Lord. The sense of spiritual revitalization, or faith, I came to find out, was indeed alive and well around the globe, through the Pentecostal and Charismatic movements.

Racism and the Pentecostal Movement: Charles Parham's Dubious Legacy

> *"The American Church of Christ is Jim Crowed from top to bottom. No other institution in America is built so thoroughly or more absolutely on the color line..."*
> **—W. E. B. Du Bois**

Despite its radical spiritual impact on the world in general, and on the peoples of the two-thirds world in particular, Pentecostalism, which is similar to other Christian movements and denominations, has had its fair share of the cancer of racism. Allan Anderson documents in *Pneuma: The Journal of the Society for Pentecostal Studies* the horrendous racism in Pentecostal circles. He notes that "in spite of the glorious claims of racial and cultural inclusivity made in early Pentecostalism, racism and cultural insensitivity have been endemic to the movement throughout its life and throughout the world" (Anderson 2005). In his analyses, he highlights the legacy of Charles Parham, the "Projector," or father of the Apostolic Faith Church, which, presumably, is the mother of the Pentecostal movement.

Parham, Allan asserts, was essentially a racial bigot and White supremacist from the very beginning. He advocated a separation of the races through his doctrinal teachings and writings. Soon after the advent of the Pentecostal movement, he was known to openly refer to Blacks as "niggers," and anyone he considered "a traitor to the white race" was a "nigger-lover" (Anderson 2005).

Parham's construct of the human race consisted of three main categories: Aryans were the descendants of Abraham, all others of European descent were the Gentiles, and the heathen were all other people-groups of the earth. In this racial scheme, African-Americans were relegated to the "heathen" column, and "Parham was soon to exclude people of African descent from being part of the Bride of Christ," that is, the Church (Goff 1988). Notably, he was often a guest speaker at Ku Klux Klan meetings.

Parham's racist actions and attitudes were indicative of his biblical beliefs, at the core of which was the doctrine of British (or Anglo) Israelism. In his books, *Voice Crying in the Wilderness* (1902) and *Everlasting Gospel* (1911), he proclaimed the racial and spiritual superiority of the White Anglo-Saxon race. He identified the throne of David with the British Royal Family, and further identified Britain and the United States with Ephraim and Manasseh, respectively, the lost tribes of Israel. That became a fundamental part of his ministry philosophy.

The impact of Parham's doctrinal beliefs on the Pentecostal Movement worldwide is also well noted. First, the formation of the Assemblies of God Church marked the beginning and completion of a totally segregated Pentecostal Movement in the United States. It was spawned by a desire to separate from Bishop Mason, the Black leader and founder of the Church of God in Christ (Robeck 2004). W. F. Carothers, a member of the Executive Presbytery of the Assemblies of God, described the "segregation in the Assemblies of God as being part of God's plan to ensure racial purity and to preserve the integrity of the races" (Carothers 2015).

The first Pentecostal church in Britain, founded by William Oliver Hutchison, embraced "British Israelism," although it had no affiliation with Parham's movement. George Jeffreys, founder of Britain's largest Pentecostal church, Elim Pentecostal Church, also became a "British Israelite."

Parham's legacy was most strongly felt in South Africa, where it resulted in even more racist splits. One pastor declared Africans "the beasts of the field," with no eternal souls. Upon the formation of the Apostolic Faith Mission in South Africa, the races were almost immediately segregated in baptisms and church gatherings. The Zion Christian Church, the largest Pentecostal Church in South Africa, eventually became identified with the racist policies of the Apartheid regime. Their mission statement in 1944 stipulated that in "race relations, the mission stands for segregation." "The fact that the Native Indian and Colored is saved does not render him European" (De Wet 1989).

Anderson's treatise on the Pentecostal Movement is another sad commentary on the history of the Church. Called to be a light in the surrounding darkness, the Church instead contributed to the darkness and, once again, became an accomplice in perpetrating evil, in the form of racism against people of other nations, especially those of African descent.

Against that backdrop, one wonders if the assertion that "Sunday morning 11:00 a.m. is the most segregated hour in America today," if accurate, is not a carry-over from the racism that has been a part of our national and church history, endorsed and promoted even by the Church. If accurate, it is an indictment of the universal Church of Christ, and the American Church in particular. It is a sad reflection of how low the Church has fallen from kingdom ideals.

The Church's Shameless Support for Eugenics

"Physical differences don't make race. What makes race are the laws and practices that affect life chances and opportunities based on those differences."
—**PBS Documentary:** *Race—Power of an Illusion*

With the cutting-edge breakthroughs and strides made in the field of science, and the progressive impact of the industrial revolution, the Church in America was confronted with a choice of whether to burrow deeper into its traditional moorings of faith, adhering firmly to its core beliefs about the sanctity of life—all human life, and thus remaining counter-cultural, or to compromise its hard-core values, reinvent itself in the name of modernity, and tow the larger society's quest for the creation of a "better" society. The moral vanguard of society, the Church, the "light of the world" and "salt of the earth," chose the latter, embracing eugenics.

The liberal wing of the Church, consisting mainly of Protestants, was particularly beholden to the call for a purer and better society through eugenics. In *Evangelical Engagements With Eugenics, 1900-1940*, Dennis Durst points out that "the evangelical mainstream in the decades following the turn of the century appeared apathetic, acquiescent, or at times downright supportive of the eugenics movement." "Evangelicals," he continues, very "often accepted eugenics as a part of a progressive, reformist vision…that fused the Kingdom of God with modern civilization" (Durst 2005).

The expectation in much of the Church was that the salvation and redemption of America specifically, and humanity in general, would occur through scientific ingenuity, and that the Kingdom of God could and would be ushered in by the cleansing of society of its misfits, using this scientific ingenuity and methods.

Consequently, the Christian religious denominations, their clergy, and religious leaders signed on. Like all lies, the eugenics movement seized on elements of truth—biblical truth, that is. For example, parallels were made between eugenics and God's call to Israel to completely annihilate Canaanite tribes and nations, lest they later become a snare to them. The iniquities of the fathers being visited upon the children to the third and fourth generations was another favorite, repeatedly elicited to buttress calls to eliminate the prospect of imbeciles and degenerates reproducing generations of their kind.

The conflation of the Calvinist doctrine of predestination (salvation for the "elect") and the ideology of Social Darwinism, predicated on theories such as "survival of the fittest" and "natural selection," meant that all economic, social, political and racial inequities were preordained, the products of divine election and/or natural selection, and, therefore, consistent with the perfect will of God. Conversion, from that perspective, thus became synonymous with physical and social reform. The Bible and the Talmud were often resorted to and used as code language for eugenics. The goal to make eugenics a national religion necessitated the inclusion of a religious element. Thus, all manner of biblical truth was manipulated to make the pitch to the religiously inclined. With time, eugenics became compatible with Christianity.

Christine Rosen, by far the most eloquent voice on the marriage between the Church and Eugenics movement, demonstrates in her book, *Preaching Eugenics,* how Christian clergy bought wholesale into a social Gospel of Progress that espoused eugenics as its main mantra. Regarding the Reverend Oscar McCulloch, she observed that the Congregational minister's call for the cessation of public assistance to the "unfit," and his advocacy of state power as a means of stopping 250 unfit families from producing generations of "murderers, illegitimate children, prostitutes, beggars, thieves and scores of…generally diseased beings," served as the initial scaffolding on which the Church later stood to champion the eugenic message. The relationship was no flirtation, but a real marriage, boasting some of the most notable preachers of the time. These preachers, "paragons of virtue," became some of the movement's most vociferous advocates, championing and providing moral validation to the nefarious pseudo-religious science of eugenics (Rosen 2004). Rosen observed that by 1927 a eugenics "Committee on Co-operation with Clergy men" was established, consisting of thirty-nine Liberal Protestants, two Rabbis, and two Catholic priests. Monetary rewards went to those preachers who preached the best messages on eugenics. In that way, the message was propagated to thousands of Americans from the pulpit as gospel truth. John Harvey Kellog, an ex-Seventh-Day Adventist Minister, the creator of the Kellogg's Cornflakes brand, and a herald of the eugenics message, preached the gospel of physical health as the key to righteous living, saying it was necessary for the will of God in heaven to be done on earth.

It is worth mentioning that on April 30, 2008, by a vote of 836 to 28, at the General Conference of the United Methodist Church, the Church unanimously voted to apologize for the involvement of Methodist churches and pastors in the American Eugenics movement. It decried its support for eugenics as a "sound science and sound theology," and apologized for the "effort to produce better human beings through breeding."

"We lament," the resolution concluded, "the ways eugenics was used to justify the sterilization of people deemed less worthy. We lament that Methodist support for eugenics policies was used to keep people of different races from marrying and forming legally recognized families. We are especially grieved that the politics of eugenics led to the extermination of millions of people by the Nazi government and continues today as 'ethnic cleansing' around the world" (Alabama Baptist News 2008).

Sad to say, the Methodist Church's involvement in eugenics was extensive and deeply entrenched in the fabric of the Church's culture. That it has apologized for its sins is very welcome news, though it still defies any real sense of human decency that such a giant pillar of the Christian faith could have become involved in egregious violations of that magnitude, in the name of science, or in the name Christ, for that matter. We are yet to hear from the Presbyterians, Episcopalians, and other religious organizations who were equally complicit in perpetrating that shameless atrocity.

Part Two:
The Solution

CHAPTER 6

The Ministry of Reconciliation

"Therefore, if any man be in Christ, he is a new creature: old things are passed away; behold, all things are become new. And all things are of God, who hath reconciled us to himself by Jesus Christ, and hath given to us the ministry of reconciliation."
—2 Corinthians 5:17 (KJV)

"Racial reconciliation isn't just a good idea because it's politically correct. The message of the Gospel is at stake."
—Afshin Ziafat

Last or parting words are usually powerful in their significance or import. Christ's last words to His disciples—in essence, the Church—stated in the Gospels (Matthew 28:18–20, Mark 16:15–20, Luke 24:44–49, and John's Gospel: 20:21) issue a clarion call to mission to all nations of the world (*panta te ethne*). Mission, for all intents and purposes, is the primary task of the Church. To be the Church is to be missional. This is referred to in missiological circles as the *Missio Dei* (*Missio* sending; *Dei* God).

God's Mission is defined by Charles Van Engen as "the people of God intentionally crossing barriers from church to non-church, faith to non-faith, to proclaim by word and deed the coming of the kingdom of God..." He emphasizes the church's involvement in God's mission: to reconcile mankind to God and bring them through faith and repentance, into the church (Engen).

David Bosch, in *Transforming Mission: Paradigm Shifts in Theology of Mission*, also observes that Missio Dei (*God's mission*, in its classical definition) is God the Father sending the Son, and the Father and the Son sending the Spirit, which is further expanded to include yet another "movement": Father, Son, and Holy Spirit sending the church into the world" (Bosch 1991). He thus puts the Missio Dei in the context of the very nature of God, as manifested in the Trinity.

John Stott's thoughts on this dimension of God's nature is even more provocative. Highlighting the essential and irrefutable missionary nature of the biblical religion in *The Whole Christian*, he notes that, "The God of the Old Testament is a missionary God, calling one family in order to bless all the families of the earth." He notes the missionary Christ, sending the church out to witness, the missionary Spirit of Acts, driving the church out from Jerusalem to Rome, the missionary church of the epistles, a worldwide community, and the missionary end of Revelations, "a countless throng from every nation" (Stott 1980).

Mission, therefore, Stott concludes, "cannot be regarded as the hobby of a few fanatical eccentrics in the church" (Stott). Mission lies at the heart of God and therefore at the very heart of the church. A church without mission is no longer a church. It is contradicting an essential part of its identity. So encompassing is this call (and wholesale its demands) that the Church loses its very essence, perhaps, even its right or reason to exist by its reluctance or refusal to be missionary in vision and practice. Newbigin underscores that the essence of the Church's existence must be understood in the context of the *Missio Dei*. His words in this regard are also insightful; he states, "What our Lord Jesus left behind, was not a creed, system of thought or rule of life, but a visible community... the Church to which He committed the entire work of salvation...to make Him and what He had done, known..." (Newbigin 1953).

Elaborating further on the visible community of which Newbigin speaks, David Heywood asserts that the centrality of this visible community as the bearer of God's mission gives to Christianity its distinctive character: incarnational, contextual, open to the world, and reflective. "Rather than following a universally applicable blueprint," he adds, "the community is called to discern the shape of God's mission for each place and time...to be renewed by the Holy Spirit so as to fulfill its mission" (Heywood 2011).

Reconciliation: The Essence of God's Mission

*"Our lack of unity and oneness is a direct
contradiction of our missiological goal:
disciples of all nations."*

—Kevin Smith

What is reconciliation? God's preeminent agenda and the shape of His mission for America at this time is Reconciliation. Generally, this means the redemption and restoration of all humanity from its "*lost*"-ness, back to fellowship with God. Reconciliation is defined as "mutual acceptance by members of formerly hostile groups of each other... Such acceptance includes positive attitudes, but also positive actions..." (Staub and Pearlman 2001).

Two Greek words drive home the meaning of reconciliation. They are *katallaso*, which is translated in the King James Bible as "to reconcile" or "to be reconciled." It denotes an exchange, which when applied to persons in relationship, suggests an exchange from enmity to fellowship (2 Cor. 5:18, Rom. 5:10). The other is *katallage*, which means "reconciliation" (Rom. 11:15, 2 Cor. 5:18–19), but was also used once as "Atonement" (Rom. 5:11). *Katallage* implies a change in the condition of mankind (from sinfulness to righteousness), a change induced by the action of God. Thus, reconciliation from a biblical perspective is the exercise of God's grace through the redemptive work of Christ to mankind, who is in enmity with God because of sin. God deals a death-blow to the sinful condition (Rom. 6:6, Ezek. 36:25–26), imputing His righteousness in Christ on the individual through repentance and faith, thus establishing the basis for a renewed relationship. He subsequently entrusts the newly reconciled individual with the same "Ministry of Reconciliation" (2 Cor. 5:18).

When limited to evangelism or soul-winning, the ministry of reconciliation assumes a vertical dimension; that is, reconciliation between God and humanity. The issue of racial healing and reconciliation, the focus of this book, falls within the purview of the ministry of reconciliation also. However, this is not on a vertical plane, but rather a horizontal one: humanity with each other, person to person or group to group, where a relationship shifts from one of enmity to one of fellowship. Staub and Pearlman again emphasize that although structures and institutions that promote and serve reconciliation are important, reconciliation must by necessity include a changed psychological orientation toward the parties involved. I could not agree more.

Racial Healing and Reconciliation: The Preeminent Mission of the American Church

"We are all one—or at least we should be—and it is our job, our duty, and our Great challenge to fight the voices of division and seek the salve of reconciliation."
—Roy Barnes

Racial healing and reconciliation is defined by Yancey as "the process by which we overcome the previous dysfunctional, unequal relationship between the races and develop an egalitarian, healthy relationship" (Yancey 1996). W. E. B. Du Bois states in *The Souls of Black Folk* (1961) that the problem of the twentieth century is the problem of race. It appears, I will wager, that America's persistent flirtation and marriage with race and racism is still the problem of the twenty-first century. It is noteworthy that America's only civil war was about racial politics, specifically the place of the Negro in American society. The genocide of Native Americans, the institution of slavery, the incarceration of thousands of Japanese during World War II, the Chinese Exclusionary Act of 1882, the Emancipation Proclamation, the Jim Crow laws promulgated in its aftermath, and the Civil Rights Movement are all attestations to the profound centrality and significance of race in American life.

It is my contention in this book that there is no better agency or greater facility for healing America's racial wounds and fostering racial reconciliation than the Church. The Church, called to be the "light of the world" and the "salt of the earth" (Matt. 5:14), the moral vanguard of our society, is the primary if not the sole entity with the divine wherewithal to facilitate racial healing and reconciliation. Yancey's assertion in this regard is noteworthy: "The more I have thought about this issue (racism)," he emphasizes, "the more I realize that the moral presence of the Church is essential in the battle against racism if racial peace is ever going to be possible in our time" (Yancey 1996). This is so because (as explained earlier), racism, at its core, is a spiritual condition, a disease of the human heart.

"Racism," according to *Facing Racism: A Vision of the Beloved Community* "is, fundamentally, a spiritual problem because it denies our true identity as children of God" (PCUSA 1999). In *Crossing the Racial Divide: America's Struggle for Justice and Reconciliation* Aaron Gallegos also notes that "racism is a spiritual issue. Neither its solutions or causes will be found (solely) through government programs, social ministries, or our own best intentions…" He advocates reaching out to God for solutions (Gallegos 1998). Since racism at its core is a spiritual malady, the panacea for it is reconciliation with God, who alone wields the capacity to heal and transform the heart.

The American Church's historical flirtation with racism and its complicity in the shaping of a racially fractured society and world make this mission of reconciliation not only an imperative, but extraordinarily complicated also, in fact, a paradox. How can the Church, a perpetrator of the sin of racism, offer the remedy for the healing of the same disease it has helped in causing? John Dawson, in *Healing America's Wounds*, highlights this paradox. Regarding prejudice, he observes that "the followers of Jesus have the potential to heal the wound" (Dawson 1994). However, he further notes of the church of America; "I see a people who sometimes mirror, more than they contrast, the national condition… Our greatest national sins are most deeply institutionalized within the Church," he states (Dawson 1994).

White supremacy, which served as the underpinnings of slavery, Jim Crow, colonialism, apartheid, eugenics, Western imperialism, and most other manifestations of racial injustice was, by and large, formulated from contrived theological and biological notions and buttressed by the Church (Lumeya 1988). In this regard, Dawson again states, "it became necessary…to dehumanize those people Europeans held in bondage…shortly…a proliferation of theories arose about the inferiority of Negroes." The challenge was that an "irreconcilable contradiction" was going to be created if the Negro or Native American was seen as human, possessing an immortal soul with the potential for salvation (Dawson 1994).

The Church's silence (and by extension, complicity) in the face of the Jewish holocaust, as Hitler unleashed his Aryan, racist fury on "inferior" Jews, is worthy of mention in this respect, and so are the Rwandan, Sudanese, and Congolese genocides. As Dietrich Bonhoeffer, eloquently asserted, "*Silence in the face of evil is itself evil: God will not hold us guiltless. Not to speak is to speak; not to act is to act*" (Bonhoeffer). Ginetta Sagan, human rights advocate and honorary Chair of the Board of Directors of Amnesty International USA, expressed it a bit more succinctly; she said, "*Silence in the face of injustice is complicity with the oppressor*" (Sagan 2000). Thus, the "light of the world," the Church (Matt. 5:14) for many "colored" people, became the pain of the world through these theories and the atrocities that subsequently followed them. To be an agent of healing and reconciliation, urgent change is needed in the Church.

Change in the Church: A Divine Imperative

The American Church as it stands today is segregated along racial, ethnic, and cultural fault lines, which is undoubtedly the legacy of its racist past. Du Bois highlighted this best in *The Color Line and the Church*, when he stated that the church in America, "is Jim Crowed from top to bottom. No other institution in America is built so thoroughly or more absolutely on the color line…" Concurring with Du Bois, Dr. King's words sound a similar tone: "It is appalling," he said, "that the most segregated hour of Christian America is eleven o'clock on Sunday morning… How often the Church has had a high blood count of creeds and an anemia of deeds!" (King 1960).

Michael Emerson and Christian Smith in *Divided By Faith* further corroborate the racism present in the Church when they charge that many churches are segregated along ethnic and economic lines and that little has changed in the more than one hundred years since Dr. King claimed that eleven o'clock on Sunday morning is the most segregated hour of the week. They observe that 92.5% of churches in the United States are racially segregated; i.e., 80% or more of individual membership in these churches represents a single (homogenous) people group. Churches in the United States are ten times more segregated than the neighborhoods in which they are located and twenty times more segregated than the public schools in their neighborhood (Emerson and Smith 2001).

Curtiss DeYoung et al. in *United by Faith: The Multicultural Congregation as an Answer to the Problem of Race*, highlight the fact that the American Church is "racially segregated" (DeYoung 2003). Only 5.5% of all Christian congregations in the US are racially mixed, they further emphasize. A recent National Congregations Study shows that nine out of ten congregations have a majority race that composes 90 percent or more of the congregation (Emerson et al. 2006). For the world or society to be segregated and racially fractured is one thing; for the scourge of racism to infect a religious institution, particularly the Church, the light of the world, the institution mandated to illuminate the darkness and point the way, is a totally different issue.

There is no doubt that a segregated and divided Church cannot foster healing and reconciliation in a divided world; only a united Church can. Some pan-Africanists, like Elijah Mohammed of the Nation of Islam and Bob Marley, the Jamaican reggae superstar, have called on Black people, in light of the atrocities mentioned earlier, to completely reject Christianity, the Bible, and the Church, and return to their ancestral forms of worship, or to Islam, allegedly the original religion of the Black Man. In this regard, Mensa Otabil's admonishment is worth noting. He states in *Beyond the Rivers of Ethiopia*: "That is not the way out! When a man is bitten by a snake," he explains, "it takes an anti-snake bite serum prepared from a snake to bring healing and restoration to that person... I totally believe that if the Bible was misused and misapplied to bind our people, we would need an anti-oppression serum prepared from the revealed truth in God's Word to bring healing, liberty and restoration to us" (Otabil 1993).

To be a force for racial healing and reconciliation, the Church must certainly undergo drastic change, just as the venom of the snake must undergo various chemical changes in order to become useful as an anti-venom serum. It has to divorce itself from its racist past, return to its "ancient landmarks," and reclaim its prophetic voice and mission of healing and reconciliation through a reinterpretation and reapplication of the same biblical authority it so woefully employed to subjugate a segment of God's people. It also means, in its quest for missional effectiveness, it must come to terms with contextual factors on the American landscape. Grappling with the seismic cultural and demographic shifts occurring in America, a result of massive migration patterns, is certainly a good place to begin. Missional effectiveness will require serious paradigm shifts.

In *Transforming Mission*, Bosch is once again masterful in his explanation of paradigm shifts in the Church vis-à-vis its mission. Mission, he says, needs to be understood as "the good news of God's love, incarnated in the witness of a community for the sake of the world." Paradigm shifts in mission, he further explains, necessitate equivalent shifts in the Church's theology of mission and praxis. Each shift in culture, he stresses, presents the Church with two options, danger or opportunity (Bosch 1991). Taking advantage of the opportunities presented requires proper contextualization.

Relating to the issue of paradigm shifts in the Church and world and the need, therefore, to contextualize its mission, Loren Mead also observes that both the Church and the world are in constant flux. However, we (the Church) bring to that constant change and unstable environment a stable and unchanging paradigm, a mind-set that sometimes lasts for centuries (Mead 1991). Eddie Gibbs, underscoring the Church's need for change, in turn says, "To assume that one can continue to function in one's accustomed style without regard to the conditions and demands of the new situation is to be as foolhardy as to turn a boat sideways to the waves in mountainous seas" (Gibbs 1986).

The most strident of the calls for change in the Church, perhaps, comes from David Olson and James Adams. They write in *The American Church in Crisis* that on any given

Sunday, the vast majority of Americans are absent from church, and if trends continue, by 2050 the percentage of Americans attending church will be half of what it was in 1990. Olson and James contend that the Church has been lulled to sleep and is ill-prepared to engage the new world. For restoration to occur, the American Church, he asserts, must address three critical shifts in our culture: from Christian to Post-Christian, Modern to Postmodern and Mono-ethnic to Multiethnic (Olson and Adams 2009). The Church, thrust into a multiracial, cultural, and ethnic ethos, needs to discern the times like the children of Isaachar (1 Chron. 12:32), and know what to change and how to renew and position itself for greater missional effectiveness in this culturally and radically different context.

In the quest for greater missional effectiveness in general, and racial healing and reconciliation in America the Church, it is my contention, must grapple with three key issues:

1. Develop a greater understanding and appreciation of the Imago Dei, the Image of God within all of humanity, and its implications for racial healing and reconciliation.
2. Address issues of social and economic justice and equity as integral to the message of reconciliation.
3. Develop a cross-cultural and multiracial paradigm by reclaiming the vision of Christ as the Reconciler of the nations (ethnos). The development of such a paradigm must be steeped in an understanding of the origin of the races, as well as the divine purpose and contribution of each of Noah's three sons to human civilization, progress, and development (The Three Branches of Noah's Sons).

RICHARD D. DONKOR

Reconciliation and the Imago Dei

"The answer to racism isn't sociological, it's theological."
—Dr. Tony Evans

The Christian life is not a call to a reclusive life or to solitary confinement as a hermit shut off in a temple or monastery, up in the woods, or on a mountaintop somewhere, totally disengaged from real life and the affairs of the world. Jesus's words regarding His Church "being in the world but not of it" (John 15:19, 17:14–16) is not a call to disassociation from the world. In fact, the contrary is rather the case. Jesus clarifies this by praying for his disciples as they are being "sent into" the world to illuminate the prevailing darkness, not to flee from it. "Pure religion in the sight of God," the apostle James also highlights, is to visit orphans and widows in their plight or distress, and to keep one's self unspotted or unstained by the world (James 1:27).

Thus, a life of solitude may be perfectly in order, if it ultimately translates to community engagement and impact in some significant or meaningful way. Jesus's example serves as a blueprint in spiritual discipline; He would occasionally remove Himself from the masses to spend time with his Father (Luke 5:16, Matt. 14:23, Mark 1:35, Luke 6:12). He would always return empowered and invigorated, ready to engage with the real-life situations of humanity. His impact on society was the result of quality time spent with his Father. Integral to the mission of the Christian, therefore, is a call to social and community engagement.

At the core of the Church and the Christian's mission to social and community engagement is the need for an awareness of, and sensitivity to, the physical, social, economic, and systemic injustices and inequities present and visible in society, among the people groups we are called to serve. The call to racial healing and reconciliation, and the removal of conditions and structures that perpetuate racism in all its varied forms, falls within this framework of social justice, equity, and service.

Despite having social, economic, and political implications, the quest for racial healing and reconciliation must not simply be relegated to the realm of politics and social science, however. Political expediency and social science have their unique place in fostering racial healing and reconciliation. Sometimes laws or practices that perpetuate inequality or injustice must be removed politically. Government may intervene and/or assist in the protection of oppressed or underserved populations. Opportunity may be created for such populations or communities by statute; however, many humanistic solutions remain superficial, only scratching the surface of the problems they attempt to solve without going to the root of the matter, which often issues from or is tied up with the spiritual decadence humanity finds itself mired in.

The ultimate solution to racism, therefore, I argue, is theological. "The answer to racism isn't sociological, it's theological," Tony Evans emphatically states. The mission and quest for racial healing and reconciliation must be founded on a firm, theological basis, one that speaks to the common humanity of all, regardless of color, class, creed, or gender. Such a theological foundation may find true meaning in the doctrine of the *Imago Dei.*

Imago Dei and Implications for Racial Healing and Reconciliation

At the core of racial healing and reconciliation is the philosophy of human dignity and excellence for all mankind, in all its varied forms and manifestations: spiritual, physical, social, and economic. This philosophy of human dignity is rooted in the theological concept of the *Imago Dei* which speaks first to the creation of mankind after the *image and likeness* of God. In Genesis 1:26–27, scripture says, "Then God said, let us make man in our image (*tselem*) and in our likeness (*demut*); and let them have dominion over the fish of the sea and over the birds of the sky and over the cattle and over all the earth, and over every creeping thing that creeps upon the earth. So God created man in His own image, in the image of God created him; male and female created He them."

After this declaration by God to Himself (the Trinity here assumed), scripture further says: God…formed man of the dust of the ground, and breathed into his nostrils the *breath of life*, and man became a living soul" (Gen. 2:7).

John the Apostle indicates that "God is a Spirit and they that worship him must worship him in spirit and in truth" (John 4:24). Thus, God, in wanting to create mankind in His own image and likeness, breathed a bit of Himself into the physical form He had made from the dust of the earth. By this act, "man became a living soul" (Gen. 2:7), thus retaining spirit-life and immortality. The phrase *"breath of life"* (Gen. 2:7) is derived from the Hebrew word, *ruach,* which translated into English means "breath," "wind," or "spirit." As the source of life, *ruach* is used about 400 times in the Old Testament to mean the "Spirit of God," the human spirit, or to denote wind as in Genesis 8:1.

The eighth psalm speaks to the special distinction and pedigree humankind enjoys among all of creation. He is made a little lower than the "angels," angels here being derived from the name of God, Elohim. "What is man that you are mindful of him, or the son of man that you visit him? For you have made him a little lower than the angels, and have crowned him with glory and honor. You made him to have dominion over the works of your hands; you have put all things under his feet" (Psalm 8:4–6).

The biblical concept of *Imago Dei,* thus, demonstrates conclusively that "mankind," both male and female, is made in the image and likeness of God. The word "angels" from the text above is from the Hebrew word Elohim, which means God. Thus, we understand from the above that God created humankind first, in His image, and second, just a little less than Himself. This makes humanity the clearest reflection of God among all creation, essentially, distinct and distinguishable from but also above all of God's creation. *Imago Dei* reminds us, therefore, that all human life is sacred and inalienable, with transcendent worth and of intrinsic value, because it originates from God. This is the key to all human dignity.

The concept of *Imago Dei* endows humanity with the spiritual capacity to know God, love God, and relate and fellowship with God in prayer, worship, and praise. *Imago Dei* grants to mankind the capacity to rule over God's creation as stewards or custodians of His (God's) property. It further gives mankind the capacity for moral decisions or choices based on conscience, the sense of right and wrong, instead of simply on our baser, animalistic instincts. *Imago Dei*, furthermore, makes humans the most creative of all God's creation, a chip off the old block, with a creative genius unmatched among all creation.

Perhaps it is important to also emphasize that "God created man" whole and complete, with no defects or deficiencies. Any distortions, wounds, or imbalance caused by any form of abuse or violence (sexual, physical, verbal, or psychological) is thus a deviation from His original intent or purpose. Any devaluation of a human being by another, whether through racism, slavery, colonialism, imperialism, segregation, capitalism, socialism, ethnocentrism, discrimination, abortion, murder, or any form of oppression, is not part of the divine plan or intent, since it denies and denigrates the essential humanity and, therefore, dignity of all mankind.

Through Adam's disobedience and subsequent fall, a distortion occurred in humanity called spiritual death. Spiritual death is the result of a fracture in the God-mankind relationship. With spiritual death came a plethora of issues, all affecting some part of this quality of dignity. The redemptive work of Christ dealt a death blow to the loss of dignity suffered in the garden, however, and provided a restorative pathway to human dignity, in all its manifestations—spiritual, physical, mental or intellectual, and financial. Through the experience of the "new birth" and the continual renewal of the mind, the full capacity and expression of God's image in mankind is progressively restored; the culmination of this restoration will occur in heaven as mankind assumes a glorified body or state.

A corollary of human dignity, also issuing out of the *Imago Dei*, is the intangible and divine quality of Excellence. Excellence is a rather unique characteristic. As an essential characteristic of God, it sets Him and everything He does apart and in a league of its own. Excellence is the very essence of who God is. In Psalm 8:1 David describes God as Excellent. Scripture tells us of an Excellent God who meticulously created all things, then looked on His creation and declared it "Good" (Gen. 1:31). The Psalmist, yet again, struck by the excellence and sheer wonder of God's creative genius in so intricately and delicately shaping the human kind, extols His Creator, Almighty God, in these words: "I will praise thee for I am fearfully and wonderfully made, marvelous are thy works; and that my soul knows well" (Psalm 139:14).

About this scripture, *John Gill's Exposition of the Entire Bible* notes how God formed man wonderfully; the structure, texture and just proportion of all its parts…with amazement…full proof of the wisdom and knowledge of God. He asserts that the eye and ear in addition to all the other parts that work in synchrony have most people filled with awe (Gill 1748).

Such a description of human excellence could not be more apropos. God's image in mankind, which places him in a class of his own with exceptional and God-endowed creativity and dominion over the earth, distinct from all other creatures, calls for the highest regard for all humanity regardless of race or ethnicity, especially by those who claim to have the highest regard for the Creator who created them. It is unimaginable for anyone to claim to serve God, yet dehumanize or despise other humans who are also made in His very image based on their color, creed, culture, or ethnicity (or gender, for that matter). If racial healing and reconciliation is to become a reality in America, first the Church must truly come to grips with its own theology, chief among the subjects being the doctrine of the *Imago Dei*.

RICHARD D. DONKOR

Healing and Reconciliation: The Place of Restorative Justice

How can the sons and daughters of former slaves and the sons and daughters of slave masters move past the sordid experiences and wounds of the past that have for centuries defined their relationship? How do the descendants of Native Americans whose homeland was conquered and annexed through mass extermination or genocide, and African Americans whose ancestors endured the pain and indignities of slavery and Jim Crow for centuries and for whom America's continued flirtation with racism remains a sore point, engage in any discourse on racial healing and reconciliation? Is racial healing and reconciliation based on the concept of the *Imago Dei* and the excellence of God's handiwork in human creation alone possible or enough without some form of restorative justice? Is the quest for racial healing and reconciliation a realistic proposition without satisfying the need for racial justice and equity?

Being a Believer in God and a consummate optimist, my personality lends itself to the affirmative on questions of this sort, including this one. Nevertheless, I would wager that finding that place of healing, reconciliation, and closure between America's polarized races will be a rather long and difficult road without some form of restorative justice. Here is why: Suppose I got into a brawl with someone, a schoolmate, friend—even a brother, perhaps, one much older, bigger, and stronger than I was—and in the process of defending myself from this bully, I lost my two front teeth. Would the passage of time (alone) be sufficient to assuage the physical, emotional, or psychological trauma and pain of that experience? How difficult or easy would it be to find closure in such a situation?

First, the absence of an apology for this unjustifiable act of hostility would make any attempt at forgiving and, subsequently, experiencing healing from the trauma (much less restoring a once-amicable relationship) extremely difficult. Question: What if through some divine intervention, however, this person realized the folly of his ways and rendered a heartfelt apology to me? Would his obvious contrition help in healing the rift between us? It most certainly would help. His acknowledgment of wrongdoing, followed by a sincere apology, should and would help ease the tension and soured relationship between us; his acknowledgment and amends would most likely help me to let go of the animus between us, relative to how deep my wounds and scars are. The process of letting go may sometimes be immediate but is more likely to be gradual or prolonged—again, depending on the emotional impact of the experience. There is, unfortunately, no definitive way of determining how long this emotional trauma may linger in my life. But the transgressor's acknowledging and taking responsibility for the atrocity perpetrated should minimize the pain and begin the process of healing and reconciliation.

Of great consequence to the healing and reconciliation process will be the two front missing teeth. Even if forgiveness is my immediate response to his contrition and apology, the continued embarrassment I might feel in my social interactions because of my missing teeth and the obvious damage to my self-image or esteem as a result might not augur well for future relations. Any time I stand in front of the mirror, smile, and observe the cavern in my mouth, I will be reminded of the unjustifiable horror and sheer brutality of the moment. Forgiving him, singularly and wholeheartedly, even without an apology from him, would undoubtedly free me from the damaging psychological effects of this trauma.

Healing, reconciliation and full restoration of our relationship would likely be tenuous, however; my missing teeth would always be feeding my scarred memories and holding me hostage, not only to a life of dented self-esteem, but probably anger, bitterness, and resentment also.

Any restitution, short of a miracle-growth formula for teeth, would have to be dentures, which (though only a simulated version of the teeth I had and therefore not perfect) would aid in the restoration of my confidence and self-esteem. Thus, attempts at healing and reconciliation in any sphere, in addition to the standard acknowledgment and sincere apology, must by necessity be combined with some measure of restorative justice (the dentures, in this example) for it to be meaningful and permanent. This illustration may well be applicable to the continuing imbroglio between White and Black America.

Jennifer Harvey, in *Dear White Christians: For Those Still Longing for Racial Reconciliation*, highlights the inadequacy of the racial reconciliation paradigm. She asserts that it is a "fundamentally flawed approach." Harvey argues against this paradigm, emphasizing that the lack of results after years of working toward achieving interracial, multiracial, diversity and reconciled communities should be an indictment of the adequacy of the paradigm of racial reconciliation. She urges a "reparations paradigm" as the panacea to the "unacknowledged history of brutal injustice." This is in reference to "White hostility to and violence against communities of color" and "legacies of unaddressed violence, oppression, subjugation, and devastation." The hope is that those who have benefited, in addition to apologizing, need to make meaningful repair (Harvey 2014). The quest for racial healing and reconciliation, thus, lacks traction, despite the great effort and resources invested in it, Harvey observes.

Emerson and Smith also sound a concordant tone. In *Divided by Faith: Evangelical Religion and the Problem of Race in America,* they underscore what they consider to be the main hindrance to racial reconciliation in America—that is, the gap in perceptions between White and Black Evangelicals about race. While Whites perceive racial reconciliation to be an individual problem, they explain, Blacks, on the other hand, consider it to be institutional, societal, and systemic. Quoting Curtiss DeYoung, they state that "systems of injustice in society and in the church, exact a heavy cost…and effectively block reconciliation… Declaring that we are equal without repairing the wrongs of the past is cheap reconciliation," they add (Emerson and Smith 2001). For most White evangelicals, the call to racial healing and reconciliation involves reducing racial strife through repentance and the forging of strong, committed relationships (Emerson and Smith 2001).

Thus, Emerson and Smith showcase the individualized perception of racism as it applies to White America, one that sees racism as simply a relational issue between people groups, especially Blacks and Whites, without due regard to the institutions and structures that maintain a system of oppression. In such an environment, the institutions and structures do the dirty work of inuring the dominant group to privilege (and doing the contrary to minority groups) without direct human instrumentation or orchestration. Emerson and Smith, quoting Carl Ellis, Head of Project Joseph, a Christian ministry, emphasize that "the question is not one of changing the hearts of individuals as much as it is dealing with the systems and structures that are devastating African-American people" To them, being sorry and apologizing is a good first step, but not enough (Emerson and Smith 2001). Cecil Murray, senior pastor of the First African

Methodist Episcopal Church in Los Angeles's statement is also instructive. He writes, "Calling sinners to repentance means also calling societies and structures to repentance—economic, social, educational, corporate, political, religious structures... The gospel," Murray continues, "works with the individual and the individual's society: to change one, we of necessity must change the other" (Emmerson and Smith 2001).

The action being proposed here is a two-pronged assault on racism with a focus on repairing the present racial chasm, by White America formally acknowledging the wrongs and the wounds of the past, while restoring a sense of justice and equity to people of color through the removal of systems and structures that have hitherto militated against efforts at upward social and economic mobility for Blacks and other minority groups. There is, undeniably, no White person alive today that is responsible for slavery and Jim Crow; neither is there a living Black person today who has ever been a slave, in terms of the kind of slavery our (African) ancestors had to endure. However, all living Blacks and Native Americans bear the legacy, wounds, and scars of White racism, slavery, and genocide, just as every living White person reaps its benefits and privileges in some form or fashion.

The Ministry of Reconciliation will resonate and gain momentum when efforts at individual healing and reconciliation are equally matched with efforts at mediating the impact of America's longstanding flirtation with racism with some sense of social and economic equity and justice. A formal recognition of, and apology for, the horrible doctrine of White supremacy upon which America was built as Europeans encountered darker-hued Native American and African populations, the decimation of Native Americans and annexation of their lands, and the enslavement, torture, and exploitation of millions of Africans in America is necessary for the healing process to begin. Skipping this first step will render any further steps either ineffective or unnecessarily difficult. Beyond this acknowledgment, America must decide how it will make restitution for these historical atrocities. We cannot simply wish the facts (and the wounds and trauma attached to those facts) away, in typical ostrich fashion. Time does not assuage the painful memories, not when one is still living with the pain.

For millions among the populations mentioned above, the smile is gone; it is gone because the teeth are gone. The wounds remain open and fresh because the cavern in the mouth is obvious to all. Slavery and Jim Crow are legally over, yes, they certainly belong in the annals of America, but the wounds and scars remain and cannot and must not be discounted. Racial healing and reconciliation through individual repentance and forgiveness, like a one-legged stool, cannot stand on its own. Social and economic justice or equity are necessary to give it balance and stability. "True reconciliation requires more than truth-telling or confession. It requires atonement and justification" (Van Patterson 2012). In this regard, the two (reconciliation and atonement/justification) then, are bedfellows.

Reconciliation: Satisfying the Demands of Divine Justice

"That He might be just and the justifier of..."
—Romans 3:25–26

The scriptures espouse a paradigm of reconciliation and justice similar to the one presented above, one of Jesus Christ satisfying the demands of divine justice, in the Father's quest to reconcile humanity to Himself. God is a merciful and loving God (Deut. 4:31, Ps. 86:15). He is also Just and Holy (Lev. 11:14, Prov. 15:9). "Shall not the judge of all the earth do right?" (Gen. 18. 25). He is a God of truth and justice: "He is the Rock, his work is perfect; for all his ways are justice; a God of truth and without iniquity, just and right is he" (Deut. 32:4). It is this just and true God who seeks reconciliation with humanity, contaminated by inheritance with the sin of its progenitor, Adam.

A Holy and Just God cannot tolerate iniquity. Sin cannot go without an equitable penalty, in His holiness. It is not in the nature of God to not deal justly with sin. His holiness demands that a price or penalty be paid for sin, which is the primary obstacle to divine reconciliation and the restoration of a dynamic relationship with Him. Beginning with the killing of an animal in Eden, using the skin as a covering for Adam and Eve's nakedness instead of their self-made aprons of leaves, God has always instituted a blood covenant and atonement as the proper way to satisfying the demands of divine justice and a return to full relationship with Him (Heb. 9:22, Col. 1:2–22, Rom. 5:10, Matt. 5:24). Without meeting this holy and divine threshold of justice, reconciliation with God is virtually impossible.

Jesus Christ fully satisfied the demands of divine justice in God's quest for reconciliation with mankind (2 Cor. 5:19, Heb. 2:17, 1 Tim. 2:5–6). In Christ, the Lamb of God, God demonstrates four attributes in His character—His holiness, justice, love, and mercy. As propitiation for our sins, Christ was all four personified. Propitiation is the act of placating or appeasing someone for wrongs done. From a biblical perspective, it refers to a gracious Father, demonstrating His love by sending His only son to pay the penalty for the sins of humanity, satisfying in the process the need to punish sin, in His Holiness and Justice. As propitiation for our sins, God's vengeance or wrath for and toward sin was vented on Christ at Calvary. Christ's substitutionary death was, thus, a vindication for divine justice, absolving humanity from all indebtedness to demands of divine justice.

Holiness, love, and mercy, as well as death and justice are all united in Christ for the fostering of healing and reconciliation between God and mankind. John Walvoord in *Jesus Christ our Lord*, states that "Christ in his death fully satisfied the demands of a righteous God for judgment upon sinners…" This sacrifice, gave believers not just forgiveness, but "justification and sanctification" (Walvoord 1969). "Reconciliation without justice," Patterson emphasizes, "is reconciliation under duress…" In addition, disregarding justice makes the cost of reconciliation too high a price (Patterson). In *The Place of Justice in Reconciliation*, He explains the nexus between reconciliation and divine justice this way.

Without Christ's sacrifice, there would be no reconciliation between God and man. "Christ is the ethical dimension of justice that satisfies God's demand for righteousness… He makes reconciliation real…" (Patterson 2012).

Reconciliation and racial justice, therefore, must go hand in hand. Without justice, any attempts at healing and reconciliation will remain superficial, and perhaps, temporary. The seal or death knell on our contemporary racial fracture lies in the acknowledgment of historical actions, the impact of such actions, and subsequent actions to redress the impact of such actions. America must seek a way to restore the front teeth, even if it means dentures. Laying the blame on those victimized by such actions, as many Whites do, is untenable and not a recipe for healing and reconciliation.

Assuming that racism is a thing of the past, as the case is with many White Americans, is also just plain ignorant. It displays a degree of disconnect with the real-life situations of many Blacks, Latinos, and minority groups, a disconnect that not only creates an aloofness to the contemporary racial crisis, but is also perpetuated by the separate lifestyles earlier alluded to by Hacker and the Kerner Commission.

Developing a Cross-Cultural and Multiracial Paradigm (The Principle of Incarnation)

The quest for racial healing and reconciliation in an increasingly multiracial and multicultural American milieu makes the need for cross-cultural perspectives, particularly in the Church, an absolute necessity. The age-old story of the four blind men and the elephant serves as a great illustration and throws light on the concept of cross-cultural perspectives or multiracial paradigm. As the story goes, the first man touched the tail of the elephant and said "The elephant is like a rope"; the second, touching the side of the elephant, exclaimed "The elephant is like a wall"; the third put his arms around its leg and shouted, "The elephant is like a tree," and the last, getting ahold of the elephant's trunk said, "The elephant is like a hose." Here, the same elephant is seen from four different perspectives. The same things might seem or look different depending on position, location, or unique vantage point (Kraft 1996).

For the most part, we all have blinders on. Our sense of reality is often warped by our history, culture, upbringing, personality, training, the influence of authority figures, life experiences, and most importantly, sin. These forces create or shape the lenses through which we interpret life. Barring any encounters that force us to learn a different way of thinking, we will remain opinionated, set in our ways of thinking and behaving, and assuming wrongly that our way of thinking and acting is normative and should be the standard operating procedure for all. This is what a monocultural perspective is all about.

Monocultural Perspective

A monocultural perspective looks at reality, including other people's reality, from one point of view only; that is, through one's own cultural lenses. Though usually unspoken, a monocultural attitude says, "It is, essentially, my way or the highway." A monocultural attitude is ethnocentric. To a person held captive by this perspective, his or her own view or perspective is often absolute (Kraft n.d.); it is or should be the ideal, the standard, or the norm, and any or every other view is either wrong or bad. A monocultural perspective has no respect for other people's ways. It is proud of its way of life and often looks down on or condemns other people's way of life, language, perspectives, and behavior, calling them either ridiculous, neurotic, uncivilized, underdeveloped, or primitive (Kraft). Questions like "Why do they do that; behave like that, talk like that; dance like that, or eat with their fingers?" often arise from monocultural people.

The fact is, for all of us, even understanding those who are like us can often be a "trip"/challenge sometimes. Trying to understand those different from us therefore, could be daunting. Our ability to positively interact or get along with people, by and large, requires that we understand their frame of reference or point of view—in other words, where they are coming from and why they think or act in ways so different, and sometimes so foreign and neurotic, to us.

In Acts 10, the Apostle Peter exhibits a monocultural and ethnocentric attitude, his prejudices shaped by his Jewish heritage. A divine and supernatural vision was needed to debunk this ethnocentric attitude and prepare him for the call to Cornelius, a God-fearing Gentile, and his household. He still was not completely delivered from it as his future behavior would reveal (Galatians 2:11–14). Religious tradition, custom, and convention had all combined to create an attitude of cultural myopia and narrow-mindedness in the servant of God. Kraft asserts that a monocultural perspective is particularly dangerous when held by people in power, as was the case in Nazi Germany. It was Hitler's ethnocentrism that shaped the Nazi party and ultimately led to the holocaust (Kraft).

It was this monocultural perspective that set the tone for Europe's encounters with Africa, also. European traders, adventurers, and even missionaries, not understanding Africa and many of its cultural practices, chose to demonize everything in their sight that they did not understand, calling it savage, neurotic, strange, uncivilized, barbaric, or animalistic. Such demonization was often followed by the imposition of a foreign culture—European in essence but labeled Christian.

Monocultural and ethnocentric attitudes also manifest themselves in the expression of faith. The way we practice or express our faith, we assume, is and should be the standard for everybody. Thus, Jewish Christians (Judaizers), for example, attempted to impose their customs (culture) upon the Gentile Christians; washing of hands (ceremonial washing/laws), covering of hair, restrictions on eating pork and other dietary patterns, circumcision, etc. The message was that unless and until the Gentile Christians *became like them culturally*, they were not full-fledged Christians (Acts 15, Gal. 6:15). "Evangelize," in this situation, means "Civilize." "Foreign-ness" is equated with evil, "strange-ness" with demonic, and "different" with uncivilized or inferior.

The demonization of cultural expressions and everything else not understood in Africa and Latin America, and the imposition of European culture by European missionaries, is a perfect example of this. For example, my African/Ghanaian name Kwabena was replaced by my "Christian name" Richard. The last time I checked, Richard is a European name, in form and meaning, with nothing Christian about it. This is the equivalent of cultural imperialism. Any deviation from the imposed custom evokes shock or some form of reaction, often negative.

It is to free us from the temptation of exporting our cultural baggage and imposing it on others that developing a cross-cultural perspective or understanding is so essential. Otherwise, we end up dehumanizing the very humans we are sent to. The truth is, no one should give up who they are to be a Christian—e.g., you don't have to be an African to be a Christian, and neither do I have to be an American to be a Christian. The Gospel is at home in every culture. Any other "gospel" (approach) amounts to Cultural Imperialism. A cross-cultural perspective allows one to see things from the other person's point of view. This is vital for intercultural engagement, necessary for racial healing and reconciliation.

In an age of globalization, one that has brought the world and its peoples so close together, a monocultural attitude or perspective can easily create a feeling of superiority. This attitude says, *we are it*; we do not need anybody, nor do we need to learn from anybody. Our hubris leads us to assume that "we are the world." But are we? The world is coming to us. Immigrants from around the world are arriving daily on America's shores (not to mention our brothers and sisters from the South of the border), and this trend will, most likely, continue. It is important to remind ourselves that the world is much bigger than just us. Thus, we cannot assume a monocultural perspective; neither can we assume an isolationist posture, which is intrinsically monocultural. Let us remember that God is NOT American; neither is He African. Thus, for the sake of healthy dialogue and interpersonal relationships with our neighbors, on the job, in our homes etc., it is necessary to develop a cross-cultural perspective.

A cross-cultural perspective is an understanding of and sensitivity to other cultural perspectives for the purpose of interaction, healing, reconciliation, or conflict resolution. Any effective form of communication, Christian or otherwise, must by necessity include a cross-cultural perspective, especially in an increasingly pluralistic environment such as America. A cross- and multicultural perspective allows us to minimize conflict because we interpret, or at least try to interpret, life experiences and situations from the point of view of the one we are dealing with, instead of from ours only. It is an attempt to walk in the other person's shoes to think and feel what, how, and why they feel and think the way they do; in essence, to try to determine what makes them tick.

Developing a cross-cultural and multiracial perspective requires immersing oneself in another's culture and way of life, often foreign, in order to understand and appreciate its dynamics. A people's culture or way of life is the vehicle for communicating a new way of life and effecting change. Christ's model serves as the perfect example for those of us who desire healing and reconciliation in a racialized, pluralistic America.

The Master's (Jesus) Example:
The Principle of Incarnation

The best example of a Cross-cultural perspective and Communication is seen in what is called the INCARNATION—God Himself taking on the form of man to redeem us (John 1:1, 14/Phil. 2:5–10). Divinity or Deity took on humanity in the person of Jesus Christ, identifying with humans by crossing "cultural" barriers and boundaries—and becoming human, as well. God participated fully in Jewish cultural life; he was dedicated in the temple on the eighth day, he learned to be a carpenter under the tutelage of his surrogate father Joseph, he was baptized in accordance with Jewish custom, he was tempted in all points as we are (Heb. 4:14–16) **not as God**, but as man. God suffered and died as a man. It called for a willingness on His part to decrease, be vulnerable and humble, and to interact with the people He came to save to ultimately redeem and restore them. Jesus is our best model for developing a cross-cultural perspective in our quest to foster racial healing and reconciliation among the races and cultures represented in the American milieu.

Erwin MacManus, in *Uprising: A Revolution of the Soul,* describes the Principle of Incarnation in these words: "Jesus did not…live His life on a mountaintop isolated from human suffering…" He came and shared our humanity, eating and walking among us in close proximity, showing us how to be in the world, but not of it. "The focus…was ministry to the entire planet" (Erwin McManus).

In *The Incarnation: God's Model for Cross-Cultural Communication,* Kraft also describes Incarnation in these terms: "In Jesus, the stereotyped God broke out of the stereotype. Though he was God… Jesus turned his back on all of this..." Kraft observes that he laid aside his rights, and power and chose to live among us as a human so we could see, hear and touch him (Kraft n.d.).

The Principle of Incarnation became the Apostle Paul's evangelistic and missionary strategy for the communication of the Gospel: In 1 Corinthians 9:19–23, he says:

> *"For though I am not obligated to any man, I have made myself a servant to all... To the Jews I became a Jew, that I might gain the Jews, to them that are under the law, as under the law, that I might gain them that are under the law... To the weak I became weak that I might gain the weak; I am made all things to all men that I might by all means save some, and this I do for the gospel's sake..."*

America's multicultural makeup makes the development of a cross-cultural perspective a missional imperative. In our schools, in our workplaces, and in our civic, social, and political institutions, the need to develop a cross-cultural perspective cannot be overemphasized. Paul's strategy was to identify with the Jew, the weak, the poor, the marginalized, and the oppressed. Such identification was to sensitize him to the needs and aspirations of that segment of the population; that just as Christ did, he might elevate them to a new plane by communicating a new and better way of life in a language that they understood. America's current racial and cultural trajectory makes this absolutely critical. May we wholeheartedly embrace a cross-cultural instead of a monocultural perspective, lest that which is supposed to be our strength, a multiracial and cultural nation, ends up becoming our bane.

CHAPTER 7

The Origin of the Races:
A Biblical Genealogy

"If anyone tells you to be colorblind, don't be. Delight in our differences."
—**Trillia Newbell**

"We're all mongrels."
—**Unknown**

There is little doubt that we are all, suddenly and unmistakably, confronted by the perplexities of our differences when chance or fate causes our paths to cross others of a different race, ethnicity, or culture. That the world consists of such varieties of tribes, people-groups, and cultures with major differences, particularly in physical features, is something we all occasionally ponder. This may occur at the store, supermarket, church, in class, or at a PTA meeting, when we perhaps encounter someone in an outfit quite different from what we are used to, or hear or overhear someone talk in an accent uniquely different from ours.

The reality of the difference and the sense of strangeness, intrigue, or fear we may feel when thrust in these situations, often betrays our own biases, prejudices, or even ignorance. While some with a fair amount of intercultural experience and competence may remain calm and indifferent, for others with less experience with such encounters, the sense of intrigue or even foreboding at the sight of a woman in a *saree* nearby, a group of Black kids hanging out at the street corner, or a man in a turban touting an unusually long beard and speaking with a thick, unintelligible accent may be cause for a quick departure from the immediate vicinity or premature exit from the store. As we make this hasty exit, forced by this weird encounter, the questions begin: "Why was he/she talking like that? Where is he/she from… India, Malaysia, Mauritania, Timbuktu? Why were they hanging out there at this time? Were they gangbangers?" All our stereotypical assumptions begin to surface.

The deeper and subliminal questions then follow, as we replay the encounter in our minds: "How come such variations in physical features?" is undoubtedly the most obvious distinction, of course. "He was much shorter and stockier… he was rather hairy; he had wider lips, hooked and longer nose, he had a rather unique smell… Was he Jewish, Lebanese or African? Perhaps Pakistani?" We begin to associate our stereotypical assumptions and biases about other cultures and ethnic groups based on the little we know and understand about this individual or group of people. For some, the arguments for and against evolution and creationism may begin to creep up when we wonder why there are such variations in the human species. Not having any answers, however, we plod on, going about our business until these same submerged questions come up at another time or place, when we are confronted by another cross-cultural encounter.

*But why such physical variations in the human species…
what do these variations mean?"* For years, I accepted the differences between the human species like most people, without
question, despite the gnawing curiosities. The physical differences were sometimes stark, for sure, but we all get accustomed to living with this reality until there is some social or
political eruption or disruption based on our racial or ethnic
differences. My personal encounter with the "White man" as
a child was simply "divine"—at least, it seemed so. Not only
were these very different people we observed fascinating and
their lighter complexion intriguing to my boys and me, but
their language and way of speaking (which we tried mimick-
ing at every least opportunity) added to our sense of intrigue
and bewilderment. Our fascination was met with equal fascination from the ones we mustered the boldness to approach
and "talk" with. Such "conversations" consisted essentially of
one basic English word, like "Yes," "No," "Come," or "Go"
from us, followed by him with one or two Twi words he had
acquired, all these interspersed with sign language to mitigate
the obvious communication barrier. Our utter innocence
and vulnerability, I am sure, were always apparent to him in
these encounters.

Even at this age we knew the White man was from
"another planet"…whatever that meant. We had no knowledge of the existence of other planets in the galaxy, that being
too deep and beyond our intellectual capacity at the time.
"Another planet" simply meant not from our world; he just
wasn't one of us. He was a stranger, a foreigner we had hap-
pily welcomed into our planet and world. Though different,
he was fun nonetheless. Physical differences did not mean
a thing. In time, the occasional presence of a White man,
woman, or child was no longer a big deal. We had become
accustomed to his presence. There were several among us,

some of them school or classmates, and some others of mixed background and heritage, "mulattoes." We did not look at them with disdain; to the contrary, their characteristically "White" features (lighter complexion, curly but fine hair, and aquiline noses in contrast with our much rounded and broader ones), accorded them a somewhat superior status in the society. Girls and guys seemed to place a higher premium on a lighter-skinned catch or date. To have a "mulatress" or anything close to it for a "chick" (girlfriend) was huge.

It was in high school that I would have serious thoughts about race, racial differences, and acts of oppression due to these differences. I was older and much more aware of my environment, as well as the racial and ethnic issues happening around the world. I had come to realize that not everyone we labeled as "White" was actually White. Up until then, Orientals (as we called Asians), Arabs, Latinos, Indians, Filipinos, and Pacific Islanders, in addition to Caucasians, were all "White folks" in my eyes. We used the same generic Twi word, *oburoni*, to describe all of them.

Keenly aware of myself and my environment, particularly, in high school, I began to ask questions: Why colonialism? Why slavery? Why racism and racial oppression? Why segregation? Why apartheid? Why can't the Black man and White man get along? Why can't they have mutual respect and live in harmony? After all, we had more in common than our differences...at least, we are all humans. Why does the White man feel superior to the Black man, and to all other races, for that matter? Why should our physical differences be the reason we hate, despise, fight, and kill each other?

These questions, ultimately, reached a crescendo. My years of anomie (as a young man) began to gradually give way to a life of soul-searching, discovery, and purpose, especially after what was a dramatic conversion to faith in Christ.

The questions above began to fuel a deep burden and passion within me to seek answers. My curiosities and propensity toward discovery and knowledge further fueled this passion to find answers. What seemed like a quest for answers to racial and political issues, in time, morphed into matters of existentialism: *Who am I? Where did we ALL (black, brown, white, yellow, red) come from? How did we get here? Why are we here? Who is God? Does humanity have divine origins?*

My journey of faith and the shaping of a Christian worldview began here. My faith provided answers to some of the questions above. Faith also gave me a sense of meaning and peace about myself as a man; a man, in general, and a Black man, in a particular context, America. The questions raised, and the answers and insights gained, also became the seeds and inspiration for this book. They have also imbued me with what now appears to be a lifetime ministry of passion and purpose—the quest for reconciliation, in all its numerous forms and manifestations.

I had never doubted the existence of God, but unbeknownst to me, the fervent prayers of my mother, made frequently while kneeling in front of her bed with her four kids, had left an indelible mark on me. Mother was a saint in the truest sense of the word, a virtuous woman who did not read or walk around with a Bible in hand daily, but nevertheless lived and exemplified the core values of a follower of Christ, in all its simplicity and purest form: faith, consistent prayer, integrity, selfless devotion, and service to her God, family, and community. To me, she was a living epistle.

Although as a child I would often giggle, holding back the laughter and with one eye open, during our family prayer times, the message of God's reality and presence was never lost on me. It was something I "felt." and knew intuitively more than cognitively. Mama's faith, impassioned prayers, and earnestness of spirit were infectious, and if such a saintly woman believed in a Creator, what reason did I have to doubt? Her life was testament enough; she knew something I did not. I embraced the creationist view of the world and all that was in it, God Almighty being the divine architect. Adam and Eve, from this perspective, were the progenitors of the human race, period.

With that settled, the next question obviously was, "If we all, indeed, had Adamic roots or origin, how come there are different races, ethnicities, cultures, and colors among "mankind"? The quest for answers to this and other questions became even more pressing upon my coming to faith in Christ and becoming keenly aware of the seeming lack of a Black presence in the Bible. Embracing my call to the gospel ministry, upon migrating to the US I was thrust into the dynamics of life in Los Angeles, with not only the sheer extent of its multiracial and ethnic composition, but also the racial tension and hostility of the LA Riots, the Simpson trial, and the swearing in of Supreme Court Justice Clarence Thomas, the only Black person on the bench. These incidents, among others, were the much-needed and perhaps final impetus to delve into a long-held passion to explore my curiosity about race.

Incidentally, a lot, if not most, of commentaries with any serious focus on a Black presence in the Bible highlight the doctrine of the "Curse of Ham," a theological concept often used by White theologians and racists to offer a rationale and explanation for the subjugation and enslavement of Black people. Growing up, as many of my contemporaries did, with the notion that Christianity was the "White man's" religion, and unconsciously inferring from that assumption that every biblical character was White, the need to search the Scriptures for answers could not have been more urgent.

Unraveling the "mystery" of the origin of the races, therefore, became the crux of my search.

What is the Origin of the Races, Cultures, and Ethnicities of the World?

The Bible provides us with some clues about the origin of the various races and cultures of the world which, though neither comprehensive nor conclusive, present us with a basic framework for further research into the subject. It is consistent with my belief in the ubiquity of the Holy Script and its ability to provide answers to timeless questions and issues that renowned archaeologist, Professor William Albright notes that *"the Bible remains an astonishingly accurate document"* revealing such a remarkable *"understanding of the ethnic and linguistic situation in the modern world, in spite of all its complexity..."* (Albright 2011). The biblical clues to this complex subject may be partially found in the genealogies of Jesus, particularly in the books of Matthew and John.

Genealogy often provides us with clues or answers about why different races, cultures, and ethnic groups exist. It addresses several things, including:

- The Development of Families
- The Development of Cultures
- The Development of Nations
- The Depraved and Deviant Nature of Man
- God's Glorious Plan of Salvation
- God's Plan of Uniting the Nations in His Love through Christ

Genesis 9:18–19 tells us about the separation of nations into distinct groups. This was done not because of superiority or inferiority, but rather *for the fulfillment of* **God's** *purpose*. Thus, separation was based on families, purpose, calling, language, etc. It was never done based on color; there is not an iota of evidence, in fact, to support that. The "brotherhood of mankind" as espoused by certain religious groups or movements (e.g., Bahai) is predicated on the fact that we all originated from a common source—Noah and his three sons: Shem, Ham, and Japheth.

"And the sons of Noah that went forth of the ark, were Shem, and Ham and Japheth… These are the three sons of Noah and by them was the whole world Over-spread" (or populated) (Gen. 9:18–19).

Each one of Noah's sons represented a nation or people-group. The three nations ultimately evolved into seventy in Genesis 10. Little wonder that Jesus sent out seventy disciples (Luke 10)—a prototype of the seventy nations. This is also consistent with His mission of reaching every nation, culture, and people-group, as Scripture outlines in Matthew 28:19: "Go…and make disciples of every nation…" (ethnos). The New Jerusalem is depicted as a multiracial and cultural mosaic consisting of the redeemed from *"every kindred, and tongue, and people, and nation…"* (Revelation 5:9). The purpose of each nation was spelled out in Genesis 9:1: "And God blessed Noah and his three sons and said unto them, 'Be fruitful and multiply and replenish the earth…'" (Gen. 9:1).

Each branch descending from Noah's three sons has its own distinctive uniqueness, characteristics, appointed purpose, and time of influence or span of time to fulfill its mission. What did each branch of the family become? Are their descendants among us today? If so, who and where are they? On these questions, I defer largely to Dr. Arthur Custance,

THE COLOR OF GOD

who does a fascinating expose on the descendants of Noah
and their contribution to world civilization (Custance 1975).

The Descendants of Shem, Japheth, and Ham

Shem was the first son of Noah. Scripture tells us
that five sons were born to him. They were Elam, Asshur,
Arphaxad, Lud, and Aram (Genesis 10:22). Out of these
sons came the *Persians, Assyrians, Arabs, Bedouins, Jordanians,
Iraqis, and Iranians, etc.—in short, most Middle Easterners of
today.* Shem, thus, is the progenitor of the Semitic tribes and
cultures. The Hebrews, who are Semitic as well, are believed
to have descended from Eber or Heber, the great-grandson of
Shem (Genesis 10:21). Abraham, the founder of the Jewish
race, was six generations after Eber.

Shem's descendants appear to have dominated the
world for 2000 years after the Hamites, producing three (3)
major religions, Judaism, Christianity, and Islam, all three
monotheistic faiths (as opposed to the polytheistic religions
and cultures that preceded them). It is noteworthy that they
also produced the Messiah, who they failed to recognize
(Custance 1970).

Japheth was probably the third son of Noah. He was
blessed with seven sons: Gomer, Magog, Madai, Javan, Tubal,
Meshech, and Tiras (Genesis 10:2). From these came most
Indo-European nations of Caucasians. For example, Gomer
had three sons, Ashkenaz, Riphath, and Togarmah. (Genesis
10:3). From them came the Germans, Celts, Scots, Irish,
French, Vandals, Visogoths, Belgians, and Scandinavians.
From Magog, the second son of Japheth, came the Russians,
Ukrainians, Chechens, Yugoslavians, Armenians, Bosnians,
Croatians, Turks, Bulgarians, Serbians, Czechs, and Slovaks.

239

Madai gave birth to the Medes, Kurds, East Indians, Aryans, Pakistanis, Parsees, Uzbekistanians, Tajikistanis, Kyrgyzstans, etc. Javan, the fourth son of Shem, is reputed to be the father of the Greeks, Spartans, Carthaginians, Romans, Italians, Cypriots, and Macedonians. Tubal is the progenitor of the Siberians, the Cossacks, the Irish, and the Spaniards, while Meshech (from who came three sons, Dedon, Zaron, and Shebashnialso), produced the Muscovites, Latvians, Lithuanians, Romanians, etc., Tiras, the last of Shem's sons, is the father of the Vikings, Swedes, Norwegians, Icelanders, and Danes, just to name a few.

It must be noted that Japheth's descendants, the Indo-Europeans and/or Caucasians, have ruled the world during the last two thousand years, making great strides in exploration and opening new worlds like the Vikings did, though, unfortunately, with much cruelty. They have made giant strides and inroads as well, in the fields of science, architecture and engineering (Custance).

Ham (also referred to as Kham or Cham) was the second son of Noah. His name means Hot, Burnt, or Dark; it also means Passionate. Ham was blessed with four (4) sons: Cush, Mizraim, Phut, and Canaan. Cush had five sons: Seba, Havilah, Sabta, Raama, and Sabtechah (Genesis 10:7). Ethiopians and Black Africans, particularly those south of the Sahara, Nubians, Australian Aborigines, Pygmy tribes, and other related groups, are from Ham.

Biblical Mizraim refers to Egypt. Six sons were also born to him: Ludim, Anamim, Lehabim, Naphtuhim, Pathrusim, Chasluhim, and Chaphtor (Gen. 10:13–14). Phut is the biblical name for Libya.

Four sons were born to Phut: Gebul, Hadan, Benah, and Adan. They comprise Libyans, Somalis, Sudanese, Tunisians, Moroccans, Cyrenicians, etc.

Canaan refers to Palestinians; Canaan had ten sons: Zidon, Heth, Amori, Gergashi, Hivi, Arkee, Seni, Arodi, Zimodi and Chamothi (or the Sidonians, Hittites, Jebusites, Amorites, Girgasites, Hivites, Arkites, Sinites, Arvadites, Zemarites, Hamathites (Gen. 10:15–17) Out of these ten sons came the Asians, Mongols, Chinese, Tibetans, Orientals, Thais, Laotians, Vietnamese, Japanese, American Indian tribes, Malaysians, Indonesians, Filipinos, Hawaiians, Maoris, Samoans, Fijians, Tongans, and other groups from the Pacific islands, including the Eskimos.

Ham's descendants, therefore, include the Egyptians, Ethiopians, Canaanites, Hittites, Phoenicians, and the Mongolians. They inhabited places like Africa, the South Pacific, Australia, Asia, the Americas, and the Pacific. Given their capacity for adaptation, Custance remarks that, "*looking at history, whichever region is considered, Africa, Europe, Australia or America,*" in essence "*in every area of the world where Japhethites have subsequently settled, they have always been preceded by Hamites*" or the descendants of Ham. "*This pattern,*" he reiterates, "*applies in every continent*" (Custance 1970).

Using the immutable significance of fossil evidence, Custance further observes that, "*the earliest fossil remains of man were "Mongoloid or Negroid*" as seen in the character of the remains and the shape of the head in various parts of the world. These earliest remains were always followed later by fossil evidence belonging to Caucasoids, who are the descendants of Japheth. It is important at this point to highlight the fact that the seventy nations that evolved from the three sons of Noah have in turn evolved into 160 major nations and many smaller ones today, for example, Mexicans are a mixture of Spaniards and Indians.

RICHARD D. DONKOR

Was Ham Cursed to Be Black?

"Racial Superiority is a mere pigment of the imagination."
—Author unknown

White theology and churches, particularly in the Civil War era, created and employed what has been known over the centuries as The Doctrine of the Curse of Ham, to foster and justify racism and slavery. The entire story is found in Genesis 9:20–27. I would like to pose a few questions in this regard:

- The Doctrine is called *The Curse of Ham*. Was Ham, indeed, cursed?
- If Ham was not cursed, who was, and why?
- Why would Ham be cursed for something his son (or grandson) did? Conversely, why would his son (grandson) be cursed for something he (Ham) did?
- If Ham was not cursed, why has this perfidious doctrine been called *The Curse of Ham*?
- Was Noah's curse about skin color? In other words, is Blackness (or a darker complexion) a curse from God?

Several issues here are worth noting:

1. First, Ham was never cursed per the biblical text. So the name assigned to the *Doctrine of the Curse of Ham* is inapplicable; a misnomer.
2. Second, the curse was placed on Canaan (again, not Ham). Canaan is the youngest son of Ham.
3. Third, Noah's curse had nothing to do with skin tone or color (in this case, Black) (Gen. 9:25–27); it

242

had everything to do with "servant hood"—that is, being a servant to his brothers. *"Cursed be Canaan, a servant of servants will he be to his brethren..."*

4. Four, when and how the linkage between skin color (Black) and the curse of "servant hood" (slavery) was created, and thereafter made so pervasive, should not be that mind-boggling. A "Christian" society or culture needed divine sanction to justify its actions and soothe its jaundiced conscience, even if that meant consciously tweaking Scripture to achieve the purpose.

Rabbi Shlomo Itzhak, a medieval French rabbi and the author of the first comprehensive commentary on the Talmud and the *Tanakh* (Hebrew Bible), explains this doctrine this way: "Some say Cham (referring to Ham) saw his father naked and either sodomized or castrated him." He further explains that Ham might have thought to himself that "perhaps my father's drunkenness will lead to intercourse with my mother and I will have to share the inheritance of the world with another brother! I will prevent this by taking his manhood from him!" When Noah awoke and he realized what Cham had done, he said, "Because you prevented me from having a fourth son, your fourth son, Canaan, shall forever be a slave to his brothers, who showed respect to me," he concludes. Rashi, as he was more popularly known, thus attributes Ham's sin to either incest or sodomy, but definitely some sexual act. He stresses that Noah's curse however had nothing to do with skin color, or the designation of Ham and his descendants to an inferior status based on color (Goldenberg).

Ibrahim Ibn Ezra, another respected Jewish commentator of the medieval era, also comments on the *Doctrine of the*

Curse of Ham. He emphasizes that Noah's curse on Canaan in Genesis 9:25 ("*Cursed be Canaan, a servant of servants shall he be unto his brethren*") speaks to Canaan's subservience to his brothers specifically, as opposed to his uncles, Shem and Japheth (His brothers were Cush, Mizraim, and Phut). Ibrahim Ibn Ezra takes it a step further by disputing those who claim Black-skinned people (the Cushim) are slaves because Noah cursed Ham, the father of Canaan. These folks forget, he insists, that the first king after the flood was a descendant of Cush; Nimrod, whose political influence and dominance over the then-known world started in Babylon (Goldenberg).

Other respected sources, such as the Amharic Commentary on Genesis, the Syriac work, Cave of Treasures, and Islamic interpreters, who were aware of the story in the Torah, have disputed this doctrine, arguing that the Torah makes no references to skin color or tone, that differences in skin pigmentation were determined not by Noah's curse, but by differences in climate and environmental determinism.

It is also necessary to point out that the Black race did not originate from the one who was cursed (Canaan in this case). Again, Ham had four sons: Cush (Ethiopia, Black Africa); Mizraim (Egypt), Phut (Libya), and Canaan (Palestine). Canaan was not Black at all; his descendants, the Canaanites, were not Negroid, but Shemitic. Cush is the father of the Black race, not Canaan. The Cushites are also referred to as Ethiopians, a derivative from two words: *Ethios* which means "Burnt" or "Dark," and *Opus* which means "Face"—so, in essence, *Burnt Face* or *Dark Face*.

Furthermore, if Adam and Eve were made from the "dust of the earth," what color were they likely to have been, dark or pale (as in White)? Adam means *ruddiness* or *reddish brown*. This implies that they were of a darker complexion. If they were indeed darker, should we then conclude that they were cursed as well, since "Blackness" or darkness is ostensibly a sign of a divine curse?

Finally, if Noah's curse indeed had to do with complexion and being dark-skinned, and if being "Black" was a curse, should not our redemption from the curse of sin and the law (Gal. 3:13–14) through the vicarious sacrifice of Christ, have turned all Black people and people of color White or pale in complexion? In other words, if a sinner when justified in Christ is made righteous (Romans 5:1, 19; 2 Cor. 5:21; Romans 10:10), why should a person of color, justified in Christ and redeemed from sin and "the curse of Blackness" not turn White, but remain Black? When you add it all up, it makes no sense. Again, a "Christian" society or culture needed divine sanction to justify its actions and soothe its diseased conscience.

In Genesis 9:1, God pronounces not a curse, but a blessing upon Noah and his sons; not just two of them (Shem and Japheth), but all three: "And God blessed Noah and his sons, and said unto them, "Be fruitful and multiply and replenish the earth..." (Gen. 9:1).

Could a drunken Noah's curse be so potent as to nullify God's blessings, keeping part of his creation (i.e., people of African descent) in subjugation for thousands of years or even perpetually? If the answer to this question is "Yes," then I need to immediately reconsider my faith in this God.

It is sad, and perhaps politically incorrect, to admit that it is this racist mentality about the purported supremacy of the White races, and by extension, inferiority of the Black and darker-skinned people-groups, that has infiltrated America's, and the West's institutions of state, including public systems, corporate structures, even universities and institutions of higher learning. It is this complex of White superiority that has for centuries shaped America's and Europe's attitudes toward Africa, Blacks, and the darker-skinned cultures around the world. It is this devious doctrine of White supremacy, therefore, that needs to be dealt a death blow, if America is to live up to the true meaning of its creed, that "all men are created equal." (It is worth noting that this creed, at the time of its formulation, referred only to "White men"; it was never intended to include Negroes or people of color.)

That Africans and most Black or Negroid people are descendants of Ham, specifically Cush (the first son of Ham) is, hopefully, a well-established fact at this point, just as much as Jews and Arabs are known to be Shemitic, and Indo-Europeans or Caucasians are known to be the descendants of Japheth. That there has been much cross-over and intermarriage between Noah's descendants, the various races, cultures, and people groups over the centuries also goes without saying. Moses married an "Ethiopian" (Hamitic or Cushite) woman, to the chagrin of his brother, Aaron, and sister, Miriam.

Today, Ethiopians, known to be descendants of Cush, a son of Ham, and therefore, Negroid, come in all manner of shades of colors, from the lightest hue to the darkest and everything in between. This seems to suggest that Ham, the progenitor of the Black races, could have fathered children who were not necessary Black. In fact, the Canaanites (who descended from Canaan, one of Ham's four sons), were not Black or Negroid at all, whereas the Egyptians (descendants of Mizraim) and Libyans (descendants of Phut) to this day feature both extremes of complexions among their ranks.

Professor Ray C Stedman (1968) emphasizes that the colored peoples of the earth, descendants of Ham, "come in varying colors: the yellow of the Chinese, the brown of the Indians, the black of the Africans, and even including some that are White-skinned" (Table of Nations). Some of the nations that evolved, such as the Hittites, are today unidentifiable as a group, and probably extinct. Why some Canaanite tribes, who were Hamitic in lineage, spoke Shemitic languages, and some Shemitic tribes also spoke Hamitic languages may be attributed to this cross-over and intermarriage, not to mention wars and conquest.

With conquest came the influence of the dominant race or culture, as in the case of the Greek or Roman invasions and conquests that made Greek and Latin the official languages of vast regions and many nations of the world. Through war and conquest came much race-mixing as well, leading to the current complexity and categories of races, ethnicities, and cultures in existence. Such a development was most certainly inevitable.

Ham and the Chinese or Mongoloid Connection

Of great interest to many curious about genealogies and the origin of the races, cultures, and people groups is the origin and place of the Mongoloid peoples on the Table of Nations. The Mongoloid people are located mainly in Asia and the Pacific Islands. While a handful of scholars have debunked any connection between them and Ham, a good and perhaps greater number emphasize, with some corroborating evidence (though still tenuous and speculative from my perspective) clues that point to such a connection. Among the latter group of ethnologists are Ray C, Stedman, Henry M. Morris, Tim Osterholm, and Arthur Custance.

Henry M. Morris observes in the Genesis Record that "descendants of Ham included the Egyptians and Sumerians, who founded the first great empires of antiquity, as well as other great nations, such as the Phoenicians, Hittites, and Canaanites." "The modern African tribes and the Mongol tribes (including today the Chinese and Japanese) as well as the American Indians and the South Sea Islanders," he continues, "are probably dominantly Hamitic in origin" (Morris).

In reference to Genesis 10:16–18, Morris further notes that the bible mentions people from the far East named "Sinim" (Isaiah 49:12). References in history that point to people in the far East named "Sinae," suggests the possibility of some of Sin's descendants going eastward, while others went south toward Canaan. Significantly the Chinese have been identified with the prefix "Sino," he asserts (e.g., Sino-Japanese War; Sinology, the study of Chinese history). Furthermore, "The name 'Sin' is frequently encountered in Chinese names in the form "Siang" or its equivalent" (Morris).

Ray Stedman concurs with Morris on the link between Ham and the Mongoloid peoples, especially the Chinese. Heth, a son of Canaan and a grandson of Ham, is the father of the Hittite nation, Stedman notes, a nation that is referenced in the Bible but one that archaeologists once said never existed. With the discovery of relics, however, they have come to agree that the Hittites were once a great and flourishing civilization (Stedman).

The name *Cathay*, an ancient name for China, is derived from the word *Khettai*, which is the Hebrew form of the word Hittite. "Certain of the Hittites," Stedman emphasizes "migrated eastward, and settled in China." Heth, father of the Hittite nation, was a brother of Sin, and both were sons of Ham (Stedman).

Both Tim Osterholm and Arthur Custance buttress the observations of Morris and Stedman above, but take the connection between the Chinese and Ham even further.

Osterholm notes that there have been questions as to where the Mongoloid who settled in the Far East fall into, in the Table of Nations. The evidence, he asserts, proves "they are Hamitic, even though some have incorrectly reasoned that the Chinese were of Japhetic stock, and the Japanese were either Japhetic or Semitic" (Osterholm). They were the descendants of the Canaanites, he asserts, who had a propensity "for sprawl." Genesis 10:15–18 suggests this inclination: "*the families of the Canaanites were spread out...*" This, it must be mentioned, is against the backdrop of Osterholm's contention that linguistic evidence points to a "Japhetic component" as well among the Chinese, that there might have been "a mixture of races," or even an Indo-European aristocracy" among them, similar to, as Barton observes, the presence of a Jewish or Semitic aristocracy at a point in Egyptian history (Osterholm).

Custance, defers to the same two names, Heth (Genesis 10:15) and Sin (Genesis 10:17) in making the case for a Hamitic connection to the Mongoloid peoples, particularly the Chinese. Both sons of Canaan and grandsons of Ham, he states are "presumed to be the progenitors of Chinese and Mongoloid" stock. He explains that the Hittites were once a powerful nation from the Far East known as the *Khitai;* they were known in Hebrew as the *Khettai,* and in Cuneiform, the earliest known form of writing invented by the Hamitic Sumerians as *Khittae.* All these names were preserved, Custance says, over the centuries in the more familiar term *Cathay,* which per the Encyclopedia Britannica was used in reference to Northern China. This name was made popular in Europe by Marco Polo. Russians still refer to China as *Kitai.*

The Cathay, Custance emphasizes, were Mongoloids and part of early Chinese stock. He reminds us that the

Hittites were depicted in Egyptian monuments "with prominent noses, full lips, high cheek bones, hairless faces, varying skin color from brown to yellowish and reddish, straight Black hair and dark brown eyes." The link between the Hittites and Cathay is revealed, he says "*in their modes of dress, their shoes with turned-up toes, and their manner of doing their hair in a pig tail...*" (Custance).

Another piece of corroborating evidence about the link between Ham and the Mongoloid people, Custance adds, is the discovery that the Hittites "*mastered the art of casting iron and the taming of horses, two achievements of great importance, and recurring very early in Chinese history—long before reaching the West,*" which, though speculative, is nevertheless suggestive of a Hittite component in early Chinese populations.

Sin (Genesis 10:17) is the other biblical personality, mentioned as the progenitor of the Chinese. The Sin-ites, an interesting people, descended from Sin, a brother of Heth and a grandson of Ham. Sin was third generation from Noah, providing a perfect timeline for some of the Chinese legends that appeared in their Book of History. Many of these legends pertained to Creation, the story of the fall, as well as Noah's flood. In fact, many ancient cultures, including the Aboriginal tribes in Australia, the Yorubas of Nigeria, and the ancient Greeks, Romans, and Indians (Indo-Aryans) all had accounts of flood stories of cataclysmic consequence, very much like the biblical account in Genesis. The chief ancestor of the Greeks was *Japetos*, which is phonetically similar to Japheth, the progenitor of the Indo-Europeans, who was believed to be the creator and ruler of the universe. The Roman version or equivalent of Japetos was Jupiter. *Satyaurata* was the Hindu/Indian Noah; he had three sons: the oldest being *Iyapeti* (Japheth), followed by *Sharma* (Shem), and *C'harma* (Ham). Although the specifics of each account differ slightly from that of the biblical, these examples still point to these ancient cultures having some knowledge of events about the flood as described in Genesis, probably passed down orally from one generation to another, as they dispersed after the great deluge (Custance).

"According to Chinese tradition," Custance remarks, "their first king called Fu-hi or Fohi (Chinese Noah) made his initial appearance on the mountains of Chin. He was surrounded by a rainbow after the world had been covered by water and sacrificed animals to God" (Custance). Again, the similarity between this Chinese version and the biblical account is obvious. The Miao tribe of southwest China also had a tradition like the Genesis account, Custance observes, "even before they met Christian missionaries." According to this tradition, God destroyed the whole world by a flood because of the wickedness of man, and *Nuah* (Noah), the righteous man, and his wife and three sons, *Lo han* (Ham), *Lo Shen* (Shem), and *Jah-hu* (Japheth) survived by building a very broad ship and taking on it pairs of animals" (Custance).

The traditional Chinese Border Sacrifice, a festival that occurred in China for centuries until as recently as 1911, involved sacrifices of a calf, instead of a bull, to Shang-Di, the Heavenly Ruler or the Creator God. Some have made a phonetic comparison of Shang-Di, the Creator God of the Chinese to El-Shaddai, the Creator God of the Hebrews. Recitations or prayers made during this sacrifice revealed an uncanny similarity to the Genesis account of Creation, where the Heavenly Ruler fashions a world out of a complete void; man falls from grace through sin, and Shang-Di institutes animal sacrifices as a remedy for sin. It is a display of mono-theistic faith that many believe the Chinese could only have obtained through some connection with Noah, his three sons and their progeny after the flood. That connection is Sin.

Sin, believed to be a third-generation descendant of Noah, provides the perfect timeline for the beginning of Chinese civilization, which started around 2235 BC. The Chinese place the origin of this civilization in the capital of Shensi, namely Siang-Fu, which interpreted means *Father Sin*. The Greeks referred to China as *Kina*, the Latin form of that being *Sina*. The Greek astronomer Ptolemy was known to have referred to China as the land of *Sinim* or *Sinae*. The Arabs in turn referred to China as Sin, Chin, Mahachin, or Machin.

The Sinae, Arthur Custance indicates, gained control over the entire land after gaining independence in Western China. In the third century BC, the *Tsin* dynasty reigned supreme, the name Tsin being a derivative of the most import-ant capital city of Sinae. Tsin was also used by the Manchu emperors for their title; it meant *pure-bred*. In time it was changed to *Tchina* by the Malays (an amalgam of Sinae and Tsin, it would appear) and subsequently brought to Europe by the Portuguese as *China*. The phrases *Sino-Japanese* war or *Sino-Soviet* border dispute as carried by many newspaper headlines years ago, or *Sinology*, Chinese Studies, were all ref-erences to the original form of the name China.

"Prior to the Mongols establishing themselves in Southern China, there were migrations of Negroid people from East Africa and the Sahara" to ancient China, Custance notes. He states that various documents and ancient texts were kept by several African cultures, not to mention the strong oral history and legends of such African migrations. Southern China is believed to have come into being because of Negroid and Mongolian mixtures.

Another point worthy of note and remark is that today China consists of mostly those from the Han dynasty. The Han race comprises about 90 percent of the entire Chinese population. Lo Han (Ham), a son of Noah we would and should recall, has been part of the flood story in Chinese tradition.

It needs to be reiterated that Arthur Custance, Stedman, or Osterholm, never claimed finality to their views; to the contrary, they indicated that their papers were "exploratory...designed to invite further exploration" or investigation. The jury, in fact, is still out on this fascinating subject. Nevertheless, that each branch of Noah's three sons contributed to world civilization in some significant way is another important dimension to the quest for racial healing and reconciliation.

CHAPTER 8

The Purpose and Contributions of Shem, Ham, and Japheth (Divine Election and Ordination)

The number three has enormous and significant spiritual import, since it is regarded in several cultures around the world as the number of Divine Perfection or Completeness. That Noah's sons are three, Ham, Shem, and Japheth, is not only ironic, but also underscores this surreal sense of divinity and spiritual significance surrounding this righteousness man and his divine purpose and mission.

The number three also has a unique place in nature. Not only does nature provide us with three forms of light—the sun, moon, and stars—it also gives us three states of matter: Solid, Liquid, and Gas. Using the three-fold cord symbolically for unions, relationships, and partnerships, King Solomon in Ecclesiastes (4:9–13) again highlights the significance of the number three. First, there is power in unity and agreement, but there is even greater and multiplied power, strength, and warmth in companionship, whether in the marital bed, business dealings, or basic interpersonal relationships: "*a three-fold cord*" Solomon states, "is not easily broken." The significance of the number three is further seen by the fact that the Creator, Almighty God Himself, is revealed in scripture as a Triune Being, One God (Deuteronomy 6:4) revealed in Three Persons, as the Father, Son, and Holy Spirit (2 Corinthians 13:14, Genesis 1:26), the One *Who Was, and Is*, and *Is to come*. Being a triune God, he creates the humankind "after His image and likeness" (Genesis 1:26) "triune" as Himself, comprising a spiritual, mental/intellectual and physical dimension (1 Thessalonians 5:23).

Both the Old and New Testaments highlight this tripartite pattern in divine and biblical revelation. For example, in the Old Testament, not only does temple worship in Israel occur in three phases—in the Outer Court, Holyj Place, and the Holy of Holies, Jonah's disobedience to God's call lands him in the belly of the whale for three days (Jonah 1:17, Matthew 12:40). God instructs Joshua to send out three spies to spy on the land of Canaan; Israel's primary offices were three-fold, that of the Priest, Prophet, and King (Deuteronomy 17:15, 18:3–5, 15), not to mention its three main feasts—Passover, Tabernacles, and Pentecost.

Continuing with the trend, the New Testament opens with the three wise men, the magi, in search of the Messiah. Upon locating him, they offer up three gifts of Gold, Frankincense, and Myrrh, signifying His Royalty, Divinity, and Death, as God's sacrificial Lamb for sin. Peter's denial of the Christ occurs three times, there are a total of three crosses at His crucifixion, and He rises from the dead on the third (third) day (1 Corinthians 15:4). Furthermore, there are three in the New Testament that bear witness in heaven (and on earth)—the Spirit, Blood, and Water (1 John 5:7). With the same biblical pattern, apparent in the story of the three Hebrew boys, Meshach, Shadrach, and Abednego, defying King Nebuchadnezzar's orders not to bow to the golden calf (Daniel 4 and 5), and Jesus's own inner circle, consisting of three men—Peter, James, and John—is it really any wonder that the progenitors of all branches of the human race should be three, the three sons of Noah?

The Contribution of Shem, Ham, and Japheth

The Creator's plan in populating the entire world with the descendants of Noah's three sons—Shem, Ham, and Japheth—after the flood, and the contributions made by each branch, provides remarkable insight into His wisdom and purpose for the nations of the world. It is an insight that should deal a decisive blow to our racial pride and arrogance and elicit a humble and profound appreciation and gratitude from each race, culture, or people group to God Almighty for its place in His grand scheme of things. Mutual respect and appreciation for each other's gifts, talents, and contributions to human development and progress should be the ultimate result.

Sanderson Beck, in his observations on Booker T. Washington (a man some have dubbed the "Black Moses") describes his educational method for the economic and social mobility of the negro as "*a harmonious trinity of the head, the hand, and the heart*" (Beck 1996). The contributions of the three sons of Noah appear to fit precisely into this "trinity." To *Shem* was assigned matters of the *heart*, specifically the task of championing the religious and spiritual life of mankind. Thus, the issues of worship were given the preeminence among the Shemitic people. We find the three most popular religions of the world—all three monotheistic, Christianity, Judaism, and Islam—originate from Shem's descendants. *Japheth*, it appears, was endued with unique intellectual or mental capabilities, and assigned tasks related to mankind's development in the realm of the *mind*. This theory/thesis is borne out by the fact that major breakthroughs in the arena of philosophy and science have come from those of Japhetic stock or lineage—Caucasians. The great strides made in the field of science today may be attributed to God's abundant endowment of Japheth's descendants with great capacity for thinking and reasoning.

Ham and his descendants (it is clear from the biblical, as well as historical and archaeological accounts, not to mention fossil evidence), spread out much more quickly than the other nations. The Canaanites, descendants of Ham, seemed to have "a propensity for sprawl" (Custance 1975). Thus, you find them in Australia, the Pacific, the Americas, and even as far as the Orient. A divine capacity was needed, it would seem, particularly in matters of survival and adaptability, as well as innovation and leadership, to conquer or tame the virgin territories to which they came and ultimately settled.

Nimrod, a descendant of Ham, is named in the Bible as the first king, world ruler, leader, and builder of great empires. A fearsome ruler who is described as "a mighty hunter in all the earth," it was Nimrod, the son of Cush and the grandson of Ham, the progenitor of the darker-hued peoples of the world, who rallied all the peoples of the Earth together to build a tower whose top would reach into the heavens (Genesis 11). This was the effort that led God to confound the language of humanity, leading to the dispersal of the nations of the world.

Lest any be inclined to minimize the genius of any branch of Noah's sons (which the current deplorable conditions of some people groups and cultures, Blacks in particular, is apt to suggest), let us not forget the great strides made by such cultures and civilizations as the *Sumerians, Phoenicians, Ethiopians,* and *Egyptians,* all of them great Hamitic civilizations of antiquity. One of the remarkable achievements of Egypt that has defied modern architecture 'til this day is how these people, without all the insights, techniques, and implements of modern architecture, were still able to build such highly advanced architectural structures. These feats, indeed, defy any theories propounded aimed at designating a people as uncivilized, with inferior human or divine capabilities.

Descendants of Ham: The Sumerian Culture and Civilization

The Sumerian civilization developed in ancient Mesopotamia, in what may be Southern Iraq today. The region and geographical location has been known as the "Cradle of Civilization" since it is known to be the first human civilization. The Sumerians are known to have developed *Cuneiform*, the first system of writing in hieroglyphic form. Their irrigation network and systems are legendary; these served to undergird their civilization, creating arable land in a region of the world known for droughts. The first forms of architecture are believed to have also come from the Sumerians. Sumerian Ziggurats were built long before Egyptian pyramids ever were. Other technological innovations, such as the wheel, V Kumar indicates, were invented by the Sumerians. The wheels, which they used for their carts pulled by donkeys, might have developed later into chariots.

For the Sumerians, they were not used as chariots or implements of war, but transportation.

The Sumerians practiced division of labor and employed a lunar calendar, Kumar adds. Our current modern system of numbers, seconds, and minutes for time, eventually translated into the sixty-minute hour and the twenty-four-hour day, may have been derived from them. The Sumerians, "have left numerous legacies for mankind including instruments of agriculture, pottery, and war trade. They invented many new techniques and skills in different wakes of life in their time including mathematics, boat and ship-making, armory and communication," Kumar emphasizes.

Noteworthy is the scriptural link between Ham and the Sumerians. Dr. Arthur Custance, commenting on this link, observes that, "There is little doubt that the basic cultures in Sumeria (and later on, in Babylonia and Assyria?), in Egypt, and in the Indus Valley, were all non-Indo-European. "It is pretty well agreed," he argues, "that these Sumerians were not Semites, being clean shaven and comparatively hairless like the Egyptians" (Custance 1975). And from their language it is quite clear that they were not Indo-European. "Their civilization developed very rapidly and achieved a remarkable level of technical competence," he adds (Custance). If the Sumerians were neither Shemitic nor Indo-European, as Custance points out, that leaves us only one other option—Hamitic.

The Genesis account states in Genesis 10:8–10 that: "And the sons of Ham: Cush, and Mizraim (Egypt), and Put (Libya), and Canaan. And the sons of Cush: Seba, and Havilah, and Sabtah, and Raamah, and Sabtechah: and the sons of Raamah; Sheba and Dedan. And Cush begat Nimrod: he began to be a mighty one in the earth. He was a mighty hunter before the LORD; wherefore it is said, "Even as Nimrod the mighty hunter before the Lord." And the beginning of his kingdom was Babel, and Erech, and Accad, and Calneh **in the land of Shinar**. Out of the land went forth into Asshur (Assyria), and builded Nineveh, and the city of Rehoboth, and Calah, and Resen between Nineveh and Calah; the same is a great city…"

Shinar, mentioned in this passage, is a reference to the region lying between the Tigris and Euphrates rivers in Mesopotamia. Shinar is believed by many scholars to be the earlier Babylonian form of the word Sumer. The cities mentioned were notable Sumerian cities or urban centers. The linkage of the "land of Shinar" above, or the land of Sumer and its inhabitants, the Sumerians, to Nimrod, the Son of Cush and progenitor of Negroid peoples, further points to a Hamitic origin for the Sumerians. The Sumerian civilization is believed to have lasted for about three thousand to four thousand years, from probably around 6000 BC to 2000 BC.

The Phoenicians: Carthaginians

Of interest to the contributions made by the descendants of Ham, in particular, are the Phoenicians, whose culture and civilization gave them political and geographic influence in the Ancient world. Notable among their legacy is their navigational prowess. They are believed to be the first to navigate around the African continent. As seafarers, they gained access and control over the Mediterranean, from thence to the Atlantic Ocean and onward to the British Isles. In the process, they opened many commercial routes and established trading posts with many nations along the Mediterranean, with whom they traded. Many inroads in the fields of mathematics (particularly), weights and measures, astronomy, sailing guided by the stars, glass and textile man-ufacturing, and the luxurious purple dye known as tyrian, have all been attributed to the Phoenicians. The best-known development, however, is their alphabet, which formed the basis of the Greek alphabet, and therefore the development of the conventional Western alphabet, and all the advance-ments it subsequently generated in Western culture.

Although some archaeological findings point to a Shemitic linguistic line, the biblical evidence, on the other hand, shows that the Phoenicians were Canaanites, and there-fore Hamitic by race, with Sidon, the first son of Canaan, as the progenitor of this once powerful Phoenician people, who were known as the Sidonians. That linguistically they were Shemitic could be a result of intermarriage or conquest. Of this, Custance observes, "the language of a people does not always indicate its physical genealogy." The Canaanites spoke languages that had Semitic origins, such as Moabite, Aramaic, and Phoenician." In fact, Hebrew is designated the "tongue of Canaan" in Isaiah 19:18. Thus, the linkage of the Hebrew tongue with Canaan signifies a linguistic bor-rowing, not a physical lineage between the Hebrews and the Canaanites" (Custance).

The ancient city of Carthage was built by the Phoenicians in North Africa, in what is today Tunisia. Carthage, the principal city of the Phoenicians, became a center of polit-ical, commercial, and military power (NS Gill). The Punic wars between it (led by their general Hannibal) and Rome are well documented in history. The Phoenicians were con-quered by the Greeks, led by Alexander the Great, and their chief city, Tyre, taken in 332 BC. The survivors of that war fled to Carthage, making it into the powerful city it became even before the rise of Rome. As previously noted, Heth, the brother of Sidon (Genesis 10:15), from whom came the

Hittites, along with Sin, his brother (Gen. 10:17) are believed to be the progenitors of the Mongols, the Chinese in particular, and all Orientals in general.

The Etruscans

The Etruscans are another people group whose place on the Table of nations has been a mystery to many researchers. Their significance is established by the fact that they made tremendous contributions to Roman culture and civilization, which today has become ours as well. Against the current pervasive backdrop that the Romans are the world's civilizers and the source almost all key inventions, Custance notes that that it is now clear that…" the Romans learned many of these things from the Etruscans. "The part played by the Etruscans," Sir Gavin de Beer states, "in the foundation of Roman civilization is immense." Cato, in turn, asserts that nearly the whole of Italy was once under Etruscan rule and influence. George Rawlinson, classical scholar and orientalist states that, "The Romans themselves notwithstanding their intense national vanity, acknowledged this debt to some extent and admitted that they derived from the Etruscans their augury, their religious ritual, their robes, and other insignia of office, their games and shows, their earliest architecture, their calendar, their weights and measures, their land surveying systems, and various other elements of their civilization." This, he contends, even fell short of the true picture, stating that "really Eritruia was the source of their whole early civilization" (Rawlinson 1878); to which list Randall Macliver adds their martial organization, not to mention probably even the very name of the city itself. So just who were these Etruscans?

Arthur Custance explains that the people of Etruria or Tuscany were known by the early Greeks as *Tyrsenoi*. They were known by the Romans, on the other hand, as *Etrusci*. However, in classic Latin times, these same people were known as the *Rasena*. Custance asserts on linguistic grounds that they originated from Asia Minor and their language was neither Indo-European or Semitic. These people called themselves Rasena, presumably after an ancestor in the tradition of Jebus (Jebusites) or the city of Sidon, named after the first-born son of Canaan, Sidon. Nimrod built the cities of Nineveh and Resen, probably, naming the second after an ancestor by name Resen (Genesis 10:12) from which the name Rasena, for his descendants, is derived. This puts the Etruscans squarely in the Hamitic line of descent.

Custance, thus, summarizes that the Rasena originated from Resen, a descendant of Ham. Starting out in Assyria, and settling in Lydia, they subsequently migrated to northern Italy, speaking a language neither Semitic or Indo-European. Being preeminently city-builders, as was their forbear Nimrod, they continued producing works of art, the exact parallels of which have been found where Genesis suggests that the city of Resen was built. Custance further proposes that Resen not only grew in importance enough to have a city in Assyria named after him, but also gave rise to a people who grew powerful enough and large enough to migrate up into Europe and into the north of Italy, from which they multiplied and became wealthy and cultured enough to inspire the Japhetic Romans to adopt a very large part of their art, law, custom, and technology as their own, making scarcely any improvement on it. Thus, from Etruria, they made a tremendous contribution to Roman civilization.

From all accounts, each branch of Noah's three sons had a divine purpose and calling in God. Each fulfilled to the

best of its ability the divine purpose and assignment designated it, thus contributing to world civilization in some form
or fashion. Jesus, it must be noted, had Shemitic, Hamitic,
and Japhetic blood. The Synoptic Gospels were written to all
three branches of Noah's sons; Mark to the Hamitic peoples,
Matthew to the Shemitic, and Luke to the Japhetic line. That
the Shemitic shepherds, Hamitic magi, and Japhetic Greeks
greeted the arrival of the Messiah demonstrates the Father's
heart and purposes for all three branches and their descendants. That all three were present and played some role in
his crucifixion further demonstrates a prophetic prototype of
the Father's desire to see the nations, all nations, united in the
Messiah, Jesus Christ.

CHAPTER 9

Racial Healing and Reconciliation: An Ideal Whose Time Has Come

"You can't hold a man down in a ditch without staying down in the ditch with him."
—Booker T. Washington

"The Whole is Greater than the sum of its parts."
—Aristotle, *Metaphysical*

In its January 16, 2015 edition, under the caption: *T. D. Jakes: We Cannot Remain Silent on This Issue,* Charisma Magazine's Steve Yount reports on a conference of "a racially, denominationally, geographically, and generationally diverse representation of nearly 100 pastors and civic and faith leaders from across the country gathered for an unprecedented summit on racial reconciliation at the Potters House in Dallas..." With the theme *The Reconciled Church: Healing the Racial Divide,* the conference, convened by Bishops T.

D. Jakes, Harry Jackson, and Pastor James Robinson, and featuring an illustrious panel including, Dr. Bernice King, daughter of Dr, Martin Luther King, former UN Ambassador Andrew Young, Dr. Samuel Rodriguez, President of the National Hispanic Christian Leadership Conference, and Leith Anderson, President of the National Association of Evangelicals, focused on practical and strategic initiatives aimed at fostering racial healing and reconciliation (Yount 2015).

I highlight the above conference and the commonality of purpose with this book to advance the notion that racial healing and reconciliation is an ideal and a dream whose time, I am convinced, has come, and whose realization will be a fulfillment, not only of Dr. King's dream, but also of the larger American dream. This is an ideal and dream whose fulfillment, I also contend (as many will presumably agree), has already began in earnest. The progress made in race relations in this country cannot be disputed or diminished by anyone; such progress has been cemented, to an appreciable degree, with the election of Barack Obama as the forty-fourth and first Black President of the United States. This was a candidacy that would, undoubtedly, have fallen short of victory without extensive support from White America, with White Iowa *flipping the script*. With that said, I am also convinced that the achievement of complete social, political, educational, and economic uplift, respect and parity for Black America, Latinos, Asians, and all other minorities in the American milieu is absolutely necessary, if not critical, in bridging America's historic as well as contemporary racial and cultural divide.

White Sensitivity: Black Empowerment

"E Pluribus Unum—Out of Many, One."

"Let us all hope that the dark clouds of racial
prejudice and the deep fog of misunderstanding will
be lifted...tomorrow the radiant stars of love and
brotherhood will shine over our great nation..."
—Martin Luther King Jr., *Birmingham Jail*

As the greatest and most influential power in the world, it is critical for its own sake and for the healing of the nations of the world that America realize the dream and ideal of racial healing, reconciliation, and equality. Perhaps one would ask, *"Racial healing and reconciliation at what cost?"* What is it going to require of us, as a nation, as a people? What postures and attitudes need to be discarded and which need to be embraced? These are critical questions and issues that must be addressed in our quest for greater equality and reconciliation.

It is my contention, first, that racial healing and reconciliation *cannot* be seriously addressed or achieved with Black America and other minority groups still occupying an inferior designation in the social and economic order relative to their relationship with White America. This is a social and economic construct, predicated upon a superior-inferior continuum or master-servant relationship inherited from antiquity, the legacy of White supremacy, slavery, colonization and Jim Crow. It is the construct under which Black America, Native Americans, Latinos, and Asians, and all minority groups, legal and illegal, are regarded as objects of others' charity, the perpetual recipients of White America's philanthropy or largesse, in the form of hand-outs. *These foreigners have turned the homeland into a Welfare society*, if you will, is the current and prevailing rhetoric and sentiment, especially in White America. Such a perspective is not tenable; there is no uplifting feeling, self-worth, or dignity in such rhetoric and sentiment, one that feeds the notion that others in the American milieu are simply parasitic. Thus, any healing and reconciliation based on a failure to recognize the basic and common humanity of all the composites in the American milieu, red, black, white, brown, and yellow, one not contingent on a shared sense of equality and mutual respect, will only be superficial.

Secondly, racial healing and reconciliation will most certainly *not* occur if, and as long as, Blacks and other minority groups continue to feel disempowered and disenfranchised, economically, academically, socially, and politically. Although the statistical evidence points to higher numbers of Whites on welfare and government subsidies than Blacks, any form of dependence on government subsidies by Blacks, Latinos, and others, even if marginal, reinforces White perceptions of a Black or Latino culture that is lazy, incompetent, crime-ridden, and always in need of handouts. These are negative perceptions or stereotypical assumptions that have been shaped over time and have become the reality of many Whites' minds, even when evidence points to the contrary.

Thirdly, racial healing and reconciliation in America will *not* be achieved just because Blacks and minorities demand it of White America. In fact, a forced request to recognize another man's humanity and accord him respect as an equal or valued partner in any enterprise is as unnatural as demanding that one love you even though they do not have the "hots" for you. This, certainly, defies basic norms of protocol in any relationship. In fact, any response to such a demand, even if affirmative, comes across as coerced and manipulative, and is likely to be shallow or superficial. *"A man convinced against his will, is of the same opinion still"* (Carnegie 1998). Except in business, contractual demands and obligations in relationships are atypical, and not normative to the forging of socially acceptable relations and interactions. Respect, in my opinion, must be earned, not demanded.

Thus, I cannot envision or advocate, to any realistic or serious degree, racial healing and reconciliation on the basis of any of the above. If healing and reconciliation is pursued because Blacks demand rights without a commensurate amount of personal and collective responsibility, and if the current social and economic order, based on White supremacy inherited from the days of slavery, colonialism, and Jim Crow, remains intact with political, social, and economic power entrenched in the dominant White culture, making Blacks, Latinos, and other ethnic groups feel disempowered or disenfranchised, the quest for racial healing and reconciliation will be stymied. The slow but encouraging signs of progress and momentum-gathering in our land, in this sphere, will evaporate. The inertia that this will create and the resultant anger and frustration could set us back.

Mutual Respect and Equality: White Man's Burden

"Injustice anywhere is a threat to justice everywhere.
We are caught in an inescapable network of mutuality,
tied in a single garment of destiny. Whatever
affects one directly, affects all indirectly."
—Martin Luther King Jr., *Birmingham Jail*

Racial healing and reconciliation will *only* fully occur when Blacks and Whites recognize each other as co-equals—that is, equal partners on an even political, social, and economic keel. The guilt, burdens, and impact of our gruesome and unpalatable history will be completely washed away when there is mutual respect and appreciation for each other, and for the collective efforts and contributions each race or ethnic group has made, historically and contemporaneously, to the great American saga. This perspective calls for the empowerment of those at the bottom of the totem pole, the Black body-politic and all minority groups in the American milieu. This has to occur on all fronts: educationally, economically, politically, and socially, in order to bring them to par with their White counterparts. It simultaneously calls for the proper education of White America on the issue of White supremacy, privilege, and racism, sensitizing the dominant American race or culture to the debilitating impact of the above, not only on other races and cultures, but also on itself. As Booker T. Washington so eloquently stated, "You can't hold a man down in a ditch without staying down in the ditch with him." Our situation, as Americans—White, Black, Latino, Asian, or Native American—can be truly described as "an inescapable network of mutuality." We are, "tied in a single garment of destiny…whatever affects one directly, affects all indirectly" (MLK Jr.). America is, indeed, stronger when we are all stronger. A weaker group in the milieu makes us all weak or weaker. This is the "inescapable network of mutuality" of which Dr. King speaks. We are in this together, as Americans, regardless of when or how we came here; either we float together or we sink together.

White America's largely mono-cultural perspective, founded on the enduring ideology of White supremacy by which many Whites still subliminally or blatantly operate, has for centuries, remained America's status quo. It has defined the character of our America, and its political, social, and economic landscape. It is, however, a negative and disempowering force that must be intentionally confronted, debunked, and replaced with a cross-cultural and multicultural perspective, one that embraces all migrant races and cultures in our current multicultural ethos. After all, with the exception of Native Americans, all of us Americans are immigrants or the descendants of immigrants, some coming here volitionally and others, forcibly.

The institutions, systems, or structures of society that sustain White supremacy, and/or any similar ideology, inimical to the ideal of racial healing and reconciliation, must be, equally, confronted, dismantled, and dismissed for good. Any bridging of the divides that haunt us and reconciliation without the full integration and empowerment of all the races or ethnic groups into the American mainstream—socially, politically, and economically—will be, again, superficial, ineffective, a farce. The dominant White power-structure in America has an indispensable, foremost and crucial role to play in this.

Mutual Respect and Equality: A Biblical Paradigm

"We should all know that diversity makes for a rich tapestry, and we must understand that all the threads of the tapestry are equal in value no matter the color, equal in importance no matter their texture."

—Maya Angelou

In an interesting encounter in the book of Galatians, The Apostle Paul makes a remarkable observation, one that I believe is relevant to the case being made here for equality and mutual respect among the various people groups represented in the American matrix. He writes: "And when James, Cephas and John, who seemed to be pillars, perceived the grace that had been given to me, they gave to me and Barnabas, the right hand of fellowship, that we should go to the Gentiles and they to the circumcision" (Galatians 2:9).

Peter, James, and John are "senior apostles," by way of ranking, relative to Paul and Barnabas. After all, the three had actually walked with Jesus in the flesh (that is, in human form), unlike Paul and Barnabas, who did not. Paul and Barnabas, who came into the faith much later, had been anointed according to their divine gifts of grace and were making giant strides in the kingdom, in pursuit of their apostolic callings and destinies. The chief apostles (Peter, James, and John) recognizing the apostolic call of God upon the lives of Paul and Barnabas, the supernatural endowments that went with the call, and the deep insights the Holy Spirit had given to the "junior" apostles, could do no other but give them *the right hand of fellowship.*

Giving of the right hand in fellowship was a sign or gesture of agreement between peers or equals. It was not one between superiors and inferiors, but rather one among equal partners in a collective enterprise, each side recognizing the other's uniqueness, differences in calling, spiritual gifts, and other endowments of grace and specialties in God's grand design. The Apostles from Jerusalem would never have done this, had they regarded Paul or Barnabas as inferior in status and ability, or erroneous in their doctrine or theology. According them the right hand of fellowship amounted to spiritual validation. By this gesture, Peter, James, and John endorsed the apostolic callings of Paul and Barnabas, accorded them full recognition, and granted them fellowship in the Church's apostolic, leadership structure for their travail and contribution to the gospel ministry. With that recognition also came the well-deserved respect that such a powerful gospel ministry to the Gentiles naturally elicited. Oftentimes, we accord recognition and respect to others when we realize we do not have in talent, skill, or experience what they have. The impact of this validation, and their subsequent partnership, interdependence, and mutual respect thus established and cemented, can only be measured by the inroads made by the Church in the Roman Empire, and the sheer impact of their combined ministries on the various nations or cultures represented therein. They "turned their world upside down" (Acts 17:6).

It is this real or perceived lack of acknowledgment by White America of the common humanity and contributions made by Black America and other minority cultures to the development of our beloved country, consistent with this biblical paradigm, that has often fueled the recurring hostility on both sides. It is this acknowledgment by White America of Black America, Latinos, Asians, Native Americans, Africans, etc., manifested not simply through grandiose speeches and empty promises (like those usually made during Black History month by politicians trying to buy votes), but through sustained, concrete actions to uplift these groups, that go to demonstrate that we are, indeed, one people, with a common destiny. It is, ultimately, positive and substantive actions, not symbolic gestures, that "redemptively" engage, uplift and empower communities that would most eloquently speak to Black America, Latinos, and other minorities, so that they may drop their pain, forgive the wounds inflicted in the past, and embrace White America and each other as partners together in this great American experience. It is a message that clearly says, "We are each other's keepers."

Black America has no interest in perpetuating "White guilt" for the sake of the atrocities of the past. Blame loses its utility or validity when there is nothing to blame someone for. White guilt (or any form of guilt, for that matter) can be removed or eased by an acknowledgment of the misdeed or a sincere apology, especially if followed by (consistent) acts of contrition. Thus, instead of White America simply (and sometimes, arrogantly) saying to Black America, "I never owned slaves...that was years ago...so just get over it, move on and get a life," as if pain, emotional wounds and hurts that have festered for centuries can easily be wished and waved away, a simple, but sincere acknowledgment of the atrocities of the past, based on an understanding and sensitivity to the issues at stake, can remove the guilt, and through the process of time, help heal the wounds of the past. This is exactly where, I believe, the Church in America can seriously lead the way. It is worthy to note that the right hand of fellowship accorded to Paul and Barnabas was not initiated by Paul, but by those supposedly senior, superior, or higher in rank than himself (namely, Peter, James, and John). This is White America's responsibility in the healing process.

Another biblical paradigm relevant to this concept of fostering racial healing and reconciliation by building mutual trust and respect between White and Black America is seen in the story of David and Jonathan:

"And it came to pass, when he had made an end to speaking with Saul, that the soul of Jonathan was knit with the soul of David, and Jonathan loved him as his own soul... then, Jonathan and David made a covenant, because he loved him as his own soul...and Jonathan stripped himself of the robe that was upon him, and gave it to David, and his garments, even to his sword and to his bow and to his girdle." (1 Samuel 18:1–3)

The word covenant, *testament* in Latin, *berith* in Hebrew, and *diatheke* in Greek, is a will, treaty, contract, pact, agreement, or alliance between two or more entities, either of equal or unequal status, eliciting certain actions, behavior or obligations from each party to the contract. Covenants, typically, elicit blessings or rewards for obedience to the tenets of the contract, as well as penalties for violation, in the case of a conditional covenant. Scripture speaks of various covenants, but that between David and Jonathan is most striking and apropos to the subject matter here.

The covenant between these two signifies a clash of subcultures within the broader Jewish culture. It is the meeting of two individuals from two very different worlds, backgrounds, classes, and socioeconomic status. Jonathan is the prince of Israel and heir-apparent to his father's throne; David, on the other hand, is a poor shepherd boy, the seventh of eight sons, whose own father, Jesse, did not think it important to have him present when the prophet Samuel arrived to anoint one of his sons king over Israel. Again, what is striking as well as paradoxical here is an alliance or covenant, forged between a future king of a nation and a poor Jewish boy from a very low estate (the country or ghetto, in our modern parlance).

To fully appreciate this analogy, it is vital to understand the status of shepherds in Israel at this time. Shepherds were a despised class, both socially and professionally. They occupied a subordinate and dishonorable place in Jewish life. Four hundred years of exile in Egyptian captivity had thoroughly rooted out Israel's nomadic lifestyle in which animal husbandry (sheepherding) featured rather prominently. The Egyptians, with their more settled agricultural lifestyle, frowned upon shepherds and their work. Shepherds were depicted in a derogatory light in Egyptian art forms. Joseph's words to his brothers sum up the Egyptian perception of this role: *"Every shepherd is an abomination* (disgusting, despicable, detestable) *to the Egyptians"* (Genesis 46:34). This Egyptian aversion for shepherds could have been nurtured because of the Hyksos, a tribe of nomadic shepherds who had held portions of Egypt under subjugation around the eighteenth century, their reign beginning around 1630. The word Hyksos itself may have been interpreted as *king-shepherds* or *captive-shepherds*. Israel, post-Egyptian captivity, acquired more land and settled into a sedentary existence, and as it did, the estimable role and place shepherds had once occupied, drastically depreciated/diminished. Shepherds were consigned to the lower labor classes and castes. It is from this thoroughly debased social context that David was divinely guided by God to challenge the Philistine giant, Goliath. The covenant that was formed between him and Jonathan, the Prince of Israel, and the implications of that covenant have much to say to America's races and cultures, which are divided not only by racial politics, but also by class. Invariably, race and class are the two sides of the same evil coin; racism begets classism, and classism reinforces racism.

"The soul of Jonathan was knit with the soul of David… and Jonathan loved him as his own soul…then Jonathan and David made a covenant, because he loved him as his own soul" (1 Sam. 18:1–3).

Jonathan's love for David and the strong mutual bond of friendship that subsequently developed caused Jonathan to give up everything; his privileged position, status in society, family ties, and loyalties, as he stepped back into the shadows and played second-fiddle to David, for David's sake. He even abdicated his right to the throne for his poor, econom-

ically-disadvantaged and socially-inferior friend and covenant partner, David. As proof of his avowed love for David,
he stripped himself of his royal garb, his robe, tunic, girdle
(belt), bow, and sword, and handed them to David. The
transfer of his royal paraphernalia to David is, again, symbolic of Jonathan's willingness to sacrifice everything, including his future kingdom, for the advancement of his friend.
Under constant threat and at the cost of his own safety and
life, Jonathan chose a covenant with David over family ties
and loyalty. He informed David of his father's devious plot to
assassinate him, sparing the life of his covenant brother and
friend on numerous occasions. "*Oh! What manner of love the
father has bestowed upon us, that a man should lay down his life
for his friend*" (John 15:13). "*For indeed, there is a friend that
sticks closer than a brother*" (Prov. 18:24). Jonathan's affection
for his friend, covenant partner, and brother is not sentimen-
tal; it is demonstrated in very practical terms.

Social mobility is displayed in Jonathan's actions, but
not the kind we are all used to and aspire toward. The type of
Social Mobility depicted, initiated, and modeled by Jonathan
is not upward, from the bottom up, but from the top down.
Scripture admonishes us not to be conceited, esteeming ourselves higher than we ought to, but instead to associate with
the ordinary or common man, those of humble pedigree
(Romans 12:16). It is exactly what Jonathan does, and he
is the initiator of it "for the lesser is blessed of the greater"
(Hebrews 7:7). He probably perceives that this is a *Kairos*
moment, a moment in history, pregnant with divine purpose, timing, and significance. The Philistine giant who
defied the armies of the God of Israel has been slain. The
yoke of oppression and the repeated threats of the enemy
against Israel have been beaten back. Specifically, Israel's
arch-enemy (the Philistines), have been defeated and are now

subservient to her. All of this is orchestrated by a divine hand through this little, teenage boy David, using nothing but a slingshot and a couple of pebbles from a stream. Jonathan does not despise the poor, socially-inferior, and underprivileged shepherd boy David; neither does he wait for David to step up to his superior royal stature or highness to ask for help or favors for his lower-level family.

Jonathan probably perceives that God has intentionally (and for reasons best known to just Him) defied conventional wisdom, matching "man" and moment in the slaying of Goliath, using (military) skills and strategy only the wilderness could hammer into a kid of David's caliber. Hidden in Israel's wilderness (the ghettoes) are, perhaps, pearls and diamonds in the rough, little heroes, potential military strategists and statesmen, divinely and sovereignly prepared and destined for the nation's deliverance in moments of national crisis. After all, David, the little shepherd boy, exemplified all the above.

With all these thoughts probably running through his mind, Jonathan, subsequently, steps down from his exalted position as prince and heir-apparent, and stoops to David's level. He has both the economic and social stature and muscle to use as he pleases. He is under no obligation to reach out to David; he can opt to either care (or care less) about David, with nothing to gain if he does, or lose if he does not. He chooses, however, to "reach down and out" and exercise his royal power and prerogative, conferred on him by his privileged birth, to empower the poor and less privileged David. Jonathan does not do this out of a sense of any guilt associated with his privileged status. In fact, he did not choose his privileged status. He was born into it, but chooses to use it for the greater good and for the benefit of another. He does it simply because he loves David as his own soul/self.

In just one fell and dramatic swoop of his royal power and privilege, Jonathan embraces David, initiates a life-long covenant with him, and by that singular act elevates him to the status of an equal, or perhaps to a status even higher, as his statements thereafter seem to indicate. When David's life is threatened by Jonathan's father, King Saul, Jonathan goes out of his way to assure him, thus: "Fear not: for the hand of Saul my father shall not find thee; and thou shalt be king over Israel, and I shall be next unto thee; and that also Saul, my father knows" (1 Sam. 23:17).

Indeed, this poor, ghetto, shepherd boy, ultimately, becomes the leader of the Jewish nation, just as Jonathan, his covenant partner and the rightful heir to the throne, had earlier declared.

How can we describe Jonathan's attitude? Surreal, saintly, celestial, and out of this world or out of the ordinary? I am convinced that if White America can muster the divine courage to similarly and with intentionality reach out and embrace Black America, not only will it rouse a sleeping giant, but a centuries-old scourge whose ghosts have haunted this nation and spawned poverty, injustice, hatred, rancor, and death, in America and around the world, would be finally dealt a lethal blow and annihilated for all eternity. A new, healed, validated, and empowered Black nation will arise from the ashes "with healing in its wings," reciprocate the gesture, and emerge as a social and economic force to reckon with. No power on earth, I am convinced, can stand against a truly United States of America as a force for good if this nation's Black and White cultures, and all the nations represented in it, come together in unity.

Racial Healing and Reconciliation:
Is It Realistic?

"I wish I could say that racism and prejudice were only distant memories, but as I look around I see that even educated Whites and African-Americans...have lost hope in equality."
—Thurgood Marshall

"It is understandable why Black America would be eager to have racial healing, reconciliation (justice and respect)," my friend began, "but what does White America stand to gain from it, especially, considering that it is currently the dominant culture, socially, politically, academically, and economically, and has all the privileges America accords its dominant culture and class? Why would someone in their right mind, with such power and privilege, want to give it up?" he queried.

Given our history, the unwillingness of each side to budge, and how difficult and long the march for justice and equality have been, and the cost in terms of lives lost and resources expended, the concept of racial healing and reconciliation, and achieving equality among, and respect for all racial groups in America's socioeconomic order, *now*, sometimes, comes across as idealistic. It certainly appears as a naïve, far-fetched, and untested proposition or theory, a pipe-dream. Little wonder that a brother posed what I thought was a rather loaded question when he read this segment of the book:

Question: Indeed, why should or would White America want to lose its privileged position and clout, reach out to Black America and other minority groups, as depicted in the biblical paradigms above, and share or give up power?" This question is as loaded as it is plausible.

Racism is indeed about power; the power one race, nation, or ethnic group wields over another or others, which assures social, political, and economic control and privilege. The current world order thrives on the matrix above, with power in all its multifaceted forms, entrenched in the Western hemisphere within a sophisticated and complex framework of race, economics, culture, and class. The very concept of racial healing and reconciliation requires, not the disempowerment of the dominant race or culture, but the empowerment of all races within a particular context, in this case, the American context, one that will require the uplift or elevation of America's racial minorities and groups to an equal status, with some form of power-sharing peaceably negotiated with the current (dominant) power structure. Navigating these sensitive contours will no doubt be a test of the character of the American people.

Suffice it to say that, since the shifting sands of time, no significant change or shift, milestone, or discovery in history or society has been met with absolute certainty. Whether it was the abolition of slavery and de jure Jim Crow calls for integration, or the adventures in aviation and aerospace by the Wright brothers and forays into space and the ultimate landing of a man on the moon, each of these was met with cynicism, at least initially. In 2008, the prospect of a Black man leading the free world as president of the United States was incredulous, only but a dream, until Iowa changed the political matrix of the Democratic primaries with its validation of the son of Kenya and Kansas, Barack Obama.

The cynicism or pessimism that one may feel about White support for racial healing and reconciliation is, therefore, not particularly strange or unique when you stop to consider the full implications of this mammoth change. It is a normal step and progression in the quest for any form of change. Arguably, most people in their right minds will not give any proposition involving giving up one's place of power and privilege a thought, much more be willing to advocate or doing it. "Freedom," Dr. Martin Luther King stated, is never voluntarily given by the oppressor; it must be demanded by the oppressed."

History is, in fact, littered with evidence that power structures, systems, and institutions, racist or not, strive to maintain their power base, meaning the status quo. Any questioning or challenge of that power or status quo is usually perceived as an affront, an attempt to undermine the power structure. This may invite the full might of its (reactionary) forces to crush or subdue this perceived threat. The American and French revolutions, the communist takeovers from the bourgeoisie classes in Russia, Cuba, and China, and the process of unraveling the evil Apartheid political machinery in South Africa (not to mention the many independence movements that evolved in Africa, Asia, and Latin America against colonialism in the fifties, sixties, and seventies), are cases in point. They all resorted to radical approaches—along with prolonged armed struggle, in some cases—in the quest for freedom, justice, and equality. Thus, unless the powers that be realize that the winds of change are not in their favor, that it is in their best interest to relinquish power, volitionally and peaceably, any change in the status quo, any power-sharing, any justice, freedom, or equality achieved must be demanded or fought for, like any other ideal.

Why should and would Whites renege on the doctrine of White supremacy and share power with Blacks, Latinos, and other marginalized groups? I am not sure if Whites, en masse, would, but I am convinced that there are many White Americans of faith and good will who understand and are sensitive to the historical injustices suffered by Blacks and other races in this God-blessed country, and are willing to live justly, equitably, and peacefully in the same neighborhoods with them. Americans in general, and most Whites, specifically, will agree that racism is an evil this country cannot tolerate. White Americans will generally agree that "all men (black, white, brown, red, and yellow) are truly created equal and endowed by the Creator with the unalienable rights of life, liberty, and the pursuit of happiness. Most White Americans, I will assume, agree with our dictum: "Out of many one," that attaining unity amid our diversity is an ideal to aspire toward; that in our unity as a pluralistic nation lies our strength; that we are stronger as a nation when each of us is stronger. Most White Americans will agree, I am sure, that in each cultural group are unique gifts, abilities, and experiences worth sharing and celebrating, just as there are, equally, negative individual and cultural tendencies in each group worth discarding, for the general good. Most Americans, White and Black, embrace diversity and cherish the ideal of equality with respect to race, class, and gender, as recent voting patterns have shown, especially among Gen Xers and Ys, and as the Supreme court has also affirmed. Finally, most Americans, Black and White, understand that "the arc of the moral universe is long, but it bends toward justice," ultimately, because God is a Just God. It is for the foregoing reasons, the *inescapable network of mutuality* we have and share, and perhaps for many more reasons than can be presented here, that I believe White America will be willing to embrace and share power with its Native American, Black, Latino, and Asian minority brothers and sisters.

Racial healing and reconciliation is an ideal whose time, I am convinced, has come. Like previous epic moments or milestones in our history, change now, as in times past, may start with just a lone voice, "the voice of one (not two) crying in the wilderness." Time, trials, seasons, and "nature's God" often test the authenticity, resolve, and resilience of any dream and its advocates before elevating or propelling the message into the national imagination and consciousness. Ultimately, the message catches fire, however, stirs the soul of a nation and generation, where a people begin to, prophetically, envision a preferred future. The vision gathers momentum and galvanizes the forces of action into a movement, until it all reaches a crescendo, a critical mass, at which point change becomes inevitable.

Edmund Burke (*The Price of Freedom*) in a letter to a member of the British Assembly, in 1791, observed that: "Those who have been once intoxicated with power and have derived any kind of emolument (compensation) from it… can never willingly abandon it. They may be distressed in the midst of all their power, but they will never look to anything but power for their relief" (Burke 1792).

Although giving up entrenched power and privilege has never been the forte of those wielding them, I feel the winds of change blowing across this God-blessed nation. I sense a growing chorus of voices on both aisles of the racial and political spectrum, who see beyond the pettiness of America's racial politics and the chasm created by it. For these voices, the sheer power of a truly United States of America is a goal and an ideal, worthy of our fervent pursuit. Despite being in the minority today, I am convinced it is only a matter of time before this broad coalition of races and cultures represented in the American milieu begins to emerge and garner strength. Like every ideal of significance, racial healing and reconciliation is a dream and an ideal whose realization is inevitable, despite the anticipated opposition from both sides. It would be phenomenal if White America led the way in the quest for healing and reconciliation of the nations—*panta ta ethne*, being the dominant race and culture. At the end of the day, however, the call for racial healing and reconciliation places great responsibility and challenge on both Blacks and Whites, and every group in between.

It is one thing to recognize that the winds of change are blowing without recourse in a particular direction and to decide to align yourself with them in order to be on the right side of history. Better, though, is the realization that we are at our strongest as a people when America lives up to its creed and highest ideal, "that all men are created equal…" and when we realize that we are better off collectively than we are individually, and allow the "better angels of our nature" (Lincoln 1861) to help us build a truly United States of America, One Nation Under God.

CHAPTER 10

Black America Today: A Dream Ambushed

Despite the immense contributions made by the descendants of Ham to world civilization, the dismal life conditions of many of that lineage of Noah's sons, on a global level, bemoans the achievements of this once-powerful people who populated the far reaches of the Earth, built the great empires of antiquity, and laid the foundation of much technological and scientific progress today, a people whose monuments continue to defy modern architectural expertise, and whose culture greatly impacted the Romans, and by extension, Western civilization.

In this segment, I discuss how for many African Americans, a prophetic people, Dr. King's dream for total emancipation and inclusion in the American dream has proved illusory. Many African Americans today are stuck in the ghettos of America, mired in poverty, shut out from the American dream. Was the American dream within reach of Black America before integration, as some have argued, or is Black America better off today because of it? I discuss the issue of Black Upward Mobility, also known in missiological circles as *Redemption and Lift*, as a major key to advancing the cause of racial healing and reconciliation. Of critical importance to achieving Black Redemption and Lift are the following:

1. Shedding any victim mentality and taking personal responsibility for the things we, as a people, can control and change.
2. The necessity of "The God factor—A Platform of Faith (Supreme Being or Supreme Court)."
3. I address the current crisis in the Black family structure, and propose a response rooted in Scripture, the Word of God.
4. I stress the insufficiency of Political Freedom without Economic and Intellectual Power and Education for total emancipation.
5. Finally, I highlight the need for economic justice and power as indispensable to Black Redemption and Lift.

The American Dream

Dr. King's dream of emancipation for Black America was not a call for it to assume an isolationist posture, politically, socially, or economically, or a return to "the motherland" (as some other Black leaders, like Marcus Garvey, and others in the Back to Africa movement advocated). To the contrary, King's dream and passion was the inclusion and full integration of Black America into American society. A proper discussion of Black America's socioeconomic development (Redemption and Lift) must, therefore, be set within the context and confines of the larger American dream.

In the *Epic of America*, author James Truslow Adams defines the American dream as "that dream of a land in which life should be better and richer and fuller for everyone, with opportunity for each according to ability or achievement" (Adams 1931). Adams contends that The American dream is not a dream pertaining to just cars and increased wages, but one that ensures social order to the end that every individual, regardless of life's circumstances, such as birth or social pedigree, can maximize his or her inherent capacities (Adams 1931).

The American Dream, thus, holds the promise that given the right conditions and climate, everyone, regardless of race, color, class, or creed could ensure their own personal success by taking full advantage of the freedoms and access to the opportunities granted by this country, utilizing God-given abilities and virtues of hard work and sacrifice. Expressed in today's parlance, this essentially means, "Picking one's self up by one's (own) bootstraps," by taking personal responsibility for one's destiny and success, through personal ingenuity and actions. Inherent in the dream is also the presumption that given the same friendly and conducive conditions, one could safely expect one's children to do better than him or herself, thus continuing the cycle of achievement and success. In time, the dream appears to have shrunk from its original tenets of freedom, opportunity, sacrifice, hard work, and entrepreneurship, to more or less, represent the mere acquisition of the tangible and mundane; in essence, plain material acquisitions, without much regard for how they were attained.

The core principles of the American dream were founded on the Declaration of Independence, which states that "All men are created equal, and endowed by their Creator with certain unalienable rights, among which are Life, Liberty, and the Pursuit of Happiness." These rights included the right to live in freedom and dignity based on one's own values, as long as those values did not infringe on the liberties of others. The right to worship freely, based on one's personal belief system, is also enshrined and ensured in the tenets of the Declaration of Independence, which formed the basis of the American dream.

It is only fair to say, however, that although Black America desires to participate in the American dream like any other American, for many descendants of African slaves, this has not been the case, and for a myriad of complex reasons. The dream has, obviously, and largely worked for White America, and other groups in the American context. For many in Black America, even the road to full citizenship and integration has been nothing but daunting, in a nation whose wealth and prosperity were largely built on their backs and at no cost. The dream working for all, including Black America, first requires the leveling of the playing field by ridding our society of institutional or systemic racism and all other forms of injustice so everyone who desires to, can compete freely and fairly. Perhaps some massive agenda of educating those who have borne the brunt of America's historical injustices, the legacy of which is still with us until this day, may be necessary also. The fact is, whether America admits the legacies of our history or not, the reality still remains, and will keep haunting us until we seriously deal with them.

Black America before Integration

*"Our American system like all others is on
trial, both at home and abroad."*
—Chief Justice Earl Warren

Although the first African slaves brought to America by Dutch traders arrived in 1619, the path to full integration into the American nation for Black America did not begin until only several decades ago, as explained below.

On May 19, 1954, the US Supreme Court handed down its ruling in the case of *Oliver Brown vs. the Topeka, Kansas Board of Education*. This unanimous (9–0) decision by the Supreme Court was a landmark, inasmuch as race relations in American society were concerned. The Court, by this decision, essentially overruled its earlier decision in 1896 in the case of *Plessy vs. Ferguson*, which rendered legal and constitutional, *separate but equal*, the segregation of American public schools based on race. Here, the court had stated that as long as educational facilities were equal, the various races could be separated without violating the Fourteen Amendment of the United States Constitution and Bill of Rights.

The Fourteenth Amendment stipulated in Section 1 that *"no state shall deny to any person…within its jurisdiction the equal protection of the laws."* In this epic case, the plaintiffs declared the purported equal status of Blacks and Whites as a charade, which only led to inferior logistics, facilities, and infrastructure for Black kids. The Court, for various reasons, agreed with this assessment and ruled the separation of educational facilities for Blacks and Whites as inherently unequal. Popularly known later simply as *Brown vs. Board of Education*, this ruling was a major step forward in the quest for civil rights in America. Blacks were legally accepted in the White world of public education, amid much public outcry, consternation, and push-back from White America, and gradually integrated into White American schools. Beyond the integration of public schools, *Brown vs. Board of Education* also precipitated several significant events in the quest for civil rights, such as the removal of *de jure* segregation (the legal segregation of American society, known as Jim Crow), the Civil Rights Act of 1964, and the Voting Rights Act of 1965. Thus, the legal embrace of Black Africans in America into the American homeland as full citizens began in earnest.

Ironically, one of the arguments that has been made on the issue of Black enterprise, empowerment, and upward mobility has been in reference to the apparent success of Black America during segregation—that is, before the integration of Blacks into White society. The implication here is that Black America, collectively, was better off before rather than after Integration.

Jeffrey L. Boney is one of the chief proponents of this persuasion. Referring to the present conditions of African-Americans (that is, since they were integrated into American society), he provocatively asserts that looking at various reports, "You'll find that Black people are statistically listed at the bottom of every good category and at the top of every negative category" (Boney). The point being made here is that integration has not been the golden era of race relations in America; neither has it promoted the educational, social, and economic uplift of Black people as was hoped for.

In yet another article, more pointed than the previous, captioned *Black Wall Street—Segregation Was Better for Blacks*, dated June 27, 2013, the author asks why Blacks discontinued their encouragement of businesses owned by other Blacks, instead patronizing White-owned businesses located in

THE COLOR OF GOD

places where they were not welcome. The rebuilding of Black Wall Street was predicated on this, he suggests. The reference to Black Wall Street, also known as, Negro Wall Street, highlights the proverbial "good old days" of Black enterprise and success, when Greenwood, in Tulsa, Oklahoma, according to the author of the article," he states. The economic prosperity of Greenwood's Black businesses, the author maintains, had a ripple effect on other Black communities around the country, allowing Blacks to employ other Blacks, supporting one another and peacefully working together, unlike today (unbiasedtalk.com 2013).

Ironically, the worst race riot in US history occurred in Greenwood, in Tulsa, in 1921, when angry White mobs destroyed America's wealthiest Black community and killed an estimated three hundred people, burning down Black enterprises. This prosperous Black enclave in the United States came to ruins after angry White mobs burned down homes and businesses, killing men, women, and children in the process, during what, for all intents and purposes, still stands as one of America's most tumultuous periods in race relations. In the aftermath of these race riots, no serious efforts were made to rebuild this once-illustrious enclave. Greenwood never recovered its glorious history and luster, particularly at a time when segregation (Jim Crow) was being abolished and Blacks were being encouraged to integrate into White society and patronize White enterprise.

Impact of Integration on Black America

In *Five Ways Integration Underdeveloped Black America*, consistent with the above perspective, the Atlanta Black Star, also highlights, in very specific ways, how integration undercut Black Progress. "After segregation ended," the article dated December 9, 2013 maintains, Black businesses such as restaurants, banks and insurance companies disappeared because, African-Americans, shifted their support, en masse, to White-owned businesses and other racial groups. "Black people," the article asserts, "spend 95% of their income at White-owned businesses...we are our own worst enemy..." it concludes (Atlanta Black Star 2013). The apparent success of Black America under segregation and before integration is implicit in these assertions.

The Atlanta Black Star article further argues, that Black wealth stagnated and declined after integration, The Black family structure collapsed, the unemployment rate among Blacks skyrocketed, the Black community became more dependent, particularly on White graces, with the perpetuation of the myth of a color-blind society, particularly after integration; integration and the myth of a color-blind society, serving to reinforce White Privilege, the unfair advantages Whites in America had accumulated and enjoyed, at the expensive of Blacks, Native Americans and other racial groups, for centuries (Atlanta Black Star 2013).

The notion of racial integration and the emergence of a color-blind American society, though only a burgeoning proposition, in real terms, was propagated through much hype and hysteria as the arrival of a new epoch in America's history, one in which Blacks had apparently attained equal status with Whites. Today, many White Americans, unfortunately, subscribe to this notion, although the reality could not be farther from the truth. Despite many Blacks and Latinos, in particular, still being mired in poverty, subject to various social, academic, and economic inequities, the myth of racial integration and equality, in large measure, has rendered any serious measures at rectifying the impact of historical racism and injustices on Blacks and other minorities, as unfair to Whites. Unfortunately, this myth persists till this day, creating blinders in the dominant White culture, to the legacy of America's "original sin," slavery, the decimation of Native Americans and the annexation of their lands, and all other forms of injustice perpetrated on minority groups.

With economic deprivation, joblessness, poverty still rampant, and political powerlessness among America's Black population at its highest, and the social oppression and lynching of Black men still a common occurrence despite the monumental strides made in civil rights, the stage was set for massive changes in America. It is against the backdrop of social, political, and economic disillusionment, turmoil and uncertainty that Dr. Martin Luther King emerges. The Black Church, specifically, the Southern Baptist Leadership Conference, served as the cradle of this emerging change. The forces of change were to be mobilized by a young Martin Luther King, an ordained minister, into a movement, the Civil Rights Movement. Under his leadership, it gained momentum, leading to monumental changes in America's racial, political and social landscape.

In his last great work before his assassination, "*Where do we go from here: Chaos or Community,*" Dr. King notes the nexus between racism and economics. The "vicious grasp" of "racism and its perennial ally—economic exploitation— provide the key to understanding most of the international complications of this generation" (MLK 1967). Thomas Jackson, drawing from David Garrow's seminal work, highlights that by November of 1966, Dr. King had transformed himself from a "reassuring reformer" into a "radical threat to America's class system and dominant institutions" (Jackson 2007). Jackson notes further from Garrow, that Dr. King recognized the "malignant kingship" between racism and

America's power and class structures, that the struggle for emancipation for African-Americans had more to do with economics than to legal issues pertaining to race (Jackson 2007). This, Jackson notes, served as the impetus for his commitment, in 1956, to achieving not only political power for the race, but also economic. Dr. King, per Jackson, sought a national effort to eradicate Black poverty and enhance Negro standards of living, by marshaling both political and social forces to that end. Though structural or systemic rationales existed for the conditions of Black people, King did not discount the place of Black pathology and the need for group self-criticism, whether related to illegitimacy or crime in order to achieve community socioeconomic ends (Jackson 2007).

It is to this group-self-criticism, related to crime, illegitimacy, poverty, ignorance and other "pathologies" that we must now turn, and seriously address, if we as Blacks in the diaspora, whether Americans, Africans, West Indians or Europeans, are to change the status quo, better ourselves, gain equality, and become a stronger force to reckon with. No one can fight success. Success speaks for itself. When America perceives the grace upon our community, manifested in our spiritual, economic, social and political strength, like Peter, James and John of Paul, it will have no choice but to give us the "right hand of fellowship."

Black America: A Dream Ambushed

*"Behold, the dreamer comes. Come now
therefore, and let us slay him…
and we will see what becomes of his dreams."*
—Gen. 37:19–20

In Matthew 26:31, Jesus uses a scripture to warn his disciples of how they will behave upon his arrest that night. You will all desert me, He said, because it is written "strike the shepherd and scatter the sheep."

As a child growing up in Ghana, West Africa, I quickly learnt that the surest way of knowing that a venomous snake that surfaces from the brushes is dead, is to cut off its head. The limb body of Goliath on the ground after being slain by David's pebble from the brook was not sufficient to demonstrate Israel's victory over the Philistine warrior, until David had cut off his head. It was by that act then that the Philistine army finally realized that their general was, in fact, dead. The cold-blooded murder of Jesus was exactly to that end, that is eradicate the potential for the dissemination of his rebellious, in the mind of the Jewish leaders, heretical, and antisocial doctrine.

The target of an enemy's attack is usually not the visionary or carrier of the dream, as the dream itself, that is, the ideology, convictions and philosophies that underlie the dream and provide impetus to it. It is these ideology and convictions that often cause panic and anxiety among those of a contrary persuasion. While the elimination of the messenger or dreamer always remains a viable and appealing option for detractors, doing away with him may not necessarily do away with the dream and its message, especially, if die-hard loyalists have already bought into it.

Violent revolutions and military take-overs of governments have always sought not just the undoing of the prevailing ideology, but the incarceration, and oftentimes, assassination of the purveyor(s) of the political, economic or religious ideology in question. Where such diabolical methods, such as murder are untenable, other less lethal and nefarious methods, like character assassination may be employed, to defame, undermine, and thus compromise the dreamer's impeccable reputation. For some very crooked and shady political systems, any means necessary to aborting the dream is not off limits; the end justifies the means.

Ironically, for Dr. Martin Luther King, the machinery and modus operandi toward his neutralization included all the above. By any means necessary, the dream had to be "aborted," because its birth would signify the emancipation and development of an entire people whose rise would be threatening to the established political, social, and economic order. Unfortunately, the dream was embodied in a person, Martin Luther King. He became collateral damage, his assassination, indispensable and critical to aborting the dream.

Question: Did Dr. King's assassination mean the assassination of the dream?

Absolutely not! To the contrary, Dr. King's assassination, gave life and impetus to the dream he lived and died for. Life comes out of death (John 14:12). Before there ever was a resurrection, there first had to be a death. Yes, his death was, undoubtedly, a setback to the fulfillment of the dream, but it was only a temporary setback. His death represented an "ambushment" and (attempted) assassination of the dream. Too late, however; the clock could not and would not be turned back. The winds of change had been set in motion and would not be stopped. Both Black and White America had bought into his dream before his death. There were loyalists on both sides of the racial and political aisle, men and women of conscience who understood that America's toxic racial, social, political, and economic trajectory was not sustainable, long-term, that an alternative course was needed, a new ethos needed to be fashioned, one in which all people, black white, brown, yellow, and red, would be judged, not by the color of their skin, but by the content of their character.

It was a vision of racial equality, harmony and justice, of "a city set on a hill" compromising a beautiful mosaic of cultures, all bound together by one creed, America's creed, that "all men are, indeed, created equal, and endowed by their Creator with the unalienable rights of life, liberty and the pursuit of happiness."

White supremacy and Black inferiority could and would no longer hold its treacherous sway over this land, the land of the free and home of the brave. Though the dreamer was assassinated, the attempted plot to assassinate the dream, was thus, thankfully, rebuffed and foiled. The messenger or vessel died, but the dream and message lives and continues on. It may have been ambushed or high-jacked, but it still lives on. It may be in a pit (like Joseph) but it still lives on; it may be in a coma and on life-supports, but it is still not dead. It may be depressed, suppressed, enslaved, imprisoned, but it still lives on. The dream lives on in the hearts and minds of men. Shame, defeat, hopelessness and misery, as in the crucifixion and death of Christ, precedes and awaits the triumphant resurrection and manifestation in Christ, of all that have suffered the indignities of America's historical flirtation with racism and bigotry. Indeed, in the words of the Negro spiritual, we shall overcome.

Black America Today

A cursory look at Black America today presents a conflicting portrait of the state of the Black nation-race, one, perhaps, more abysmal on an international level than even America. Since 1957, when the Civil Rights Act was enacted, we have seen giant strides made by Black America. Laws extending equal rights and protection have been instituted.

The Voting Rights Act of 1965 made it possible for Blacks to vote without any inhibitions (at least on paper). Through Richard Loving, a White man, and his wife, Mildred, a Black woman, laws prohibiting anti-miscegenation were passed in 1967 by the US Supreme Court, legalizing and removing the stigma surrounding interracial marriages in the United States.

In the political and governmental arenas, great progress has been made also. We have had Blacks run as candidates for mayor and governor of major cities and states in the union and win. We have seen Black presidential candidates; the most formidable of them before President Barack Obama being the Rev. Jesse Jackson, vie for his party's nomination for president and greatly influence the political landscape. Condoleezza Rice is the first Black woman to serve as National Security Adviser and Secretary of State of the United States. We have seen a Black man in our life time become the Chairman of the Joint Chiefs of Staff and Secretary of State, in the person of General Colin Powell. Today, a Black man occupies the White House, the highest elected office in the land, all these, indeed, unthinkable a generation ago.

In the areas of sports and entertainment, Blacks have dominated, and are still dominating. Names like Oprah Winfrey, Denzel Washington, Halle Berry and Tiger Woods, have become household names and a testament to the possibilities available to African Americans in America today, fifty-plus years after the death of Dr. Martin Luther King and the advent of the Civil Rights movement. Thurgood Marshall and currently Clarence Thomas, Black justices, have served on the Supreme Court, the highest court of the land. We have seen the emergence of a Black middle class, albeit slowly, but nevertheless real, living in suburbia with all the conveniences and comforts of the White *brotherhood*—or sisterhood, if you so choose. In every area of human endeavor, from academia to golf, we see evidence of a Black presence and excellence, made available to Black Americans by virtue, and in fulfillment, of the dream. The other side of the coin, however, tells a completely different story of Black America. Unfortunately, it is often an embarrassing topic to discuss in a public forum, but nevertheless a necessary one, in my opinion.

In *Liberal Views, Black Victims*, Walter E Williams cites the high incidences of murder and violent crime in cities such as Baltimore, Detroit, and Washington, DC, cities densely populated by blacks. "This high murder rate is, and has been," he emphasizes "a Black problem." Citing statistical data from the Bureau of Justice, Williams further hammers the point. Between 1976 and 2005, he adds, Blacks, who comprise 13% of the population, committed over 52% of the nation's homicides and were 46% of the homicide victims. Ninety-four percent (94%) of Black homicide victims had a Black person as their murderer. Williams further drives the point home by emphasizing the sharp contrast between Black homicide rates and that of Japanese-Americans, which is almost negligible—1 per 100,000 (Williams 2016).

Cynthia Tucker, a syndicated columnist and editor for the Atlanta-Journal Constitution, also addresses the paradox in Black America. The success of the Civil Rights movement, she explains, enabled millions of Black Americans to join the nation's economic, political, and cultural mainstream. She underscores the fact that there are two Americas—both Black. One comprises the "accomplished, the educated, the pragmatic" whereas the other is populated with the "marginalized, the undereducated and the incarcerated." Herein lies the paradox: "As the middle class," Tucker explains, "has risen to new heights, the Black underclass has become more deeply mired in a troubling web of pathologies." A symptom of these pathologies is seen in Black incarceration rates. Black men and women, Tucker contends, made up 40% of prison inmates by 2006 compared to 34% in 1950, a period in American history when prejudice in the criminal justice system was more acute, with arrests and incarceration having become "a rite of passage" in poor Black neighborhoods (Tucker 2007).

The National Urban League's annual report for 2007 buttress these findings even further. Over 30 percent of young Black men drop out of high school—a higher rate than is observed for any other group. The dropout rate in inner-city schools is higher than that, by some estimates. On any given day, roughly 12 percent of all Black men, that is 1 out of 8, between the ages of 16 and 34, are incarcerated, while roughly twice this number are either on parole or probation. Many non-custodial fathers have steep child-support orders in arrears up to 65 percent of their meager earnings. Some of these "arrears" are due to "periods of incarceration." Between 4.5 and 5 million are ineligible to vote due to felon disenfranchisement laws. Out of these, over 2 million are Black (National Urban League 2007).

Issues of criminality in the Black community are as real as they are often personal, hitting close to home. Several years ago, I held a Financial Empowerment Seminar in a Black church, with a view to hire some for the company I worked for at the time. Almost three quarters of the church membership had felony convictions or a criminal history of some kind, making them ineligible for the opportunity I was offering.

Homicide accounts for 31 to 51 percent of mortality in fifteen- to thirty-four-year-old Black men, compared to only 7 to 10 percent in White males in the same age bracket.

The college completion rate for Black males is only 36 percent. Out of the number of African-American students who enrolled in 4-year degree programs between 1995/96–2001, only 43 percent graduated, compared to 63 percent for Whites.

In an article titled *Murder City in the Wall Street Journal*, Henry Payne highlights the violence in the city of Detroit, which FBI reports have concluded surpasses that of Chicago and New York, with its murder rate at 47 per 100,000 residents. The city is 81% Black, with a third of its residents living below the poverty line. The nuclear family is all but non-existent in the city. "According to academic research, over 50% of all Black men in Detroit are high-school dropouts." "In 2004, 72% of those drop-outs were jobless." "By their mid-30s, 60% have done prison time." "Among Black dropouts in their late 20s, per a University of California, Berkeley study, more are in prison (34%) than are working (30%)," a situation the author appropriately describes as "Cultural homicide" (Payne 2007).

The issue of Black cultural pathologies dates as far back as the sixties, when the Moynihan report was released. Daniel P. Moynihan, then assistant secretary of labor, based his report on the findings of E. Franklin Frazier, the notable Black historian whose book: *The Negro Family: A Call for Action*, provided a model for Black studies. Moynihan's report, labeled the Black family as "dysfunctional," a condition that was causing "the tangle of pathology" to tighten. The report also blamed the increasingly disparate levels of economic, educational, and social state of the Black community on a family structure that was becoming "highly unstable and in many urban centers approaching complete breakdown." This breakdown of the family, according to the report, can be traced to the legacy of slavery, growing urbanization, discrimination, and a tradition of matriarchy (Moynihan 1965). As is to be expected, these designations created no little uproar, especially in the Black community and some segments of the White establishment.

It is my conviction that for real or proper, as opposed to superficial, healing and reconciliation, based on race, to occur in America, the Black community has to negotiate its place on the American landscape from a position of strength, not weakness. Relationships and partnerships are negotiated in every department of life. Individuals, communities, businesses, and countries need each other, particularly in a globalized world and economy, and are in constant negotiation with each other for deals and mutually beneficial partnerships. Mutually-respectful relationships and partnerships tend to be more durable than those established with one partner strong, and the other, weak.

The ability to walk away from any deal or negotiation and not feel a sense of loss, lack of appreciation, or abuse is negotiating from a position of equality, strength, independence, or control. It is impossible for any one side to manipulate the other to their advantage when both sides are equally strong. Negotiating from a position of strength means both sides have something to offer, something the other side either wants or needs. It means bringing value to the table. The market only pays for value. One's stock value goes up in the marketplace when who you are, and what you have or bring to the table, is indispensable.

Thus, it will not be our common humanity alone that unites us and determines how we treat each other, but also the value each racial or ethnic group brings to the table. It is this sense of value that Black America and other minority groups must fight for. Not only does the marketplace pay for value, but life will also give us only what we are willing to fight for—nothing more, nothing less. This calls for serious introspection on our part. It also calls for doing away with negative and debilitating forces that militate against our personal or individual as well as group achievement and success. In this quest, I discuss six (6) factors which I believe are key to Black *Redemption and Lift,* or *Upward Social and Economic Mobility,* and ultimately, to racial healing and reconciliation. They are the following:

- Change: From Victim to Victor: Toward a Paradigm of Personal Responsibility
- The God Factor: A Platform of Faith (The Supreme Being and the Supreme Court)
- Family Matters: Setting the House in Order
- Breaking the Mental Shackles: Education, the Great Equalizer
- Economic Justice and Empowerment: The Check Marked Insufficient Funds

Join me as we address these in our next chapter.

CHAPTER 11

Black Redemption and Lift

*"I am thankful to all those who said, No.
Because of them, I did it myself."*
—**Wayne W. Dyer**

Early in elementary school, all of us are taught and become familiar with the meaning and importance of the equal sign. Basically, it means something on the left side of the equal sign or symbol, usually, a number, amounts to, or is "equal to" the number on the right side. If the number on one side changes, either by adding to or subtracting from it, the number on the other side must, of necessity, also change by the same amount added or subtracted. This is necessary for the equal sign to still be applicable, otherwise, the equal sign will be unfit and inappropriate for the equation.

The same principle may be applied to real life. It is often said that the meaning of insanity is doing the same things repeatedly and expecting a different result. Put another way, and in more practical terms, the meaning of insanity can be, for example, expecting to win or become more successful while remaining the *same person, with the same thinking, atti-*

tudes, and habits. That is untenable, mathematically, as it is practically. Life just does not work like that.

For change to occur in our circumstances, there must be a commensurate degree of change on the other side of the equation. Change on one side always requires, and must receive, reciprocal change on the other for the equal sign to still hold true. In real life, this may mean the learning or acquisition of new information. The new knowledge and insights gained from the new information then shifts our thinking, mentality, or paradigm in such a way that it translates into a reciprocal change in our behavior, work ethic, performance, and, ultimately, results. The entire trajectory of our lives and circumstances changes as well, consequently.

The price tag for freedom or progress in any field, therefore, is change. A definite change in racial attitudes, behavior, and actions needs to occur for racial healing and reconciliation to become a reality. A certain change is needed in White America for the debilitating complex of White supremacy or superiority to be eliminated. A change in the mentality of Blacks is necessary to rid ourselves of the equally debilitating inferiority complex and other negative attitudes that militate against our progress. Change in the Black body-politic is a prerequisite to achieving socioeconomic parity with our White counterparts and other groups in the American milieu. Socioeconomic parity is impossible without change in the Black body-politic. Such parity, again, is essential, for the sake of real healing and reconciliation based on race. Any change in destiny for the better, requires an equivalent change in direction. Charles Darwin said it this way: "It is not the strongest of the species that survives, or the most intelligent, but the species most responsive to change" (Darwin 1988).

Ancient Greek philosopher, Heraclitus, on the other hand, said, "Change is the only constant thing in the universe" (Mark 2010).

It is totally nonsensical to be lost, and to be aware that you are lost because you took the wrong turn and drove in the wrong direction but then, keep going in the same wrong direction. The common-sense thing to do is to stop, consult your Thomas guide or GPS navigation system, perhaps, for rerouting, or ask someone who knows the area well for help, and then turn around. Thus, as the ancient Chinese philosopher and writer, Lao Tzu says, "If you don't change direction, you may end up where you're headed."

Sticking to a particular way of life or behavior, when the times call for change, or a rigid adherence to a specific behavior pattern when the behavior in question is not producing the desired results, is as ridiculous as wearing winter clothes in scorching summer temperatures and vice versa. Fluidity must replace rigidity when times are changing. Professor Eddie Gibbs, in *Followed or Pushed,* debunks any such inclination to rigidity in changing times, describing such behavior "as foolhardy as turning a boat sideways to face the waves in the middle of a storm" (Gibbs 1986). You know as well as I do what outcome awaits this person—disaster. Changing times require an equivalent change in mentality, attitude, behavior, and performance.

Change: Toward a Paradigm of Personal Responsibility

"The soft-minded man always fears change; he feels security in the status quo, and he has an almost morbid fear of the new. For him the greatest pain is the pain of a new idea."
—**Martin Luther King Jr., Strength to Love (1963)**

In 2008, Barack Obama, ran as a candidate president of the United States on a mantra of, and call for *Change*. Such a call is vast in its implications for America, as a whole. For African Americans, Latinos, and other minorities, who have yet to feel fully socially and economically integrated into mainstream American society, this call was especially significant. Obama's call resonated with the nation. For many African Americans, it signified the dawning of a new era, an era of hope. Obama's candidacy symbolized and stirred the hopes of a generation; it lifted the cloud of impossibility and the stalemate that many minorities in this American cauldron had come to accept as their lot. Suddenly, the American dream, until now only a fleeting illusion, a mirage, had become a probability once again.

Tears flowed freely and uncontrollably, tears of both joy and disbelief, as Obama broke barriers, becoming the first Black man to win the nomination of major political party in America's history. Even more astounding was when he won the presidency. An epoch passed into the history books as a new one emerged, equally historical and powerful in its precedence. For me, it marked the rising of new nation, the United States of America, one that, at least symbolically, was beginning to live up to the true meaning of its creed, that all men are created equal. It signified the rising of a new Black America who, by his victory, had been given a shot in the arm in the attempt to attain equality in the land of their birth. Furthermore, it marked the emergence of a new generation of Americans in whose realm of reality, racism, and racial conflict had no place. It signified the readiness of a nation to deal with its racial demons and heal the wounds of its racial past, by embracing an African American for its highest office, the result of both White and Black Americans forging a strategic partnership.

Barack Obama's election was not only symbolic, but also prophetic in its implications. It reminds me of a time in the Bible when Israel found itself in the wilderness as she made her way from Egyptian captivity to the Promised Land. The Israelites, under the leadership of Moses, came to a place in the wilderness where certain skills were needed which Israel did not have. Clarity of vision and direction was needed. The context called for a people who were comfortable with, and knowledgeable of, the wilderness terrain, a people who could help the nation of Israel make its way through the dangers of the wilderness, of wild beasts and thorns. The survival skills needed to navigate this wilderness terrain lay in a man called Hobab, a Midianite, a dark-skinned people-group. It was Hobab, the Midianite, that God used to provide clarity of vision and direction in the wilderness. Numbers 10:29–32 tells the story.

Eyes in the Wilderness

"And Moses said unto Hobab, the son of Raguel, the Midianite, Moses father in law. Come with us and we will do thee good… Leave us not I pray thee for thou knowest that we are to encamp in the wilderness, and thou mayest be unto us instead as eyes…if thou go with us, whatever good the Lord do unto us, the same will we do to thee."
—*Numbers 10:29–32*

Who was Raguel, the Midianite? The name Raguel is sometimes rendered "Reuel" as in Exodus 2:18. The scripture above refers to him as Moses's father-in-law. In Exodus 3:1 as in Exodus 18:1–8, his name is Jethro, a Kenite shepherd (Judges 1:16) and Priest of Midian. One of Jethro's daughters, Zipporah, is given to Moses in marriage after Moses serves the seven daughters at the well. Moses's marriage to Zipporah is met with contempt from Aaron, and his sister, Miriam, their contempt for Zipporah being that she is Ethiopian, or a Cushite, of African descent (Numbers 12:1). The displeasure from the two seems to stem from her darker complexion, an obvious characteristic of the Cushites or Ethiopians (Jer. 13:23). It stands to reason, in any case, that if Zipporah was Ethiopian (*Ethios*—dark or burnt, *Opus*—face), or Cushite, Cush being the oldest son of Ham, and the progenitor of the African races, that her father, Jethro (also Raguel or Reuel), and brother, Hobab, would all have had to either be Ethiopian or Cushite or, at least, had some African roots.

That Moses would entreat Hobab, a dark-skinned man, to guide God's people as they encounter the wilderness terrain is quite striking in its implications. Moses would not have sought Hobab's help under normal circumstances, but Hobab and his people, have adaptation and survival instincts and skill-sets, endowed by nature's God, upbringing, geographical location, and life experience, unknown to Israel. Survival instincts, creativity, keener vision, a ruggedness, resilience, fortitude, the ability to avoid traps in the dark, terror by night, the ability to work with very little, and making something happen when there is nothing are skills that one raised in that environment, like Hobab, brings to the table. It is simply a result of being in touch with the wilderness terrain. Ironically, this is how Blacks, for the most part must live, not only in America but the world over—life has taught us to survive, no matter what. We have been shaped by our life-circumstances to make things happen out of nothing. It is little wonder that Hobab and his people should be called at this time to serve as "eyes" to Israel in the wilderness.

Prophetically, Barack Obama's election to the presidency, as always, is a call for a special or particular kind of leadership for a special time and place. God has a way of always matching "man" and moment, with respect to leadership. He (God) rules in the kingdoms and affairs of men. He gives it whosoever he wants or chooses, and sometimes places the least important of men over them (Daniel 4:17), irrespective of our politics or preferences. He is the judge, He puts down one and sets up another (Ps. 75:7); after all, He is no respecter of persons (Acts 10:34). He takes the foolish things to shame the wise, the weak to confound the mighty and those disregarded and despised for His purposes (1 Cor. 1:26–28).

President Obama's election was a call from among the lowly and socially, less-significant, to utilize valuable, time-tested character traits, shaped by America's racial politics in the life of a Black kid, the offspring of biracial parents. As the son of a full-fledged or indigenous Cushite from Kenya and a White mother, a daughter of Japheth, from Kansas, his creative adaptation, perspectives, instincts, and worldview, informed by his experiences, would be rather unique. These, combined with the grace of God, were earmarked not only to provide vision, purpose, and direction, but also bring stability to a country on the brink of a major national and financial crisis, in essence, become "eyes" in the wilderness. Obama's election, besides, was a call to break with the past routines and convention, and chart a new course—with unconventional people, the least among us, with unconventional skills as partners.

For Blacks and all people of color, as well, it is a prophetic call to break with the past and begin to look at life afresh and through different lenses. It is definitely not a call to continued servitude, as slaves or as second-class citizens in an oppressive and racist system, but a call to fulfilling prophetic destiny as a people, through humility, introspection, service, and leadership in tough times, by embracing and effecting change, first in our lives, and then in the status quo. For Moses and Israel, forging a strategic partnership with Hobab and his people was necessary because of the peculiar times, circumstances, and the skills that Hobab and his people brought to the table. Until now, Hobab is an obscure figure, a virtual unknown in the Bible; he is insignificant. However, when the times call for change, for fresh and visionary leadership, with a fresh perspective in tumultuous times, the son of Jethro, the priest of Midian, a Cushite, is the man for the hour. Change, for Black America, and all Blacks in the motherland and in the diaspora, therefore, means rising to the challenge of the new situational demands of our time, not just in America, but globally. It is a call to leadership through servanthood and service in turbulent times.

Another important piece of the request from Moses often forgotten about, is the assurance He gives Hobab, Jethro's son, as an inducement or incentive, perhaps, to come along with Israel: "If thou go with us, whatever good the Lord do unto us, the same will we do to thee" (Numbers 10:32). Another translation says, "*If you come with us, we will share with you all the blessings the Lord gives us*" (NLT). For anyone still with any inclination to think or believe that Blacks are a cursed people, therein lies another truth, a blessing. There is no indication in the scriptures that Hobab did not oblige Moses. For all intents and purposes, therefore, Hobab and his people, served as "eyes" in the wilderness, providing vision and direction, with an expectation of sharing in the covenant promises of God to His people, Israel. May it be eternally known and emphatically stated that Blacks are a blessed people.

Change: Requirement for Success and Leadership in Black America

Change is a requirement for progress and success in every sphere of life. The only constant thing in the universe, Einstein says, is change. The times require us, as a country, society and community, to change. The demands of racial healing and reconciliation require us also to change. Change is critical for the socioeconomic advancement of Black America. Achieving parity with our White counterparts and other ethnic groups in the American milieu is impossible without change. Some changes are harder to achieve than others, and some are spiritual, physical, mental, and even subliminal. Nevertheless, the journey of change must begin somewhere. A journey of a thousand miles always begins with the first step. It is time to take the first step. Let us examine the concept of change further, and some particular areas of change we need to look at as a community.

First, whatever you can tolerate, you will never change. No one changes when conditions are tolerable or going well. **Question:** When was the last time you changed, or saw someone change when everything was going well and either you or they were comfortable? The worst time to recruit a person for another job they know very little about is when they just got a major promotion on their current job, with great benefits. Most people refuse to change when they do not hurt enough. If the status quo serves you well and you are satisfied with it, why change it? If one is satisfied with being on welfare, with bad credit, or living from paycheck to paycheck, why would they change that? If being in a relationship is so important to you that you choose to stay in it, despite the abuse, you would never change it. Changing one's life from failure to success, or poverty to prosperity, thus, begins with a strong dissatisfaction with the status quo. A strong, emotional "why" precedes every major form of change. The rewards or benefits of change must outweigh the cost and pain of not changing before any form of change occurs. It is the equivalent and essence of a cost-benefit analysis.

Without change, death is certain. Every living organism grows and growth requires change. Growth and change are both evidence of life. Without change, death is certain. One theory that has been propounded by scientists to explain the demise and extinction of the dinosaurs, some 65 million years ago, pertains to their inability to change and adapt to the colder temperatures of the ice age, known as the Mesozoic Era.

What about Blackberry? There was a time Blackberry was the phone to have, with Fortune Magazine naming Blackberry the fastest growing company among the one hundred fastest-growing companies in the world in 2009. Its parent company, launched in 1999 under the name Research in Motion, made Wall Street and Capitol Hill buzz with its usage, primarily because of its email capabilities, making it the prized-possession and phone of choice for many. Emails were received, in real time, with its "push email" feature. In 2010, Blackberry was purported to enjoy the highest market share in the smartphone industry in the US. The company's fortunes begun to encounter a downturn, however, when Apple introduced its iPhone, with touchscreen features. The iPhone gained instant traction among consumers, including the business community, whose patronage of Blackberry had helped propel it to the top. It was followed by several Android mobile gadgets, together making the Blackberry look unexciting and antiquated. The inability to discern the movement of the market from keyboards to touchscreen navigation, from mere communication devices to full-blown, hand-held, on-the-go entertainment centers, to change and innovate accordingly, made it extremely difficult for Blackberry to maintain its competitive edge, leading to its eventual demise.

Consider the Swiss watch industry, also: In the mid-1970s, Quartz technology shifted the balance of power from the Swiss, historic leaders in the global watch industry, to a rising giant from Asia, Japan. The Swiss were shut out from the market for *two* reasons: First was their refusal to *change and respond* to the new wave of digital, electronic watches. Secondly, watches had become fashion accessories and status symbols instead of mere timepieces. The failure to recognize this new trend and respond accordingly also cost them their market share. We should, therefore, never fight change but rather consider it **a** friend, not an enemy. It is the chisel of God for our growth and success. It is life's manure for nurture and progress. Success, progress, and prosperity tend to find those who change and innovate the most, with changing times; they often win the most.

As African Americans, we need to intentionally change the largely distorted self-image and identity crisis shaped by negative stereotypes from the society we live in. The sad thing about this is that many of us have bought wholesale into these negative stereotypes and live them out in our daily lives. We often act based on our self-perception. You do not have to tell me you feel less than or inferior; I can tell from the way you behave or act that you have an inferiority complex. If you think of and see yourself as a fool, you are going to act a fool; if you think you are God's gift to women or vice versa, you are going to act as such. On the other hand, if you think, believe, and see yourself as a child of the living God, created for good works, endowed with creative power and genius, to make a difference in your world, you will behave in ways consistent with that belief and mind-set.

The good thing is that we have the power not to succumb to these negative stereotypes, but instead break that mentality and cycle, and choose to think, believe, and act differently from every negative stereotype imposed on us by our environment. We are not second-class citizens or inferior; to the contrary, we are fearfully and wonderfully made, in God's sight (Ps. 139:14). We are a people of purpose and destiny, with a mission to fulfill on Earth.

Change means to stop equating ignorance and lack of education with being Black or "cool," and conversely, equating education, knowledge, and speaking well with being or acting White. Even in Africa (Ghana, to be precise) this mentality is prevalent. A well-educated person may be referred to by parents or family as *Me Buroni* (Twi) or me *Blofo nyo* (Ga), literally translated, "My White man or woman." Being average and mediocre are no Blacker than education, excellence, or speaking well are White. Good standards, manners, communication skills, etc., are good and equal opportunity; they belong to every human being and will work for anyone, regardless of color, race, or ethnicity.

In a world where the color Black has an evil and sinister connotation, and White represents all that is pure, positive, and celestial, one can understand how standards of excellence are equated with White, and mediocrity and all that is negative and contrary to excellence, with Black. Being Black is no accident of creation. I am, and you are "fearfully and wonderfully made..." and in the very image of God. Not only do we have to quit confusing the resident (the real you—your spirit) with the residence, we also need to understand how intricately, and delicate God made even our bodies. Being fearfully made speaks to the intrinsic and inestimable value of all humans. The capabilities of the human being, the number of cells in our bodies (in the billions!) and how they all function, synergistically, is beyond human comprehension. It can only be fully explained by an amazing Creator, who knows the exact number of hairs you have on your head (Matthew 10:30), and custom-made every single individual, ethnicity, and people group according to their unique purpose on earth.

Change means shifting from blaming racism and the White man for all our woes. If you are upset about your situation, stop blaming your parents, your family, boss, racism, or the White man. Allow your anger or frustration to become the fuel you need to rise above your circumstances. Anger and resentment do not achieve much, especially if directed at the wrong thing or person. "The wrath (anger or resentment) of man does not work the righteousness of God" (James 1:20). Blaming the White man for everything is granting him too much power over my life. It is as if to say, "This man is so powerful, and he has so messed me up and so impacted my life and destiny, that I am paralyzed beyond recovery, and unable to do anything for myself." No one says it like that, but our actions oftentimes speak louder than what we are not saying.

There is no doubt that the White man has committed some atrocious acts. That the legacies of his actions are still with us is also indisputable. That the White Man is yet to properly "'fess up to the mess" he has committed is also true. That America and the world are still grappling with the vestiges and wounds of colonialism, neo-colonialism, slavery, apartheid, imperialism, etc. are all very true. However, blaming him for all our woes is equally wrong, and two wrongs, per the sages, do not a right make. Blaming everything on racism and the White man paralyzes not him but you. He becomes a corpse or noose around your neck all over again.

The blame game has been with us since Eden. Adam blamed both God and Eve: "It was the woman you gave me," he charged (Gen. 3:12). Ruling governments blame the opposition, players blame coaches, employees blame employers, wives blame husbands, Republicans blame Democrats, atheists blame God, Marxists blame religion and the bourgeoisie, while many Africans, Native Americans, and two-thirds of world cultures and people-groups lay the burden of all mishaps squarely at the feet of witchcraft and demon spirits. The blamed return fire, blaming the blamer, all the above players mentioned above, invariably, caught in an apparent web of vindictiveness and finger-pointing. The blame game thus continues unabated.

When we point the (accusing) finger instead of owning our mistakes, we only shift the spotlight and responsibility from us to others. Momentarily, this absolves us of the guilt, burden, and shame of our own foibles (or junk...if you will). In so doing, we gain relief, but only temporarily, the act of blaming another only turning us into hopeless, paralyzed victims of our circumstances instead of victors and arbiters of our own destinies. Long term, passing the buck, most importantly, robs us of the opportunity for critical introspection, growth, character transformation and formation, all intangible, yet extremely valuable assets which accrue to us through the very pressure or pain we despise and try to avoid or escape.

"Smart leaders own their decisions, their actions, words and outcomes, good and/or bad and therefore reap the benefits of taking responsibility" (Wilson). When we reorient our thinking to embrace the fear, vulnerability required, and possible reprisals for "'fessing up" to, or owning our mistakes and flaws, the pain and pressure automatically become the manure or fertilizer for personal nurture and development, critical keys for our eventual coronation in a highly competitive world.

Change implies a willingness to do a critical self-evaluation, attentively listening to divergent views, especially from our loyal opposition. It also implies embracing some of the voices of criticism of our community to see if there is any validity to what others, both within and outside the community, are saying. Change also implies subsequently addressing those issues in our culture which are inimical to our advancement. It is important to understand that not every "negative" thing that is said about us is false or racist. It is ignorant and foolhardy to turn a deaf ear to every criticism that is leveled at us and label it racist, even if constructive.

Racism is real, so our sensitivities and paranoia are not unfounded, but so are our issues. For example, as African Americans, we know that the Criminal Justice System is unfavorable toward us; it is racist in a lot of ways. Racial profiling for Blacks and Latinos, especially, are not illusions; they are part of our reality as Blacks or Latinos in America. It is a major factor in why the Criminal Justice System is disproportionately biased against Blacks leading to the incarceration of thousands of Black and Latino young men. President Bill Clinton, the man Toni Morrison referred to as America's "first Black President," came under fire for policies put in place by his administration that led to the incarceration of thousands of Black and Latino men. One statistic put the prison population of Blacks at 40%, although the Black population is only 13% of the entire America population. By the same statistic, Whites make up only 39% of the prison population, although Whites represent 64% of the American population (Center for American Progress 2015).

However, knowing that the system is already stacked against us, we also need to ask ourselves, what is it in our culture, if anything, that allows our kids to play into the very trap that has been set for them, knowing well that the system is already out to get them? My point is that, at the end of the day, one cannot simply place all the blame on the system. There are external forces arrayed against us beyond our control, but there are internal forces within our control, and those are the ones that need to be identified and addressed as a community. The ability to admit and accept our flaws is not a sign of weakness, but of humility and strength.

Criticism can have positive and constructive effects. Critiquing one's self is a healthy habit to form. Scripture admonishes us to "examine" ourselves (2 Cor. 13:5). Also, to judge or examine ourselves, that we be not judged (1 Cor. 11:31). The implication here is that if we would personally search our own selves and rectify our wrongs, no one would have anything on us, unless they falsify the evidence, because we would have already done our homework. Embracing criticism, therefore, has the power to reveal blind spots in our lives that hopefully we can rectify in order to grow or make progress as a community. It is why we often say, "Check yourself before you wreck yourself."

Change also means social and economic uplift and parity for Black America and all minority groups. This requires a radical shift within the Black community itself, from a paradigm of dependency, to a self-reliant, "do it yourself" approach. Social and economic uplift and parity for Blacks and minority groups calls for an intentional change of a mentality that embraces welfare dependency, illegitimacy, and dysfunction as an authentic Black alternative. It calls for a mentality that intentionally resists the culture of low expectations and mediocrity, as well as self-destructive and nihilistic tendencies to which a lot of our children, growing up without fathers or father figures, are beholden to. Social and economic uplift requires vision and self-motivation, instead of depending on someone or a system, such as welfare, that long-term, only stifles your creative and productive capacities and keeps you broke. There is no self-worth in welfare, especially, when it becomes a permanent feature of one's life. We are called to be productive; "Be fruitful and multiply and replenish the earth and subdue it...and have dominion..." (Gen 1:26) were the first and foremost instructions to Adam and Eve. I recommend a self-help approach to Black redemption and lift, because what happens if the one you are depending on to motivate or pump you up never shows up? I am afraid that if we wait on America to come to grips with its social responsibility to its poor and marginalized, we might be waiting a long time. We have already waited a long time and in continuing to wait, we will miss out on the great promises and opportunities that a strategic moment in our history has offered us.

Change from a victim to a victor mentality by taking personal responsibility for yourself and your destiny. It strikes me as quite interesting any time I see people on the sidewalk or street corners, sometimes homeless, begging for food, money, or handouts. My first instinct is to carefully observe the dynamics at work—that is, who they are, their race or ethnicity, their disposition, whether they are high, drunk, or sober, and what is written on the signs they are carrying. Nine times out of ten, they happen to be either White or Black. Occasionally, you may see someone Asian among them, but that is very rare, in my experience. Among the White and Black individuals holding the sign, you will usually find a Latino brother, not holding a sign begging for alms like the others, but a bouquet of flowers or several bags of oranges, offering them for sale for very little. Usually, the

Latino man can hardly speak any English, whereas the White and Black individuals communicate in fluent English.

This scenario is not a one-time event, but something I have observed for years in Palmdale and Los Angeles, where I have lived for almost half my adult life. Several issues become apparent here. First, the Black and White brothers are probably American, while the Latino brother is most likely not. Second, the two speak English fluently, and probably have no language or communication barriers, whereas the Latino guy probably does. Even though I have no way of proving this, my guess is that the Black and White brothers have no problems with their residency in America; they often look like "bona fide Americans"—born and raised in America, or at least having migrated to America when they were much younger. The Latino brother, based on mere conjecture, probably has problems with his legal residency in the US. If all these assumptions are indeed the case, how do we explain the differences in attitude? Why would someone born here in America, with no communication barriers, and possibly no issues with legal residency, end up begging for food and money on street corners, while another, with all the decks stacked against him (language, papers etc.) stand at the same street corner, hustling to make something happen out of nothing?

This is, obviously, no scientific enquiry; however, it is evident that the life experiences of these groups of men have fashioned them into who they are. It is these experiences that have shaped their sense of responsibility, and it is this sense of responsibility, in turn, that drives each of them to do whatever they deem necessary to make life in America meaningful and worth living for them. I am not sure what this Latino man had to go through to get to America, but if my "relatively easy" experience (almost ten years on the waiting list) compared to what others must endure to get to America is anything to go by, he must have gone through some very challenging circumstances to finally get here. The struggle it took for him to finally make it to America, perhaps, a lifelong dream, is enough motivation for him, to be responsible and make it work. Furthermore, there is family, perhaps, comprising not only a wife and kids back home in his country of origin, but also an extended family consisting of a father, mother, siblings, aunties, uncles, and cousins, all counting on him for their sustenance. It is this level of expectation on him to deliver, and the accountability that goes with it, that serve as the force or fuel to his sense of personal responsibility. Despite his obvious struggles, this man does not see himself as a victim, but a victor. He is not waiting for anyone to pick him up; he is propelled intrinsically to lift himself from the doldrums, and ultimately his family, as well. His sense of purpose, his reason for being, a strong and emotional why, shaped by his struggles and life-experiences, propel him to higher heights. If you have had to swim through shark-infested waters to get to America, the land of opportunity, you do not easily squander your opportunity.

"If first class citizenship is to become a reality for the Negro, he must assume primary responsibility for making it so" (King 1960.).

Les Brown in turn says, "Accept responsibility for your life…it is you who will get you where you want to go, no one else" (Brown n.d.).

John Maxwell also emphasizes that the day we truly grow up, that is: "The greatest day in your life and mine is when we take total responsibility for our attitudes" (Maxwell n.d.).

One of the biggest hurdles to taking responsibility for your life and aiming for the top is a victim mentality. A victim mentality is toxic and self-sabotaging. It is disempowering because it dwells on the wounds of the past, thereby taking the responsibility for failure and ineptitude from an individual and consistently places it on others. It dwells on past failures because it derives its power from negative events in the past. It is difficult to be a possibility-thinker or future-oriented with a victim mind-set. After four hundred years under Egyptian captivity and servitude, Israel developed such a mentality. Though they prayed to be delivered from slavery and bondage, their foremost instinct upon encountering any challenge pertaining to their future, was to blame Moses for delivering them from Egypt, and to demand a return to the place of bondage, apparently (and in a morbid way) now a comfort zone, much more appealing than the liberty and prosperity which lay in their future (Ex. 16:3, Num. 14:4). It is a visionless, colonial mentality that is fixated on the past and its hurts. Steve Maraboli says a victim mentality is like holding your own breath and blaming others for your inability to breathe (Maraboli n.d.).

A victim mentality and success are incompatible; they have nothing in common. Like oil and water, they are poles apart. We either choose to remain victims or change and take responsibility for our actions and destinies. The call to racial healing and reconciliation will demand of us as a community, to rid ourselves of any tendency toward a victim mentality. Achieving any degree of upward mobility will not come by dwelling on the past, but rather on the future. We cannot drive forward looking in the rearview mirror. Dwelling on the past is a recipe for disaster on the road of life. We cannot change the past. Dwelling on the pain of an abusive relationship one endured ten, twenty, or thirty years ago, simply makes one toxic and unattractive, to one's own detriment. Toxicity and success are not the best of friends. Let the past and its failures guide us into making better and more productive choices and decisions, but keep your focus on today and tomorrow, i.e., the present and future. The apostle Paul puts it best when he states in Philippians 3:13–14: "This one thing I do, forgetting what is behind and straining toward what is ahead, I press on toward the goal to win the prize for which God has called me heavenward in Christ Jesus."

Paul's attitude should be our attitude.

When I let go of the past, as well as the victim mentality associated with it, and take personal responsibility for my actions, first, it puts me, not someone else, in charge of my life and destiny. Secondly, it is a recognition that I am exactly where I am in my life because of the person I am, and/or have chosen to be. In other words, I am the sum-total of the decisions and choices I have made till this point. Thirdly, I also recognize that I cannot get to where I want to get to if I stay who or where I am. My actions, every single one of them made based on sound choices and decisions and consistent with my core values, beliefs, and principles, henceforth will become vital and integral to my future success. My business, relationships, performance, and results, now my personal responsibility, will grow, get better, and increase (or not) in direct proportion to the personal mistakes and flaws I own and the changes I am willing to personally make to overturn them. In other words, the day I decide to embrace change and actually begin the journey of change is the day my business, marriage, performance, or life also begins to turn around for the better. I have the power. The power to change and succeed is mine. Nobody controls or manipulates it because it is in my hands. This is the attitude that turns lives and destinies around. It is a *winner's* or *victor's* attitude and mentality.

RICHARD D. DONKOR

The God Factor: A Platform of Faith (The Supreme Being or Supreme Court)

"We are a religious people whose institutions presuppose a Supreme Being."
—Supreme Court Justice William Orville Douglas

There is no doubt that the *ministry of reconciliation* (2 Cor. 5:18), specifically racial healing and reconciliation, is at the crux of God's call and agenda for His Church, the Body of Christ, in America. It is my conviction that the Church in America stands at the precipice of internal, monumental shifts, a revival if you will, that will usher in a wave of healing and reconciliation based on race among its ranks, and cause black, white, brown, yellow, and red Christians, and the multiplicity of colors and cultures in between, to worship and celebrate Christ together, without any inhibitions or hesitation.

A divided church cannot bring healing to a divided world; only a united church can. For the broader American society to experience not superficial, but authentic healing and reconciliation among the plurality of races gathered here, the church needs to get its act together. It must be the "city on a hill," the light that, indeed, illuminates the prevailing darkness of racial rancor and polarization. God, undoubtedly, must be at the center of such a move. God must be at the forefront of any efforts at bringing Whites and Blacks together. God must be the facilitator of the major changes that need to occur on both sides, and in the Black community, with the unique challenges confronting it, if upward socioeconomic mobility is to be achieved. Human instrumentation alone will not do it. Social or political intervention may make a dent in our racial politics, but none can permanently put centuries of hate, mistrust, and suspicion away and behind us. America needs God—a return to and faith in God—to achieve these monumental tasks.

There is no denying, therefore, the need and centrality of faith in all human endeavors. "Unless the Lord build the house," Scripture says, "they labor in vain that build it" (Ps. 127:1). Afeni Shakur, the mother of the famed rapper Tupac Shakur, highlighted the importance of engaging and involving God Almighty, the Supreme Being and Creator, in our human, even political discourse. To her, the biggest mistake the Black Panther Party made "was to take God out of the movement" (Shakur 2003). It is this ingredient, faith and reliance on the grace and power of a living and loving God who rules in the affairs of men, that America cannot afford to miss, as we continue our quest for racial healing and reconciliation, the need for Black redemption and lift to achieve that end, and the critical changes that need to occur in the Black body politic, some of which have been already highlighted in the previous chapter, to achieve this. *The God Factor: Establishing a Platform of Faith* from where everything springs, thus, is the focus of this chapter. Will America look to its political, economic, social, and judicial institutions, like the Criminal Justice System or Supreme Court alone, to institute law and order or heal the historical divides between its people-groups, or will it trust the Supreme Being, the God who rules in the kingdom of men, on whom and on whose principles, we claim our country was founded, to effect legitimate and lasting change in its racial discourse—the politics of race?

"Faith," Helen Keller once stated, "is the strength by which a shattered world shall emerge into the light" (Kellee n.d.). "Faith is taking the first step," Dr. King stated, "even when you don't see the whole staircase." Paul the Apostle describes it as "the substance of things hoped for" and "the evidence of things unseen" (Heb. 11:1). Faith is that intangible but real force that adds substance to our hopes, connects humanity to divinity, the natural to the supernatural, making the unseen or invisible visible and the impossible possible. It is that basic trust in a divine power and presence that elevates the human spirit from the mundane and ordinariness to the place of extra-ordinariness, where exploits become the norm, the mediocre becomes excellent, and the low and inferior achieves dignity, self-esteem, and confidence. By faith, the weak, the broken-hearted, foolish, fearful, the incompetent, impotent, and skeptical are touched and elevated to become power-houses, repositories, and exemplars of God's goodness, grace, and loving kindness. By faith, barren wombs are made fertile, impenetrable darkness encounters light, unconquerable mountains of adversity are leveled and become a plain, valleys of despair are filled with hope again, and crooked paths are made straight. Hence, Jesus's words that "all things are possible to him that believes" (Mark 9:23).

Dr. Martin Luther King, in *Strength to Love* (King 1963), discusses how fallen humanity often feels the need to assert its independence from God. "At times we feel we don't need God," he states. He argues, however, that there are times when disappointment, disaster, and grief descend on our lives, tearing us apart. Those times call for a deep and abiding faith in God. Some have made pleasure, money, even science, their gods. Science has given us the atomic bomb, and with it have come all manner of anxiety and fear. With all the money, we worship and idolize, we often still come to points in our lives when we realize that there are things like love and friendship money cannot buy. In an unpredictable world characterized by stock market crashes and bad business investments, money, Dr. King admonishes, may well be "an uncertain deity" to depend on. None of these transitory gods, he mentions, can fill the void in the human heart; only God can. "It is faith in Him that we must rediscover," he concludes (King 1963). I totally concur not only with the need for rediscovering our faith, but also its revitalization. Nothing fills the void in the human soul like faith does. For the mammoth challenges facing our nation, and the nations of the world, the need and centrality of faith cannot and must not be discounted. Righteousness, indeed, does exalt a nation, but sin is a reproach to any people (Prov. 14:34).

Secular Humanism: The Anti-God Campaign

"Remove not the ancient landmarks your fathers have set..."
—*Proverb 22:28*

"Religion is the sigh of the oppressed creature, the sentiment of a heartless world, and the soul of soulless conditions...it is the opium of the people."
—Karl Marx

Despite our need for God and faith to be integral components of our personal and national lives, there is an emerging phenomenon significantly impacting America, and most cities of the world today, that seeks to undermine the place of faith in our national discourse. This phenomenon known as postmodernity, with its twin corollaries of secularism and pluralism, both cultural and religious, are already militating against the God Factor, particularly, in the public square.

Postmodernity is the intellectual and cultural ethos that is increasingly becoming dominant in contemporary society. It has been described as "a cultural shift of seismic proportions, which affects every area of society" (Gibbs 2001). William Easum calls it a transition from the industrial to the "Quantum Age" (Easum 1997), a change from a world of slow incremental change to one which is discontinuous, unpredictable and chaotic, without any clearly defined contours. The postmodern ethos rejects any leanings toward prepositional truth. Knowledge is no longer objective and certain. There is ambivalence about the truth and any leanings toward absolute truth is met with caution and suspicion. "To each his own" best describes this ethos and the cultural mood it fosters.

Post-modernity is tolerable of other viewpoints because of the assumption that there are a lot of gray areas to truth. This tolerance carries over to the accepting, affirming and celebrating of diversity and pluralism, whatever form it takes. Furthermore, post-modernity is characterized by an accelerated pace of change. The collapse of the Berlin wall, the disintegration of the Soviet Union, the pace of development in certain fields of study, such as Genetic engineering (cloning), are but a few cases that point to this acceleration.

Living with paradox and absurdity is a call that post-modernity will make on nations, as well as the Church. It will continue to render distinctives irrelevant, especially distinctives pertaining to church life, such as modes of baptism (e.g., *Infant Baptism/Anabaptism, Calvinism/Arminianism* etc.). Consequently, the postmodern mind-set feels comfortable affirming, both traditional, classical Christian doctrines such as "*resurrection*," as well as such non-Christian beliefs as "*reincarnation*." For them it is not a matter of "either/or," but a matter of "both/and." For people, raised under classical Christian traditions, this may be absurd, even heretical, but not to the postmodern generation.

Added to this cultural phenomenon, is the increasing drift toward cultural and ethnic pluralism. With postmodernity, has come religious pluralism. Most American cities today are multi-faith. Immigrants from Hindu, Buddhist, Sikh and Muslim backgrounds comprise the American multireligious milieu. In such a context, Newbigin says, "an appeal to the Bible is simply an expression of one's personal choice among a host of choices." The gospel, rendered relative in a pluralistic American context, implies that any "confident statement of ultimate belief or claim to absolute truth about God, or anything for that matter, is liable to be dismissed as ignorant, arrogant, and dogmatic" (Newbigin 1989).

In America, and most western industrialized nations of the world, the dogmatism or absolutism of the past, has given way to a pluralistic, syncretistic view of religion, with the gospel as just one other player among several. The atheistic view of God under modernity which assured the "death of God" (Cox 1966) has been replaced by a pantheistic world-view, which assumes the existence of God, but yet asks the question, "Which God?" It is the secularization of postmodern society, with its attendant cultural and religious pluralism, that have some calling the inclusion of "One Nation Under God" in our Pledge of Allegiance, "In God We Trust" on our coins, and any attempts at reintroducing traditional American values into our social systems and culture, like prayer in schools, offensive, and a violation of their civil rights. It is against this backdrop, that the call for the revitalization of faith is made. It is also against this backdrop that the calls for racial healing and reconciliation, as well as for change, and upward social and economic mobility for Black America are made.

For Black America removing that "ancient landmark" (Prov. 22:28) of faith in a God who is Supreme and above all, is and would be a recipe for disaster. A return to the faith that sustained our forefathers and mothers, as they made their way through the "middle passage" to the Americas, or to Europe, is non-negotiable; it is a must. Thankfully, although only 13% of the total population of the US, Blacks comprise about 25% of worshipers in America's mega-churches. It is no accident that the values we espouse as a nation and the human rights we enjoy as a people were founded on Judeo-Christian principles. America's Civil Rights Movement was galvanized under the banner of the Southern Christian Convention, and under the able leadership of Dr. Martin Luther King Jr., an ordained minister.

In the Supreme Being, and our faith in Him, lie the amazing grace that sustained our forebears. In that selfsame faith, lies the amazing grace that will lift and lead America, and all its people groups to the place of redemption, healing and reconciliation. Again, may we never remove this ancient landmark of faith as a people. The day we do, is the day the process of our demise as a nation, begins, for God is keenly interested and serves as an active participant in the affairs of men and nations.

God Rules in the Affairs of Men: The Rise and Fall of Nations in Bible Prophecy

"Blessed be the name of God forever and ever, for wisdom and power are his; and he changes the times and seasons, he removes kings and sets up kings..."
—*Daniel 2:20–21*

"God has made the world and all things therein... And has made of one blood all nations of men to dwell on the face of the earth and has determined the times (kairos—seasons

336

of opportunity) before appointed (i.e., history—birth,
development, decline or death) and the bounds of their
habitations (i.e., geography) that they should seek the Lord..."
—*Acts 17:26–27*

Contrary to popular belief, God is keenly interested in how nations are founded and governed. The Bible is a book about nation-building. In it, God provides humanity with a template on the subject, starting with the call of Abraham. In Genesis 12:1–3, He enumerates a litany of blessings he would bestow upon Abraham and his posterity for his obedience, beginning with "I will make you a great nation" (v. 2). The values inculcated in the citizenry, the caliber of leadership He desires, systems of governance to be employed and principles for a humane and civil society, not to mention dietary and business principles for sustaining the health, success, and prosperity of His people, are all outlined, and revealed in time.

It is important to note that God's system of government starts with a solid religious foundation for His people. This is to serve as a prototype and guide to all human leadership and governance, because "righteousness exalts a nation, but sin is a reproach to any people" (Prov. 14:34). This righteous standard of living is to be woven into the fabric of the community and citizenry, God's people, through a solid and dynamic relationship with God, beginning with those who lead His people. It was up to the leadership and those in authority to seek Him, and then transfer this pursuit of, and allegiance to God to the people. Acts 17:27, captures this thought; it explains how God sets the geographical boundaries of nations, and determines their birth, growth and development, as well as their death.

The purpose was for the nations to seek after God, reach out to Him and find Him (Acts 17:27). Satan's temptation in the garden was to thwart this pursuit of God on mankind's part, resist God's authority and assert his independence from God, to his own demise. That modus operandus is still in vogue and remains an operative strategy of the devil till this today. When leaders resist the authority of God, violate His commandments, and become gods unto themselves, the impact of their actions is felt, not only by them, but also by the nations and people they lead. That God rules in the kingdoms and affairs of mankind, is undeniable. His sovereignty over nations, empires and civilizations is revealed in the biblical encounters below.

The Babylonian, Medo-Persian, Greek, and Roman Empires

"But God is the judge, He puts down
one and setteth up another."
—*Psalm 75:7*

"And when ye shall see Jerusalem compassed about
with armies…and they shall fall by the edge of the
sword and shall be led away captive into all Nations
and Jerusalem shall be trodden down of the Gentiles
until the times of the Gentiles be fulfilled."
—*Luke 21:24*

This prophecy by Jesus in response to a question posed by his disciples about the end-times, has a direct bearing on the dream of King Nebuchadnezzar, the despotic king of Babylon, its interpretation and prophetic implications, as recorded in the second chapter of the book of Daniel. The prophecy foretold the repercussions of Israel's rebellion and persistent violation of God's laws, the fall of Judah and the Babylonian captivity of the Jews, an event that was to complete Israel's dispersion among the nations. It also addresses prophetically, the rise and fall of various empires and kingdoms, leading up to Christ's return to earth to set up His kingdom and usher in His millennial rule: This event occurs after *"the times of the Gentiles be fulfilled"* Let us get to the details of this end-time prophecy.

Babylonian Empire: During the time of the Babylonian captivity of Judah, Israel's southern neighbor, King Nebuchadnezzar has a rather puzzling dream, which defies all interpretation by the magicians, sorcerers and wise men of the land. It takes Daniel, a captive Jewish man *"in whom the spirit of God is..."* to finally bring any meaning and understanding to bear on his dream. The dream was of eschatological significance, foretelling *"what shall be in the latter times"* (Dan. 2:28).

The King's Dream (Daniel 2:28–44): In the dream, Nebuchadnezzar "saw a great image...this image's head was of fine gold, his breasts and his arms of silver, his belly and his thighs of brass, his legs of iron, his feet part of iron and part of clay;..." (Daniel 2:31–33). Then he saw "a stone which smote the image upon his feet that were of iron and clay, and brake them to pieces" As the stone smashes the legs of this image, the entire structure collapses, and gets broken into several tiny pieces, no bigger than particles of dust on the ground; the particles are blown away by the wind. The stone that initiated this process however is retained, "till it became a great mountain, and filled the whole earth" (Daniel 2:34–37).

Daniel's Interpretation: Daniel's interpretation of Nebuchadnezzar's dream foretold the times, seasons and succession of powers, empires and civilizations that were to occur before Christ's millennial reign on earth. "Thou art this head of gold" Daniel told the king, for "Thou, O king, art a king of kings, for the GOD OF HEAVEN hath given thee a kingdom, power and strength and glory." The "death" of this once great empire, the Babylonian empire, is depicted in Isaiah's prophecies found in Isaiah 13:1–22 and 14:4–23.

The Persian Empire: "And after thee" Daniel continues, "shall arise another kingdom inferior to thee…" This inferior kingdom symbolized by the less valuable metal, silver, is seen in the dual **Medo-Persian** (breast and arms) alliance led by another despot, King Darius, which invaded, overthrew, and reduced Babylon to ashes in 539 BC.

The Greek Empire: "And another third kingdom of brass, which shall bear rule over all the earth…" (Dan 2:39). The Greek Empire, "the kingdom of brass" became one of the greatest empires that ever existed. Around 334 BC, the Greeks under the leadership of Alexander the Great, conquered the Medes and the Persians, who had dominated the world for about two hundred years. The empire was born around 1650 BC (birth). It had its *season of opportunity* (growth and development) and finally declined and disintegrated (death) around 350 BC, after dominating the then known world for over three hundred years. At the peak of its grandeur, known as the classical age, many discoveries were made, discoveries which formed the basis of many of the breakthroughs in modern science, medicine, math and the arts still in use till this day. Hippocrates, the physician correctly identified many diseases, Mathematicians like Pythagoras and Euclid discovered rules of math and geometry, and philosophers like Aristotle, Socrates and Plato conducted studies of life and its meaning, which are still of great value today As remarkable and glorious as this Greek era was, it also, like all others, came to an end (i.e., died).

Roman Empire: "And the fourth kingdom shall be as iron, forasmuch as iron breaketh in pieces and subdueth all things: and as iron...shall it break in pieces and bruise...and the kingdom shall be divided...and as the toes of the feet were part of iron, and part of clay, so the kingdom shall be partly strong and partly broken" (Dan. 2:40–43).

Following on the heels of the Greek Empire, in might and majesty, was the Roman Empire, symbolized in Nebuchadnezzar's dream and Daniel's interpretation of it by "legs of iron." The Roman Empire is perhaps the greatest in recorded history. The Romans, as the prophecy indicated, subdued all that they surveyed. At its zenith, it stretched from Asia Minor in the East, to Britain and Portugal in the west. All the lands around the Mediterranean were included in the empire, with a total population of about 60 million. Its military might, inroads in the fields of government, political structures, e.g., democracy, freedom of speech, human rights, architecture, writing—alphabets, the arts, science, medicine and philosophy were unmatched. The enduring nature and impact of the Roman Empire is seen in the fact that Western culture and civilization today traces its roots to the values, social and political order of the Romans. As it had been foretold by the prophet Daniel, the empire was subsequently divided into the Eastern and Western segments, the Eastern with its capital in Constantinople (previously Byzantium) and the West with its capital in Rome. Rome's glory faded over time as it experienced incessant invasions from the Huns, Vandals and Visigoths, to name a few. The empire fractured into many smaller states, weakened as a result, ultimately declining and "dying" around 500 AD

From these accounts, it is obvious that no one nation, empire or civilization, has a monopoly over God's purpose, season of opportunity or time-table. Neither does any civilization or nation have forever to accomplish or fulfill its God-ordained purpose on the world stage. Many from various fields of endeavor, political, social and economic, have touted the fall of the United States from its number one spot as the world's greatest power, and the emergence of China as the next super-power. Whether these sages are right or wrong, one thing is certain; each one of the nations and civilizations mentioned had a season of opportunity and a specific contribution it was destined to make in this theater of life, amidst all the rivalry and quest for national prestige and dominance from other nations. Seeking God, and extending His kingdom, influence, peace and prosperity to the nations of the world and to all mankind, will always stand as the barometer for greatness. It is what great nations do, with the Abrahamic covenant, serving as a blueprint, for all eternity.

Benefits of Religion

There is a substantial and still growing amount of evidence that points to the enormous dividends to be derived from the regular exercise of one's religious beliefs and practices. The correlation between religious beliefs and practices and individual, family, community, and by extension, national well-being, has been noted in every department of life, including reductions in divorce rates, criminal inclinations and delinquency, births out of wedlock, health problems, and even prejudice, leading researcher, Patrick Fagan, to conclude that "No other dimension of life in America-with the exception of stable marriages and families, which

THE COLOR OF GOD

in turn are strongly tied to religious practice, does more to promote the well-being and soundness of the nation's civil society than citizens' religious observance" (Fagan 2006). I cannot agree more.

Patrick F. Fagan is William H. G. Fitzgerald Research Fellow in Family and Cultural Issues in the Richard and Helen DeVos Center for Religion and Civil Society at The Heritage Foundation.

Family Matters: Setting the House in Order, the Black Family

"A lack of economic opportunity among Black men, and the shame and frustration that came from not being able to provide for one's family, contributed to the erosion of Black families."
—**Barack Obama**

Another area of grave concern, critical to Black advancement but needing serious attention, is the state of the Black family. In an article captioned Murder City, on the city of Detroit, published in the Wall Street Journal by Henry Payne on December 8, 2007, the nuclear family is all but non-existent in a city which is 81% Black, per the author. Academic research shows that over 50% of all Black men in Detroit are high-school dropouts, per Payne's article; 72% of those drop-outs were jobless, in 2004 and by their mid-thirties, 60% have done prison time. Whereas in 1960, 25% of children were born to single mothers, twenty years later, that is 1980, that number has almost doubled to 48%; 80% of the city's Black children, were born to single parent households. Together with the gun-violence and murder rate, the author appropriately describes the situation in the city as "Cultural homicide" (Payne 2007).

In a *Newsweek* article captioned "Endangered Family," Michele Ingrassia highlights the decimation of the institution of marriage in the Black family. Two out of three first births to Black women under thirty-five are now out of wedlock. In 1960, it was two out of five. Quoting Larry I Bumpass, a demographer at the University of Wisconsin, Ingrassia observes that, "a Black child born today has only a 1-in-5 chance of growing up with two parents until the age of 16." The adverse repercussions of these trends; higher crime rates, low education and an increase in welfare rolls, affect all of society, not just Black families. This trend, however, is not about the poor underclass. She notes that whereas 65% of poor unmarried Black women have children, which is twice the rate of Whites, an equally distressing 22% of unmarried Black women earning over $75K or above, also have children out of wedlock, ten times the rate of Whites in the same income bracket (Ingrassia 1993).

Much of the reporting on the state of the Black family can be traced to fifty years ago, when Senator Patrick Moynihan caused a firestorm by declaring that fatherless homes were "the fundamental source of the weakness of the Negro Community." His 1965 report, *The Negro Family: The Case for National Action,* highlighted the "tangle of pathology" (USDL 1965) the Black family structure was caught in and the urgent need for a concerted national effort to stem, as well as, turn the tide.

As bad as the situation was then, it has grown much worse today, with a majority of Black families with children (about 62%) headed by one parent. It is worthy of remark that during our last presidential election, then Senator, Barack Obama, called out Black fathers on this same issue, much to the chagrin of some among the liberal ranks. The Rev. Jesse Jackson reacted to this by threatening to cut off his...His unseemly remark was, unfortunately, caught on tape.

A myriad of reasons can be assigned to this dismal state of affairs within the Black community: racism, structural inequities in development, unemployment, poverty, a lack of social responsibility to our poor and marginalized, and the list goes on. I have no doubt that government does have a role in helping create the necessary conditions for growth and empowerment, particularly, in the inner cities of America, where the majority of the Black underclass resides. Sadly, conservative administrations have been known to pay lip service to the issue of *family values*, by demonstrating no commitment to the subject in real terms, by creating the necessary empowerment zones in the inner cities for families in those neighborhoods to flourish, thus, undermining their own rhetoric. Liberals, on the other hand, have tried to demonstrate how much they value families, the old-fashioned, by throwing more money at the problem. A call for family values simply implies valuing families enough to want to create the necessary conditions for their stability, health and empowerment. This is no liberal or conservative issue or agenda, but a human and a national one, requiring both liberal and conservative insights and policies to permanently solve. The solution always seems to lie somewhere between these two polarities.

However, the one theme commonly lacking and often not mentioned in any discussions on the state of the Black family, especially in liberal circles, is the crucial place of *personal responsibility*. This phrase has today become taboo to liberals and a code phrase for conservatives, unnecessary bickering points in the culture wars raging between the Left (Liberals) and the Right (Conservatives). At the same time, it is obvious to everyone that government can only do so much, and where it cannot or refuses to do its job (for whatever the reason), it is incumbent on us as a community, to find ways to take care of ourselves, our own and each other. Any shying away, therefore, from the call to personal responsibility, is as ignorant as those caught up in the war of words surrounding the use of the phrase. Obviously, there are some issues beyond our control, whereas there are others within our control. There are problems external to us, and others "internal" to us; it is those within our control that we must begin addressing as a community.

Until the Black community aggressively addresses the issues and values that shape Black family life, the pathologies alluded to by Patrick Moynihan and other conservative figures, will continue to plague us, and perhaps, even loom larger. We can then forget about any talk about redemption and lift, or upward mobility, and simply stand by and watch as groups migrate to America, and socially and economically bypass us. We might as well continue the same blame game—blaming racism and the White man for what he did to our ancestors. As tough or challenging as it currently is, it will only get tougher if we do not seriously address this crisis in the Black family; whether it pertains to our kids acting delinquent, dropping out of school, teenage pregnancies, births to unwed mothers, drug-and-gang activity, joblessness, all of which are associated with poverty, both spiritual and natural. If a Black man, with a father from Kenya, Africa, raised by a single mother and grandparents, like most of us, a guy who experimented with drugs in his youth, can become the president of the United States, what excuse do we still have? It is easy to come up with a thousand and one excuses why it cannot be done, when really, all we need is one reason—only one—to do it. That *one reason* represents or answers the question "Why? Your Big, Emotional Why" is the beginning point for success in any and every enterprise.

Successful family life does not happen automatically; it is often forged through pain and "struggle," especially, in a culture and environment where 50 percent of all marriages end in divorce, and the institution, to all intents and purposes, is fast becoming a relic. Perhaps, a better appreciation of the principles that govern the marriage institution, for those who seek to do better, will help us enjoy this sacred union much better.

The concept of the traditional marriage and family is being tested to its very foundations, particularly, in the West. Marriage and family, indeed, are fast becoming relics of the past, with many alternative patterns having crept into this sacred institution. The gamut or variations of relationships and family patterns is ever widening: Some have decided marriage is not for them and are choosing a single lifestyle with no kids. Some have chosen to have kids but never get married, while yet others have also chosen cohabitation, avoiding any marital ties or commitments that bind them. They may choose to have kids or not; again, another variation in a postmodern and secularized world.

Some also have a morbid fear about committing their entire lives and lifetime, to someone in marriage. After all, if I have seen my parents go through an ugly divorce, perhaps not once or twice, my aunties and uncles, and perhaps, even grandparents likewise go through it, with devastating consequences, what would make marriage appealing to me? Why should I go into something so scary and potentially hurtful? There is a legitimate concern, even fear, here. Perhaps, I can offer a little hope.

Your parents' negative experience does not have to be your experience. Someone's negative experience does not have to be your experience. No one inherits their parents' failures or successes. We may inherit the consequences of their successes or failures, but never the success or failure itself. To assume that because your parents or a dear relative had a major setback in their marriage, that you are also going to have a setback in yours, is not only superstitious, but an unnecessarily allowance for Satan to gain a foothold in your soul and torment you for no reason. You do not put your life on hold because someone missed the boat. You learn from their mistakes and chart a new course for your life.

The fact that an accident occurred on the freeway, killing those in the car, does not make you stop driving if you are a driver, does it? If you drive yourself to work, do you stop driving because someone, out of their own carelessness, or just unfortunately, suffered a mishap on the road? We hear of plane-crashes occasionally. We do not stop traveling by airplanes or stop flying because one airline crashed. The point is, a thousand people having an accident, does not imply that you or I will get into an accident too. Likewise, your parents' reality does not have to be your reality. Your past does not have to equal your future. You are different, your name is different, and your destiny is different, and you will do better where they failed, if you acquire the proper knowledge needed to succeed and apply it. Knowledge is power.

We must face life with faith and optimism, always expecting the sun to rise after the sunset, the rainbow to appear on the horizon after the dark, gloomy and ominous clouds have disappeared—and they will disappear. There is light at the end of the tunnel. Marriage and family are for you, if you want them. We just got to do it His way. The key is knowledge; applied knowledge.

A Theology of Restoration for the Black Family

Family is the foundation of human society, the bedrock of any nation. It is where everything originates. Before there ever was a thing called, church, school, government, there was first the family.

God is the Creator of all, including the family. The Bible begins in the Book of Genesis with the institution of Marriage and Family—between Adam and Eve—and ends in Revelation with the Marriage between Christ and His bride, the glorious Church. It is worthy of note that Jesus performed His **first miracle** at a marriage ceremony (a wedding) when He turned water into wine. Again, the biblical account says it was God (not Adam) who said, *"It is not good for man to be alone"* (Gen. 2:18). God did not even seek Adam's consent or permission; in fact, He put him to sleep and went about His business. This implies that marriage and the family are *God's idea*—they are His prerogative.

Since marriage and family are God's idea (i.e., divine institutions) for you and I to be successful at them, we must do it His way; i.e., *God's way,* using His principles, guidelines and His guidance.

God is a God of Order not chaos. He established authority and order in the family and in the home by making *Man* the *head of the union and household.* Being all-knowing, He knew the man (Adam) was going to need a wife, helper (Eve), but yet still waited on that. He created the man first, established him in his leadership role and gave him responsibilities before creating the woman.

Headship or Leadership is extremely critical to the smooth running of any entity on earth, be it a household, school, corporation or government. The entire operation of that entity is controlled and directed by and from the head.

This is the reason why you can *amputate a leg,* but you cannot *amputate a Head.* It is the reason why you can have a *heart transplant* but never a *Head Transplant.* Any reversal of God's order, whether in the home or elsewhere, will result in chaos. Leadership is usually vested in one person, not two. It is one captain per ship, not two.

Out of the Family came Communities, out of Communities came Human Societies and out of Societies come Nations.

The health of a nation reflects its families, of which the man is the head. To ascertain the character and health of a *nation,* first look at the character and health of its *societies,* then its *communities,* its *families* and finally, *its men.*

The condition and character of America's Black men is the barometer for evaluating and determining the character and condition of the Black nation. Herein lies the problem. Any successful attack on and emasculation of the Black man spiritually, physically, mentally, and financially has devastating consequences for the nation.

The first thing God gave man (Adam) upon creating him was a Job, responsibility (not a wife) *"The Lord God took the man and placed him in the garden to Dress it and to Keep it..."* (Genesis 2:15) Men need to ensure that they have a job, a career or business running which can provide for a family before they embark on the journey of starting one.

The man is to be the custodian of God's Laws and Word, not the woman. God entrusted His commandment, law and Word to Adam, not his wife, Eve. To Adam God gave the commandment, outlining what the consequence of *disobedience would be "of the fruit of the tree of the knowledge of good and evil, thou may not eat for the day thou eat of it, thou shall surely die..."* (Gen. 2:17).

The Enemy's target is Men—Satan's target was Adam, not Eve. Eve was just the means to that end. God confronted and queried Adam (not Eve) about their act of disobedience: "And the Lord God called unto Adam, and said unto him "Where art thou?... Hast thou eaten of the tree, whereof I commanded thee that thou should not eat?" (Gen. 3:9–11).

Note the following biblical Examples: Moses, David, and Jesus's eras. Just as Adam, the male-man was the target of the enemy, so were the men and the boys (potential men) the enemy's target.

Moses's Era

Pharaoh (the slave master) issues an order for the Hebrew baby boys to be slaughtered:

"If it be a son, kill him but if it be a daughter, then she shall live." (Ex. 1:16)

Jesus's Era

Herod issues a decree to kill all the Hebrew *male* children:

"When Herod saw that he was deceived by the wise men, he was very angry and he sent and slew all the male *children that were in Bethlehem...from two years old and under..."* (Matt. 2:16).

David's Era

Men are the defense against or entry points for enemy attacks on the family—spiritually, physically, emotionally, and financially. Men need to be "present" for the health and stability of the nuclear family. When the men were away, removed from their wives and children, the families became easy prey for the enemy.

"When David and his men came to Ziklag, the Amalekites had invaded the city and burned it with fire, and their wives, and sons and daughters were taken captives..."(1 Sam. 30:1–6).

Adam

Adam, not Eve, was the target of the enemy's intrigues in the garden. He was the head of the household and the *custodian* of God's Law. If only Eve had eaten the fruit, humanity would not have had a problem, because she was not the custodian of the law and, therefore, not the target. A blow to the head is always a sure way of neutralizing the opponent. Adam was the head.

Absentee Fathers: A National Epidemic

"Being a Male is a matter of birth, being a Man is a matter of choice; any male can make babies (even dogs can have puppies and cats, kittens) but it takes a Real Man to be a Real Father."
—Dr. Ed Cole, Christian Men's Network

Are fatherless homes "the fundamental source of the weakness of the Negro Community," as Senator Patrick Moynihan declared? Without equivocation, the answer is a resounding Yes! It is not the only problem, but most definitely, a major source of Black community weakness. A large portion of the spiritual, emotional, psychological, and economic problems of the Black community can be traced to this national epidemic—absentee fathers.

The national furor generated over Moynihan's report, and the relentless assault it received at the hands of social scientists and academics, most of them liberal, who saw his thesis as an attempt to "blame the victim," contributed in no small measure to the lack-luster "national action" he had called for as a response to problem. Today, after virtually a whole generation of Black kids have become victimized by poverty, drug addiction, street gangs and crime, teenage pregnancy, and the criminal justice system, there appears to be some consensus among social scientists that Moynihan might have been right after all.

Bryce Christensen writes in *The Family in America* that, "the research linking Black family break-up to Black misery is compelling-and depressing." He adds that more black children were living in abject poverty because of them being in single parent households due to the breakdown of the family (Christensen 1989).

For instance, a 1989 study, showed that among Black families, more than seven out of ten poor children live in families without a father" (Wetzel 1990). A 1991 report also concurred with this finding, stating that a "changing Black family structure in the 1960s accounted for roughly 65% of the increase in official poverty among Black children" (The Future of Children). The correlation between absentee fathers and poverty of children could not be starker. Christensen furthermore states that black children from single parent families have poorer grades and more problematic behavior than their peers from intact homes. In addition, they are more likely to drop out of high school. Christensen, further, comments on the loss of tens of thousands of Black males from fatherless homes—adolescents and young adults—to street crime (Christensen 1989). Sociologists, in their studies of inner-city Blacks, show more than little evidence, he says, that "boys reared in father-absent homes gravitate to gangs apparently in part because these boys lack a healthy, domestic exemplar of masculine identity…," leading Courtright to conclude that the "root cause of Black inner-city male violence" was due to the "decline of the stable two-parent families and…an entrenched culture of poverty…" (Christensen 2005). According to Scott Johnson in *US News and World Report*:

- 40% of America's homes today have no father figure.
- Almost 60% of all men incarcerated grew up in homes without a father figure.
- Life expectancy of men is seven years less than women.
- 3 out of 4 retarded kids are boys.
- Men are twenty-five more times likely to be committed to a mental institution.
- 3 out of 4 kids aborted are boys.
- 3 out of 4 kids given up for adoption are boys (Johnson 1995).

Also:

- 63% of Youth suicides are from fatherless homes.
- 90% of all homeless and runaway children are from fatherless homes.
- 85% of all children that exhibit behavioral disorders are from fatherless homes.
- 80% of rapists motivated with displaced anger come from fatherless homes.

- 71% of all high school dropouts come from father-less homes.
- 70% of juveniles in state operated institutions are from fatherless homes.
- 85% of all Youth sitting in prison are from father-less homes (parent-less statistics).
- Nearly 2 out of 5, i.e., 40% of children in America live in a fatherless home (Johnson 1995).

The common thread running through these statistics is that men or boys are usually the worst victims of the adversities that befall the Black family, bearing the brunt of Satan's nefarious intrigues in various negative and brutal ways. The absence from home of dad has serious adverse repercussions on the children they leave behind. A father's presence in the home, on the other hand, creates a sense of calm, security and assurance. The question: "*Who am I*" or "*Where did I come from?*" that is, issues over one's identity and self-esteem, are resolved when a dynamic and loving relationship is forged between dad and child. The story of *Roots* represents one man, Alex Haley's, search for this identity, the realization of which helped an entire race discover who they were and resolve some of the issues regarding its identity.

America's youth are busy with the same search. A father's love also establishes and reinforces the self-esteem of his children. Today, many young girls are out on a hunt for this love, real unconditional love, the kind they never got from daddy—because he was never there. They end up looking for this love in all the wrong places—drugs, peers, alcohol, and other young men, who just like them, are looking for the fatherly love they never had also, leading to many heartaches. The result is unwanted pregnancies and illegitimate babies, which inexorably, perpetuates the "tangle of pathology" Moynihan referred to (Moynihan 1965). A child's sense of security, protection, and preservation are vested in their father. There is a sense of calm just knowing that Dad is around.

The Black Man: An Emasculated and Endangered Species

"We live in the most incarcerated country in the world. There are more Black men under correctional control today than were under slavery in 1850."
—John Legend

The current state of the Black man has led to some labeling him an Endangered Species. Stereotypes applied to him abound; lazy, a buffoon, ignorant and lacking in natural intelligence, barbaric, with a propensity toward criminal behavior—a gorilla in the midst, one to be feared, his most notable attribute being his sexual prowess and his bent toward the artistic and athletic impulses.

From Male Domination to a Legacy of Matriarchy

Gender roles and power within the Black family in America have changed. The Black man, probably, with a criminal record hanging over his life and following him everywhere, with no higher educational qualification to his credit or vocational training and skills to count on, and therefore, jobless, feels a sense of emasculation. This is especially the case if his wife is college-educated, works a decent job on the nicer part of town, drives a decent car, and by virtue of the above, fits in perfectly with a different crowd, belonging to a different and higher echelon. Invariably, in societies where some form of racial, ethnic, or tribal oppression has occurred or persists, the power structure and systems of state are designed to neutralize the oppressed, in order to entrench itself and perpetuate the status quo. The target of such an effort is always the male, in this case, the Black male. It was the same in Pharaoh's Egypt, where Israel was enslaved for four hundred years.

Africa, for the most part, is a male-dominated culture. With the passage of time, development, women being educated and enlightenment, that mentality has waned, but only to a degree. The birth of a male child is still met with much pomp and celebration. Historically, this was a military, economic and cultural imperative, to the extent that a man could divorce his wife simply for not giving him a son, an heir. In no way, however, was this male-domination supposed to denigrate or discount the unique place and role of womanhood in African society. As the Black man was captured and forcibly brought into the new world, the process of his emasculation began. His place as head of the household and role as provider were completely erased, as he worked the fields and he was addressed as "boy," while his "wife" was promoted to "house-nigger" to undertake domestic responsibilities.

Thus, The Black male lost his sociological role as father and his economic function as provider. The structure of the Black family under slavery is what has persisted till this day. Reducing the man to a subordinate station in the family structure and hierarchy, thereby, neutralizing his potential power in the broader society was the agenda. Jill Bishop highlights this alteration in the gender status of the Black family under slavery. The robust communal spirit which accentuated familial networks, with the Black male taking centerstage as father and provider, was replaced by an equal, almost competitive role for the Black woman. There always seemed to be an external power to check or reign in the Black male (Bishop 1996).

Thus, the roles were flipped, with the Black woman taking center stage in family affairs and decisions. The Black husband will often defer to his wife to make decisions about finances, vacations, and issues regarding the kid's education, not because he is incapable of making them, but because he believes she is better equipped to make them, especially in cases where the wife is better educated. By virtue of her higher education, she knows her way around the White world better, speaks better, and is more confident. The Black man on the other hand is often uneducated, unemployed/jobless, has a few stripes with the law under his belt, a felon, unable to secure a job as a result. He has no choice, but to depend on his wife, an option that further robs him of his masculinity—morally, socially, and economically.

Already trapped and humiliated by his circumstances, and often feeling abused and disrespected by his assertive, Black wife, and sometimes his children, over whom he now has little or no authority because of his circumstances, the option to leave becomes very appealing—and he does leave, but only to repeat the cycle—hooking up, shacking up, having babies out of wedlock, unable to properly care for the new family, feeling humiliated and, ultimately, abandoning them. This is the quagmire in which the Black man in America is immersed. It is this quagmire, his distorted self-mage and emasculation, that must give way to a rediscovery of his true identity and masculinity in God.

Restoration of the Family: Hope for America

"Behold I will send you Elijah the prophet, before the coming of the great and dreadful day of the Lord; And he shall turn the heart of the father to the children and the heart of the children to their fathers, lest I come and smite the earth with a curse."
—Malachi 4:5–6

The restoration of the family, the return of fathers to their biblical roles and duties as Priests, Prophets, Kings and Role models, and the proper training and raising of our kids in the ways of God is the greatest spiritual and social need of our time. Without it, our nation and civilization are cursed, as the scripture above indicates. May we together rise up to the challenge, lest we fail irreparably as a nation and our civilization perish.

Boys to Men: Black Males—a Return to Biblical Fatherhood

Fatherhood by its very meaning, presupposes the fathering of children—i.e., reproduction (1 Cor. 4:14–16). However, it is critical not to limit fatherhood to just a biological function. A clear distinction between *Fatherhood* and *Fathering* needs to be made because there are too many irresponsible little brats (boys) going around fathering babies with equally immature and vulnerable girls, girls who are looking for love in all the wrong places. The result is often the entrapment of these young unwed mothers in a lifetime of poverty, and the birth of poor, fatherless, babies who grow up to perpetuate the very cycle of irresponsibility and dependency that our communities need to get rid of.

"Being a Male is a matter of birth, being a Man is a matter of choice; any male can make babies, but it takes a Real Man to be a Real Father" (Cole 2009).

Fatherhood: A Biblical Paradigm

In John 17:18–21, 26, Jesus says: "I have declared to them, YOUR NAME…" (John 17:18–21, 26). What name? Jehovah, El Shaddai, El Ohim, Jehovah Shammah, Nissi, Rapha, Tisdkenu? Were these the "NAME" that Jesus was referring to? No! It was the name "Father."

God has a keen interest in the concept of Fatherhood and in the attitudes, responsibilities and role of fathers; so special is this interest that He even decided to share in the title of father. In response to a request by His disciples to teach them how to pray, he taught them to begin prayer by addressing God as father: "Our Father, which art in heaven…" (Matt. 6:9). Jesus further said: "I am the Way, the Truth and the Life; no one comes to the Father except by me" (John 14:6).

Very often, we miss the purposes of God by focusing only on Jesus, the Son. Some erroneously pray to Jesus and present their petitions to Him, believing that He is the ultimate. God's purpose however is not that we come to the Son, but that through the Son we come to the Father. *Jesus is thus the "Way." The Father is the Destination. "Whatever ye shall ask the Father in my Name, he will give it to you…"* (John 16:23)

Biblical Role of Fathers: Priest, Prophet, Role Model, and King

Fathers as Priests: Hosea 4:6, Malachi 2:7. Fathers have a priestly responsibility to their families. A priest is an Intercessor, an advocate, mediator or intermediary. He represents the family before God; he is the *go-between* between God and the family, presenting the petitions of the family to God and pleading its case. The Father's role is to *lead* in the spiritual life of the family, inculcating an attitude of worship, ushering the family into the presence of God for prayer and the study of God's word—in essence nurturing a closer and more intimate family relationship with God. As priest, he is also the *spiritual protector* of the family: the *gatekeeper*, so to speak, who like a watchman or security guard, watches every "entry point" into the family or household for any foul activities. Part of his job description is to provide a "covering," a shield for the family, fending off demonic attacks from Satan, "the terminator," in his capacity as protector, and always pleading God's mercy, grace and favor upon the family.

A father's role and duties to his family cannot and must not be delegated. A loving, fulfillment of his divine role and responsibilities, in simple childlike obedience to God's word, will bring with it manifold blessings in every department of life. The father's best equipment and resources for this role are Prayer and God's word. The following biblical examples of fatherhood should provide further insight into the priestly role of fathers.

- **Passover:** God entrusted the protection of Israel's families from the angel of destruction and death, to the fathers, the head of each household (Exodus 12).

- **Job exercised his priestly role as father** by interceding consistently before God on behalf of his family, especially the children (Job 1:1–5).
- **Epileptic Boy:** Dad exercises his intercessory ministry as he persists in seeking out divine help and deliverance from Jesus and his disciples on behalf of his son (Matt. 17:14–17).

Fathers as Prophets: "Thus Says the Lord"

One of the major issues confronting America today is the issue of spiritual, especially biblical, illiteracy. A generation or two ago, one did not have to be a Christian to know the stories of Adam and Eve, Noah's Ark, Jonah in the Belly of the Whale, and Nativity stories regarding the birth of Christ. America has, undoubtedly, undergone drastic changes. The society is no longer a "churched culture," and with that has come a mass ignorance of basic biblical knowledge, knowledge that we took for granted growing up. Many kids, unless they probably attend a parochial Christian institution/school, have never heard about Adam and Eve, Moses, Job or Jonah, much more know some detail about the biblical stories or lessons involving them. Recently, in a class session in college, one girl, supposedly an adult, expressed her utmost surprise (too much laughter in the class) upon learning that Christmas was the commemoration of Christ's birth. Apparently, it had never occurred to her that Christmas had anything to do with Christ. Her level of ignorance as a college girl and an adult was as shocking as it was disappointing. The spiritual education of the family, especially children, falls under the purview of the prophetic role and responsibility of fathers. The YMCA, YWCA, or the Youth department of your church could assist, but this is the role of dad, not them.

Fathers need to declare God's word to and upon their children. The word of God is light; it illuminates the darkness around us and provides light for the lives and paths of our children, especially in the face of the unparalleled demonic activity in the world today. The word of God is also a cleansing agent; compared to water, it washes (Heb. 10:22–23), cleanses and purifies our children from any worldly and ungodly pollution or contamination, especially when lovingly taught and applied.

Our children live in a time and day when the appeal of the demonic could not be greater. There is an unprecedented deluge and battle of the demonic, raging for the minds and souls of our children in the form of drugs, gang activity, pornography, sexual promiscuity, alcoholism, some rap music, rock and roll as well as various anti-Christ philosophies. The prophetic role of fathers does not only entail teaching our children the word of God but also helping them to properly interpret its principles and applying them to the many complex issues today's youth are confronted with. In this, *thus saith the Lord*" should be our watch phrase as Fathers.

Fathers as Role Models

"In the book of Corinthians, Paul asks the Corinthian church, his spiritual children, to be followers of him and imitators of his example: 'Wherefore I beseech thee, be ye followers of me...'" (1 Cor. 4:16)

Fathers are the representatives of God to the family; they reflect God's image. Consistently modeling this godly image in front of our children has the ultimate and positive result of transmitting God's image to them through our example. The Heavenly Fathers image manifested through Earthly fathers is ultimately caught and duplicated in the children's lives. It is like making several photo copies of an image—the master copy. The image of God thus becomes the normative lifestyle and pattern of behavior for the children as God begins to manifest His life through them through the visible representation and manifestation of God's character through their Dad. The father's example as a role model worthy of emulation is therefore critical to the kind of children we raise or produce in our community

Fathers as Kings: Revelation 5:9–10

Fathers are also called to be Kings. The word "king" can sometimes have a negative connotation in that it implies one person having uncontrolled, unlimited power, with everyone at his beck and call. It often refers to an autocratic system of governance. In its exclusive application to biblical Fatherhood however, it implies an authority vested in the father by God, for the purpose of protecting, training and raising children, and in the process, administering loving censure, discipline, and correction. It does not at all imply a dictatorial, unquestioned, abusive, and insensitive style of ruling, usually characteristic of kings, No! Far from it. God has not called us as fathers to be King Kongs in our homes.

One of the most remarkable testaments to the kingly role of fathers is found in the story of Abraham. Abraham is called a "friend of God"; he is trustworthy because of the way he trains and raises his children. Thus, he gains favor with God; "divine secrets,"—that is, God's intentions for the city of Sodom and Gomorrah, are made known to him. In Genesis, God explains why He chose Abraham: "Shall I hide from Abraham that thing which I do?…for I know him, that he will command his children and his household after him and they shall keep the way of the Lord to do justice and judgment that the Lord may bring upon Abraham that which he had spoken of him…" (Gen. 18:17–19).

A father's duty is to instruct, i.e., "command" his children and entire household in the ways of God.

The Apostle Paul also explains the kingly authority and role of fathers in the home, but not until he had established a nexus between a father's leadership at home with his leadership role in the house of God (Church). Home life is the basis for leadership in God's house.

In his teaching in 1 Timothy 3:4–5, he spells out various principles which are quite instructional to parents, fathers and leaders, eager to take on the mantle of leadership and exercise their kingly authority. Regarding the qualifications of a bishop, Paul says, he should be "One that rules his own house well, having his children in subjection with all gravity; for if a man know not how to rule his own house, how shall he take care of the church of God" (1 Tim. 3:4–5).

He further instructs fathers in these words: "And you fathers, provoke not your children to wrath, but bring them up in the nurture and admonition of the Lord" (Eph. 6:4–5).

In Colossians, he adds a further dimension to the instruction: "Fathers provoke not your children to anger, lest they become discouraged" (Col. 3:21).

A Couple of Points to Note

1. A father can "provoke" a child to wrath through cruelty, ridicule, loss of temper, abuse, or misuse of his parental authority.

2. Such provocation may cause children to "become discouraged." This means children may lose heart; in essence, the spirit of dominion within every child given by God to conquer the world could be crushed, if discipline is excessively cruel or severe. A child's "winning instinct or streak" or "fighting spirit" could be broken or shattered if fathers are overly harsh with them.

3. The tendency of parents, particularly fathers, in the correction and disciplining of children is to say "no" to the inappropriate things they say or do. However, correction should not always be about what they are not to do, but more so about what they can do or need to be doing. No's to everything is not enough, especially in the absence of nothing to say "Yes" to. Fathers need to offer that positive direction.

4. "Bringing them up in the nurture and admonition of the Lord…" This refers to the mode of raising and training our children. The scriptures further admonish us to "*Train a child in the way he should go, and when he is old, he will not depart from it*" (Proverbs 22:6). Parents, fathers especially, have a divine responsibility to train children in the ways of God. God's promise is that they will not depart from what was taught them in their later years. They may take a detour along the way; make mistakes, trip and fall along the way—especially

during their teenage years. Ultimately, however, and because of the foundation earlier laid, God assures us of their return to the "ancient landmark" (i.e., what was taught to them as children). "*Nurture*" refers to their spiritual education and formation. "*Admonition*" points out one's duties and responsibilities. When children are properly "trained" per the precepts outlined above, they become "responsible" citizens and contribute to the spiritual, social, and economic well-being of their community, society, and ultimately the nation. The proper training and raising of our kids as a society is a biblical imperative, one we cannot shirk or simply ignore. It is the greatest need of our time.

5. Functioning as a dad, a good dad, is never an easy job. Personally, as a dad, I have felt inadequate, oftentimes. Other times, I have felt like a complete failure. It is important, however, that we hold on to God, to His word and grace, to help us live up to our divine roles and responsibilities. His grace is sufficient.

Emancipation Proclamation: Let My People Go

"Without Commerce and Industry the people Perish."
—Marcus Garvey

The Emancipation Proclamation which ended *de facto* slavery in America took place in April of 1865. Much progress has been made in Black America, no doubt. I am, however, of the opinion that it could have been accomplished sooner, considering that it has been over 150 years since slavery occurred. I believe that African Americans should have long been fully integrated into American society for America to be what I believe the Framers meant it to be "One Nation (under God) with Freedom and Justice for All."

The lack of full integration into the American mainstream for Black America, socially and economically, speaks volumes; a push for legal and physical emancipation does not amount to much, without a commensurate push for mental or intellectual, and economic emancipation. Legal emancipation can only be consolidated, and its benefits fully realized, through mental and economic emancipation. Without it, the free but former slave will continue to languish in the doldrums, eating the crumbs that fall from the master's table, because he has no seat at the table. An individual in that state may even prefer or wish to return to a life of servitude in exchange for a morsel of bread and shelter at the shanty slave quarters. Generations of Black Americans that have been dependent on government assistance or subsidies for generations, unable or unwilling to get off the welfare system, are in this cycle of perpetual servitude.

In his memoirs, Booker T Washington recounts a moving story about what the Emancipation Proclamation meant to his family, and the reaction of the freed slaves to the news. He writes...

> We were told we were free, and we could go where and when we pleased. My mother leaned over and kissed her children, while tears of joy ran down her cheeks...for some minutes there was great rejoicing, and thanks giving, and wild scenes of ecstasy. After the initial jubilation had worn off, however, a strange

feeling of seriousness, even gloom, began to descend upon some of the former slave population. A new and somewhat disturbing thought had occurred to them. Financially they were now responsible for themselves. They could no longer rely on the master for food and shelter. As free people, they had to find their place in society…it was very much like suddenly turning a youth of 10 or 12 years out into the world to provide for himself…some of the slaves were 70 or 80 years old… gradually, one by one, stealthily at first, the older slaves began to wander from the slave quarters back to the "big house" to have a whispered conversation with their former owners as to their future. (Schroeder 1998)

Cry Freedom: Let My People Go

"What I ask for the Negro is not benevolence, not pity, not sympathy, but simply justice…if the Negro cannot stand on his own legs, let him fall… All I ask is give him a chance to stand on his own two legs…"
—**Frederick Douglass**

Decades of Black political agitation, primarily through the civil rights movement, have led to the removal of *de jure* segregation, racist laws that were obviously inimical to Black social and economic uplift. From emancipation from slavery, the enactment of civil and human rights laws, ranging from the desegregation of hotels, theaters, restaurants, and housing, to the integration of the public-school system, voting rights for both men and women and equal employment opportunities; these are all testaments to the indomitable spirit and quest for freedom and justice manifested by Black America's leaders, both past and present. The sacrifices they made, oftentimes with their lives, are what have brought us, thus, far.

Political freedom and rights, however, only serve as a starter; a means to an end; they do not, in and of themselves, translate into, or guarantee economic power and/or freedom. Political freedom and rights unmatched with an equal focus on economic freedom and justice, will eventuality lead right back to bondage and servitude, perhaps, of a different kind. For many nations or people-groups formerly colonized by Western European nations, whether in Africa, Asia, or Latin America, this has been the experience, the most recent and most visible case being Black South Africa. Years of struggle, sometimes through the barrel of the gun for political freedom, are often undermined upon achieving independence from the colonial master, by the lack of economic development, freedom, and empowerment

"Poverty is not an accident; like slavery and apartheid, it is man-made and can be removed by the actions of human beings" (Mandela 2005).

Mason Weaver, in a New Visions commentary paper by The National Center for Public Policy Research, asks the question *"What is the goal of the Black community? Economic power or Political power?"* Weaver argues that "if the culture (Black culture that is) has no strong semi-independent economic base, then it resembles a plantation, not a community" (Weaver 1997). The feeling of perpetual oppression that Blacks feel, he explains, whether it be through the drug menace, crime, bad schools, high taxes or welfare, are attributable to lack of financial resources than any deficiency in political. Weaver illustrates his point by drawing attention to the various communities represented in the American multicultural milieu. He emphasizes that these communities, such as the Japanese, Korean, Arab Americans, or Jewish Americans with so much clout and strong traditional political agendas and priorities, seem less interested in how many congressmen and/or how strong their congressional caucus is, but are rather more interested in economics. This is because, he stresses, "economics, not politics, is the path to achieving real personal freedom." Weaver thus persuasively suggests that "Economic freedoms are not decided by political parties or a social culture, it is decided by the individual willing to sacrifice all he has for all he desires. That is freedom and that is America." I cannot agree more. Booker T. Washington's account of the slave reaction to the news of emancipation attests to this sobering, reality as well (Schroeder 1992).

A parallel of Black America's socioeconomic status, that is, political emancipation without the attendant economic emancipation, is similarly reflected in the African context. In the late 1950s and early 1960s, the winds of change began to blow on the continent of Africa, especially along the Western coast. Some of Africa's brightest sons, such as Dr. Kwame Nkrumah, Nnamdi Azikiwe, Sekou Toure, and Jomo Kenyatta and Kenneth Kaunda in East Africa, began to lead the charge for Africa's independence from colonial rule. The dream of political freedom led to an anticipation of economic freedom for the peoples of those former colonies. The collective hopes and aspirations of many of these peoples have been dashed. Instead of political freedom, economic development, and prosperity, the continent has been a symbol of chaos, discontent, deprivation, disease, political unrest, and instability.

It is ironic that Dr. Martin Luther King Jr. was assassinated as he prepared to lead a Poor Peoples March on the nation's capital, his quest for and transition from civil rights to economic empowerment for all people, never fulfilled in his lifetime.

If Black America, is ever to fulfill its divine purpose, and become a force to reckon with, economic emancipation must keep pace with political agitation. It is my intention to focus more attention on this issue, in the follow-up to this book. Black America is still holding the "Check Marked Insufficient Funds."

Breaking the Mental Shackles: Education, the Great Equalizer

*"Emancipate yourself from mental slavery,
none but ourselves can free our minds."*
—Bob Marley

"Free your mind, the rest will follow"
—En Vogue

Emancipation from mental slavery and bondage is yet another critical corollary to the process of Black America's redemption and lift. Political agitation and freedom may create the necessary conditions for all manner of freedoms, including economic emancipation, where exploitation of local resources by the master, gives way to more control by the indigenous and legitimate owners of such resources. However, where mental, intellectual inferiority or ignorance exist, such resources may amount to nothing more than a decorative or show piece. Real socioeconomic transformation occurs with the removal of any mental blocks or shackles, the acquisition of fresh knowledge and insights, and the application of such insights for capacity-building and community political, social, and economic development and transformation.

"Political activity alone cannot make a man free. Back of the ballot, he must have property, industry, skill, economy, intelligence and character" (Washington 1990).

Mental Shackles

"As a man thinks...so is he..."
                                        —*Proverb 23:7*

"For lack of knowledge, my people perish..."
                                        —*Hosea 4:6*

As I pondered this subject in relation to Black America, my mind went back to certain experiences in my childhood. One of them stood out clearly for me, and it was this: Growing up in Ghana, Africa, I became aware of two breeds of chickens. I am talking about a culture in which chickens are usually raised in the backyard poultry farm. The two breeds of chicken consisted of the local breed and what was called the *White man's chicken*, in local parlance. The local breed was more agile, less picky about what they were fed, harder to catch if let loose; its meat was also slightly tougher. Whereas some preferred the local chicken for food, many others preferred the White man's chicken. The *abrofo-kokor* (literally translated "White man's chicken") was not often reared in the backyard, out in the sprawling and expansive poultry farms which were structured for commercial purposes and dotted the landscape. They were reared for commercial purposes, and thus fed with scientifically—engineered poultry feed and treated to more intensive care and supervision. Their proper care usually made them fatter, thus, providing more meat at the dinner table. However, they were more docile; they hardly ran when we chased them as kids. This was no abuse at all, but a childhood pastime for most kids.

So occasionally, when my parents chose to go for the high-prized, fatter poultry farm-bred, *White man's chicken*, my job was to tie a thin string around one leg and tie the other end of the string to a post of some sort. This was to ensure that that they would not be able to escape even if they did try. Consistent with their rather compliant temperament, these poultry chickens would stoop, sit or squat, upon realizing, perhaps, instinctively, that they could not get away because of the string, and as long as no one bothered them, they would continue sitting at the same spot for hours. Hopefully, you get the picture, because this is where it gets interesting. Not only was it amusing seeing a live chicken so up close, but our keen sense of play made us try some things out, one of which still stands out in my mind. Once the chicken sat down, we would go behind it, and with a pair of scissors, cut the cord that prevented their escape. To our surprise, that chicken would still sit there and if unperturbed, would continue sitting there to perpetuity. Even when shooed, they would hop, once or twice and sit back down again, at that same spot and in that same position.

The story is quite like that of the elephant, or the flea circuses of the eighteenth century, when fleas were conditioned to jump only so high, instead of their ability to jump over fifteen feet. In the case of the elephant, the baby elephant when captured would be tied with a thick chain to a stake for the first five years of its life. After the many attempted pulls to free itself failed (in the five years), the elephant, finally, succumbed to its circumstances. At this point all that was needed was a thin rope tied to a little post to keep it harnessed. The now giant elephant still stuck with the program, stayed harnessed, controlled by a thin rope and a post it could effortlessly pull out of the ground, but would never attempt to.

The question is, "What is it that keeps the poultry chicken or elephant from attempting to change its circumstances? What is it that keeps it sitting when it can stand, walk or even fly away and escape the wrath to come, or in the case of the elephant, just walk off?"

Obviously, breaking the shackle, string or stake that holds them down, for both the elephant and the chicken, requires some mental rehabilitation. Their thinking is "skewed." The problem though, unknown to them is two-fold: the first is *conditioning* and the second is *ignorance* (not necessarily stupid, but a lack of knowledge). Both creatures have been *conditioned* to think they are in a situation beyond their control; hence they refuse to challenge their circumstance (status quo), and instead succumb to it. Their imprisonment, bondage or captivity is ensured by reason of their mental chains. These chains have them so shackled that they do not even attempt to escape anymore; this is mental conditioning at its best, or should I say, its worst. Secondly, we can attribute their captivity, mental as it were, to a *lack of knowledge*, i.e., ignorance. *If only the elephant and the chicken knew that they were free.* If they only knew that they could walk away into freedom. Their ignorance of this reality however, made their enslavement complete.

> *When you control a man's thinking,*
> *you do not have to worry about his actions.*
> *You do not have to tell him not to stand*

here or go yonder. He will find his "proper place" and will stay in it. You do not need to send him to the backdoor; he will go without being told. In fact, if there is no backdoor, he will cut one for his special benefit. His education makes it necessary. (Woodson 2010)

Harriet Tubman tells a story which is not only moving and painful, but also quite insightful and relevant to what is being discussed here. She tells of how she grew up like a "neglected weed, ignorant of liberty, having no experience of it." It takes a special person to pursue something they have never tasted. Most people not having a clue what it felt like to be free, would have settled comfortably into bondage, accepting it as the norm which they did, but not Harriet Tubman. "I had crossed the line," she recounts, "I was free but there was no one to welcome me to the land of freedom. I was a stranger in a strange land." The journey to heroism can often be quite lonely. She then proceeds to make a powerful and profound statement, relevant to our discussion. She says, "If I could convince more slaves that they were slaves, I could have freed thousands more" (Tubman n.d.).

To be in bondage or prison, like the slaves Harriet Tubman mentions, and not know it or assume that that is your God-given lot in life is quite pathetic. Equally pathetic, however, is to be liberated and not know it (like the elephant and the chicken) and continue sitting in bondage, living rather comfortably beneath your divine potential. Unfortunately, that is exactly what conditioning and ignorance do to the ignorant and has done to many who were colonized or enslaved, many of them Black folks.

Slavery, colonialism and racism have had the adverse effect of creating a monopoly over the minds of many African-Americans, and Blacks in the diaspora. It is another form of slavery, this time not physical but mental, where one sees himself or herself as a helpless victim to his or her circumstances. For many of our people, it has been difficult seeing the possibilities in a society that has told them for centuries that they are less than.

Let us not forget, however, that the cord that held down the chicken was cut; the thick chain that held the elephant in check as a baby was broken and replaced with just a thin rope and a little stake in the ground. Is it not ironic that a thicker chain holds the elephant down when it's a baby (about fifty pounds), and in contrast, a much thinner, less strong, chain holds it captive, when it is fully grown and at about five thousand pounds. The fully-grown elephant surrenders and conforms to its circumstances because in its mind, the thin rope or chain is more powerful than it.

It is time to destroy this monopoly over your mind, ingrained by your circumstances. It is a prison of the mind, which is internal, not external; it is within us. We are slaves to our own mentally-created limitations. Your situation is not bigger than you; your crippling habits and addictions, poverty, lack of education, etc., are not bigger than you. You may think you are helpless, a victim, forgetting that the obstacles are limited to only how you think. You are only where you are because of mental and self-imposed barriers which have stifled your success. You can better yourself. You can change your mind-set and live a life without limitations; you can "de-condition" and recondition your mind to believe again. Harriet Tubman did it. Booker T. Washington did it as well. We can do it too.

"Whatever the mind can conceive, and my heart can believe, I can achieve." (**Muhammed Ali**)

"If you keep thinking what you've been thinking, you'll keep doing what you've been doing and you'll keep getting what you've been getting." (**Unknown**)

Little wonder, Bob Marley, in Redemption Song, admonishes us as a people to "*emancipate*" ourselves "*from mental slavery,*" urging that "*none but ourselves can free our minds*" (Marley 1980). The correlation between our thoughts (mentality) and our ways (actions /behavior) is uncanny. Our "ways" (our actions or behavior), the scripture says, are a direct result of our thought life (mentality). The Almighty calls on us to let go of the old, dehumanizing and debilitating thoughts which have crippled, enslaved and caused us to live beneath our potential as a people, and begin to live as God's people, designer-labeled, in His image (Gen. 1:26–28).

"My ways are not your ways, neither are my thoughts your thoughts, for just as the heavens are higher than the earth, so are my ways and my thoughts higher than yours" (Isaiah 55:8).

The Prison Door Is Open; Why Stay In?: Living a Life without Limitations

"Thoughts are things; what you think about you bring about"
"if you think you can, you can, and if you think you can't, you're right."

—Mary Kay Ash

A powerful story used as an introduction for the 1997 movie *Good Will Hunting* is that of George Bernard Dantzig, once a student at the University of California, Berkeley. Noted as a conscientious student, one who studied rather late into the night, Dantzig had overslept and therefore showed up to class about twenty minutes late one day. He saw two problems on the board, and assuming they were homework assignments, promptly copied them down and went home to work on them after class was over. The story notes that he seemed to think that the problems were a bit more difficult than usual, but he proceeded to solve them anyway and returned them to his professor, Jerzy Neyman, a couple of days later. Six weeks passed and one Sunday morning, at about 8:00 a.m., Dantzig and his wife were awakened by banging on the door. It turned out to be his professor who informed him that one of the answers to the two questions had been prepared for publication. Unknown to Dantzig, the professor had mentioned to the class before he arrived that these problems were "unsolvable statistical theorems." Legend had it that even Einstein was unable to solve them (Affleck et al. 1997).

The moral of the story is this: Dantzig was a man without any mental limitations. Since he was late to class, he had not heard and therefore not been subjected to the doubt, fear and sense of impossibility that the professor's words might have conveyed to the rest of the students. If it had been unsolvable for hundreds, perhaps thousands of years, if even Einstein was unable to solve it, how could I? His lateness to class was a blessing in disguise. George however solved the problem because he had no idea or knowledge that he couldn't. George B. Dantzig died on May 13, 2005, at the age of ninety.

Education: The Great Equalizer

"Education is the key that opens the golden door of freedom."
—George Washington Carver

"He who opens a school door closes a prison."
—Victor Hugo

"Education then, beyond all other devices of human origin, is a great equalizer of the conditions of men—the balance wheel of the social machinery…it gives each man the independence and the means by which he can resist the selfishness of other men."
—Horace Mann

Education has been called the Civil Rights issue of our time. It may well not be just that, but also the human rights issue of our time, the great equalizer, which opens the door to all possibilities. It is the path to upward social mobility. As a community, we need to not only value intellectual achievement, but also raise expectations for our kids, parents, and teachers. If our children begin to think that dealing drugs is the most effective way for upward social mobility, we have a serious problem.

The Supreme Court's decision in 1954, *Brown vs. the Board of Education's* was a landmark victory for Black Americans, paid for by the toil and blood of our forebears. It paved the way for Blacks to be fully integrated into the America Public School system (National Center Staff). It did away with the previous prejudicial school system of *Separate but Equal* enacted through *Plessy vs. Ferguson* in 1896, where school segregation was enforced by law (History.com). Today any kid in America has the right and the ability to go to school, a right and an ability not enjoyed by many kids in other parts of the world. I personally left an institute for higher education and learning because of daunting financial demands after the death of my parents, which occurred three months apart from each other. Despite all the challenges that the American economy is going through, college education is still available to any and everyone who is serious about educating themselves. It makes no sense to me, for any one not to go to college when Federal and state governments are willing to help, financially, not to mention all the scholarships one can qualify for through academic achievement, excellence, and other means.

By far, and especially for people of color, education provides the safest and most effective means for upward social mobility, and everything else an individual can dream of. It is indeed the *Great Equalizer*. Racism still exists and racial disparities persist, undoubtedly, but all key indicators point to higher income levels for those who choose to pursue higher or college education.

CHAPTER 12

The Multiracial and Cultural Church Christ's Agent of Racial Healing and Reconciliation

As sociologists and economists ponder and analyze the problems, aspirations and despairs of America's ethnic groups and migrant populations, legal and illegal, and as politicians attempt to win elections, sometimes, by exploiting the racial and cultural divisions, playing one race or ethnic group against another (e.g., Willie Horton-Bush and Dukakis debacle, 1988), the questions that confront the Church, in my view, among others, are as follows:

- Is God in the mass migrations of various people groups to the US?
- If so, what are the spiritual and missiological implications of these trends for the Church?

- How should the Church respond to the racial and cultural dynamics reshaping our society today (e.g., the increasing Browning of America), and the prospect of the dominant culture, White America, becoming the new minority (by 2050)?
- How can the Church be better positioned and ready to respond to a possible escalation in race and ethnic tensions, a scenario Pannell captures in his book, *The Coming Race Wars* (Pannell), in light of the extreme racial, cultural and political polarization in our country?

Undoubtedly, the implications of America's contemporary, pluralistic and urban culture for missiology are vast and manifold. It is my contention that employing the dynamics of multicultural churches as a church planting strategy is the most effective missiological response to the questions raised above, for engaging the plurality of cultures represented in America with the gospel of Jesus Christ, and particularly, for fostering racial healing and reconciliation in contemporary urban settings of America.

The multiracial and cultural church is the panacea for America's racial wounds, and the most credible witness of God's love for all humanity in a racialized, multicultural society. It is also, by extension, the foremost agent for fostering racial healing and reconciliation in a racially-polarized context. There is, indeed, no greater agency and facility for healing America's racial wounds and fostering racial reconciliation than the Church, specifically the Multicultural or ethnic church. Yancey's assertion is again noteworthy here; "the more I have thought about this issue (racism), the more I realize that the moral presence of the Church is essential in the battle against racism if racial peace is ever going to be possible in our time" (Yancey 1996). The Church, called to be the "light of the world" and the "salt of the earth" (Matt. 5:14), the moral vanguard of our society, is the primary, if not the sole entity with the divine wherewithal to facilitate racial healing and reconciliation. This is so because (as explained earlier), racism, at its core, is a spiritual condition, a disease of the human heart. "Racism, according to *Facing Racism: A Vision of the Beloved Community* is, fundamentally, a spiritual problem because it denies our true identity as children of God" (The Initiative Team on Racism and Racial Violence). In *Crossing the Racial Divide, America's Struggle for Justice and Reconciliation*, Aaron Gallegos also notes that "racism is a spiritual issue. Neither its solutions or causes will be found (solely) through government programs, social ministries or our own best intentions... The forces that perpetuate racism through our society are rooted in spiritual realities that require us to call out God for spiritual solutions" (Gallegos 1998). Since racism, at its core, is a spiritual malady, its panacea would be authentic transformation and reconciliation with God, who alone wields the capacity to heal and transform the human heart.

The American Church's historical flirtation with racism, and its complicity in the shaping of a segregated and racially fractured society and world, makes the Church's mission and the ministry of reconciliation, not only an imperative, but simultaneously, complicated; a paradox. How can the Church, a perpetrator of the sin of racism, offer the panacea for the healing of the same disease it has helped in causing? John Dawson in *Healing America's Wounds* highlights this paradox. Regarding prejudice, he observes that "the followers of Jesus have the potential to heal the wound. However, he further notes, "When I look at the Church of America, I see a people who sometimes mirror, more than they contrast, the national condition…our greatest national sins are most deeply institutionalized within the Church," he states (Dawson 1994).

The Church's complicity is seen through its use of theologically-contrived theories, such as the *Curse of Ham and his descendants,* to confer a status of genetic inferiority on all people of color, especially, those of African descent (Lumeya 1988). Attributes of brute strength and accolades pertaining to the athletic and artistic impulses of darker-hued people were gratuitously conferred, not to mention their sexual prowess and voracious appetite for carnal pleasure, while every other attribute was denigrated, labeled subhuman, and consigned to an inferior designation. This was often done with the divine sanction of, and endorsement by the Church. In this regard, Dawson again states, "it became necessary… to dehumanize those people Europeans held in bondage… shortly…a proliferation of theories arose about the inferiority of Negroes" (Dawson 1994).

The challenge here lay in the fact that, an "irreconcilable contradiction" was going to be created if the Negro or Native American was seen as human, possessing an immortal soul with the potential for salvation (Dawson 1994). A status of superiority, conversely, was true for all of Aryan or Caucasian descent. These were stereotypes legitimized, at best, from theology to biology. White supremacy, which served as the underpinnings of slavery, Jim Crow, colonialism, apartheid, eugenics, Western imperialism etc. were formulated from these contrived notions and buttressed by the Church (Lumeya 1988).

The Church's silence, and by extension, complicity, in the face of the Jewish holocaust, as Hitler unleashed his Aryan, racist fury on "inferior" Jews, the Rwandan, Sudanese, and Congolese genocides are worthy of mention, in this regard.

As Dietrich Bonhoeffer, eloquently asserted, "Silence in the face of evil is itself evil: God will not hold us guiltless. Not to speak is to speak; not to act is to act" (Stewart 2016). Ginetta Sagan, human rights advocate and honorary Chair of the Board of Directors of Amnesty International, USA, expressed it a bit more succinctly; she wrote, "Silence in the face of injustice is complicity with the oppressor" (Segan 2000). Thus, the "light of the world," the Church (Matt. 5:14) became, for many "colored" people, the pain of the world through these theories, and the atrocities that subsequently followed.

Change in the Church: An Urgent, Divine Imperative

The American Church as it stands today is segregated along racial, ethnic and cultural fault lines, undoubtedly, the legacy of its racist past. Du Bois, the preeminent Black-American scholar and social scientist, who died and was buried in Ghana, West Africa, my country of origin, highlighted this best in *The Color Line and the Church*, when he stated that "The American Church of Christ is Jim Crowed from top to bottom. No other institution in America is built so thoroughly or more absolutely on the color line..." (Du Bois 1929). Concurring with Du Bois, Dr. King's words sound a similar tone in a sermon on March 31, 1968, just days before his assassination: "It is appalling, he says, "that the most segregated hour of Christian America is eleven o'clock on Sunday morning... How often the Church has had a high blood count of creeds and an anemia of deeds!" (King 1987).

Emerson and Smith in *Divided By Faith* further corroborate the racism Du Bois and King excoriate in the Church, when they charge that so many churches are segregated along ethnic and economic lines, and that little has changed in the more than one hundred years since it was first observed that eleven o'clock on Sunday morning is the most segregated hour of the week (Emerson and Smith). They assert, besides, that 92.5% of churches in the United States are racially segregated—i.e., 80% or more of individual membership in these churches represents a single (homogenous) people group. Churches in the United States are ten times more segregated than the neighborhoods in which they are located and twenty times more segregated than the public schools in their neighborhood (Emerson and Smith). Between 1990 and 2007, a period of seventeen years, the United States population, in general, increased by 56,819,471.3, whereas church attendance in the United States increased by a paltry 446,540 people (DeYmaz 2007).

In *United by Faith: The Multicultural Congregation as an Answer to the Problem of Race*, the authors DeYoung et al also highlight the fact that the American Church is "racially segregated." Only 5.5% of all Christian congregations in the US are racially mixed (DeYoung et al), they further emphasize. A recent National Congregations Study shows that nine out of ten congregations have a majority race that composes 90 percent or more of the congregation (Emerson et. al). Similar figures have been found in other national congregation surveys as well (Dougherty and Huyser). For the world or society to be segregated and racially fractured is one thing; for the scourge of racism to infect a religious institution, such as the Church, the Body of Christ and the light of the world, mandated to illuminate the darkness and point the way, is a totally different issue.

Unfortunately, a segregated and divided Church cannot foster healing and reconciliation in a divided world;

only a united Church can. Some Pan-Africanists, like Elijah Mohammed of the Nation of Islam and the late Bob Marley, the Jamaican reggae superstar, have called on Black people, in light of these atrocities, to completely reject Christianity, the Bible and the Church and return to the Black man's original and ancestral forms of worship, or to Islam, allegedly, the original religion of the Black Man. In this regard, Mensa Otabil's admonishment is worth noting. He states in *Beyond the Rivers of Ethiopia*.

"That is not the way out! When a man is bitten by a snake," he explains, "it takes an anti-snake bite serum prepared from a snake to bring healing and restoration to that person... I totally believe that if the Bible was misused and misapplied to bind our people, we would need an anti-oppression serum prepared from the revealed truth in God's Word to bring healing, liberty and restoration to us" (Otabil).

To be a force for racial healing and reconciliation, the Church must undergo drastic change, just as the venom of the snake must undergo chemical changes in order to become an anti-venom serum. The Church has to, certainly, divorce itself from its racist past, return to its "ancient landmarks" and reclaim its prophetic voice and mission of healing and reconciliation through a reinterpretation and reapplication of the same biblical authority it so woefully employed, to subjugate a segment of God's people. It also means, in its quest for missional effectiveness, it must come to terms with contextual factors on the American landscape. The significance, as well as, the contours of the seismic cultural and demographic shifts occurring in America, a result of the massive migration patterns is, certainly, a good place to begin.

In *Transforming Mission*, David Bosch, the illustrious South African theologian and missiologist, is masterful and eloquent in his explanation of paradigm shifts in the Church vis-a-vis its mission. Mission, Bosch says, needs to be understood as "the good news of God's love, incarnated in the witness of a community for the sake of the world." Paradigm shifts in mission, he further explains, necessitates equivalent shifts in the Church's theology of mission and praxis. Each shift in culture, he stresses, presents the Church with two options: danger and opportunity (Bosch 1991). The need for proper contextualization in mission, thus, cannot be overemphasized.

To the issue of paradigm shifts in the Church and world, and the need, therefore, to contextualize its mission, Loren Mead also observes that, both the Church and the world are in constant flux. We (the Church) however, bring to that constant change and unstable environment, a stable and unchanging paradigm, a mind-set that sometimes lasts for centuries (Mead 1991). Eddie Gibbs, underscoring the Church's need for change, in turn, says, "To assume that one can continue to function in one's accustomed style without regard to the conditions and demands of the new situation, is to be as foolhardy as to turn a boat sideways to the waves in mountainous seas" Gibbs. The most strident of the calls for change in the Church, perhaps, is Olson. He writes in *The American Church in Crisis* that on any given Sunday, the clear majority of Americans are absent from church, and if trends continue, by 2050, the percentage of Americans attending church will be half of what it was in 1990. Olson contends that the Church has been lulled to sleep and is ill-prepared to engage the new world. For restoration to occur, the American Church, he asserts, must address three critical shifts in our culture: from Christian to Post-Christian, Modern to Postmodern and Mono-ethnic to Multiethnic (Olson). The Church, thrust into a multiracial, cultural and ethnic ethos, needs to discern the times like the children of Isaachar (1

Chron. 12:32), and know what to change, how to renew and position itself for greater missional effectiveness in this context.

"Of the children of Isaachar, men who understood the times, and knew what Israel ought to do..."

The Multiracial Church Vis a Vis the Homogenous Unit Principle In a Pluralistic, Multiracial and Ethnic Context

Of great consequence to God's mission of reconciliation, particularly, healing and bridging the racial divides in the Church and the broader American society, is the homogenous unit principle. In an increasingly multiracial, cultural and ethnic milieu, it is my contention that more multiracial, ethnic and national churches need to and should be planted in the Name of the One who "broke down the middle wall of division and hostility" (Eph. 2:14) that is Jesus Christ.

In *United by Faith*, the authors boldly declare that "Christian congregations when possible should be multiracial...the twenty-first century must be the century of multiracial congregations" (DeYoung et al). This paradigm is in sharp contrast to the Homogenous Unit Principle, first espoused by notable missiologist, Donald McGavran, *The Bridges of God*, and later popularized by Church Growth advocate, Peter Wagner. Based, in part, on McGavran's finding that "people like to become Christians without crossing racial, linguistic or class barriers" (McGavran 1955), Wagner in *Your Church Can Grow: Seven Vital Signs of a Healthy Church* defines a Homogenous Unit as: "a group of people who consider each other to be our kind of people. They have many areas of mutual interest; they share the same culture;

they socialize freely…when they are together, they are comfortable, and they all feel at home" (Wagner 2011). In every day parlance, we could interpret the Homogenous Unit Principle to mean, "Birds of the same feathers flock together."

Wagner's argument for this principle is three-fold: First, the church's "focus here is on" or should be "Evangelism, not Christian Nurture." How to establish an effective base for winning the unsaved to Christ, thus, becomes paramount. Second is the cultural or sociological factor: This means that a common culture, background or interest, will serve as a natural basis or attraction for building and nurturing durable, significant relationships). Cultural pluralism, Wagner adds, has come to stay in America and Christians who do not feel either comfortable with it or understand its full implications "will continue to reject the homogenous unit principle," as a "denial of the Doctrine of Christian unity and a return to racism and discrimination" (Wagner 2011).

Wagner's statements above appear to "absolutize" the homogenous unit principle, making it into a prescriptive methodology or guide, leaving no room for dissent or equivocation, whatsoever. He posits as either "uncomfortable" with cultural pluralism or not aware of its "full implications" regarding Evangelism and/or church growth, any contrarian and his or her views regarding this principle. First, the fact of our pluralistic character as a nation has already been amply stated in this literature review. It is my conviction that America's cultural diversity must not only be affirmed; it must also be celebrated. In no way, however, should it be used to endorse Schlesinger's "separatist impulse," fueled by race, culture or ethnicity, and there is no better context for this than the Church, the earthly Jerusalem. The Heavenly Jerusalem is depicted as comprising of people redeemed from "every kindred and tongue and people and nation" (Rev.

5:9–10). It would seem to me that, the Lord would want His Bride to have a foretaste of this experience on earth. Thy will be done earth as it is in heaven was Jesus prototype of prayer, as he taught his disciples how to pray. His desire is to, ultimately, establish His kingdom (rule) on earth, as it is in heaven (Matt. 6:10).

Second, evangelism, as opposed to spiritual nurture is the other reason presented by Wagner and proponents of the Homogenous Unit Principle. Evangelistic effectiveness, however, does not depend solely or primarily on people's comfort level with each other by way of a shared culture or interest. These may be platforms that may allow for more interaction and easier communication of the gospel, but wrestling souls from the grip of Satan in the name of the Lord (which is what evangelism entails) is fundamentally, and essentially a spiritual issue, not social or cultural. The Apostle Paul emphasizes the spiritual nature of the Christians' battle: "For we wrestle not against flesh and blood, but against principalities and powers…" (Eph. 6:12). If our gospel is hidden, from the unsaved, Paul again says, it is because "the god of this world has blinded their minds…" (2 Cor. 4:4). Jesus emphasized the spiritual nature of soul-winning when he stated the need to first "bind the strong man" before attempting to plunder his goods (Matt. 12:9). If conversion is primarily (but not solely) a spiritual matter, then Christian or Spiritual Nurture, which leads to spiritual health, maturity and discipleship, may well be the real key to evangelistic viability, since spiritual babies cannot wage spiritual battles. Little wonder that Christ appointed the ministry gifts of apostle, prophet, evangelistic, pastor and teacher to "equip" (train, equip, coach, nurture, empower, disciple) the saints for the "work of the ministry" (Eph. 4:11–12) the beginning point of which is evangelism. Evangelistic effectiveness is, essentially, therefore, the natural outcome of a spiritual "income" and nurture, and not a sociological or cultural enterprise. Furthermore, homogeneity does not have to be limited to race, culture or ethnicity, particularly in such an increasingly fragmented, multiracial and ethnic environment, where polarizing forces motivated by the demonic, are bent on using race and ethnicity to create a wedge among us. The segregation of the Church has been the unfortunate development, however. Michael Emerson's indictment of the homogenous (or segregated) church through his research findings in *Divided by Faith* is worth noting: "The segregation of the local church unintentionally perpetuates systemic racism in society, he concludes" (Emerson and Smith).

In a modern world, a growing proportion of humans lives in urban areas where they are exposed to cultural influences of many kinds, in a continuous process of mutual exchange and influence between different groups. In such an environment, each person naturally becomes a part of several communities at the same time (Newbigin).

The call to, and cost of Discipleship and disciple-making, the focus of missions and evangelism (Matt. 28:18–19) furthermore, make it imperative that the Church reevaluate the homogenous unit principle, especially in our current context. If Church growth alone is the focus of our evangelistic and missionary enterprises, then it would seem that Jesus failed woefully. In sheer numerical terms, Jesus's ministry in three years does not appear to be particularly productive; only 120 were in the Upper Room waiting for the promised Holy Spirit. His call for complete self-denial and commitment to the kingdom and its principles of discipleship was too harsh, costly and honest for many in the multitudes that thronged him to keep up with the program. The call to community with those unlike us, culturally and ethnically, is vital for fulfilling the call to discipleship.

The words of David Watson in *Called and Committed* are particularly instructive in this regard. In discussing corporate life in the Church based on radical biblical principles, he states that; "Christ's calling is to a radical alternative society which will by its existence and values, profoundly challenge the existing society," unfortunately "the Church," he says, "consists largely of comfortable clubs of conformity" (Watson). What is more uncomfortable than worshipping or fellowshipping with people who are culturally "strange" or foreign, people you have been brought up to believe are out to get you, and therefore to fear, never to trust and if possible, avoid all your life.

Watson draws from *Schopenhauer's Porcupines: Intimacy And Its Dilemmas: Five Stories Of Psychotherapy*, in which Luepnitz, the German philosopher, likens people to a pack of porcupines on a freezing winter night. The subzero temperature forces them to come together for warmth. But as soon as they come together, they jab and hurt each other. So they separate, only to attempt, repeatedly to huddle together again (Luepnitz). Watson calls on the Church to resist this temptation, one that I believe the Church has already succumbed to. It is a temptation to separate, to pull back to a safe and comfortable distance, to erect cultural barriers and to protect ourselves from the vulnerabilities of close interracial or cultural relations, thereby destroying or weakening the love and unity which Jesus commanded, for which he prayed, died and sent His Spirit to accomplish.

It behooves us, the Church, to keep reminding ourselves that the call to discipleship is a call to Community, a real, authentic community, Watson emphasizes (Watson). Sunday morning should forge such racial, cultural, and ethnic community among Christians, of all cultures, races, and ethnicities, instead of the stark, non-Christ-like reality currently confronting the Church which highlights our differences instead of our similarities. The authenticity, unity, and strength of a multicultural, racial, and ethnic community is, and will be our key to missional effectiveness in a culturally and ethnically pluralistic America.

Extracting people from their cultural matrices and placing them in artificial settings for worship, what, in *Your Church Can Grow: Seven Vital Signs of a healthy Church* calls "cultural circumcision" (Wagner 2011) is not what is being advocated here. What is, is a multiracial and ethnic church planting paradigm that acknowledges, affirms and celebrates cultural differences, but nevertheless points to a "Super Culture"; God's super culture in Christ, to the end that we all, black, white, brown, yellow and red, may "come into the unity of the faith…to the measure of the stature of the fullness of Christ" (Ephesians 4:13). This speaks to a certain maturity forged by our unity as the Body of Christ.

An important nursery of the Church's maturity is the "unity of the faith…" (Ephesians 4:13). The unity the apostle espouses is one that transcends every possible line of division, natural and/or spiritual, in the Church. To reach and mobilize a people-group, homogenous in all respects, to faith in Christ without teaching them to "observe all things whatsoever Christ commanded" (Matt. 28:18–19), is to short-sell the gospel message and compromise a crucial tenet of discipleship. "The Christ who is presented in Scripture for our believing," Newbigin says in *The Open Secret*, "is lord over all cultures and His purpose is to unite all of every culture unto Himself in a unity that transcends, without negating the diversities of culture" (Newbigin 1995).

The paradigm being espoused becomes even more so critical in a post-modern, secular and pluralistic cultural environment, where many can trace their lineage to three, four or more different racial and ethnic groups. In fact, Tiger Woods is a prime example of this. He referred to his ethnic identity as "Cablinasian"—for Caucasian, Black, Indian and Asian. Doubtless, with increased migration to the US and intermarriage among America's ethnic groups, will come increased heterogeneity in the population. Armed with this expectation and paradigm, a new theology of missions should be enunciated, one that posits the homogenous unit principle not as a rule, stipulation, or an absolute, but rather as sociological insight, strategic and complementary to the missionary enterprise.

Multiracial and Cultural Churches: A Panacea to America's Race Problem Multiracial and Cultural Church Defined

The multiracial or multicultural church, it is my contention, is the answer to the race problem, both in the Church and in the broader American society. As DeYoung, Curtiss, Emerson, Yancey and Kim define it, in *United by Faith*, a multicultural church is a church congregation with no more than eighty percent (80%) of its membership belonging to one racial or ethnic group (DeYoung et al). DeYmaz explains that leading researchers and sociologists in the Multiethnic Church Movement define a multiethnic (or, multiracial) church in terms of an eighty-twenty rule. In other words, when a congregation reaches 20% diversity, they will describe it as being multiethnic/multiracial. For example, that 20% could represent White people in an African American church;

or it could represent a more general population that is 10% African American, 5% Latino and 5% Asian in a congregation that is otherwise 80% White (DeYmaz 2007).

David Daniels III, in his article, *God Makes No Difference in Nationality—The Fashioning of a New Racial? Nonracial Identity at the Azusa Street Revival* highlights the impact of the Azuza Street Revival on the racial environment of the era. Utilizing the radical statement applied to the revival by Pastor Frank Bartleman that the "The Color Line was washed away in the blood," Daniel observes that "the new racial identity at the Azusa Street Revival looked beyond the racial divide of the era and reflected a racial vocabulary, symbolism and vision that differed drastically from the dominant society of that day" (Daniels 2006). The radical statement Bartleman used, Daniels further writes, captured the aspirations of Christians who had rejected the "racial etiquette of the era" and embraced a new ethic, one that reached beyond the color line that separated the races. The Azusa Street revival, it is well known brought together people of different races and nationalities, some of who testified publicly of being cleansed from their prejudice by this experience. Of this, Daniels additionally highlights that, "In addition to a color-blind congregation, Seymour and the Azusa Street revival developed a nonracial identity. Besides a variety of nationalities integrating a previously all-Black revival, what is astonishing about the Azusa Street revival is the conversions that occurred in the racial consciousness of Whites such as Frank Bartleman, G. B. Cashwell, and others. These individuals had admitted to being prejudiced but experienced a conversion in racial consciousness that led them not only to reject prejudice and willingly associate with other races, but also to educate their networks about interracial association" (Daniels 2006).

From a missional or missiological perspective, the planting of multiracial and cultural church, therefore, is the greatest need of the hour. It is a biblical response, demonstrating God's original intent for His Church and for all people. It symbolizes the inclusive call, nature and message of Christ to "whosoever." There is no better testament to Christ as the only "repairer of the breach" in an often hostile, racially-polarized world than the multicultural church. Olson and Adams write *In the American Church in Crisis,* that in a mono-ethnic world, Christians, pastors, and churches only had to understand their own culture... In the multiethnic world, pastors, churches, and Christians need to operate under the rules of the early Church's mission to the Gentiles (Olson and Adams 2009). In modeling the early church, the multicultural church exhibits, not a cheap or easy fraternity among people of the same kind, but a costly discipleship where we may struggle or grapple with our differences, culturally, but in the process, learn to decrease that Christ may be exalted in and through us, Olson writes (Olson).

The biblical paradigm of the church is multiracial and multicultural. It is the heart of the Father to bless the ecumenical family of nations through Abraham and his seed. Thus, prophetic utterances depicting God's heart for, and call to the nations, are repeatedly enunciated throughout scripture. In Isaiah 2:2–3 and repeated in Micah 4:2. In Mark 11:7, Jesus states that his house shall be called a house of prayer, again for "all nations." The Great Commission spelt out in Matthew 28:18–18 and Luke 24:44–49, furthermore, are a call to reach and make disciples of all nations. The heavenly Jerusalem depicted in Revelation 5:9 and 7:9 speak of the multitudes gathered from "every nation, tribe, people and language." America today is a nation of nations. The nations of the world have virtually converged upon the United States.

In such a multicultural and ethnic context, there is no better credible witness than the churches that reflect the cosmopolitan nature of American society as it stands, today, i.e., multicultural churches. Writing the foreword to the book, *One New People, Models for Developing a Multiethnic Church*, by Manuel Ortiz, Harvey Conn speaks to the Church's call to the nations. In a day of fear and distrust, the multiethnic church, he emphasizes, is a sample of recomposition in Christ. E pluribus Unum is a visionary slogan in politics; in the multiethnic church, it is a response of the Holy Spirit to culture wars. It is well worth more than a quick glance by a fractured society seeking unity in too many superficial solutions, and by a church that often doesn't realize the treasure it has been given (Ortiz 1996).

The DNA of the Church was multiethnic and cultural from its very advent. In *United by Faith*, the authors emphasize that the first-century church was united by faith. This unity occurred as local congregations strategically implemented the Jesus's vision of a house of prayer for all nations. Early congregations of the Church of God were culturally diverse. In Jerusalem, they bridged the diversity of culture found among the Jewish people of the time. Outside Jerusalem, congregations bridged the separation between Jews, Samaritans, and Gentiles. Followers of Jesus Christ continued to establish multicultural congregations...their broad inclusiveness only decreasing when the church became more aligned with the Roman Empire. It was then that the church became divided buy faith (DeYoung et al 2003).

The credibility of the church, with respect to race relations in America comes into focus here. The multiracial church should serve as a lighthouse in a cynical and racially polarized world, beholden to the sin of racism. Light leads the way; it shows the possibilities. Christ's call is for us to be blameless, examples in a crooked and perverse world among whom we shine as lights (Phil. 2:15). Paul, writing to the Ephesian church, appeals to the people of God, the church in Ephesus, to "walk worthy of the vocation placed upon them" (Ephesians 4:1). The apostle Peter also reminds us that judgment must begin in God's household, with God's people (1 Pet. 4:17). Paul admonishes the Corinthian church to also judge or examine itself, adding that if it did, it will not come under God's censure (1 Cor. 11:31), since judgment is to begin in the house of the Lord. The biblical injunction to judge or examine ourselves becomes critical, considering the above. The call to self-examination is a call to establish the Church's credibility, which credibility serves as the only platform or credentials we presumably have for outreach to the world. Since Sunday morning 11:00 a.m. has been perceived as the most segregated hour in America because of the racial, ethnic, and cultural polarization in the church, there is no better day and time of the week to demonstrate the love of God for all humanity than the same day and hour, Sunday morning 11:00 a.m.

The multiracial cultural church demonstrates this love, and by extension, its credibility, by embracing all races, cultures and ethnicities. After all, we can only "revenge all disobedience" when our "obedience is fulfilled" (2 Cor. 10:6). For an entity like the Church, whose history in this regard has been anything but glowing, this is an imperative. Regarding the church's credibility as a faithful and effective witness of our hope in Christ, Mark DeYmaz asserts his belief in the unity and diversity of the multiethnic local church, as an authentic and tangible display of the love of God for all people. It provides us, he says, with the most effective means for reaching the world with the gospel, as made clear by none other than Christ himself on the night before he died (John 17:20–23).

In other words, the intrinsic desire of a healthy multiethnic church, its very motivation, is to see people come to know Christ in a personal way (DeYmaz 2007). Dr. King's appeal is instructive in this regard "first, the church must remove the yoke of segregation from its own body. Only by doing this can it be effective in its attack on outside evils…" (King). For in an increasingly diverse and cynical society, DeYmaz, in leading a healthy multiethnic church, concludes, people will no longer find credible the message of God's love for all people when it's preached from segregated pulpits and pews (DeYmaz 2013).

In summarizing, there is no gainsaying that the Ministry of Reconciliation, both vertical and horizontal, lie at the top of God's missional agenda for America, a nation increasingly becoming multiethnic and cultural. The Church, called to be the light of the world, is at the forefront of this mission and ministry of reconciliation. Since racism is primarily a spiritual condition, the Church is the only entity on earth with the divine capacity to foster real healing and reconciliation. However, a racially and ethnically divided Church is anathema to this mission. A segregated Church, reinforced by a separatist impulse, as seen in the Homogenous Unit Principle cannot bring healing to a divided world. Change within the Church, therefore, is an urgent, divine imperative. The multicultural church offers the best hope for healing and reconciliation in a pluralistic America.

CONCLUSION

In part 1 of this book, *The Color of God, America, The Church and the Politics of Race*, I have examined the issue of race in America, its nuances, morbid tentacles, reach or impact, to ascertain the most effective means by which racial healing and reconciliation may be achieved, particularly, in our nation's urban contexts. That race has been an integral part of our sordid history has been established. That it is a social construct aimed at social, economic, and political dominance has also been established. That the Church has been complicit in the creation of America's racial fragmentation, certainly, leaves much to be desired. The arrival of multitudes of immigrants to America's shores only complicates an already complicated problem, changing its designation from a "melting pot" to a "salad bowl." Will the center hold?

This was Schlesinger's deepest concern. Tracing this history has only been necessary to determine a better way forward. Having contributed actively to the creation of a fragmented culture, the Church cannot now remain passive or silent; it must engage the society in the effort to dismantle the vestiges of racism that still dots America's institutions and cultural landscape. "We will have to repent not merely for the vitriolic words and actions of the bad people but for the appalling silence of the good people," Dr. Martin Luther King stated (King). A segregated Church certainly cannot bring healing and reconciliation to a divided world; only a united Church can. Consequently, the Church has to undergo seismic change, and become a prophetic prototype of the heavenly Jerusalem on earth, a kingdom comprising every tongue, people, tribe and nation (Rev 5:9–10, 7:9).

The concept of the Homogenous Unit Principle needs reexamination, considering the increasing multicultural context America's Church is called to engage with, and for the sake of racial healing and reconciliation. Contrived racist theologies and theories formulated to buttress the subjugation of people of color, especially, those of African descent, also need to be revisited, reinterpreted and recontextualized in light of this present discussion; it is unthinkable that such doctrines were used to rebuild the very walls for which Jesus Christ died to break down (Eph. 2:14). In light of all the arguments presented in this book, I make an unequivocal claim that racial healing and reconciliation is an ideal whose time has come. This ideal calls for the creation of a just, equitable and egalitarian, multiracial America, one in which every race, culture and ethnicity has a stake in the continued growth and development of our beloved country.

In part 2, I discuss the subject of Black Redemption and Lift, as critical to real, as opposed, to superficial healing and reconciliation. For Black America, particularly, and all other descendants of African slaves in the diaspora, in general, it is time to fulfill our prophetic mission and destiny of being "eyes in the wilderness" and channels of blessing to our world. To achieve this, we need to break the shackles that hold us bound, spiritually, socially, mentally, and economically, and reverse the adverse impact and legacy of centuries of historical and present-day racism on our lives, our families and posterity. Like Joseph, sold into slavery by his brothers, who attained the heights of power and achievement in a land that was initially foreign to him, I declare that it is time for the Black-Body politic to change, heal, be restored and elevated to the very heights of spiritual, mental, educational, social and economic achievement. A strong Black community and culture means a strong America, and a better world. Black Redemption and Lift is not only necessary for the cause of racial healing and reconciliation, but also for the betterment of our country.

Only few people have gone through what we have been through and survived. It is time to let go of the wounds of the past, whether White America acknowledges the atrocities it has perpetrated and the pain she has caused, or not. This is imperative, for the "wrath of man, scripture says, does not work the righteousness of God" (James 1:20). Our sense of spirituality necessitates that we trust God and forgive. Forgiveness will bring to us, healing we can then offer to others.

"If you want to go fast, go alone, if you want to go far, go together" (African Proverb). The multiracial and cultural church presents the Church with the most effective means to engage a racially, culturally and an ethnically, pluralistic America. There is no better context to validate, show respect, and express appreciation for those of other cultures than to sit down with them, talk, eat, worship, and have your kids play together in an environment of love and mutual acceptance. This is what the multiracial and cultural church context is about. What Jesus did by his death and resurrection, had cosmic dimensions, theologically, touching the ecumenical family of nations. A theology of mission that captures His passion for the nations as depicted in the New Jerusalem, should be most welcome in an ethnically polarized such society, as ours, often racked and polarized by ethnic and racial animus. In the multicultural church, the dialogue toward racial healing, reconciliation and justice can, at least, begin.

To fulfill God's mission in post-modern pluralistic America, the Church of Jesus Christ cannot allow itself to be held hostage by the mentality and methods of its racist past. It must dare to be countercultural. It must balance individual or personal salvation with a community orientation and action. This means that the Church must be an instrument of justice, not love alone. Justice, in today's world, is a manifestation of love. In the words of Newbigin, "where justice is denied, love is certainly denied." "For the Biblical writers," he continues, "to know the Lord was not a matter of intellectual contemplation or mystical union, it was a matter of doing justice and mercy in concrete terms" (Newbigin 1995).

The Church must consequently be a voice for the millions of immigrants fleeing political tyranny, religious persecution and economic deprivation. It must continue to champion the cause of healing and reconciliation among the races, for regardless of which ship we all came on, whether the Mayflower or the Amistad, today, we are all in the same boat; we either choose to float together or we sink together. Church leaders must not sweep the issue of racism, whatever its form, under the carpet and pretend it does not exist. Those who claim there is no problems are the problem. The ignorance, fear and suspicion, which are usually at the root of most racial and ethnic tensions, must be dispelled through cultural awareness and sensitivity seminars, and other forms of interracial dialogue. The Doctrine of the Curse of Ham needs to be researched and reinterpreted in our Bible commentaries for the sake of future generations. How can we tell a little Black or Latino child that God loves him or her, when this same God has permanently cursed and banished him or her to a life of perpetual servitude because of his or her race, color or hair texture? Black kids need to know that there was a Black presence in the Bible, that some of the earliest Church fathers like Augustine were Black Africans, and that the first Christian university was built in Africa. This will help dispel the notion that Christianity is the "White man's" religion. Furthermore, church leaders must endeavor to model diversity at every level of leadership in their churches, and joint worship services and/or community-impact programs (e.g., street/graffiti cleaning) between local churches with different racial and ethnic compositions should be encouraged. Our churches should reflect the demographic makeup of our immediate communities and never again should we, the Church, allow the Name of the one who broke down the middle wall of division among the races/nations, i.e., Jesus Christ, to be used to rebuild those same walls again.

The hope of reconciliation, between God and humanity, as well as between all races, cultures, and people groups lies in Christ, whose death and resurrection removed every hostility between all peoples of the earth. At his birth, three categories of people from three different cultural groups came looking for him. They were the shepherds, from the family of Shem, the Greeks, who represented Japheth's line, and the three wise men from the family of Ham (Custance 1970). Each of the three branches or families of Noah's sons, representing the races, played a role in his crucifixion and death, also. The moral responsibility was accepted by Israel in Matthew 27:25. The physical burden and responsibility was borne by Simon of Cyrene, obviously, a Black man, and therefore belonging to the family of Ham, and the executive decision and responsibility assumed by the Japhethic line, the Romans (Matt. 27:26). It is to this unity of purpose, each race, culture and ethnicity playing its part and making its divine contribution to human development, that Christ calls us. To Christ, therefore, each culture, race and people-group must come and rediscover its purpose. Just as Joseph's coat of many colors was dipped in the blood of the lamb, so must the nations be dipped in, and cleansed by the precious of the Lamb of God, Jesus Christ. The blood-soaked, multicolored garment of the beloved son, Joseph, was then presented to the father, Jacob. Even so will Christ present His chaste Bride, the Church, comprising the nations, cultures, races and people groups of the world, redeemed and cleansed by His blood, to His Father, united as one, their differences washed away and undone by the color of the blood by which they are cleansed. As we strive to replicate the Father's Kingdom and will on earth, and in America, may we always be reminded of the source of the sweet melodies we enjoy each Sunday, at our churches. Both, the black and white notes of the piano or keyboard, working harmoniously together, make these melodies possible. This is the Father's desire for His kingdom, a kingdom comprising "every, kindred, tongue, people and nation (Rev. 5:9). Let your kingdom come, Lord.

REFERENCES

ABC News. *"Halle Berry Cites One-Drop Rule: Is Her Daughter Black or White?"* Accessed May 25, 2016. http://abcnews.go.com/Health/halle-berry-cites-drop-rule-daughter-black-white/story?id=12869789.

Abu-Lughod, Janet L. 1999. *Sociology for the Twenty-First Century: Continuities and Cutting Edges.* Chicago: University of Chicago Press.

"Action." *Public Productivity and Management Review* 20, no. 3: 243. doi:10.2307/3380975.

Adams, Guy B. 1997. "Racism, Community, and Democracy: The Ethics of Affirmative

Adams, James Truslow. 1931. *The Epic of America.* Boston, MA: Little, Brown, and Company.

Adams, Maurianne, Lee Anne Bell, and Pat Griffin. 1997. *Teaching for Diversity and Social Justice: A Sourcebook.* New York: Routledge.

Affleck, Ben, Matt Damon, Robin Williams.1997. *Good Will Hunting.* Directed by Gus Van Sant.

Alabama Baptist Newspaper. 2008. http://www.thealabamabaptist.org/print-edition-article-detail.php?id_art=6697&pricat_art=8.

Albright, William. 2011. *Welcome to Vision Viewpoint Blog.* Blog, Reformation Hope Church.

Alexander, Elizabeth. 2009." The Venus Hottentot (1825)." *Callaloo* 32, no. 3 (2009): 725–728. doi:10.1353/cal.0.0506.

Alexander, Leslie M. 2012.*African or American? Black Identity and Political Activism in New York City, 1784-1861.* Urbana, IL: Univ. of Illinois Press.

Allen, Theodore W. 1997. "The Invention of White Race: Racial Oppression and Social Control." *Racism: Essential Readings*: 357–79. doi:10.4135/9781446220986.n35.

Allport, Gordan Willard. 1958. *The Nature of Prejudice.* Garden City, NJ: Doubleday.

Alumkal, Antony W. 2004. "American Evangelicalism In The Post-Civil Rights Era: A Racial Formation Theory." *Sociology of Religion* Vol. 65, No. 3 (Autumn 2004), pp. 195–213.

Anderson, Allan. 2005. "Dubious Legacy of Charles Parham: Racism and Cultural Insensitivities Among Pentecostals." *Pneuma* Vol. 27 (Spring 2005): 51–64.

Angelou, Maya. 2014. *Rainbow in the Cloud: The Wisdom and Spirit of Maya Angelou.* New York: Random House.

Ash, Mary Kay. 1985. "Quote by Mary Kay Ash." Goodreads Inc. http://www.goodreads.com/quotes/83216-if-you-think-you-can-you-can-if-you-think.

Atlanta Black Star. 2013 "Five Ways Integration Underdeveloped Black America." http://atlantablackstar.com/2013/12/09/5-ways-integration-underdeveloped-black-america/.

Baca, Jimmy Santiago. 1952. *A Place to Stand.* New York: Grove Press.

Barkan, Elliott. 1986. *Freedom's Doors: Immigrant Ports of Entry to the United States.* Philadelphia, PA: Balch Institute for Ethnic Studies.

Barkun, Michael. 1999. *In God's Country: The Patriot Movement and the Pacific Northwest*. Pullman, WA: Washington State University Press.

Barnes, Roy. 2001. Brainy Quote. Accessed May 26, 2016. http://www.brainyquote.com/quotes/quotes/r/roybarnes246329.html.

Bartlett, Bruce R. 2009. *Wrong on Race: The Democratic Party's Buried Past*. New York: Macmillan.

Baum, Gregory, John Aloysius Coleman, and Marcus Lefebure. 1982. *The Church and Racism*. Edinburgh: T. & T. Clark.

Beck, Sanderson. 1996. "Booker T. Washington and Character Education." *Literary Works of Sanderson Beck*. http://www.san.beck.org/BTW.html.

Berranger, Olivier de. 1997. "French Catholics Apologize for World War II Silence on Jews." CNN. Last modified October 1, 1997. http://www.cnn.com/WORLD/9710/01/france.catholics/.

Bishop, Jill. 1996. *The Black Family in America*. "Family Structure Changes: 1950s to 1990s." http://www.bishopfamily.com/essays/family_structure_changes.htm

Black, Edwin. 2003. *War Against the Weak: Eugenics and America's Campaign to Create a Master Race*. New York: Four Walls Eight Windows.

Bosch, David Jacobus. 1995. *Believing in the Future: Toward a Missiology of Western Culture*. Valley Forge, PA: Trinity Press International.

Bosch, David Jacobus. 1991. *Transforming Mission: Paradigm Shifts in Theology of Mission*. Maryknoll, NY: Orbis Books.

Bradt, Steve. 2010. "One-drop Rule Persists." *Harvard Gazette*. Last modified December 9, 2010. http://news.harvard.edu/gazette/story/2010/12/one-drop-rule-persists/.

Bray, Michael. 1994. *A Time to Kill: A Study Concerning the Use of Force and Abortion*. Portland, OR: Advocates for Life Publications.

Breen, Tom, and Renee Elder. 2011. "North Carolina Facing up to Legacy of Sterilizations." Kaylee A. Remington, On the Docket. Last modified June 20, 2011. https://kayremington.files.wordpress.com/2011/06/afghan-weddings.pdf.

Briggs, John C. 2010. *The Lincoln-Douglas Debates: The Lincoln Studies Center Edition, Edited by Rodney O. Davis and Douglas L. Wilson*. Ann Arbor, MI: Michigan Publishing, University of Michigan Library.

Briggs Jr., Vernon. 1999. "Immigration Policy and the Plight of Unskilled Workers." *Center of Immigration Studies*. March 11. http://cis.org/articles/1999/briggstestimony031199.html.

Brown, Les. Goodreads Inc. https://www.goodreads.com/author/quotes/57803.Les_Brown.

Buchanan, Patrick J. 2011. *Suicide of a Superpower: Will America Survive to 2025?* New York: Thomas Dunn Books.

Burke, Edmund. 1792. *The Works of the Right Honourable Edmund Burke, Collected in Three Volumes*. London: Printed for J. Dodsley.

Byrne, Terry. "A Tangled Web of Racial Tension." *The Boston Globe* May 9, 2015. Accessed 2016. http://www.highbeam.com/doc/1P2-37935445.html?refid=easy_hf.

Camarota, Steven A. 2007. *Immigrants in the United States, 2007: A Profile of America's Foreign-Born Population.* Washington, DC: Center for Immigration Studies.

Carnegie, Dale. 1998. *How to Win Friends and Influence People.* New York: Simon and Schuster.

Carothers, W. F. 1915. "Attitude of Pentecostal Whites to the Colored Brethren in the South," *The Weekly Evangel.* August 14, 1915, 2. http://www.academia.edu/10825872/ The_Dubious_Legacy_of_Charles_Parham

Carver, George W. "Education is the Key to Unlock the Golden Door of Freedom." Brainy Quote. Accessed May 19, 2016. http://www.brainyquote.com/quotes/ quotes/g/georgewash157103.html.

Center for American Progress. 2015. https://www. americanprogress.org/about/mission/.

Christensen, Bryce. 1989. "From Home Life to Prison Life: the Roots of American Crime." In *The Family in America.*" Rockford Institute Center on the Family in America, Vol. 3 No. 4.

Christensen, Bryce. 2005. "Intolerable Tolerance: When Tolerance Turns Against the Family." Sutherland Institute. Last modified October 25, 2005. http:// sutherlandinstitute.org/uploaded_files/sdmc/ intolerabletolerance.pdf.

Christerson, Brad, Michael Emerson, and Korie L. Edwards. 2005. *Against All Odds: The Struggle of Racial Integration in Religious Organizations.* New York: New York University Press.

Bonhoeffer, Dietrich *Christian History.* 2016.

Chua, Amy. 2009. *Day of Empire: How Hyper-powers Rise to Global Dominance and Why They Fall.* New York: Anchor Books.

CNN. 2008. "Barack Obama is 'President of the World.'" http://www.cnn.com/2008/POLITICS/11/05/international.press.reaction/index.html?iref=24hours.

CNN. 2015. "Kids' Test Answers on Race Brings Mother to Tears." http://www.cnn.com/2010/US/05/18/doll.study.parents/.

Cohen, Richard J. 2009. "Major Civil Rights Group Demands CNN Remove Lou Dobbs from the Air." Letter to CNN. http://www.huffingtonpost.com/2009/07/24/major-civil-rights-group_n_244532.html.

Cohen, W. B. 2003. *The French Encounter with Africans: White Response to Blacks, 1530-1880*. Bloomington, IN: Indiana University Press.

Cole, Ed. 2009. *The Ed Cole Library.* http://www.edcole.org/index.php.

Colson, Chuck. 1999. "The Silence of the Sheep." http://www.breakpoint.org/bpcommentaries/entry/13/13418.

Coomaraswamy, Rama P. 1978. "Studies of Comparative Religion." The Destruction of the Christian Tradition (Part 1). http://www.studiesincomparativereligion.com/Public/articles/browse_g.aspx?ID=322.

Corsi, Jerome R. "Obama's Birth-certificate Guardian out of Job." *WorldNetDaily*. http://www.wnd.com/2010/12/237733/.

Cox, Harvey. 1966. *The Secular City; Secularization and Urbanization in Theological Perspective*. New York: Macmillan.

Custance, Arthur C. 1958. "Does Science Transcend Culture?" University of Ottawa.

Custance, Arthur. 1970. "Doorway Papers." http://www.custance.org/.

Custance, Arthur. 1975. *Noah's Three Sons.* Grand Rapids, MI: Zondervan.

Daniels, Jessie. 2009. "Summertime and Swimming Pool Racism." *Racism Review.* http://www.racismreview. com/blog/2009/07/08/swimming-pool-racism/.

Darwin, Charles. 1988. *On the Origin of Species, 1859.* New York: University Press.

Daniels III, David. 2006. "God Makes No Difference in Nationality—The Fashioning of a New Racial? Nonracial Identity at the Azusa Street Revival." *Enrichment Journal.* http://enrichmentjournal. ag.org/200602/200602_072_nodifference.cfm.

Davies, Philip J. 1987. "Dianne M. Pinderhughes, Race and Ethnicity in Chicago Politics: A Reexamination of Pluralist Theory. Champaign, IL: University of Illinois Press.

Davis, Rodney O. and Douglas L. Wilson. 2008. *The Lincoln-Douglas Debates: The Lincoln Studies Center Edition.* Champaign, IL: University of Illinois Press.

Dawson, John. 1994. *Healing America's Wounds.* Ventura, CA: Regal Books.

Deci, Edward L. 1995. Why We Do What We Do. New York: Penguin Group.

De Wet, C. 1989. "The Apostolic Faith Mission in Africa: 1908–1980. A Case Study in Church Growth in a Segregated Society." Unpublished PhD dissertation. Cape Town: University of Cape Town.

DeYmaz, Mark. 1997. *Building a Healthy Multi-Ethnic Church: Mandate, Commitments, and Practices of a Diverse Congregation.* San Francisco, CA: Jossey-Bass/ John Wiley.

DeYmaz, Mark, and Harry Li. 2013. *Leading a Healthy Multi-Ethnic Church: Seven Common Challenges and How to Overcome Them.* Grand Rapids, MI: Zondervan.

DeYoung, Curtiss Paul, Michael Emerson, George Yancey, and Karen Kim. 2003. *United by Faith The Multiracial Congregation As an Answer to the Problem of Race.* Oxford: Oxford University Press, 2003.

Dinnerstein, Leonard and David M. Reimers. 1999. *Ethnic Americans: A History of Immigration.* New York: Columbia University Press.

Dixon, Jeffrey C. and Michael S. Rosenbaum. 2004. "Nice to Know You? Testing Contact, Cultural, and Group Threat Theories of Anti-Black and Anti-Hispanic Stereotypes." *Social Science Quarterly* 85:257–280.

Dorrien, Gary J. 2012. *The Obama Question: A Progressive Perspective.* Lanham, MD: Rowman & Littlefield Publishers.

Dougherty, K. D. and K.R. Huyser. 2008. "Racially Diverse Congregations: Organizational Identity and the Accommodation of Differences." *Journal for the Scientific Study of Religion*, 47: 23–44.

Douglass, Frederick. 2011. "Frederick Douglass's America: Race, Justice, and the Promise of the Founding." The Heritage Foundation. http://www.heritage. org/research/reports/2011/01/frederick-douglass-s-america-race-justice-and-the-promise-of-the-founding.

Douglas, William O. 1952. "Zorach V. Clauson, US Law." LII /Legal Information Institute. https://www.law. cornell.edu/supremecourt/text/343/306.

Drost Michael. 2009. "Museum Slaying Suspect Charged; Police Weigh Hate Crimes, Rights Offenses." *The Washington Times* June 12, 2009. http://www.highbeam. com/doc/1G1-201667662.html?refid=easy_hf.

D'Souza, Dinesh. 1995. *The End of Racism: Principles for a Multiracial Society.* New York: Free Press.

D'Souza, Dinesh. 2010. "How Obama Thinks." *Forbes*, September 9.

Du Bois, W. E. B. ca 1929. "The Color Line and the Church." *Credo*, November: 4.

Du Bois, W. E. B. 1935. *Black Reconstruction: An Essay Toward a History of the Part Which Black Folk Played in the Attempt to Reconstruct Democracy in America, 1860-1880.* New York: Russel & Russel.

Du Bois, W. E. B. 1961. *The Souls of Black Folk: Essays and Sketches.* Greenwich, CN: Fawcett Publications.

Durst, Dennis. 2005. "Evangelical Engagements with Eugenics, 1900–1940." *U.S. Politics Online*: A Political Discussion Forum Archives. http://www.uspoliticsonline.net/threads/13360-Evangelical-engagements-with-Eugenics-1900-1940.

Dyer, Wayne W. nd. "Quote by Wayne W. Dyer." Goodreads Inc. http://www.goodreads.com/quotes/531513-i-am-thankful-to-all-those-who-said-no-it-s.

Easum, M. William and Thomas G. Bandy. 1997. *Growing Spiritual Redwoods.* Nashville, TN: Abingdon Press.

Edwards, George C. 2008. "Exclusive Interview: President Jimmy Carter." *Presidential Studies Quarterly* 38, no. 1:1-13. doi:10.1111/j.1741-5705.2007.02625.x.

Ellis, David, Jeanne McDowell, Sylvester Monroe and James Willwerth. 1992. "LA Lawless." "Can We All Get Along." Vol. 130. no. 19. *Los Angeles Times Magazine*, May 11. 28–31.

Emerson, Michael O. and Christian Smith. 2001. *Divided by Faith: Evangelical Religion and the Problem of Race in America.* Oxford: Oxford University Press.

Emerson, Michael O., Rachel Tolbert Kimbro, and George Yancey. 2002. "Contact Theory Extended: The Effects of Prior Racial Contact on Current Social Ties." *Social Science Quarterly* 83:745–761.

En Vogue. 1992. "*Free Your Mind.*" Audio. East West. September 24.

FactCheck. 2008. "Born in the U.S.A." FactCheck. http://www.factcheck.org/2008/08/born-in-the-usa/.

Fagan, Patrick F. 2006. "Why Religion Matters Even More: The Impact of Religious Practice on Social Stability." The Heritage Foundation. http://www.heritage.org/research/reports/2006/12/why-religion-matters-even-more-the-impact-of-religious-practice-on-social-stability.

Fisher, Irving. 1913. *In Good Health Magazine.* Battle Creek, MI.

Floyd, Thomas. 2011. "Olsen's Prediction after Lost Season Coming True." *The Washington Times* July 15, 2011. http://www.highbeam.com/doc/1G1-261404933.html?refid=easy_hf.

Flynn, Tom. 2016. *The Anti-God Campaign—Secular Humanism.* https://www.secularhumanism.org/index.php/13.

Fold3. "The Children of Nazi Germany." https://www.fold3.com/page/285875536_the_children_of_nazi_germany#description.

Fox News. 2011. "N.C. Forced Sterilization Victims Voice Grief, Pain." http://www.foxnews.com/health/2011/06/23/nc-forced-sterilization-victims-voice-grief-pain.html.

Franklin, Robert M. 2007. *Crisis in the Village: Restoring Hope in African American Communities.* Detroit, MI: Fortress Press.

Fraser, Steven, ed. 2008. *The Bell Curve Wars: Race, Intelligence, and the Future of America.* New York: Basic Books.

French, Talmadge L. 2014. *Early Inter-Racial Oneness Pentecostalism G.T. Haywood and the Pentecostal Assemblies of the World (1901-1931)*. http://public. eblib.com/choice/publicfullrecord.aspx?p=1879167

Gallegos, Aaron. 1998. *Crossing the Racial Divide: America's Struggle for Justice and Reconciliation*. Washington, DC: Sojourners.

Galton, Francis. 1873. "Africa for the Chinese." Sir Francis Galton F.R.S: 1822–1911. http://galton.org/letters/ africa-for-chinese/AfricaForTheChinese.htm.

Galton, Francis. 1907. *Inquiries into Human Faculty and Its Development*. London: J. M. Dent & Sons.

Garces-Foley, Kathleen. 2007. *Crossing the Ethnic Divide: The Multiethnic Church on a Mission*. Oxford, UK: Oxford University Press.

Gardner, Amy and Krissah Thompson. 2010. "Tea Party Groups Battling Perceptions of Racism." Washington Post. http://www.washingtonpost.com/wp-dyn/ content/article/2010/05/04/AR2010050405168.html.

Gardiner, William J. 2009. "Reflections on the History of White Supremacy in the United States." Unitarian Universalist Association | UUA.org. http://www. uua.org/sites/live-new.uua.org/files/documents/ gardinerwilliam/whiteness/white_supremacy_us.pdf.

Garvey, Marcus. 2013. "Marcus Garvey—New World Encyclopedia." New World Encyclopedia. http://www. newworldencyclopedia.org/entry/Marcus_Garvey.

Gilman, Sander L., Sara Baartman, and Zola Maseko. 2000. "The Life and Times of Sara Bartman: The Hottentot Venus." *The American Historical Review* 105, no. 5: 1849. doi:10.2307/2652212.

Gibbs, Eddie and Ryan K. Bolger. 1996. *Emerging Churches: Creating Christian Community in Postmodern Cultures.* Grand Rapids, MI: Baker Academic.

Gibbs, Eddie. 1986. *Followed or Pushed.* Bromley: MARC Europe.

Gibbs, Eddie and Ian Coffey. 2001. *Church Next: Quantum Changes in Christian Ministry.* Leicester: Inter-Varsity.

Gilbreath, Edward. 2015. "Is Racial Reconciliation a Top Priority for Your Church?" *Charisma Magazine,* February.

Gill, John. 1748. *John Gill's Exposition of the Entire Bible.* 2012 Amazon digital.

Gill, John. 1810. *An Exposition of the Old and New Testament.* London, UK: Mathews & Leigh.

Gill, N.S. "Carthage and the Phoenicians." http://ancienthistory.about.com/od/aneplacesgeography/a/Phoenicians.htm.

Giroux, Henry A. 2009. "Youth and the Myth of a Post-Racial Society Under Barack Obama." http://www.truth-out.org/archive/component/k2/item/83774:youth-and-the-myth-of-a-postracial-society-under-barack-obama.

Gobineau, Arthur, and Adrian Collins. 1967. *The Inequality of Human Races.* New York: H. Fertig.

Goff, James R. 1988. *Fields White Unto Harvest: Charles F. Parham and the Missionary Origins of Pentecostalism.* Fayetteville: University of Arkansas Press.

Goldenberg, David M. *The Curse of Ham: Race and Slavery in Early Judaism, Christianity, and Islam.* Princeton, N.J.: Princeton University Press, 2003.

Gould, Stephen. 2009. "Saartjie's Speech and the Sounds of National Identification." *Mosaic* (Winnipeg), June 1.

Graham, David. 2015. "Rupert Murdoch Says Ben Carson, Unlike Obama, Would Be a 'Real Black President.'" *The Atlantic.*

Grieco, Elizabeth. 2005. Unauthorized Immigration to the United States. MPI report.

Griffin, John Howard. 1961. *Black Like Me.* Boston: Houghton Mifflin.

Grove, Lloyd. 2010. "America Not Yet Post-Racial: The Verdict from the Aspen Ideas Festival, by Lloyd Grove." *The Daily Beast.* http://www.thedailybeast.com/articles/2010/07/08/america-not-yet-post-racial-the-verdict-from-the-aspen-ideas-festival.html.

Guardian, The. 2007. "Flesh Made Fantasy" *The Guardian.* https://www.theguardian.com/books/2007/mar/31/featuresreviews.guardianreview12.

Hacker, Andrew. 1992. *Two Nations: Black and White, Separate, Hostile, Unequal.* The Macmillan Company, New York, 1992. Revised: Scribner, 2003.

Hakim, Joy. 2003. *Freedom A History of the US.* Princeton, N. J.: Oxford University Press.

Haney-López, Ian. 1996. *White by Law The Legal Construction of Race.* New York: New York University Press.

Hartman, Chester W. 2006. "Apologies/Reparations." In *Poverty & Race in America: The Emerging Agendas,* 40. Lanham, MD: Lexington Books.

Harvey, Jennifer. 2014. Dear White Christians: For those Still Longing For Racial Reconciliation. Grand Rapids, MI: William B. Eerdmans Publishing Company.

Herrnstein, Richard J., and Charles A. Murray. 1994. *The Bell Curve: Intelligence and Class Structure in American Life.* New York: Free Press.

Heibert, Paul G. 2008. *The Gospel in Human Contexts: Anthropological Explorations for Contemporary.* Grand Rapids, IL: Baker Academic.

Heywood, David. 2011. *Reimagining Ministry.* London: SCM Press.

History.com. Staff. 2016. http://www.history.com/topics/Black-history/march-on-washington.

History Commons. 1923. "United States vs Bhagat Singh Thind." *History Commons.* http://www.historycommons.org/entity.jsp?entity=bhagat_singh_thind_1.

History.com Staff. 2009. "Plessy vs Ferguson." http://www.history.com/topics/Black-history/plessy-v-ferguson.

Hitler, Adolf. 1925. "*Mein Kampf* (II.II)." Wellesley College. Last modified July 18, 1925. http://academics.wellesley.edu/Polisci/wj/100/mk3.html.

Hit on the Head.com. 2013. "Black Wall Street-Segregation was Better for Blacks." www.unbiasedtalk.com/uncategorized/black-wall-street-segregation-was-better-for-blacks/.

Hollinger, David A. 2006. *Cosmopolitanism and Solidarity Studies in Ethnoracial, Religious, and Professional Affiliation in the United States.* Madison, WI: University of Wisconsin Press.

Holmes, Oliver W. 1927. "Buck vs Bell Opinion." DNA Learning Center. https://www.dnalc.org/view/15759-Oliver-Wendell-Holmes-.html.

Holmes, Rachel. 2007. *African Queen: The Real Life of the Hottentot Venus.* New York: Random House.

Hoover, Will. 2008. "Obama's Hawaii Boyhood Homes Drawing Gawkers." *The Honolulu Advertiser* Accessed April 25, 2016. http://the.honoluluadvertiser.com/article/2008/Nov/09/ln/hawaii811090361.html.

Hoyt Jr., Carlos. 2012. "The Pedagogy of the Meaning of Racism: Reconciling a Discordant Discourse." *National Association of Social Workers* 57, no. 3 (July/August 2012).

Hugo, Victor. "Quote by Victor Hugo." Goodreads Inc. http://www.goodreads.com/quotes/18929-he-who-opens-a-school-door-closes-a-prison.

Huyser, Kevin D. Doughtery and Kimberly R. 2008. "Racially Diverse Congregations: Organizational Identity and the Accommodation of Differences." The Society for the Scientific Study of Religion 47 (1): 23–44.

Ingrassia, Michelle. 1993. "Endangered Family." *Newsweek*. August 30. 16–27. http://www.holysmoke.org/fem/fem0119.html.

Jackson, Thomas F. 2007. *From Civil Rights to Human Rights: Martin Luther King, Jr., and the Struggle for Economic Justice*. Philadelphia, PA: University of Pennsylvania Press.

Jaffa, Harry V. 2000. *A New Birth of Freedom: Abraham Lincoln and the Coming of the Civil War*. Lanham, MD: Rowman & Littlefield Publishers.

James, M. Annette, ed. 1992. *The State of Native America: genocide, colonization and resistance*. Boston, MA: South End Press.

JBHE. 2008. "Bob Jones University Apologizes for its Racist Past." *The Journal of Blacks in Higher Education*. www.jbhe.com/news_views/62_bobjones.html.

Jefferson, Thomas. 1853. "Notes on the State of Virginia." https://archive.org/details/notesonstateofvi01jeff.

Jensen, Robert. *What Is White Supremacy, Challenging White Supremacy Workshop*, San Francisco, CA.

Jensen, Robert. 2005, The *Heart of Whiteness: Confronting Race, Racism, and White Privilege.* San Francisco, CA: City Lights.

Johnson, Scott. 1995. "A Father for Our Father." *US News and World Report.*

Jovicevich, Alexandre. 1961. *Les Lettres D'Amabed De Voltaire. Édition Critique Et Commentée.* Edited by Alexandre Jovicevich. Paris: Éd. Universitaires.

Joyner, Rick. 1996. *Overcoming Racism.* Charlotte, NC: Morningstar Publications.

Keller, Hellen. "Quote by Hellen Keller." http://www. goodreads.com/quotes/106925-faith-is-the-strength-by-which-a-shattered-world-shall.

Kerner Commission, Report of the National Advisory Commission on Civil Disorders. 1968. Washington, DC: US Government Printing Office. https://www. ncjrs.gov/pdffiles1/Digitization/8073NCJRS.pdf.

King, Martin Luther Jr. 1960. "The Rising Tide of Racial Consciousness." http://kingencyclopedia. stanford.edu/primarydocuments/Vol5/6Sept1960_ TheRisingTideofRacialConsciousnessAddressatthe Gold.pdf.

King, Martin Luther. 1963. *Strength to Love.* Detroit, MI: Fortress Press.

King, Martin Luther Jr. 1967. *Where do we go from here: Chaos or Community?* Boston, MA: Beacon Press.

King, Martin Luther Jr. 1986. *Stride Toward Freedom: The Montgomery Story.* San Francisco, CA: Harper & Row.

King, Martin Luther Jr. 2003. *A Testament of Hope: The Essential Writings and Speeches of Martin Luther King, Jr.* James M. Washington, ed. New York: Harper One reprint edition.

KJV Zondervan Study Bible. 2002. New York, NY: Zondervan.

Klassen, Ben. 1981. The White Man's Bible. Lighthouse Point, Fla. (PO Box 5908, Lighthouse Point 33064): Church of the Creator.

Klein, Joe. 2008. "Obama's Victory Ushers in a New America," Time.com (November 5, 2008). Online: http://www.time.com/time/politics/article/0,8599,1856649,00.html.

Knickerbocker, Brad. 1999. "When the Hate Comes from 'Churches.'" Christian Science Publishing Society. http://culteducation.com/group/871-christian-identity/3693-when-the-hate-comes-from-churches.html.

Kopp, Claire. 2012. *Becoming Female: Perspectives on Development*. New York, NY: Springer. 1st ed. 1979.

Kraft, Charles H. 1996. *Anthropology for Christian Witness*. Maryknoll, NY: Orbis Books.

Kraft, Charles. n.d. "The Incarnation, God' Model for Cross Cultural Communication." Brookhaven Presbyterian Church." http://brookhavenpres.com/?s=Kraft

Kumar, V. 2011. "Who Were The Sumerians?" http://vkumar.expertscolumn.com/article/who-were-sumerians.

Lattanzio, Vince. 2009. "Campers' "Complexion" No Problem for New Pool." NBC 10 Philadelphia. http://www.nbcphiladelphia.com/news/archive/Campers-Complexion-No-Problem-for-New-Pool.html.

Legend, John. 2015. "Oscar Speech on Incarceration." The Oscars 2015, Hollywood, January 28, 2015.

Lemon, Don. 2012. "It Only Takes One Drop—In America—CNN.com Blogs." In America—You Define America What Defines You. CNN.com

Blogs. http://inamerica.blogs.cnn.com/2012/01/15/don-lemon-it-only-takes-one-drop/.

Lincoln, Abraham. 1861. "Abraham Lincoln: First Inaugural Address. U.S. Inaugural Addresses." Bartleby.com. http://www.bartleby.com/124/pres31.html.

Luepnitz, Deborah Anna. 2003. *Schopenhauer's Porcupines Intimacy and Its Dilemmas: Five Stories of Psychotherapy*. New York: Basic Books. http://site.ebrary.com/id/10732948.

Lumeya, Nzash U. 1988. *The Curse on Ham's Descendants Its Missiological Impact on Zairian Mbala Mennonite Brethren*. Masters thesis, Fuller Theological Seminary School of World Mission.

Lynn, Richard, and Tatu Vanhanen. 2002. *IQ and the Wealth of Nations*. Westport, CN: Praeger.

Lyon, K. Brynolf and Archie Smith Jr. 1998. *Tending the Flock: Congregations and Family Ministry*. Louisville, KY: Westminister John Knox Press.

Macdonald, Andrew. 1978. *The Turner Diaries*. New York: Barricade Books Inc.

Malkin, Bonnie. 2008. "Barack Obama has made Martin Luther King's Dream a Reality, Australia's Kevin Rudd says." *The Telegraph* (Sydney), November 5. http://www.telegraph.co.uk/news/worldnews/barackobama/3384764/Barack-Obama-has-made-Martin-Luther-Kings-dream-a-reality-Australias-Kevin-Rudd-says.html.

Mandela, Nelson. 1996. Address to the Joint Houses of Parliament, Westminister Hall, London, England July 11.

Mann, Horace. "Horace Mann Quotes." https://www.goodreads.com/author/quotes/279932.Horace_Mann.

Mantle, Burns, and Garrison P. Sherwood. 1933. *The Best Plays of 1909-1919,* New York: Dodd, Mead, & Company.

Maraboli, Steven. Steve Maraboli Quotes. https://www.goodreads.com/author/quotes/4491185. Steve_Maraboli

Mark, Joshua J. 2010. "Heraclitus of Ephesus." Ancient History Encyclopedia. http://www.ancient.eu/Heraclitus_of_Ephesos.

Marley, Bob. 1980. "Redemption Song." Audio. Island Records.

Marshall, Thurgood. 1992. "Thurgood Marshall—The Liberty Medal Acceptance Speech." Genius. http://genius.com/Thurgood-marshall-the-liberty-medal-acceptance-speech-annotated.

Martinez, Elizabeth. n.d. *What Is White Supremacy, Challenging White Supremacy Workshop,* San Francisco, CA, page 16.

Maxwell, John C. "Quote by John C. Maxwell." http://www.goodreads.com/quotes/179068-the-greatest-day-in-your-life-and-mine-is-when.

Maxwell, Zerlina. 2012. *Ebony.* November 29. Accessed 2012. http://www.ebony.com/news-views/its-not-halles-fault-199#axzz46gGnEYD6.

Marx, Karl. "Contribution to the Critique of Hegel's Philosophy of Right 1844." Marxists Internet Archive. Accessed July 3, 2015. https://www.marxists.org/archive/marx/works/1843/critique-hpr/intro.htm.

McDaniel, Anita, and Clyde McDaniel. *21st Century African American Social Issues: A Reader.* Mason, OH: Thomson Learning Custom Pub., 2003.

McGavran, Donald A. 1955. *The Bridges of God: A Study in the Strategy of Missions*. New York: Distributed by Friendship Press.

MacIver, David R. *The Etruscans*. New York: Cooper Square Publishers, 1972.

McManus, Erwin Raphael. 2006. Uprising: A Revolution of the Soul. Nashville, TN : Thomas Nelson.

McNeill, Starlette. "The Most Segregated Hour." The Race-less Gospel. Last modified September 16, 2012. http://racelessgospel.com/2012/09/16/the-most-segregated-hour/.

Mead, George Herbert. 2013. George Herbert Mead in the Twenty-First Century. Edited by Krzysztof Skowronski F. Thomas Burke. New York, NY: Lexington Books. https://books.google.co.za/books?id=2Vfl9w_mmjgC&printsec=frontcover#v=onepage&q&f=false.

Mead, Loren B. 1991. *The Once and Future Church: Reinventing the Congregation for a New Mission Frontier*. Washington, DC: Alban Institute.

Mead, Walter Russell. 2010. "The American Interest." Is This Lobby Different From All Others? March 12. http://blogs.the-american-interest.com/2010/03/12/is-this-lobby-different-from-all-others/.

Meckler, Mark, Jenny Beth Martin, and MacMillan. *Tea Party Patriots: The Second American Revolution*. New York: Henry Holt and Co, 2012.

Menzie, Nicole. 2014. Sin of Racism Will Continue until Church Gets Its Act Together, quote: The answer to racism isn't sociological, it's theological." (Dr. Tony Evans). New York, NY.

Mercurio, John. 2002. "CNN.com—Lott Apologizes for Thurmond Comment—Dec. 10, 2002." Breaking News, Daily News and Videos—CNN.com. http://

www.cnn.com/2002/ALLPOLITICS/12/09/lott. comment/.

Metzler, Christopher. 2008. *The Construction and Rearticulation of Race in a "Post Racial America."* Bloomington, IN: Author House.

Migration Policy Institute. 2003 Annual Report. Financial, Washington, DC: Migration Policy Institute.

Morgan, David. "The World Welcomes Obama's Victory— CBS News." Breaking News, US, World, Business, Entertainment & Video—CBS News. Last modified November 5, 2008. http://www.cbsnews.com/news/ the-world-welcomes-obamas-victory/.

Morris, Henry M. *The Genesis Record: A Scientific and Devotional Commentary on the Book of Beginnings.* Grand Rapids, Michigan: Baker Book House, 1976.

Morrison, Toni. 1998. "Comment." The New Yorker. Last modified October 5, 1998. http://www.newyorker. com/magazine/1998/10/05/comment-6543.

Moynihan, Patrick. 1965. "BlackPast.org." *The Moynihan Report The Black Family.* http://www.Blackpast.org/ primary/moynihan-report-1965.

Mydans, Seth. 1991. "Special to New York Times: Tape of Beating by Police, Revives Charges of Racism." *New York Times.* New York, New York: New York Times, March 7.

Myrdal, Gunnar, Richard Sterner, and Arnold Marshall Rose. *An American Dilemma; The Negro Problem and Modern Democracy.* New York: Harper & brothers, 1944.

Nagourney, Adam. "Obama Elected President as Racial Barrier Falls." *New York Times,* November 4, 2008. http:// www.nytimes.com/2008/11/05/us/politics/05elect. html?_r=0.

National Center Staff. 1954. "National Center." Brown vs. the Board of Education's. http://www.nationalcenter. org/brown.html.

National Enquirer. "SEN. JOHN EDWARDS CAUGHT WITH MISTRESS AND LOVE CHILD!" National Enquirer. Last modified July 22, 2008. http://www.nationalenquirer.com/celebrity/ sen-john-edwards-caught-mistress-and-love-child/.

National Urban League. 2007. "National Urban League, 2007 Annual Report." Benchmark Printing. http://nul. iamempowered.com/sites/nul.iamempowered.com/ files/report_attachments/NUL07AnnRepFinal_0.pdf.

NBC News. "White House Disputes Carter's Analysis— Politics—Capitol Hill | NBC News." Msnbc.com. Last modified September 16, 2009. http://www.nbcnews. com/id/32869276/ns/politics-capitol_hill/t/white-house-disputes-carters-analysis/#.Vz4i5fkrLIU.

Neiwert, David A. 1999. *In God's Country: The Patriot Movement and the Pacific Northwest*. Pullman, Wash: Washington State University Press.

Nemeth, Charles P. 2011. *Criminal Law, Second Edition*. Hoboken: CRC Press.

Newbell, Trillia. 2015. "Lifeway Leadership." The Gospel and Racial Reconciliation. March. http://www.lifeway. com/leadership/2015/04/09/10-quotes-from-the-erlc-leadership-summit-on-race/.

Newbigin, Lesslie. 1953. *The Household of God: Lectures on the Nature of the Church*. London: SCM Press.

Newbigin, Lesslie. 1989. *The Gospel in a Pluralist Society*. Grand Rapids, MI: W.B. Eerdmans.

Newbigin, Lesslie. 1995. *The Open Secret: An Introduction to the Theology of Mission*. Grand Rapids, MI: W. B. Eerdmans.

Newton, Thomas. 1786. *Dissertation on the Prophecies, Which Have Remarkably Been Fulfilled, and Are Fulfilling in the World.*

NLT. *Holy Bible: New Living Translation.* 1996. Wheaton, Ill: Tyndale House Publishers.

Obama, Barack. 2008. "A More Perfect Union. *The Wall Street Journal.* http://blogs.wsj.com/washwire/2008/03/18/text-of-obamas-speech-a-more-perfect-union/.

Ogilvie, Matthew. 2001. "Children of a White God: A Study of Racist "Christian" Theologies by Matthew C. Ogilvie." The Human Nature Review. http://human-nature.com/nibbs/01/ogilvie.html.

Ogletree, Charles. 2010. President Obama's Harvard Professor. *Black Star News.* http://www.Blackstarnews.com/others/extras/charles-ogletree-president-obamas-harvard-professor.html.

Olson, David T., and James Adams. 2009. *The American Church in Crisis Groundbreaking Research Based on a National Database of Over 200,000 Churches.* Grand Rapids: Zondervan.

Ortiz, Manuel. 1996. *One New People: Models for Developing a Multiethnic Church.* Downers Grove, Ill: InterVarsity Press.

Osterholm, Tim. "Table of Nations and Genealogy of Mankind." Roots Web: Free pages. Accessed May 24, 2016. http://freepages.folklore.rootsweb.ancestry.com/~sturnbo/files/oldest/Table%20of%20Nations%20and%20Genealogy%20of%20Mankind.htm.

O'Sullivan, John. 1845. "Annexation." Grinnell College. Last modified 1845. http://web.grinnell.edu/courses/HIS/f01/HIS202-01/Documents/OSullivan.html.

Otabil, Mensa. 1993. *Beyond the Rivers of Ethiopia.* Bakersfield, CA: Pneuma Life.

Parkman, Francis, and Francis Parkman. *The Conspiracy of Pontiac.* New York: Collier Books, 1962.

P. Scott Richards, PhD, Allen E. Bergin, PhD. 2005. A Spiritual Strategy for Counseling and Psychotherapy, Second Edition. New York, NY: American Psychological Association.

Pannell, William E. 1993. *The Coming Race Wars? A Cry for Reconciliation.* Grand Rapids, Mich: Zondervan Pub. House.

Parent-less Statistics. Families Civil Liberties Union. Accessed May 19, 2016. http://www.fclu.org/parentless-statistics/.

Parham, Charles Fox. *A Voice Crying in the Wilderness.* Baxter Springs, Ka: Apostolic Faith Bible College, 1910.

Parham, Charles Fox. *The Everlasting Gospel.* [Baxter Springs, Kan.]: [Apostolic Faith Church], 1911.

Parkman, Francis. 1851. *Conspiracy of Pontiac and the Indian War after the Conquest of Canada.* University of Nebraska tenth edition, 1994.

Patterson, Cameron. 2012. *The Place of Justice in Reconciliation.* Seattle, WA: Seattle Pacific University.

Payne, Henry. 2007. "Murder City." The Wall Street Journal. http://www.wsj.com/articles/SB119707331734217730.

PBS So Cal. 2016. *Race the Power Of Illusion.* http://www.pbs.org/race/000_General/000_00-Home.htm.

PCUSA. 1999. "Facing Racism: A Vision of The Beloved Community." Violence, the Initiative of Racial Violence. Presbyterian Church (USA), 22. https://www.pcusa.org/resource/facing-racism-vision-community/.

Pearlstone, Zena. 1990. *Ethnic L.A.* Beverly Hills. CA: Hillcrest Press.

Perkins, Spencer, and Chris Rice. 2000. *More Than Equals: Racial Healing for the Sake of the Gospel.* Downers Grove, Ill: InterVarsity Press.

Pettigrew, Thomas F. and Linda R. Tropp. 2006. "A Meta-Analytic Test of Intergroup Contact Theory." *Journal of Personality & Social Psychology* 90:751–783.

Pew Research Center. 2008. http://www.people-press.org/2008/08/21/more-americans-question-religions-role-in-politics/.

Peyronnin, Joe. 2010. "Why Now Senator Graham?" *The Huffington Post.* Last modified May 25, 2011. http://www.huffingtonpost.com/joe-peyronnin/why-now-senator-graham_b_309718.html.

Pickett, Justin T., Daniel Tope, and Rose Bellandi. ""Taking Back Our Country": Tea Party Membership and Support for Punitive Crime Control Policies." *Sociol Inq Sociological Inquiry* 84, no. 2 (2014): 167-90. doi:10.1111/soin.12033.

Pinderhughes, Elaine. 1989. *Understanding race, ethnicity, and power: the key to efficacy in clinical practice /.* Edited by Collier Macmillan. Vol. XV. New York, NY: Free Press.

Politifact. 2009. "'Birthers' Claim Gibbs Lied when He Said Obama's Birth Certificate is Posted on the Internet." http://www.politifact.com/truth-o-meter/statements/2009/jul/28/worldnetdaily/birthers-claim-gibbs-lied-when-he-said-obamas-birt/.

Pocock, Michael, Gailyn Van Rheenen, and Douglas McConnell. 2005. *The Changing Face of World Missions: Engaging Contemporary Issues and Trends.* Grand Rapids, MI: Baker Academic.

Pounder, C. C. H, Larry Adelman, Jean Cheng, Christine Herbes-Sommers, Tracy Heather Strain, Llewellyn Smith, and Claudio Ragazzi. 2003. *Race the power of an illusion*. San Francisco, Calif: California Newsreel.

Rawlinson, George. 1878. *The Origin of Nations In Two Parts, On Early Civilizations, On Ethnic Affinities, Etc.* New York: Scribner, Welford, & Armstrong.

Richardson, Christopher M., and Ralph E. Luker. 2014. *Historical Dictionary of the Civil Rights Movement*. 2014.

Rieff, David. 1992. *Los Angeles: Capital of the Third World*. New York: Simon & Schuster.

Rittner, Carol, John K. Roth, and Wendy Whitworth. 2004. *Genocide in Rwanda: Complicity of the Churches?* Newark, Notts., UK: Aegis.

Robeck, Cecil M. 2004. "The Past: Historical Roots of Racial Unity and Division in American Pentecostalism." Cyberjournal for Pentecostal-Charismatic Research. http://www.pctii.org/cyberj/cyberj14/robeck.html://.

Romo, Oscar I. 1993. *American Mosaic: Church Planting in Ethnic America*. Nashville, Tenn: Broadman Press.

Rosen, Christine. 2004. *Preaching Eugenics: Religious Leaders and the American Eugenics Movement*. Oxford: Oxford University Press.

Rothenberg, Paula S. 1998. *Race, Class, and Gender in the United States: An Integrated Study*. New York: St. Martin's Press.

Rothschild, Matthew. 2008. "A Historic Vote, Defying Racism." *The Progressive*, November 4, 2008.

Russell, Cheryl. 2000. *Racial and Ethnic Diversity: Asians, Blacks, Hispanics, Native Americans, and Whites*. Ithaca, NY: New Strategist Publications.

Rush, Benjamin. 1799. "Observations Intended to Favour a Supposition That the Black Color (As It Is Called) of the Negroes Is Derived from the Leprosy." *Transactions of the American Philosophical Society* 4.

Sanders, Katie. 2015. "John Legend's claim that 'we live in the most incarcerated country in the world.'" PUNDIFACT. February 23. http://www.politifact.com/punditfact/statements/2015/feb/23/john-legend/fact-checking-john-legends-claim-we-live-most-inca/.

Schapiro, Rich, and James G. Meek. 2009. "Holocaust Museum Shooter's Ex-wife Says His Racism Ate Him Alive." *NY Daily News*. http://www.nydailynews.com/news/world/holocaust-museum-shooter-neo-nazi-james-von-brunn-ex-wife-vowed-boots-article-1.374005.

Schlesinger, Arthur M. 1998. *The Disuniting of America: Reflections on a Multicultural Society*. Whittle Books, 1991. Revised/Expanded edition. New York: W. W. Norton.

Schroeder, Alan. 1992. *Booker T. Washington (Black Americans of Achievement)*. New York: Chelsea House Speech.

SCOTUS. 2010. "Charles Kerchner, Jr., et al., Petitioners v. Barack H. Obama, President of the United States, et al." Supreme Court of the United States. Last modified July 2, 2010. http://www.supremecourt.gov/Search.aspx?FileName=/docketfiles/10-446.htm.

Seattle Times. 2003. Southern Legend Strom Thurmond Dies. The Seattle Times.http://community.seattletimes.nwsource.com/archive/?date=20030627&slug=strom27.

Sagan, Ginetta. 2000. *The Guardian*https://www.theguardian.com/news/2000/sep/14/guardianobituaries.

Segura, Liliana. 2009. "Racism Is the Prime Cause for Debunked Obama Birth Certificate Conspiracy Theory." *AlterNet.* http://www.alternet.org/story/141587/

racism_is_the_prime_cause_for_debunked_obama_birth_certificate_conspiracy_theory.

Shahid, Aliyah. 2011. "Hawaii Governor Drops Mission Prove Obama Was Born in State." *NY Daily News.* http://www.nydailynews.com/news/politics/neil-abercrombie-hawaii-governor-drops-mission-dispel-birthers-prove-obama-born-state-article-1.150834.

Shakur, Afeni. 2003. Talking Drum 1998-2003.http://www.thetalkingdrum.com/afeni.html.

Sharp, Rob. 2008. "The Chosen Ones: The War Children Born to Nazi Fathers in a Sinister Eugenics Scheme Speak Out. *The Independent.* http://www.independent.co.uk/news/world/europe/the-chosen-ones-the-war-children-born-to-nazi-fathers-in-a-sinister-eugenics-scheme-speak-out-771017.html.

Singleton, Marilyn M. 2014. "CGS: The Science of Eugenics: Americas Moral Detour." CGS: Center for Genetics and Society. http://www.geneticsandsociety.org/article.php?id=8261.

Smedley, Audrey. 2012. "RACE—The Power of an Illusion. Background Readings. PBS: Public Broadcasting Service. http://www.pbs.org/race/000_About/002_04-background-02-06.htm.

Smith, Efrem. 2012. *The Post-Black and Post-White Church Becoming the Beloved Community in a Multi-Ethnic World.* San Francisco: Jossey-Bass.

Smith, Kevin. 2015. The Front Porch. http://thefrontporch.org/authors/kevin-smith/.

Smith, Will. 2012. "Race and Prejudice in America Today: A Series—White Supremacy and White Privilege." Daily Kos. http://www.dailykos.com/story/2012/12/27/1174353/-Race-and-Prejudice-in-America-Today-A-Series-White-Supremacy-and-White-Privilege.

Smollett, T., John Morley, William F. Fleming, and Oliver Herbrand Gordon Leigh. 1901. *The Works of Voltaire: A Contemporary Version*. Paris: E. R. Du Mont.

Society for Pentecostal Studies (US). 2004. *Pentecostalism and the Body: 33rd Annual Meeting, Marquette University, March 11-13, 2004*. [United States]: The Society.

Somashekhar, Sandhya, Wesley Lowery, Keith l. Alexander, Kimberly Kindy, and Julie Tate. 2015. "Ferguson: Police Still Killing Unarmed Black Men One Year Later | The Washington Post." *Washington Post*. http://www.washingtonpost.com/sf/national/2015/08/08/Black-and-unarmed/.

Sowell, Thomas. 1994. *Race and Culture: A World View*. New York: Basic Books.

Sowell, Thomas. 2015. "Race, Politics and Lies." RealClearPolitics—Opinion, News, Analysis, Video and Polls. http://www.realclearpolitics.com/articles/2015/05/05/race_politics_and_lies_126484.html

Spencer, Margaret B. 2010. "Study: White and Black Children Biased Toward Lighter Skin *AC 360*. CNN, May 14, 2010.

Staub, E., and L.A. Pearlman. 2001. *Healing, Reconciliation, and Forgiving After Genocide and Other Collective Violence*. In R.G. Helmick and R.L. Petersen (Eds.), Forgiveness and reconciliation: Religion, public policy, and conflict transformation, pp. 301. Radnor, PA: Templeton Foundation Press.

Stedman, Ray C. 1968. "The Three Families of Man Genesis 9:18–28." http://www.raystedman.org/old-testament/genesis/the-three-families-of-man.

Stern, Gail F. 1989. *Freedom's Doors: Immigrant Ports of Entry to the United States.* Philadelphia: Balch Institute for Ethnic Studies.

Stewart, Ryan. 2016. "11 Bonhoeffer Quotes to Remember a Pastor Who Resisted Evil Unto Death." Sojourners on line, https://sojo.net/articles/11-bonhoeffer-quotes-remember-pastor-who-resisted-evil-unto-death.

Stolarik, M. Mark. 1988. *Forgotten Doors: The Other Ports of Entry to the United States.* Philadelphia: Balch Institute Press.

Stott, John. 1980. "The Whole Christian," *Proceedings of the International Conference of Christian Medical Students,* ed. Lee Moy Ng (London: ICCMS and Christian Medical Fellowship.

Stuart, Clark D. 2012. *The 100.* Bloomington, IN: Trafford Publishing.

Sullivan, Andrew. 2009. "Barack Obama Citizenship Conspiracy Theories." Sunday Times. http://www.sonyebooklibrary.com/article/WHEBN0020617631/Barack%20Obama%20citizenship%20conspiracy%20theories.

Sundstrom, Ronald Robles. 2008. *The Browning of America and the Evasion of Social Justice.* Albany, NY: SUNY Press.

Tasker, David. 2008. "Divine Fatherhood, Re-Examining the Paradigm." *Journal of Asia Adventist Seminary,* 2008, Vol. 11 Issue 2, p. 109 11 (2): 109.

Daily Mirror, The (London). 2008. "It's the Black House: Obama is New President." November 4.

Thernstrom, Abigail and Stephan Thernstrom. 2000. "Civil Rights: What Went Wrong?" *Wall Street Journal.* New York, NY, January 17. http://archive.frontpagemag.com/readArticle.aspx?ARTID=22141.

Thernstrom, Stephan. 2000. "New Life for the "One Drop" Rule." http://www.tysknews.com/Depts/Constitution_Issues/one_drop_rule.htm.

Thompson, Krissah. 2009. "Harvard Scholar Henry Louis Gates Arrested." Washington Post. http://www.washingtonpost.com/wp-dyn/content/article/2009/07/20/AR2009072001358.html

Tocqueville, Alexis de, and Henry Reeve. 1840. *Democracy in America*. London: Saunders and Otley.

Tubman, Harriet. "Profile of Harriet Tubman." http://www2.lhric.org/poCantico/tubman/profiles.htm.

Tucker, Cynthia. 2007. "*As Black Middle Class Rises, Underclass Falls Still Further.*" http://articles.baltimoresun.com/2007-12-03/news/0712030044_1_black-bill-oreilly-middle-class.

Tutu, Desmond. 1999. *No Future without Forgiveness*. New York: Doubleday.

Tutu, Desmond. "Quote by Desmond Tutu." http://www.goodreads.com/quotes/33011-when-the-missionaries-came-to-africa-they-had-the-bible.

Tzu, Lao. "Lao Tzu Quotes." http://thinkexist.com/quotation/if_you_do_not_change_direction-you_may_end_up/214079.html.

Unbiasedtalk.com. 2013. http://www.unbiasedtalk.com/uncategorized/black-wall-street-segregation-was-better-for-blacks/.

UNESCO. 1950. "The Race Question." http://unesdoc.unesco.org/images/0012/001282/128291eo.pdf.

USDL. 1965. The Negro Family: The Case for National Action. United States Department of Labor. Office of Policy Planning and Research. Detroit, MI: University of Michigan Library.

US News & World Report. 1983. "Los Angeles has become the Mecca for people from so many lands that the police speak forty-two languages." March 21, 1983, 49–53.

Van Engen, Charles Edward. 1996. *Mission on the Way: Issues in Mission Theology.* Grand Rapids, MI: Baker Books.

Van Soest, Dorothy., and Betty. Garcia. 2003. *Diversity Education for Social Justice: Mastering Teaching Skills.* Alexandria, VA: Council on Social Work Education.

Viles, Peter, Audrey Singer, and Harry Pachon. 2009. CNN Breaking News. http://www.cnn.com/TRANSCRIPTS/0412/09/ldt.01.html.

Weaver, Mason C. 1997. "Too Much Political Power, Not Enough Economic Independence." National Center for Public Policy Research—A Conservative Organization. https://www.nationalcenter.org/P21NVPower197.html.

Wagner, C. Peter. 1989. *Strategies for Church Growth: Tools for Effective Mission and Evangelism.* Ventura, CA: Regal Books.

Wagner, C. Peter. 2010. *Church Planting for a Greater Harvest: A Comprehensive Guide.* Eugene, OR: Wipf and Stock Publishers.

Wagner, C. Peter. 2011. *Your Church Can Grow: Seven Vital Signs of a Healthy Church.* Eugene, OR: Wipf and Stock Publishers.

Wallenstein, Peter. 2014. *Race, Sex, and the Freedom to Marry: Loving V. Virginia.* Lawrence, KS: University Press of Kansas.

Wallis, Jim. 2007. *America's Original Sin: Racism, White Privilege, and the Bridge to a New America.* Brazos by Amazon.

Walvoord, John. 1969. *Jesus Christ Our Lord.* Chicago, IL: The Moody Bible Institute.

Washington, Booker T. 1990. *Up from Slavery: An Autobiography*. Raleigh, NC: Alex Catalogue.,

Washington Times. 2008. *Who Decided to Call Obama Black?* July 8. http://www.washingtontimes.com/news/2008/jul/08/who-decided-to-call-obama-a-Black-man/?page=all.

Watanabe, Teresa. 1999. "Rude Awakening on Racism Gave Minister New Mission." *LA Times*. http://articles.latimes.com/1999/jul/25/news/mn-59449.

Watson, David. 1982. *Called & Committed: World-Changing Discipleship*. Wheaton, IL: H. Shaw Publishers.

Weaver, Mason. 1997. "What is the Goal of the Black Community? Economic Power or Political Power?" *New Visions Commentary Paper*. Washington, DC. The National Center for Public Policy Research.

Wegman, William. 1992. "America on Trial, Fire and Fury." *Newsweek*. http://www.biblio.com/book/newsweek-may-11-1992-america-trial/d/535752943.

West, Cornel. 1994. *Race Matters*. New York: Vintage Books.

Wetzel, James R. 1990. "American Families: 75 Years of Change." *U.S. Bureau of Labor Statistics*. http://www.bls.gov/mlr/1990/03/art1full.pdf.

Williams, Walter E. 2016. "Liberal Views, Black Victims." http://walterewilliams.com/liberal-views,-black-victims/.

Wilson, William J. 1978. *The Declining Significance of Race: Blacks and Changing American Institutions*. Chicago: University of Chicago Press.

Winkle-Wagner, Rachelle. 2010. "So Educated: The Educational Consequences of the Post-racial Myth." So Educated. http://www.soeducated.com/2010/11/educational-consequences-of-post-racial.html.

Wise, Tim J. 2009. *Between Barack and a Hard Place: Racism and White Denial in the Age of Obama*. San Francisco: City Lights Books.

Wood, Daniel B., Christian Science Monitor. 2002. "LA's Darkest Days." *Christian Science Monitor*. Los Angeles. April 29.

Woodson, Carter Goodwin. 2010. *The Mis-Education of the Negro*. New York: CreateSpace Independent Publishing Platform.

Woodson, Carter G. and Willie Lynch. 2009. The Mis-Education of The Negro by Carter G. Woodson and The Willie Lynch Letter. New York, NY: Classic Books America.

Yancey, George 1996. *Beyond Black and White: Reflections on Racial Reconciliation*. Grand Rapids, MI: Baker Books.

Yancey, George. 1999. "An Examination of the Effects of Residential and Church Integration on Racial Attitudes of Whites." *Sociological Perspectives* 42:279–304.

Yancey, George 2003. *One Body, One Spirit: Principles of Successful Multiracial Churches*. Downers Grove, IL: InterVarsity Press.

York, Chris. 2015. "BBC Britain First Documentary 'We Want Our Country Back' Sparks Lively Debate." *Huffington Post*. Britain, UK, June 16.

Yount, Steve. 2015. "T.D. Jakes: 'We Cannot Remain Silent on This Issue.'" *Charisma News*. http://www.charismanews.com/us/47925-t-d-jakes-we-cannot-remain-silent-on-this-issue.

Zangwill, Israel. 2007. "The Melting-Pot [EBook #23893]." *archive.org*. http://archive.org/stream/themeltingpot23893gut/23893.txt

Zeskind, Leonard. 1999. "Analyst Leonard Zeskind Discusses Extremism in America." Southern

Poverty Law Center. https://www.splcenter.org/fighting-hate/intelligence-report/1999/analyst-leonard-zeskind-discusses-extremism-america.

Ziafat, Afshin. 2015. "10 Quotes from the ERLC Leadership Summit on Race." Life Way Christian Resources. Last modified April 9, 2015. http://www.lifeway.com/leadership/2015/04/09/10-quotes-from-the-erlc-leadership-summit-on-race/.

Thank you for reading my book.

The Color of God
America, the Church, and the Politics of Race

Please visit my website for other follow-up information:

www.thecolorofgod.com

Rick Donkor is available as a guest speaker and/
or consultant for your business, church or ministry
organization. He may be reached at:
colorofgodbook@gmail.com